Power Excel and Word

Power Excel and Word

Dan Gookin

San Francisco London

Associate Publisher: Dan Brodnitz

Acquisitions and Developmental Editor: Pete Gaughan

Production Editor: Erica Yee

Copy Editor: Sally Engelfried

Compositor: Chris Gillespie, Happenstance Type-O-Rama

Proofreaders: Laurie O'Connell, Nancy Riddiough

Indexer: Ted Laux

Cover design and Illustration: Richard Miller, Calyx Design

Library of Congress Card Number: 2004109319

ISBN: 0-7821-4379-2

Manufactured in the United States of America

10 9 8 7 6 5 4 3 2 1

Contents at a Glance

Contents

About the Author

Dan Gookin is a writer and computer guru whose favorite saying is "Computers are a notoriously dull subject, but that doesn't mean I have to write about them that way."

Combining his dry wit with an entertaining and engaging writing style, Dan has written more than 90 books about computers, including the international bestsellers *DOS for Dummies* and *PCs for Dummies.*

All told, his books have been translated into over 30 foreign languages and have sold over 15 million copies. Dan's current titles include *Troubleshooting Your PC for Dummies,* as well as *Dan Gookin's Naked Windows XP* from Sybex.

Introduction

It's easy to learn Word. Excel is different, but it's not that difficult to get to know the basics. Using either program, just about anyone can slap together a document or fill in a grid with numbers. Both Word and Excel are forgiving to the beginner, and most people are happy to use them at that level. But my guess is that you're different. You want more!

Greetings, budding *power user*!

Trust me, there is *power* in Word and Excel. It's not really hidden; the power is there if you know where to look and have a helpful guide—like this book—that shows you the ropes.

Unlike other books, this one respects you and what you already know about Word or Excel. I see no reason to bore you with the basics or bother you with simple tricks that anyone can figure out. No, the reason I wrote this book is to help you unlock the potential of Word and Excel, to go beyond the beginner level and show you how to use the same programs everyone else does, but at a higher level. The end result is that your stuff will look better, you'll be a smarter user, and you'll end up looking more attractive and making more money. Who wouldn't want that?!

About This Book

This book is not my personal love poem to Word. It's not my sonnet to Excel. You see, when it comes to using a computer, I'm on *your* side. I get frustrated just like you do. For example, have you ever done something sweet in Excel only to forget what it was or how it worked just a few hours later? Or perhaps you think you have all of Word's formatting tricks down pat, and then someone you know shows you a document that makes your jaw drop. Well, this book contains the solutions to those puzzles, the answers to those questions, and the remedies to the ills that plague anyone using the two most popular programs from Microsoft Office, Word and Excel.

Above all, this book has *attitude*. I'm not out to try and teach you how to worship your software. I don't want to justify some of the mysterious ways Word does things or to get all gushy over the basics in Excel. No way! So rather than bore you with what you already know or can figure out on your own, I'm here to show you the best and most useful parts of Word and Excel. It's what I call the nifty stuff, the handy and useful things, the shortcuts, the tips, and the special features that will give your creations that extra-added *wow* factor.

What's Covered Here

This book covers the two main programs in Microsoft Office, Word and Excel. These programs either come bundled with Office, or you may have bought them separately. Either way, it's upon those two main programs I've decided to concentrate all my fire power.

In another unusual approach, unlike any other book on Microsoft Office, this one covers an amazing *three editions* of the Office suite: Office 2000, Office XP (also called Office 2002), and Office 2003. So you're getting six programs covered in this single book. Such a deal!

NOTE *Even though the editors and I didn't officially test the material, we're pretty certain that most of it works for Office 97 as well. So, in a way, this book is valuable to Word 97 and Excel 97 users as well.*

And don't think that my approach leads to clutter! The silent truth is that these different versions of Office are all truly similar to one another, similar enough that there are only scattered places in this book where separate steps or figures are required. The information in this book is crafted and presented so that it doesn't really matter which version of Office you have; all the tricks, tips, and solutions work without anyone feeling left out.

This book covers such intermediate Office topics as:

- Precisely formatting a paragraph in Word
- Using drawings and pictures inside a document
- Using tabs to set up a "cast list"
- Knowing when to use a table in Word and when to just insert an Excel worksheet
- Formatting a worksheet so that only certain pages print
- Redoing Excel charts on-the-fly
- And many, many more!

What You Won't Find in This Book

This book covers only Word and Excel. It does not cover Outlook, PowerPoint, OneNote, Publisher, Access, FrontPage, PhotoDraw, or any other programs included with various editions of Microsoft Office.

Macros are covered briefly here. I show how to record a macro, but I just don't have enough room to get into the meaty information on programming. Alas!

This book doesn't cover how to use Windows, any version. I assume that you can use Windows in at least a basic manner. That's all this book cares about.

Conventions

This book refers to the Microsoft Office as "Office." The applications are referred to by their common names: Word and Excel. Though the official names all include the words "Microsoft" and "Office" and probably some ™ or ® thing there somewhere, they're not used here.

If there are any differences between the various versions of Office, these will be indicated in the text. For example, if Word 2000 does something differently from Word XP or Word 2003, then that's noted. Fortunately, such instances are rare; I would say that over 95 percent of Office is generic enough that there was no need to continually include separate steps.

Do note that the figures are mostly of Office 2003, though some specific figures for Office 2000 are also included. (Office 2003 and Office XP are visually similar.)

This is an active book with many steps and tutorials that show you how things get done. The steps are numbered, often with comments (or even substeps) between them:

1. Pick up the phone handset. You should hear the irritating noise the phone company calls the "bong" (snicker, snicker).
2. Dial **1234**. Each number makes a charming sour noise as the key is pressed.
3. Wait for someone to answer.

The stuff you type (Step 2) appears in **bold text.**

Key combinations are specified using the + character. Ctrl+D means to press the Ctrl (control) key and type a D, just as you would press Shift+D to get a capital letter D when typing.

NOTE *Note icons flag information that needs to be, well, noted. They're asides or supplemental information to what's already written in the text. They also provide warnings for things to avoid doing.*

The Windows key on your keyboard is labeled "Win" in this book. So if I tell you to press Win+D, it means to press the Windows key, tap the D key, and then release both keys.

About You!

Greetings, gentle reader! To get the most out of this book I am assuming the following things about you. Let me put on my Computer Book Author Psychic Turban and describe you:

- You're very attractive, underpaid at work, and underappreciated by your family.
- You have a computer with Microsoft Office installed, edition 2003, XP (or 2002), or 2000.

- You're well versed in your version of Windows.
- You understand enough about Microsoft Office to consider yourself an *intermediate* user.
- Yes, whether you accept it or not, you *are* an intermediate user.
- You're willing to learn more about Office so that you can become a more efficient and impressive computer user, at least better than the doofs you work with.
- You have some secret talent, such as rolling your tongue or wiggling your ears.
- When you show up at the Post Office, invariably there will be a line.
- I can see by the Ten of Swords that your former lover is trying to win you back but the county jail stationery just isn't tugging at your heart.

Okay! Okay! Time to remove the Psychic Turban!

What Now?

Now you're ready to start reading the book!

Where to Start Reading

You do not need to read this book from front to back. It's designed so that you can start anywhere. For example, you don't have to complete a tutorial in Chapter 1 to do the exercises in Chapter 3. Feel free to dive in and start reading anywhere.

Chapters 1–9 cover Microsoft Word, from words to paragraphs to documents. Chapters 10–15 cover Microsoft Excel, from navigating worksheets to making complex charts out of web-based content. You can start reading in any chapter in any order. The book is cross-referenced so if something is covered in an earlier chapter you'll know where to look.

Where You Can Get More Information

As a computer book author, it's my duty to provide you with as complete and accurate information as possible. If anything appears confusing or you require additional information, then I feel I owe it to you to give you that information. Therefore I'm offering my e-mail address should you have any questions regarding this book or its subject:

`dgookin@wambooli.com`

I promise to reply to all e-mail sent to me. However, I cannot troubleshoot your PC, nor can I provide answers to questions on topics not directly covered by this book.

I also offer a free weekly newsletter that contains tips, how-tos, bonus lessons, and Q&As for this and all my books. You can read more information about my free "Weekly Wambooli Salad" newsletter at:

`http://www.wambooli.com/newsletter/weekly/`

In addition to the newsletter, supplemental information specific to this book can be found on my website at:

`http://www.wambooli.com/help/office/`

Any errors, omissions, or additional information—including new information, updates, and special how-tos—can be found on that page.

And for general information about myself, fun quizzes, trivia, and a list of other books I've written and stuff, go visit:

`http://www.wambooli.com/`

Now you're ready to go forth, read, and enjoy your Excel and Word power!

Chapter 1

Life beyond the Basic Word

PRETTY MUCH ANYONE CAN use a computer and figure out how to use Word. The program has been so successful that it's essentially unchanged from its Word 97 version. The name of the game is to get your stuff down on paper and make it look good. The rules are easy. This chapter here elaborates on some of the more basic concepts you may not know, plus a few new rules and tricks designed to help you make your word processing chores all the easier:

- Helpful hints on properly saving your stuff
- Password protection advice
- Better ways to cut and paste and search and replace
- Resetting defaults without messing with `NORMAL.DOT`
- Making the spell checker behave
- Printing a document backward
- Setting margins for printing on three-hole-punch paper
- Printing two pages per sheet

Saving and Opening Documents Can Be Torture if You Don't Know a Few Things

Save now! Save early! Save often!

The three biggest issues whenever you save a document (in Word or in any application) are

- The document's name
- The document's location
- The document's type

The Save As dialog box (Figure 1.1) handles all these details for you, which is basic baby Windows stuff. Of course, that doesn't mean you can't screw them up. So heed these words of advice before getting into the intermediate-level knowledge nuggets:

FIGURE 1.1
Your typical Office Save As dialog box

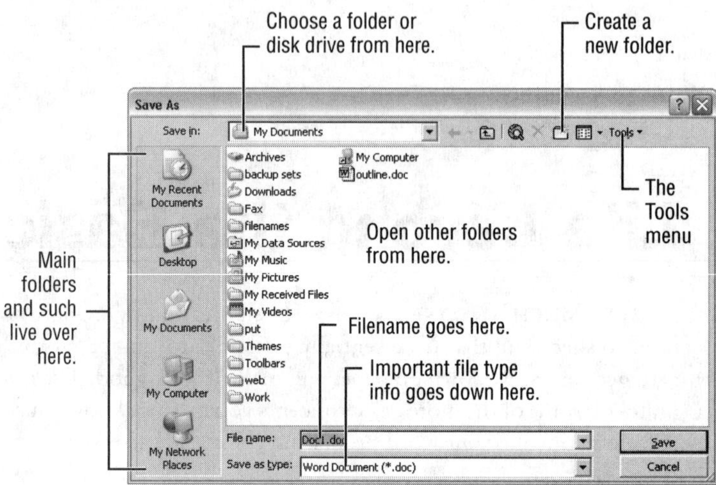

First, the document name must be descriptive of the contents. You have up to 200 characters to use for the name, including numbers and letters and a smattering of symbols, but brief is best.

Second, be thoughtful of the file's final folder destination. Don't just shove everything into the My Documents folder. Organize. Use subfolders. In fact, the filename can be simpler if the folder it lives in is more descriptive. Consider this: The file is named `14.DOC`. But it lives in the October folder. And that lives in the 2004 folder. And that lives in the Letters to the Editor folder. Consider:

```
Letters to the Editor/2004/October/14.doc
```

versus a single file in the My Documents folder:

```
Letter to the editor on October 14.doc
```

Finally, there is the document file type, which is found in the bottom part of the Save As dialog box. You can use that list to save or *export* your document into a variety of different word processor formats. Most often you'll be using the Word Document format (thus a `.doc` extension on the file), but be careful not to neglect the power that drop-down list gives you—and to avoid the confusion that can result should you choose the wrong option.

Why Save a Document in Another Format?

The primary reason for *not* using the Word Document file format is to share your stuff with some loser, uh, I mean someone who doesn't have Word as his or her word processor. For example, if they

MAKING A LONGER RECENTLY USED FILE LIST

Without otherwise scolding Word into action, the recently used file list keeps track of only the last four files you've opened, saving their names at the bottom of the File menu. You can adjust the number of filenames Word remembers up or down, depending on your whim:

1. Choose Tools ➤ Options.
2. In the Options dialog box, click the General tab.
3. Adjust the value by the "Recently Used File List" item (which must be checked on). Values can go from 1 through 9. To choose zero, just uncheck the box.
4. Click OK.

I personally like having only four items, though when I'm doing a big project and shuffling files quite a bit, six seems like a more logical value.

have WordPerfect, you can choose one of the WordPerfect file formats from the Save as Type drop-down list (Figure 1.1).

Another instance may be where you have to save a document in plain text format. For example, say you deleted something important in Windows and you have to replace it by creating a list and saving it to disk as an ASCII or text file. If so, choose "Plain Text (*.txt)" from the Save as Type drop-down list.

NOTE *The best non-Word format to choose is the Rich Text Format (`*.rtf`). That format is the most common among all the major word processing applications for most computers. In fact, I would save a document as RTF instead of attempting to save in WordPerfect or even HTML format; it's just that much more common—and better.*

Should I Ever Have to Save a Document as a Web Page?

My advice is never to use any web page or HTML format in the Save As dialog box, and by all means avoid the File ➤ Save as Web Page command. These options are designed for those who use Word as their web page editor. The problem with that is that Word is not a very good web page editor. (I've even gotten Microsoft personnel to admit that—off the record.)

There may be some time when you need to "share" your precious Word document with others, and the suggested format may just be HTML. If so, then go ahead and use the File ➤ Save as Web Page command to create the HTML document. I suppose if your hands are tied to doing that, then do that you must. But don't make it a habit if you can help it.

Why Does the Document Open All Weird?

Again, you can blame the Save as Type drop-down list for any weirdness that happens when you open a document, though in this case the weirdness takes place in the Open dialog box with the Files of Type drop-down list, as shown in Figure 1.2.

FIGURE 1.2
The typical Open dialog box for Office

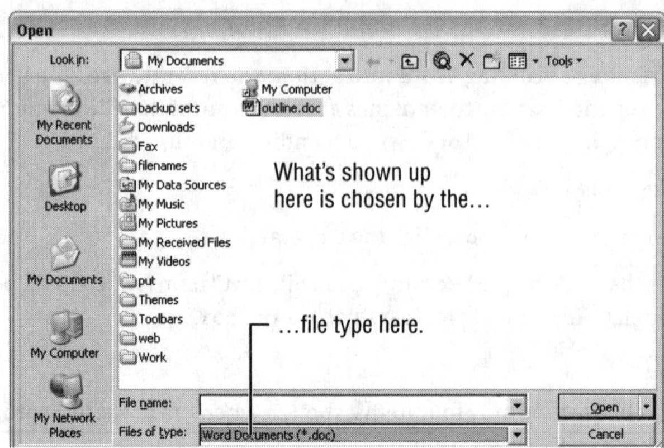

The Files of Type drop-down list not only tells Word which types of files to display in the Open dialog box, but it tells Word how to open the files as well.

For example, if you choose the option "Recover Text from Any File," then Word dutifully does that—even to its own files. So if that option is chosen and you open a Word document, you will see junk on the screen.

The solution is to pay attention to the file type choices in the Open dialog box. If the document looks like junk, then follow these steps:

1. Immediately close the weird document; do not save it to disk.
2. Choose File ➤ Open to bring up the Open dialog box again.
3. Confirm that the proper type is chosen in the Open dialog box.
4. Open the file.

NOTE *Be careful* not *to save the file if it's opened in a weird format. If you do so, then you cannot recover the original. Uh-oh! (As a suggestion, consider using Windows to make a copy of the original; then work on the copy only.)*

JUST YOUR BASIC OPEN AND CLOSE KEYBOARD COMMANDS

Here are the keyboard commands used in Word, as well as other Office and Windows applications, for the standard operations of opening, closing, and saving documents:

Ctrl+S Save the document to disk, or summon the Save As dialog box if the document has yet to be saved.

Alt+F, A Specifically summon the Save As dialog box.

Ctrl+O Open a document previously saved to disk.

Ctrl+W Close a window, prompting to save the document if it's unsaved.

Continued on next page

JUST YOUR BASIC OPEN AND CLOSE KEYBOARD COMMANDS *(continued)*

When used with the Shift key, the commands apply to all open Word windows:

Shift+Ctrl+S Save all open documents.

Shift+Ctrl+W Close all open windows.

Finally, from before Windows was standardized, there are some leftover keyboard commands from the very early days of Word:

F12 Summon the Save As dialog box (even for an already-saved document).

Shift+F12 Save the document to disk.

Ctrl+F12 Summon the Open dialog box.

Can I Password-Protect My Document?

Certainly! After summoning the Save As dialog box, use the Tools menu to modify the way the file is saved to disk. (Refer to Figure 1.1.)

1. In Word 2003/XP, choose Tools ➤ Security Options; in Word 2000, choose Tools ➤ General Options. The Save or Security dialog box appears, such as shown in Figure 1.3. It's very similar for all versions of Word, though the location of the open and modify password text boxes is different.

2. If you like, enter an open password. This password prevents the document from being opened unless the person knows the password.

FIGURE 1.3
Entering a password or two for your document

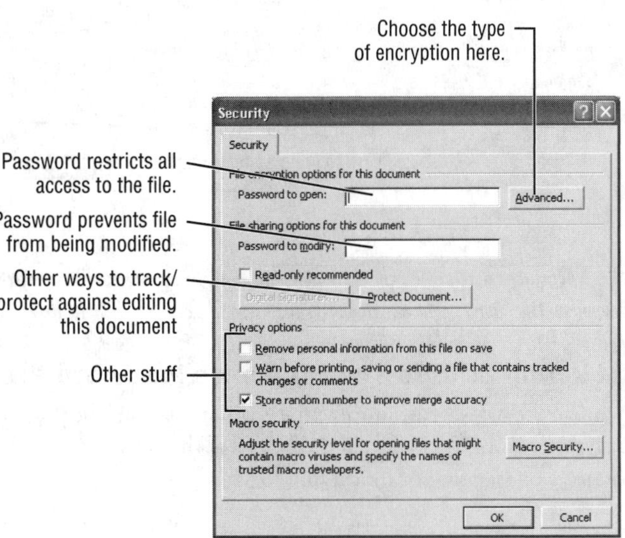

3. If you like, enter a modify password. This password allows the file to be opened as a "read-only" document. If they know the password, however, then they can modify the document.

NOTE *Passwords are case-sensitive. They consist of up to 15 letters and numbers. Do not forget them or you're screwed!*

4. Click OK after entering one or both passwords. If you don't enter any passwords, then the document is not protected.
5. Confirm the password(s). Type them again to ensure that you remember them. Don't forget them!
6. Continue using the Save dialog box to save the file to disk.

The password-protected file doesn't look any different on disk, nor does it look any different when you're working on it in Word. But once you close the document, the password encryption takes over, and only by knowing the password can you get at the document's contents.

When you go to open a password-protected document, either in Word or by double-clicking the document's icon in Windows, you'll be presented with a Password dialog box or two. The first may be required for merely opening the document—that's the open password.

A second dialog box, such as the one shown in Figure 1.4, is the modify password dialog box. Note that there is a Read Only option in that dialog box in case you do not know the password; only by entering the password can you modify the document.

FIGURE 1.4
Oops! Better know the password to modify that document!

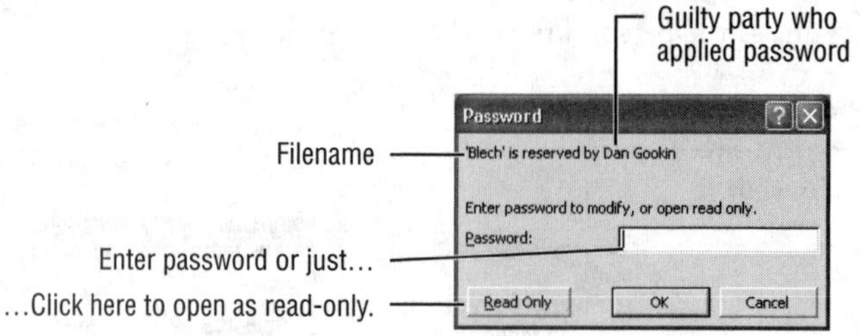

NOTE *Actually, you can use the Save As command in any read-only Office document to save that document to disk using another filename. Then you can open that second document for editing. (Sneaky, but it works.)*

Can I Remove the Passwords from a Password-Protected Document?

To remove the passwords, simply repeat the steps from the previous section, but leave both password input boxes blank. Click OK, and that resets the passwords back to nothing, and there are no more restrictions on opening or modifying the file.

But I Forgot the Document's Password!

You're screwed. Really. Don't be dumb: follow these handy password-remembering rules:

- If you feel you're going to forget your password, then write it down! But don't write it down on a sticky note and stick it on the monitor. Instead, put it in your day planner, perhaps on the bottom of the page with your birthday. But whatever you do, write that password down so you can at least find it later.
- Shorter, memorable passwords work best.
- Passwords mixing letters and numbers are also good, such as the number and street where you used to live or where a relative lives.
- There is also a school of thought that absurdity often makes a memorable password. For example, stick together two obnoxiously unrelated words like "baby-meat" or "armored-nun."

Finally, there is really no hope if you forget your password. Microsoft cannot help you, nor are there any secret tools or tricks available on the Internet. So remember that password!

I Can't Find My Document!

If you're missing a document, then you have a few tricks you can pull before you consider tossing the computer before an oncoming train.

First, check the File menu. Is your document down near the bottom, in the list of recently used files?

Second, check the Documents or My Recent Documents submenu from the Start button. Is the file listed there?

Third, you can use Window's Find or Search command to look for the document, but you can also use the Find or Search command in the Open dialog box to help you quickly find your document based on its contents. Follow these steps for your version of Word.

Finding a Wayward Word File in Word 2003/XP

1. Summon the Open dialog box.
2. From the Tools menu, choose Search. The File Search dialog box appears, and like its ancestors it's too vast and ugly to reproduce on these pages. But fortunately it's not as complex or weird as the Word 2000 variation.
3. Make sure that the Basic tab is showing, not the Advanced tab.
4. Type some words from your document into the Search text box. For example, that letter to the editor you wrote comparing the snow plow driver to Adolf Hitler. If you lost that document, then consider searching for the words "Hitler" and "snow plow" to find what you want.

   Fortunately, all the other settings are made for this type of search (the most common), so…
5. Click the Search button.

6. Eventually a list of matches appears, which you can sift through. Click the file you want to check out.

7. Click the OK button.

8. Back in the Open dialog box, click the Open button to open the file.

If the list appearing in the File Search dialog box is *way too long,* then you'll need to rethink your approach. Try using more specific words, or click the Advanced tab and heed these instructions:

1. From the Property drop-down list, choose Contents. Not "Comments" but "Contents."

2. Enter the words you're searching for in the Value text box. For example, "Hitler" and "snow plow."

NOTE *If the words appear together in your document, then surround them with double quotes. "Snow plow" searches for the word "snow" followed by "plow." But if you type each word individually, then the document can contain either word in any order any number of words apart.*

3. Click the Add button.

4. Now you can enter another bit-o-information to search for. From the Property drop-down list choose "Creation Date."

5. From the Condition drop-down list choose an option, such as "On" or "On or After" or "This Week."

6. If you chose a condition that requires a date, then enter the date in the Value text box.

7. Click the Add button.

8. Now you have two search criteria, which should be enough. Click the Search button.

And off Word goes to look for the document matching your specifications.

Locating Lost Documents in Word 2000

1. Summon the Open dialog box.

2. From the Tools menu, choose Find. The Find dialog box appears, but it's much too complex and obtuse to show here in a figure.

3. From the Property drop-down list, choose Contents. The Condition drop-down lists self-modifies to say "Includes Words."

4. Type some words from your document into the Value text box. For example, if you lost the document about how you cheated the Brundlemans at cards, then searching for the words "Brundleman" and "cards" would most likely yield successful results.

5. Click the Add to List button. Ah-ha! This is the step everyone forgets (and the reason they changed all this with Word XP). If you forget to click the Add to List button, you'll be reminded to do it later.

6. Optionally choose a location from the Look In drop-down list. It already shows you the My Documents folder, which is an ideal place to look. But if you feel the file is on a disk in another drive or a specific folder, then choose it from the list as well. To search the entire computer, select My Computer from the list.

7. Put a check mark by "Search Subfolders" so that the search expands down into the very depths of your disk drive's folder structure.

8. Click the Find Now button. Word scurries around the folders you told it to look in and finds all files matching your search criteria. They appear in a tree structure that unfolds in the Open dialog box.

NOTE *If a multitude of files were found, then consider redoing the search with more specific information, or even repeating steps 3 through 5 and adding a range of dates to narrow the search.*

9. Ctrl+click to select all the files found.

10. Click the Open button to open all the selected files. Now you can sift through each of them in Word until you find the one you want.

Yes, it's possible to open more than one file at a time in the Open dialog box. The Open button opens any and all selected files shown in the list.

Fixing the Stupid Menus!

Tired of the menus in Office changing size on you? Sick of having to click the "show more" chevron to see the entire menu? Me too! A program should never conceal its options. So to fix Word's timidity of its own menus, follow these steps:

1. Choose Tools ➤ Customize.
2. Click the Options tab in the Customize dialog box.
3. In Word 2003/XP, click to select "Always Show Full Menus;" in Word 2000, remove the check mark by "Show Full Menus after a Short Delay."
4. Click OK.

That way the menus stay open and visible all the time. It's also the way I prefer to use Office applications, and the way they're shown in the screen shots in this book.

How Do I Save a Document to Drive A?

You can save a document to any disk in your system, whether it's another hard drive or a removable disk such as a floppy, Zip, or writable CD or DVD. The secret is to choose that disk from the Save In drop-down list at the top of the Save As dialog box (see Figure 1.1).

Please don't try to save to Drive A—or any removable disk—as opposed to using the hard drive. The hard drive is designed to be your primary file storage location. Use it! Then, after the file is safely saved on the hard drive, consider using the Save As command to save a *copy* of the file to a removable disk. Or you can use Windows to simply copy the document to a removable disk.

NOTE *Floppy disks are notoriously unreliable. They're fine for backups or for moving files between computers, but not for permanent storage.*

Word Crashed! What Can I Recover?

Word is smart about document recovery. If there is anything to recover, then you'll see that file appear in a window the next time you start up Word. The window will have the original file's name followed by the text "(Recovered)."

In Word 2003/XP, point the mouse at the recovered file, and a menu button appears. Click that button to select a recovery option.

In Word 2000, use the Save As dialog box to save that recovered file back to disk and overwrite the original.

Yes! It's okay to overwrite an original file with a recovered version. I would say 99 percent of the time that's the option I've chosen. (The other 1 percent of the time the recovered file was no different from the original.)

Of course, to make Word recover files, you need to turn on the AutoRecovery feature:

1. Choose Tools ➤ Options.
2. Click the Save tab.
3. Put a check mark by "Save AutoRecover Info Every" (if a check mark isn't there already).
4. Enter a time interval to save the AutoRecover information. Ten minutes is okay for most people.
5. Click OK.

Now your computer is semiprotected against bad things happening. Word will automatically save your documents (whether you do or not) every 10 minutes or so. Of course, nothing gets hurt by your pressing the Ctrl+S key combination every few minutes just to be safe.

NOTE *If there are no recovered documents after a crash, then don't worry. Your stuff was probably all up-to-date and there was nothing necessary for Word to recover.*

A Gaggle of Nifty Word Formatting and Editing Tricks

Just when you think you know every Word trick there is, some doofus pops up and shows you something new, something useful, something you wish you would have known for the last project you did. Well, for the next few pages I plan on being your personal doofus and showing you what I think are some handy, unknown, or under-used tools in the Word toolbox.

How Do I Select Only One Sentence of Text?

A sentence is an irregular beast, not a single word or paragraph. Therefore selecting it using the mouse or the keyboard requires tedious skill...unless you know this trick: Press the Ctrl key and click the mouse somewhere in the sentence. Zloop! The entire sentence is selected and ready for action!

And for your passing enjoyment, Table 1.1 lists other quick and nifty ways of instantly selecting text.

TABLE 1.1: SELECTING CHUNKS OF TEXT IN WORD

To Select This Chunk of Text	Take This Action	Or This One
Word	Double-click the word.	With the insertion point in the word, press the F8 key twice.
Sentence	Ctrl+click the sentence.	With the insertion point in the sentence, press the F8 key three times.
Line	Click in the margin to the left of the line.	
Paragraph	Double-click in the margin to the left of the paragraph.	With the insertion point in the paragraph, press the F8 key four times.

Can I Change the Capitalization without Retyping the Whole Sentence?

The easiest way to change capitalization of a word is to put the insertion point in the word and press Shift+F3. That changes the capitalization to one of three modes: Initial Caps, ALL CAPS, or all lowercase. Keep pressing Shift+F3, toggling back and forth until you get the capitalization you want.

As an alternative, you can select the text you want to recapitalize and choose Format ➤ Change Case from the menu. Doing so displays five options for changing the case of the selected text, as shown in Figure 1.5. Select an option and click OK.

FIGURE 1.5
Even more ways to change the case

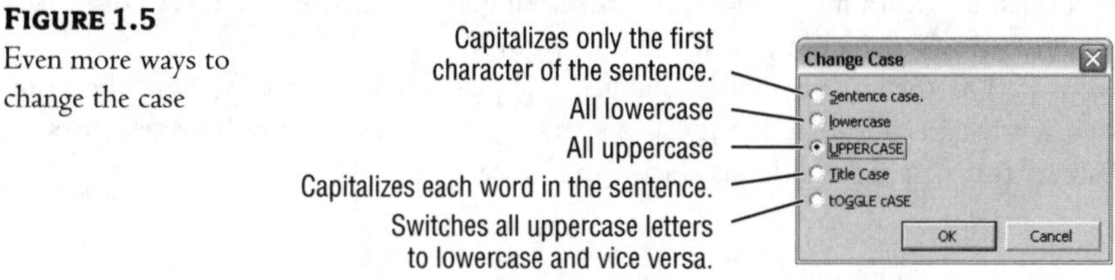

NOTE *Despite the earnestness of the Change Case command (Shift+F3) referring to its Initial Caps command as "Title Case," it is a common convention not to capitalize prepositions, articles, or conjunctions in a title. So, words such as* of, in, and, on, by, with, for, *and so on are not capitalized, well, unless they appear at the start or end of the title. (I asked my editor about this issue and she trembled in fear, citing some obscure tome called the* Chicago Manual of Style. *But then she also mentioned about 1,600 exceptions. So I suppose whatever you capitalize in your title is okay with me.)*

How Can I Paste in Text without Pasting in All the Formatting?

I suppose it's handy that when you normally paste text into Word, all the text's original formatting follows along like so much emotional baggage. For example, if you copy text from a web page into Word, you'll notice that any formatting the text had on the web page automatically follows that text into Word.

If you don't want the formatting to follow the text—for example, you want the text to appear in the document using the document's own formatting styles (just as if you had manually typed the text yourself), then you need to know how to Paste Special. Obey these steps:

1. Choose Edit ➤ Paste Special. The Paste Special dialog box appears.
2. Choose "Unformatted Text" from the list.
3. Click the OK button.

And the text is pasted into the document *minus* any formatting it may have had. The end result is text that appears as if you've typed it yourself.

In Word 2003/XP, you can choose the Unformatted option *after* you paste the text by clicking the Paste Options button that appears after the text has been pasted. Choose "Keep Text Only" from the pop-up menu, and it's the same thing as pasting in unformatted text.

NOTE *If there isn't an "Unformatted Text" option, then there is no text in the Clipboard to paste. Also note that you can Paste Special only from the Paste Special dialog box, not from the Clipboard task pane in Word 2003/XP.*

What the Heck Is Wrong with This Formatting?

Most of the e-mail questions I get regarding Word deal with some sort of weird formatting, such as a blank at the start of each line or a border following random paragraphs. Fortunately, nothing in Word is truly hidden from you. And while Word lacks a Reveal Codes command (that I so loved back in the days of DOS WordPerfect), it does have a Show Formatting command.

To see what evils lurk in a paragraph's formatting, press the Shift+F1 key combination. This has two different effects, depending on your version of Word.

In Word 2000, the mouse pointer changes to a question mark–arrow, which you can use to point-and-click at any text in Word. Doing so displays a pop-up cartoon bubble that lists the formatting for whatever text you clicked on, as shown in Figure 1.6.

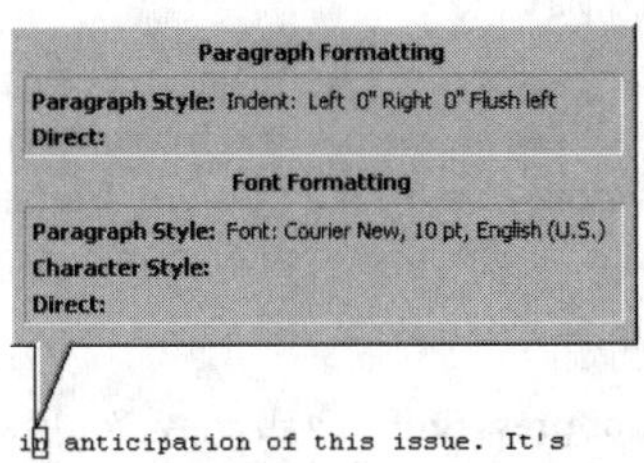

FIGURE 1.6 Checking the text formatting in Word 2000

The problem here is that only information is displayed. It's up to you to figure out where the problem lies, not only from the terms used in the description but from knowing which Word commands control those formatting options. (Fortunately all formatting options exist in the Format menu.)

In Word 2003/XP, information about the formatting appears in the Reveal Formatting task pane, as shown in Figure 1.7. This is very similar to the information shown for Word 2000, but with the advantage that you can click the underlined (blue) links to get at the proper dialog boxes required to fix things.

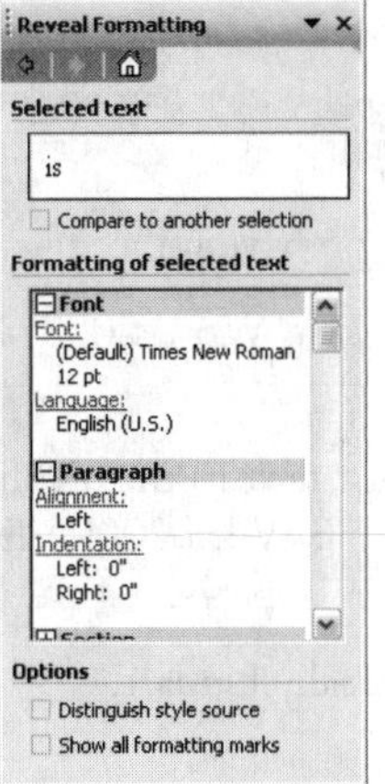

FIGURE 1.7 Checking the formatting in Word 2003/XP

How Come Changing the Format of One Paragraph Changes the Formatting of Them All?

I encountered this problem a while back and it bugged the bejoobies out of me: whenever I made one line of text bold, every other paragraph in the document bolded up. Very annoying, until I figured out that it was a Style issue.

THE MIGHTY F2 KEY

One of the easiest ways to copy or move a block of selected text in Word is to employ the handy F2 key. Unlike any of the other 10,000 ways to copy or move text, F2 is a breath of fresh air, giving you an immediate command versus a combination of commands or windows or prayers and incantations. It works like this:

1. Select the text you want to move or copy.
2. Press the F2 key to move that text, or press Shift+F2 to copy. You'll see "Move to Where?" or "Copy to Where?" appear on the status bar.
3. Click the mouse where you want the text moved. You can scroll to anywhere else in the same document, but you cannot use this trick to move or copy between two different documents.
4. Press the Enter key to move or copy the text.

Note that moving or copying text in this manner does *not* place that text into the Clipboard for repasting. No, the F2 command is more of a quick-move/quick-copy command than a traditional copy- or cut-and-paste operation.

Styles can be programmed to be automatically updated. So when you modify a paragraph in a document, all other paragraphs formatted with that style also change. This can be handy if you like to mess with styles after they're created, but it can also be a pain in the butt. To fix it, you must visit the Style dialog box:

1. Put the insertion pointer in the paragraph having the style you need to fix.
2. Choose Format ➤ Styles and Formatting in Word 2003/XP; choose Format ➤ Style in Word 2000.
3. Choose Modify from the drop-down list next to the highlighted style in the Styles and Formatting Task Pane in Word 2003/XP; in Word 2000, click the Modify button in the Style dialog box. The Modify Style dialog box appears.
4. Uncheck the item that reads "Automatically Update."
5. Click OK.

With the Automatically Update option disabled, your document's paragraphs can be modified without changing the underlying style. Or, conversely, if you do want styles to be updated on the fly, then you can check that option so that changes to one paragraph affect all other paragraphs of the same style. (But either way, I find it annoying.)

Why Would I Want to Search and Replace Styles?

Word's Search and Replace function is powerful enough to wreak havoc on even the most innocent of things, such as a style. So suppose you discover that for some arcane legal reason all your *italic text* has to be changed into boring old underline. Here's how you can do that without wasting a ton of time by using the Search and Replace command:

1. Press Ctrl+Home to zip to the tippy-top of your document.
2. Choose Edit ➤ Replace. The Find and Replace dialog box appears, ready to "Find What" and "Replace With." But you need more information than that, right?
3. Click the More button. More stuff appears!
4. Click the Format button.
5. Choose Font from the pop-up menu. The standard Font dialog box appears.
6. Choose Italic in the Find Font dialog box, or select whatever font attributes you're searching for.
7. Click OK.

   Now notice in the Find and Replace dialog box how the text "Format: Font: Italic" appears below the Find What text box. That means Word is searching for a format, not a specific chunk of text. The format it's searching for is any text that's italic. Time to select what to replace the italic text with:

8. Click the mouse in the Replace With text box.
9. Click the Format button.
10. Choose Font from the pop-up menu.
11. Choose the solid underline from the Underline Style drop-down list. That's the replacement style.
12. Click OK. Now under the Replace With text box you'll see "Format: Underline." You're searching for italic text and replacing it with underline—a style or formatting search and replace instead of a text search and replace.
13. Click the Replace All button to convert all your document's italic text into Underlined text.

You can search and replace any formatting attribute with any other formatting attribute, including text color, paragraph formatting, even styles you've created. Just choose the proper formatting command from the Format button.

NOTE *Word remembers the last formatting item you searched and replaced! To clear the formatting information from the Find and Replace dialog box, click the No Formatting button. If you forget to do this, then Find and Replace will not behave as you expect it to.*

Where Was I Last Editing?

A handy key to remember is the Shift+F5 combination. Pressing Shift+F5 returns the insertion point back to the place in your document where you last edited. So if you're scrolling through text reading, or bouncing from here to there editing, remember Shift+F5 to return to where you once were.

Is There an Easier Way to Edit a Document Full of Pictures?

Word doesn't do desktop publishing very well. Instead of forcing too many pictures into Word, I recommend using a "real" desktop publishing program, such as Microsoft's Publisher or Adobe's InDesign. But anyway...

If you're suffering through a document that has lots of pictures and it seems to be slowing things down, then shift into this mode:

1. Choose Tools ➤ Options.
2. Click the View tab in the Options dialog box.
3. Put a check mark by "Picture Placeholders."

That replaces the images in your document with placeholders, which makes scrolling around work a lot easier. When you're done editing, simply repeat the above steps to reactivate the pictures.

Why Would I Need the Document Map?

The Document Map is one of those seldom-used features that can really save you time both navigating a larger document and getting "the big picture" on what you're writing.

To switch on the Document Map, choose View ➤ Document Map from the menu, or click the Document Map button on the toolbar. A slice of the screen is split off to show you the various headings in your document, as illustrated in Figure 1.8.

Alas, if your document lacks headings, doesn't use the Headings styles, or is too short, then the Document Map isn't of much help.

Choose View ➤ Document Map again, or click the toolbar button, to make the Document Map view vanish.

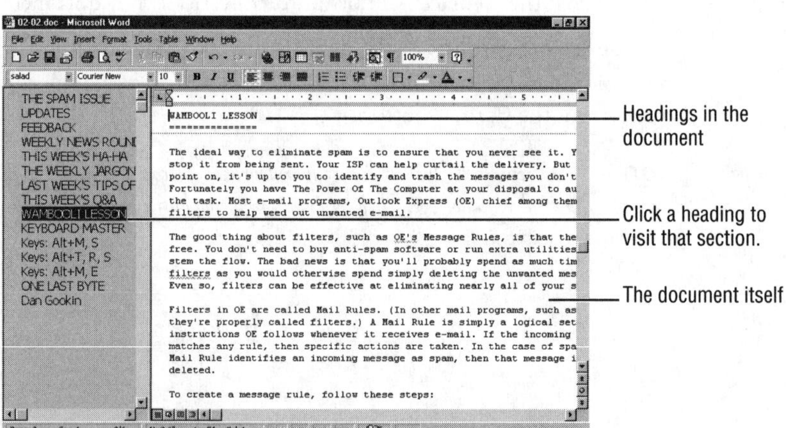

FIGURE 1.8
Viewing the Document Map

What's the Point of NORMAL.DOT?

NORMAL.DOT is a template file, not a document. As such, it is the standard (or "default" if you want) template used by Word whenever you open a new document and don't specify any other template. It contains the standard settings for any new document, such as Times New Roman font at 12 points, single-spaced, and so on. (See Chapter 5, "Using Styles and Templates to Save Oodles of Time," for more information on templates.)

If you want to change the way Word starts new blank documents, then you merely need to edit the NORMAL.DOT template and update the settings. NORMAL.DOT can be opened like any template file in Word, edited, then saved back to disk. The secret is to choose "Document Templates (*.dot)" from the Files of Type drop-down list in the Open dialog box.

A better way to make subtle changes in the NORMAL.DOT file is to take advantage of the various Default buttons located in many of Word's dialog boxes. These buttons can be used to modify the NORMAL.DOT template without having to go through the ordeal of trying to find it on disk and opening it.

For example, say you want all your new documents to be in the Bookman font at 10 points. Just choose Format ➤ Font and select Bookman as the font and 10 points as the size. Then click the Default button. Word asks if you want to save that change to the NORMAL.DOT template, making it stick for all new documents you open (Figure 1.9). Click Yes to make it so.

FIGURE 1.9
Changing the default font

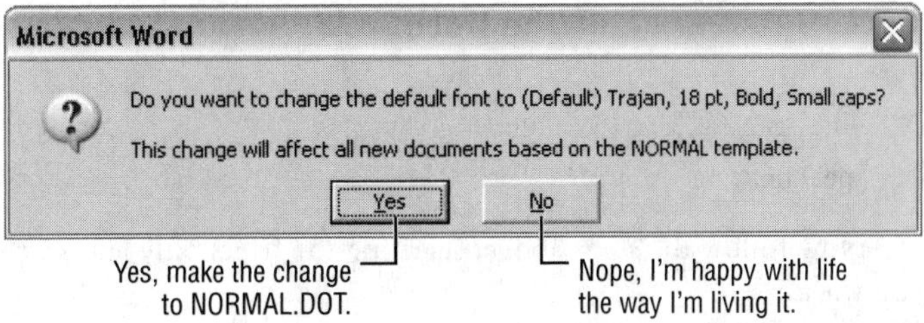

There are other Default buttons in other formatting dialog boxes as well. These also modify the settings of the NORMAL.DOT template. Use them to change the settings for your new, blank documents.

NOTE NORMAL.DOT *also contains any modifications you make to the toolbars or other aspects of Windows. So if you modify the toolbar and are eventually asked to "Save the Changes to* NORMAL.DOT*?" click the Yes button to keep your modifications.*

NOTE *It's a bad idea to over-modify the* NORMAL.DOT *template. If you find yourself making too many modifications, consider moving them all from the* NORMAL.DOT *template into another, custom template file you create. That way you can leave* NORMAL.DOT *basically "nude," which may come in handy. Refer to Chapter 5 for information on copying and deleting information in a template file.*

What's the Best Way to Alphabetically Sort a List of Items?

Word is entirely capable of sorting text. The problem is that the Sort command is hidden in the Table menu. I suppose that's because Sort is a more powerful tool when it comes to messing with tables. But in any event, you can also use the Sort command to sort just any text. Here's how:

1. Select the text you want to sort. For example, it can be a list of items, each on its own line. If you sort paragraphs, then only the first word in the paragraph is used for the sort.
2. Choose Table ➤ Sort. The Sort Text dialog box appears, but you needn't pay any attention to it; it's already set up to sort alphabetically, A to Z.
3. Click OK. And your text is sorted.

Often what you want to sort is an inline list of items. For example:

```
My favorite fruits are apples, oranges, bananas, pears, grapes, cherries and
peaches.
```

To sort the list of fruit, first edit the paragraph so that each fruit appears on a line by itself:

```
My favorite fruits are
apples,
oranges,
bananas,
pears,
grapes,
cherries and
peaches.
```

Now follow the steps above, selecting the fruits only and sorting them by name. You'll end up with:

```
My favorite fruits are
apples,
bananas,
cherries and
grapes,
oranges,
peaches.
pears,
```

Now re-edit the paragraphs back into a single sentence, moving the "and" and the punctuation into the proper positions, and you have a sorted list.

This Chunk of Text Is in Latin; How Can I Tell the Spell Checker to Ignore It?

The easiest way to avoid spell-checking foreign words is to format that chunk of text with the foreign language's attribute—yet another seldom-used feature of Word. Here's how:

1. Select the portion of text in a foreign language—or select any chunk of text that you merely don't want Word to spell-check, such as a code listing, filler block, or whatever you tire of seeing flagged as "misspelled."
2. Choose Tools ➤ Language ➤ Set Language. The Language dialog box appears, described in Figure 1.10.

FIGURE 1.10
Setting a new language for the spell checker

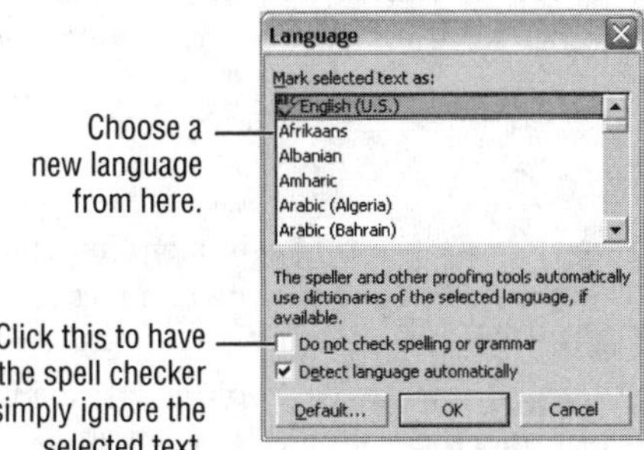

3. Scroll through the list until you find Latin.
4. Click OK.

Now the Latin text will be identified as such. In fact, if you had the optional Latin dictionary installed, Word would spell check the Latin text.

Optional dictionaries exist for all the languages listed in the Language dialog box. Alas, I've had a heck of time trying to find or order them from Microsoft. So unless you meet with better luck, I suggest merely using the Language dialog box to mark your foreign language text as "Do Not Check Spelling or Grammar." That way, you won't have to suffer through all the red and green wavy lines.

Printing Fun

The final step to the word processing process is getting your stuff down on paper, the hard copy, the printing part. This normally doesn't even receive a second thought. That is, until you come across one of the issues covered in the following sections.

PRINTING KEYS

The printing keyboard shortcut is one of the basic Windows shortcut keys: Ctrl+P.

Another handy keyboarding combination worth knowing is the command to quickly summon the popular Page Setup dialog box: Alt+F, then U. The F is from File and the U comes from the word "Setup." Try to remember those special words as opposed to any others that the F-U combination might make you think of.

Note that some of the items here are printer specific. Your printer's manufacturer, not Microsoft, creates the printer driver, the software used to control the printer. Printing is the spot where Word hands over control to that other software. So how your printer works may be subtly different than what's described below.

How Can I Stop Printing?

I find the most satisfying way to stop printing is to stand up and immediately yell at the printer, "Stop, you idiot!" This is quite satisfying, but sadly this method has been found to be less than effective in most situations.

First, use your printer's queue list to try to stop the document from printing.

Because your printer is printing, there should be a tiny printer icon that appears in the System Tray/Notification Area on the right end of the taskbar. Double-click that little printer icon to open your printer's window and view the queue list.

Click to select your document in the list. Then choose Document ➤ Cancel from the menu (or Document ➤ Cancel Printing, depending on your version of Windows).

Wait patiently. Eventually the document will stop printing.

If the document doesn't stop printing, and the printer keeps spewing out page after page, then consider turning off your printer. Do this only as a last resort: Turn off the printer. Wait a few moments, and then turn the printer on again. Eject a page from the printer just in case a page was "stuck" in the printer when you turned it off.

How Come the Document Comes out of the Printer Backward?

Many ink printers and a few laser printers spew out their documents face up in the printer tray. The result here is that page 1 is always on the bottom of the stack, meaning that you have to reshuffle your printer's output. *And aren't computers supposed to save you time!?*

Anyway, it's entirely possible to have your printer send out its pages in reverse order, providing that you remember these steps in Word:

1. Bring up the Print dialog box. Choose File ➤ Print or press Ctrl+P.
2. Click the Options button. This summons a second Print dialog box with a few special options custom to Word.

3. Click to check "Reverse Print Order." That's the secret!
4. Click OK.
5. Click OK to print in reverse order, and the pages come out of the printer backward!

Now the last page prints first. If your printer spits out pages face up, then on top of the last page comes the next-to-last page, and so on all the way down to page 1, which prints on top the pile.

Can I Print on Both Sides of the Page?

Printing on both sides of a page is tricky. Well, it's tricky unless you have a printer that's capable of printing on both sides of the page. If you do, then you'll see the "Print on Both Sides" option deep in the printer's Properties dialog box.

For example, in Figure 1.11 you see the Properties dialog box for my HP color LaserJet, which has a dual-sided printing option attached. Alas, most printers lack this option, so you'll have to do things like this:

1. Save your document to disk, all nice and neat and ready to print.
2. Summon the Print dialog box. Choose File ➤ Print or use the handy Ctrl+P keyboard shortcut.
3. In the Print dialog box, choose "Odd Pages" from the Print drop-down list. Figure 1.12 shows where to find this.

   First you want to print pages 1, 3, 5, and so on. Those will go on one side of the paper.
4. Click OK to print.

FIGURE 1.11
An option for printing on both sides of the page

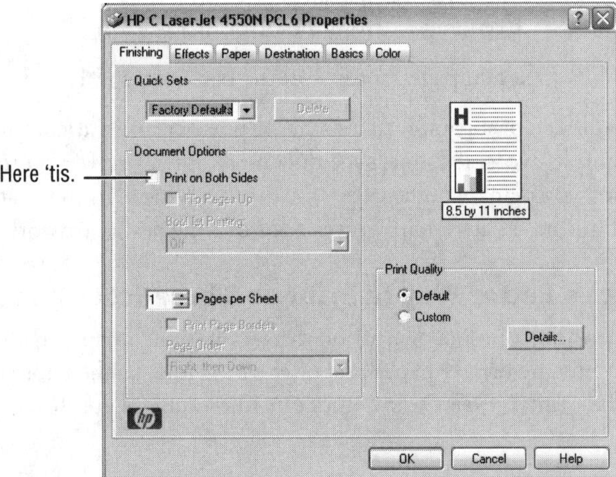

FIGURE 1.12
Printing odd pages, then even pages

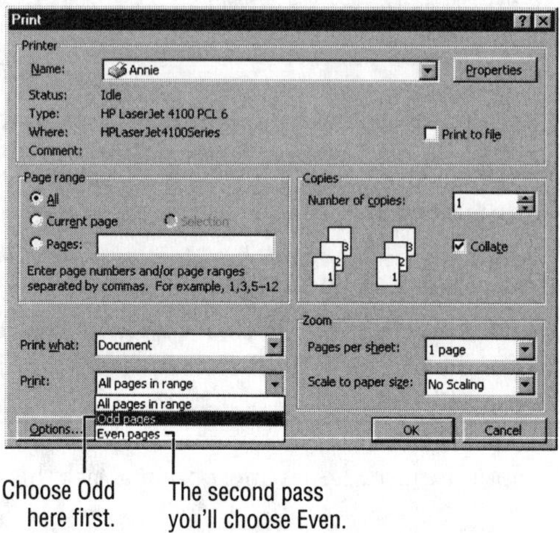
Choose Odd here first.
The second pass you'll choose Even.

And the printing goes on.... When the printing is done, gather the sheets and put them back into the printer's paper tray, but oriented so that printing takes place on the back side.

Further, you need to ensure that the first page is on top and the last page is on the bottom of the stack. That's because page 2 needs to go on the back of page 1, and so on. (See the previous section on printing in reverse order, if that helps you stack up your pages properly.)

When the odd pages are properly ordered and oriented in the printer, you're ready to print on the even side.

1. Choose File ➤ Print.
2. Choose "Even Pages" from the Print drop-down list.
3. Click OK, and page 2 prints on the back of page 1, and so on for the rest of your document.

Yes, this can be a pain. It takes a bit of practice and patience to get it right. I recommend starting with a simple two-sided, one-page document. Then move up into longer documents. And if this is something you plan on doing often, look into buying a printer that has a dual-sided or duplex printing option built in. That certainly saves a lot of time and guesswork.

Is There a Better Way to Print on Three-Hole-Punch Paper?

I prefer printing out lots of stuff on three-hole-punch paper. Rather than mess with a paper punch, I prefer to buy my printer paper prepunched. As long as the paper is properly oriented when you stick it into the printer, everything comes out fine—unless you forget to adjust the margins.

Generally speaking, I prefer a 0.5" margin on the left side of three-hole-punch paper. That gives enough room so that my text isn't too close to the holes. To set the margins that way, you use the Page Setup dialog box:

1. Choose File ➤ Page Setup.
2. Click the Margins tab (if you need to). Figure 1.13 shows you what's up with the Page Setup dialog box.

FIGURE 1.13
The Page Setup dialog box

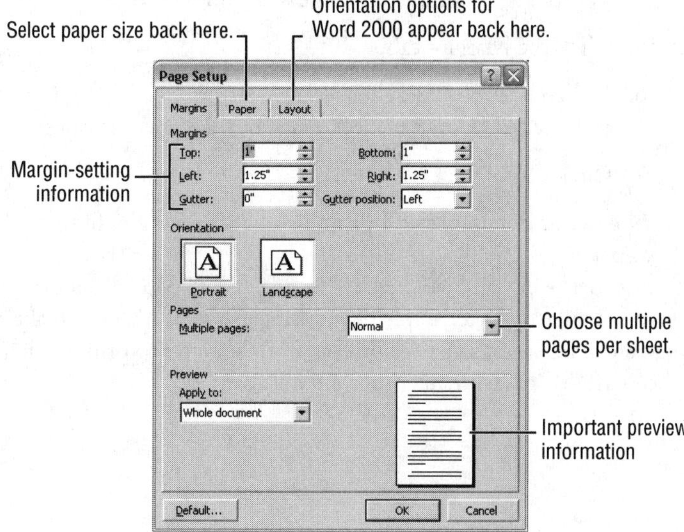

3. Adjust the Gutter margin up to 0.5". The "gutter" is a typesetting term for the edge of a page that is used for binding. Also note in Word 2003 that you can set the Gutter Position for a document, though for three-hole-punch paper the position is Left, which is already defined.
4. Click OK, and the margins are properly set for three-hole-punch page printing.

The margins you set for the page are different from the margins set for individual paragraphs. In fact, the values you use for a paragraph's margin are all relative to these page margins. (Paragraph margins are set by using the Format ➤ Paragraph command.)

How Can I Print Two Pages on an 11 × 14 Sheet?

It's simple to direct Word to print two or more "pages" on a sheet of paper. The problem comes, however, when you want to fold the paper in some way to make a book. Word lacks the smarts to intelligently print for binding purposes. (For that task you need a desktop publishing program, such as Microsoft's Publisher or Adobe's InDesign.) In any event, you can print more than one page on a sheet of paper if you follow these steps:

1. Choose File ➤ Page Setup.
2. Click the Paper or Paper Size tab.
3. Select Legal size paper from the Paper size drop-down list.
4. Change the Orientation to Landscape. Note that this is done in the Paper Size tab for Word 2000, but in the Margins tab for Word 2003/XP.
5. Click the Margins tab.
6. In Word 2003/XP, choose "2 Pages per Sheet" from the Multiple Pages drop-down list; in Word 2000, put a check mark by "2 Pages per Sheet."
7. Click OK.

Now your document will print two pages on a single sheet. In this case, an 8.5 × 14 sheet of legal paper.

Again, the big problem here is binding. While Word can print two pages on a sheet of paper, it's very difficult to glue or staple the multiple pages together to make a book. If you attempt it, then the pages will be out of sequence. In fact, it's just better to print the pages, cut them out (with a scissors), then paste them (with glue) into a book form.

Chapter 2

Alas, There Is No Such Thing as a "Simple" Document

THE ART OF WORD processing is a fairly easy one. In fact, I know a great many people who get by in Word using just a few basic features. That's fine. Yet, by not understanding some of the other basic features, folks are missing out on some wonderful shortcuts and terrific insights. I know the argument is, "Why waste tricks on a basic boring document?" But my answer is, "Why not?"

It's shameful the amount of time people waste over doing things that could be done automatically by the computer. I could offer example after example, but instead I thought I would present this chapter full of simple document sins and solutions. Yeah, it's more solutions than sins, so don't expect anything racy. The purpose here is to expose some of the more basic things Word does, tricks that will help you save time when you work on the typical document or letter.

- Understanding a document's margins
- Properly formatting paragraphs (a variety of choices)
- Paragraph spacing: before, after, and in the middle
- Some tips for writing so-called simple letters
- Fudging your document's length without affecting word count

Measuring Your Way around a Document

One of the secret keys to unlocking the mystery of Word is to know how the frustrating program measures things in a document. It's enough to drive you mad! In fact, writing this chapter did drive me mad. I had to spend several days in a nice soft room to recover. But when I came out, I had an epiphany. It was one of those undiscovered truths that helps us understand the universe. And that is that it doesn't really matter how Word measures things in a document. What matters are the results. When you know what it looks like, then you can work backward to get those results while freely ignoring any details.

Where the Hell Are My Margins?

They say that the computer HAL went nuts in *2001: A Space Odyssey* because it was given two sets of conflicting instructions. Well, the reason most Word users go insane is that you're given two sets of margins to deal with: the page margins and the paragraph margins.

Making Sense of Page Margins

The page margins tell Word where to offset the text in your document from the edge of the paper.

And there is the key word: *paper!* Page and paper go hand-in-hand in Word. Whenever you think of something on a page, consider it as part of the piece of paper that prints. In a way, that's utterly different from your document, which consists of words in paragraphs. Those paragraphs have their own margins as well.

Page margins are set in the realm of the Page Setup dialog box, Margins tab. To get there, choose File ➤ Page Setup.

NOTE *Keep in mind that most printers have absolute margin limits. For example, most laser printers cannot print on the outside half-inch of a page. Also, most inkjet printers need a larger margin at the top or bottom of the page in order to feed the paper through the printer.*

Headers and Footers: The Ugly Exceptions

Unlike all the other text in your document, headers and footers are not bound by the box created from your page margins. Nope, they're set differently, normally outside (above and below) the page margins. This is an odd exception, specifically because your header or footer can grow larger (top to bottom) depending on how much junk you place there.

To set the header and footer margins on a page, follow these steps:

1. Choose File ➤ Page Setup.
2. In Word 2003/XP, click the Layout tab to find the Header and Footer settings; in Word 2000, locate the Header and Footer settings in the bottom of the Margins tab. The measurements "From Edge" refer to the top edge of the paper for the Header and the bottom edge for the Footer.
3. Change these settings as necessary. For example, if you really, *really* want a one-inch margin all the way around your page, you'll need to change the settings for Header and Footer to 1.0″ instead of the 0.5″ .
4. Click OK.

Also note that large headers and footers do push into the text. So if your header has a huge graphic in it, that header pushes *down* and causes the top margin for text on the page to go down as well. (The best way to see how this affects your document is in Print Layout view.)

Get Your Mind out of the Gutter!

The *gutter margin* is used to create extra space on any given edge of the page for binding purposes. So, for example, if you're planning on sticking the pages into a folder, then you probably want a little extra room on the binding side, so that the text doesn't "run into the gutter."

If your document needs a gutter, then Word lets you set one in the Page Setup dialog box. You can specify whether to put the gutter on the top or left edge of the page; then you set the gutter's depth by using the Gutter gizmo.

Paragraph Margins

Most Word users become more confused with paragraph margins than they do page margins. This is most likely for two reasons:

- The paragraph margin measurements are relative to the page margin on the left.
- The Ruler tends to distort things by putting a zero-inch mark where the paragraph starts. Stupid Ruler.

Figure 2.1 shows the Ruler with all the important features labeled.

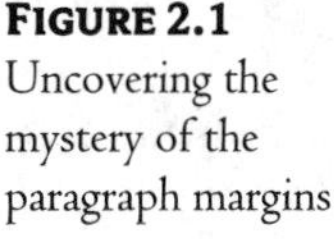

Figure 2.1
Uncovering the mystery of the paragraph margins

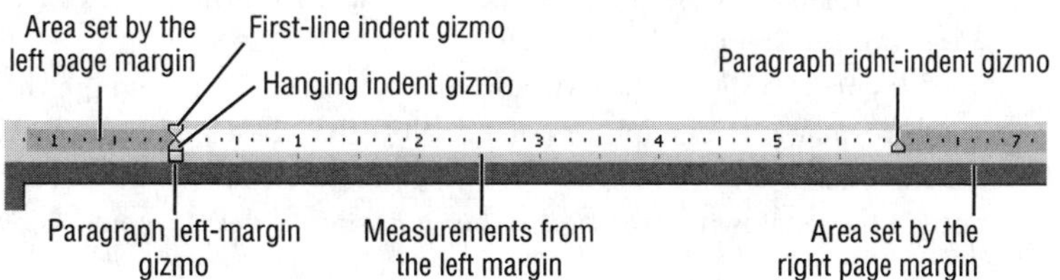

To best see how this works, switch to Print Layout view by choosing View ➤ Print Layout from the menu. Further, you may have to choose a Zoom value less than 100% to see the full page (left to right) on your monitor.

Print Layout view shows both horizontal and vertical rulers. The gray area is defined by the page margins. The white part of the ruler is what's used when setting paragraph margins.

Note that the paragraph's left margin is set at zero inches, which is *not* the edge of the page but rather the left margin offset. This is where most Word users get confused; paragraph measurements are from the *margin*, not the edge of the page!

The indent gizmos on the ruler are used to control the paragraph's margins manually. Otherwise, you use the Format ➤ Paragraph command to summon the Paragraph dialog box and set things up there by entering measurements. The next section discusses all the options and such.

USE THE PREVIEW WINDOWS AND PAGE PREVIEW COMMAND

Setting margins here and there and testing how things look can be a major pain! First, I recommend writing your text and worrying about margins and all that later. But second, and most importantly, take advantage of the various Preview panes in the margin-formatting dialog boxes. Use them to get an idea of what kind of formatting you're getting into.

Finally, don't forget about the Print Preview command (File ➤ Print Preview). It uses both horizontal and vertical rulers to show you just how your document will lay out on a page—a very valuable tool, not to be overlooked by any margin-manipulating maven.

I Want to Indent My Paragraph Like This!

Say hello to my handy visual formatting guide for soothing your paragraph ills!

The problem with paragraph formatting is the terminology: hanging, indent, offset, justified. These terms, like the fine print when you lease a car, mean nothing! So instead of trying to fool your brain into understanding them, I've come up with the visual sample formatting guide for the next few pages. Hopefully there's a paragraph format here that you like and want to use. If so, then follow the handy steps required to format your paragraph that way.

Figure 2.2 illustrates a sample preview paragraph. This gives you a quick idea of what the paragraph formatting should look like, complete with the approximate settings of the paragraph margin gizmos on the ruler.

Figure 2.3 shows the settings required inside the Paragraph dialog box, which you can access via the Format ➤ Paragraph command. Note that these measurements apply only to the Indentation part of the dialog box (which is why only it is shown). And you can adjust values to exact amounts other than those shown in the figure (but you should get the general idea).

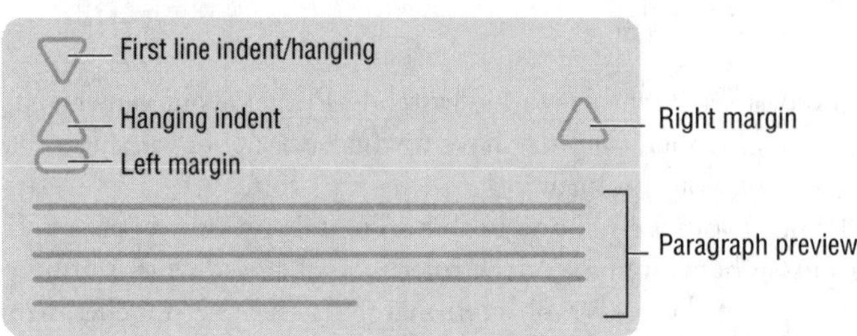

FIGURE 2.2
The sample paragraph-formatting example

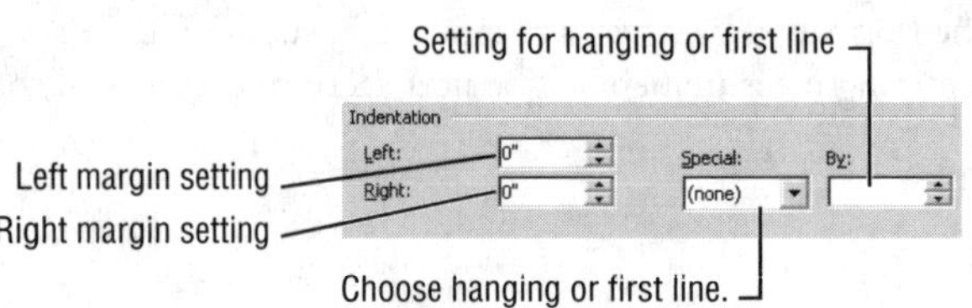

FIGURE 2.3
The example's sample Paragraph dialog box settings

Finally, ensure that the Ruler is visible when you use Word. Choose View ➤ Ruler if you don't see the Ruler on your screen.

NOTE *The following sections do not cover the basics of paragraph alignment: Left, Right, Centered, or Justified. Most of these operations take place on paragraphs that have been formatted either with Left or Justified alignment.*

Paragraph Formatting Lingo and Gizmos

Can't tell the formatting players without a scorecard? Here's a quick rundown of what the heck all these things are.

Alignment: Left The paragraph is lined up on the left margin but not on the right.

Alignment: Centered Each line of the paragraph is centered on the page.

Alignment: Right The paragraph is lined up on the right margin but not on the left.

Alignment: Justified The paragraph is lined up on both the left and right margins.

Indentation: Left The left edge of the paragraph is offset from the page's left margin by a given amount.

Indentation: Right The right edge of the paragraph is offset from the page's right margin by a given amount.

Indentation: Special: First Line The paragraph's first line is indented by the given amount.

Indentation: Special: Hanging The paragraph's first line is offset ("out-dented") from the rest of the lines by a given amount.

What's the Point of the Dull, No-Format Paragraph?

The point is that this is the prototype paragraph (the one shown in Figure 2.2). It's the one you want to recover to when your paragraph modifications have gone berserk and you need a small dose of sanity.

The typical paragraph Word starts out with has both the left and right margins offset at zero (even with the page margins). There is no first-line indent or hang. Yawn.

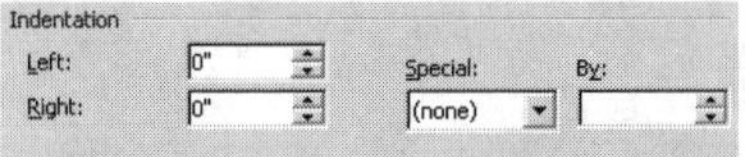

To compensate for the lack of first-line indent, most of these style paragraphs are typically followed by a vertical space. That's done either by tapping the Enter key twice after typing the paragraph or by adding space after the paragraph in the Paragraph dialog box. (This is covered later in this chapter.)

NOTE *Also note that this formatting is what's required to undo some of the more complex examples that follow. So when you want to return to plain and boring, reset your paragraph's margins to the values described in this section.*

Why Would I Want to Indent the First Line?

If you don't have any spaces between paragraphs, then indenting the first line tells the reader where the new paragraph starts. Otherwise your document will be one long Great Wall of Text and potentially intimidate your readers into a state of unconsciousness.

The first-line indent is a popular alternative to no first-line indent. By using a first-line indent, you also avoid the necessity of having to double space between paragraphs; the indented first line makes it easier to see paragraph breaks on a page.

The typical first-line indent is half an inch, as shown below. You can make the indent as wide or as narrow as you like.

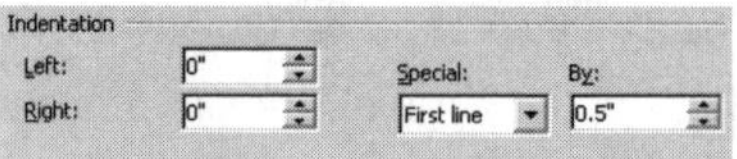

NOTE *By automatically formatting a paragraph with an indented first line, you no longer need to press the Tab key to start a paragraph. See? Computers can* make your life easier!

What Is a Hanging Indent and Why Would I Need One?

Hanging indents aren't common, but they can be ideal for certain types of lists, descriptions, or special items because the unusual paragraph formatting is appealing—especially how it stands out on the page.

A hanging indent paragraph looks like the first line is reverse-tabbed over beyond the margin, but that's not the case. Essentially, a hanging indent is where the first line is *not* indented but the rest of the paragraph is, as shown above.

KEYBOARD SHORTCUTS FOR THE INSTANT HANGING INDENT

Amazingly enough, Word has a keyboard combo to instantly create a hanging indent paragraph.

Ctrl+T Press Ctrl+T once, and the paragraph is hung-indented one-half inch. Press Ctrl+T again to indent another half inch, and so on. But if you go too far, there is a companion key:

Ctrl+Shift+T This key combination unhangs an indent by half an inch or merely undoes what's been done by the Ctrl+T key combination. (This keyboard shortcut has no effect on a paragraph without a hanging indent.)

Note especially how the left margin (shown below) is not changed by the hanging indent. Even though the indent gizmos on the ruler (above) look different, the margin indentation in the Paragraph dialog box has not changed. This has been known to drive people nuts.

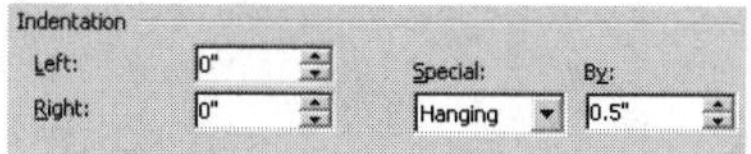

CAN THE INDENT ALSO HANG BEYOND THE PAGE MARGIN?

Okay. Sure. Whatever.

The quick way to hang an indent into the page margin is to drag the top first-line indent gizmo on the ruler to the left, into the gray area. That leaves the other items set on the left margin.

The harder way to do this is in the Paragraph formatting dialog box, shown below. In that case you must enter a negative value for the Left indent that is equal to the positive value of the hanging indent. Me? I can't understand that while I'm not intoxicated.

COME ON: IS THERE A *REAL* NEED TO HAVE A HANGING INDENT?

The true advantage of hanging indents comes when you create lists of things, what I call "item-tab-paragraphs." Figure 2.4 illustrates how the example looks on the page.

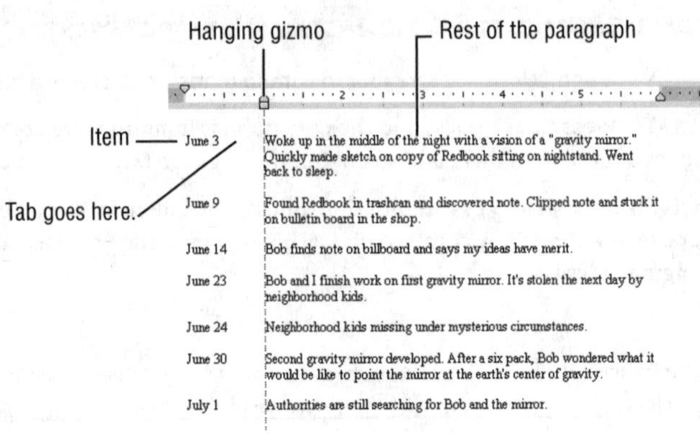

FIGURE 2.4
An example of an item-tab-paragraph

To make this happen, first type your paragraphs:

1. Type the item. It can be a date, location, term, or whatever.
2. Press the Tab key. Don't worry if the paragraph looks ugly at this point; you need the tab there for when you finally create the hanging indent.
3. Type the rest of the paragraph. Again, it won't line up right at this stage. Don't worry! You're just getting information down. Formatting comes after.
4. When you've finished typing all your paragraphs, you're ready to format. Select all the paragraphs.
5. On the Ruler, drag the hanging gizmo over to the left. As you drag, a line drops down onto the page, showing you where the indented paragraph's left margin will fall. Use that as a guide as you drag the hanging gizmo. Wait until all the paragraphs are lined up properly.
6. Release the mouse button to view your paragraphs. If you need to adjust the indent, drag the hanging gizmo farther to the right or back to the left. Or if you're picky, find a half-inch tick to line the gizmo up with.

The end result looks something like Figure 2.4. Note that even in that figure, the hanging indent could be moved farther to the left to tighten up the space after the item.

NOTE *The worst way to accomplish this same thing is by using spaces instead of the Tab key. Never use spaces! Any time you have to use more than one space, you should be using the Tab key instead! See Chapter 7 for more information on tabs.*

What If I Need a Continuation Item-Tab-Paragraph without an Item?

Just press the Tab key to start the line; then type the paragraph. Any text before the tab lines up at the left margin. Otherwise, when you press the Tab key, you slide the rest of the text over to the hanging indent margin.

How Can I Right-Align the Item and Then Left-Align a Paragraph?

This is a tough one to explain, but visually compare Figure 2.5 with Figure 2.4. Notice how in Figure 2.5 the items are lined up along their right edge, whereas in Figure 2.4 they're lined up along their left edge? This trick can easily be accomplished by following these steps:

Start by typing your paragraphs. Always do this first before you format, but note how the tabs are laid out:

1. Start each paragraph with a tab.
2. Type your item. And remember, these items must be short; otherwise the paragraphs will be too narrow and the whole thing will look damn ugly.
3. Press the Tab key again. Note that sometimes when you press the Tab key it appears as if the text doesn't move much. That's okay! Avoid the temptation to press the Tab key twice. Once is enough! The tab is in there, even if you can't see it. Trust me.
4. Type the rest of your paragraph. Yes, it will look ugly at this stage. But this is the best way to set up for the rest of the formatting.

After entering all your paragraphs, you're ready to format. This is where the ugliness clears up, but it also requires a bit of eyeballing and some finesse. Pay careful attention:

1. Select all the paragraphs.
2. Drag the hanging gizmo over to about the 2″ mark on the ruler. No, this isn't where you want it; it's just temporary.
3. Click the Tab well on the Ruler until you get the right tab symbol.

   The Tab well is found on the far-left end of the Ruler. The right tab symbol is a backward "L."

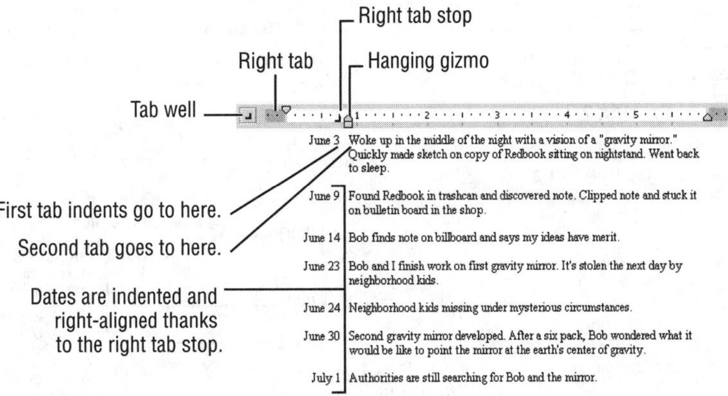

Figure 2.5
Say hello to the tab-item-tab-paragraph.

4. Click the mouse on the 1″ mark on the ruler to set the right tab there. You'll notice that the formatting is now better than it was before. All you need to do is adjust the offset of the right tab and hanging gizmo to perfectly line up your paragraphs.
5. Slide the right tab gizmo to the left. Slide it over as far as you can without shoving your items over to the left margin. For the dates in Figure 2.5, I chose the 0.75″ mark.
6. Click the hanging gizmo over to the left. You can put it as close to the text as you like, such as one tick away, as I chose in Figure 2.5. Or you can back the text off a bit for a more dramatic effect. But don't back the text too far over to the right or the paragraphs will scrunch up and wreck the right-align effect of the items.

The key to making this work is remembering the tab-item-tab sequence when you type the initial paragraphs. Then keep the right tab and hanging gizmo close together, as shown in Figure 2.5, and it can look pretty neat.

Is There Such a Thing as an Item-Tab-Item-Tab-Paragraph?

You can have as many items sitting on the first line of a paragraph as you have room for. Generally speaking, however, if you have more than two items at the start of a paragraph, then what you really need there is a *table* and not a paragraph. Refer to Chapter 7 for information on creating a table. Otherwise, you can set up the items as shown in Figure 2.6.

The idea here is that you start your paragraph with an item, press the Tab key, type the next item, and then press Tab again to type your paragraph. The first tab stop sets the position of the second item, and the hanging gizmo sets the position of the rest of the paragraph.

Start, as with previous examples, by typing your paragraphs ahead of time:

1. Start each paragraph with the first item.
2. Press the Tab key.
3. Type your second item. Both items must be short, as shown in Figure 2.6. Anything longer and you really need to use a table instead of this paragraph-formatting trick.

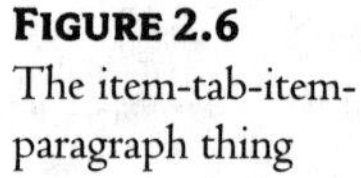

FIGURE 2.6
The item-tab-item-paragraph thing

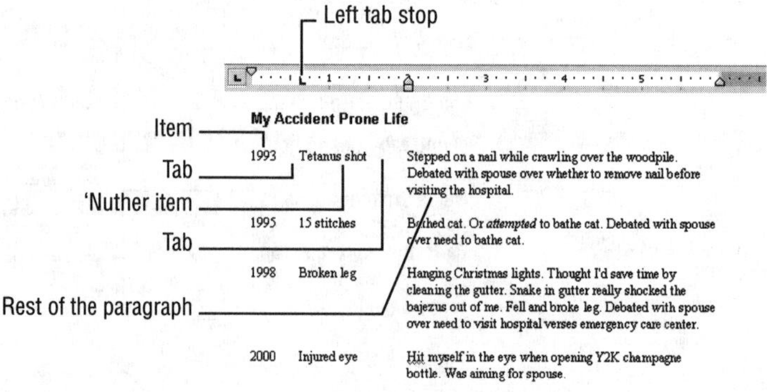

4. Press the Tab key again.
5. Type the paragraph. Forget that it looks ugly! This job you're doing with the Tab key makes it all line up better in a second.

When you've finished typing the paragraphs, you're ready to format them:

1. Select the paragraphs that you want to format.
2. Choose a left tab stop from the Tab well.

   The left tab stop looks like a fat letter "L." You may have to click the Tab well a few times until you get this symbol.
3. Click the Ruler at the 1″ stop to set the left tab stop there. This indents the second item in each paragraph. If you need to adjust the tab stop to the left or right, do so by dragging it with the mouse. (It's an eyeball thing; set the tab stop where it looks good for whatever list you're making.)
4. Drag the hanging gizmo to the 2″ spot on the ruler. That lines up the paragraph text (the third item). You can slide the hanging gizmo to the left or right to adjust how it looks with the rest of the text.

In Figure 2.6 I set the tab at 0.625″ and the hanging gizmo at 2″ exactly. Again, this is an eyeball thing, which is why it's best to use the Ruler instead of messing with the Tabs and Paragraph dialog boxes.

I Want to Have the Paragraph First and Then the Items on the Right Side of the Page.

Then what you need is a table. See Chapter 7.

When and How Would I Use a Block Quote?

Specifically, you block-quote any chunk of text that's too long to stick in double quotes in the middle of a paragraph. So when you decide to stick the "Gettysburg Address" into your document, you block-quote it to make it stand out special.

The block-quote text is simply a paragraph with both the left and right margins sunk in, typically one inch. To move the left margin, use the left-indent gizmo (the rectangle under the triangles); otherwise you have to move both the hanging and first-line gizmos separately.

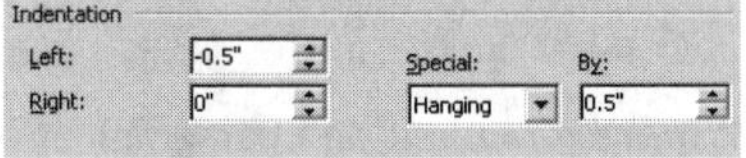

NOTE *When you use a block quote in a document, you do not have to put quotation marks around it. Simply introduce the quote, such as, "Here is what James Madison had to say about tyranny," and then contain the entire quote in the block or blocks that follow.*

How Do I Make a Block Quote with the First Line Indented?

It's unusual, but it can be done just as it would with any paragraph of text.

Indented block quotes simply share the same formatting as shown in the previous section, but with the addition of a half-inch (or less) offset with the first line of text.

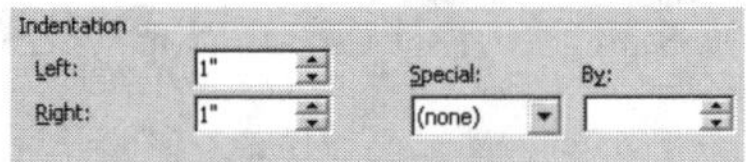

Which Is Better: To Indent Each Paragraph or Double Space between Paragraphs?

Deciding how to format your paragraphs depends on your mood. There are no hard-and-fast rules; in professional publishing, it's up to the "house style" as to which way to go. But, generally speaking, all documents are formatted one way or the other, rarely mixed.

To format indented paragraphs, simply set the first-line indent to 0.5″ or whatever you like. This can be done on the Ruler or in the Paragraph formatting dialog box, which is covered earlier in this chapter.

To automatically follow a paragraph with a space, you need to use the Paragraph dialog box: Choose Format ➤ Paragraph, and in the Spacing part of the dialog box, set the amount in the After text box. By working the gizmo in the After text box, you can set a space of 6 pt (six points) or 12 pt (12 points) after each paragraph you type.

This is automatic, so you don't need to double-press the Enter key at the end of a paragraph. Oh, and you can also manually type in any point value you like. For example, some twisted individuals prefer to follow fancy headings with only 3 pts of space. When your number is set, click OK.

Indenting a Paragraph by Keys

Word has a handy keyboard combo for indenting a paragraph one-half inch on the left margin. This isn't the same as a block indent, but it's close:

Ctrl+M Each time you press Ctrl+M, the paragraph's left margin is indented one-half inch. (The right margin is not affected.)

Ctrl+Shift+M Pressing this key combination unindents the left margin by one-half inch, effectively undoing whatever the Ctrl+M key combination has done.

Making Points

The *pt* abbreviation in Word stands for points. This is a typesetter's measurement, but you're already familiar with it in that Windows uses points to measure how large fonts are.

Typical values for points between paragraphs are 6 and 12. If you truly want a "blank line" between paragraphs, then choose a point size to match the point size of whatever font you're using. For example, if you're using 12 pt Times New Roman, then a 12-point space after each paragraph will give you your blank line.

This change applies to all selected paragraphs or any new paragraphs you type. Word automatically inserts the given number of points of "air" after each paragraph.

You can also use the "Spacing: Before" item in the Paragraph dialog box to add that much more space between your paragraphs. However, I typically use only the "Spacing: After" item to keep all my paragraphs consistent and to keep myself sane when I try to track down weird formatting errors.

NOTE *The best way to ensure that the blank space follows all your paragraphs is to create a style in Word and apply that style to all your paragraphs. See Chapter 5, "Using Styles and Templates to Save Oodles of Time."*

I Hate the Way This Paragraph Breaks Up!

One way to control (or at least attempt to control) the way a paragraph breaks up between two pages is to take advantage of the Line and Page Breaks tab in the Paragraph dialog box, shown in Figure 2.7. Use the options there, described in the figure, to help you keep your paragraphs from being mangled between two pages.

NOTE *Word does try its best to heed your instructions about not breaking up paragraphs. However, there are some cases where breakup must occur.*

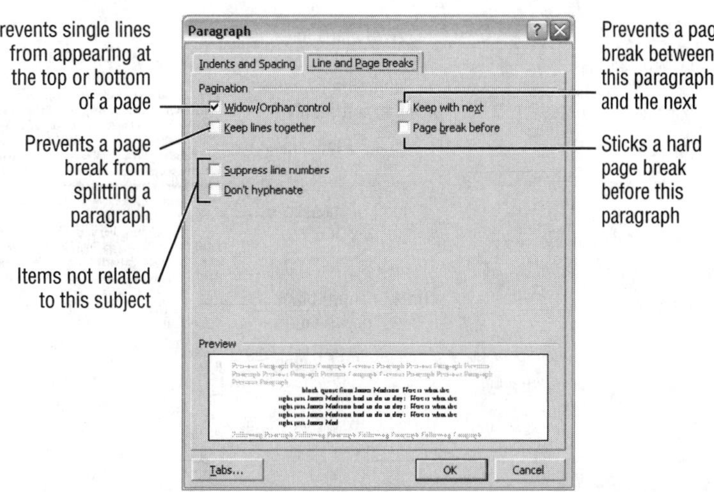

FIGURE 2.7
The other side of the Paragraph dialog box

Stuff You Can Do Better When You're Writing a Simple Letter

While desperately trying to think up things you can do with a word processor, software developers inevitably claim, "You can write a letter." Sometimes there's more detail: "You can write a letter home" or "You can write a letter to a long-lost friend." Whatever. In the age of e-mail, do people still write letters?

Yes, you bet they do! And they write them as badly as they compose their e-mail. My favorite letter is the quasi-legal-sounding letters I get from annoying neighbors and political enemies. I'd happily list one here as an example of "what not to do," but that would spawn a whole raft of new quasi-legal-sounding letters, so I shall be more bland in the examples that follow.

Where Does My Address Go on a Simple Letter?

Honestly, it does not matter where you put your address on a letter! Such things used to fall under the guise of *etiquette*. Remember Ms. Manners? Ha! You thought I had her killed, but I didn't. She's still with us and as full of recommendations as ever. Of course, back when we had social classes and an aristocracy, you could get into serious trouble when writing a malformed letter. Today, in the age of e-mail, no one really cares. (Sorry, Ms. M.)

Still, according to the information I've dug up, the traditional way to format a simple, personal letter is shown in Figure 2.8. Note that neither your address nor their address needs to go anywhere on the letter. (Even so, I've seen letters where the recipient's address goes above the salutation.)

A typical business letter is shown in Figure 2.9. Your address is considered to be part of the letterhead (which is included in the document header in the figure). If not, then your address follows the closing. Otherwise, Figure 2.9 holds all the secrets.

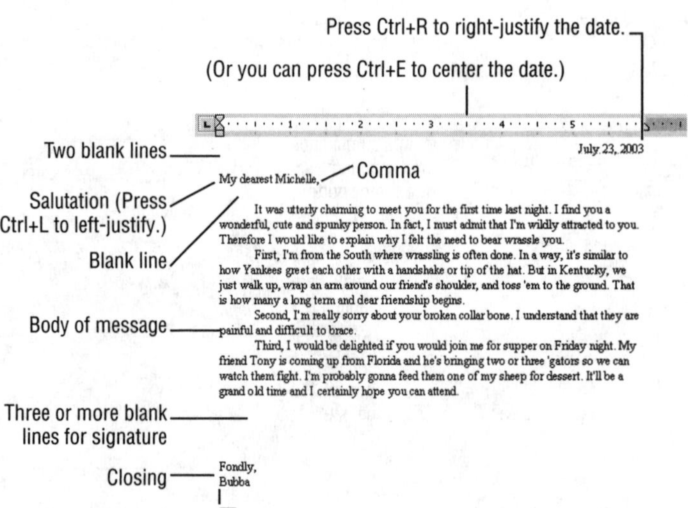

July 23, 2003

My dearest Michelle,

It was utterly charming to meet you for the first time last night. I find you a wonderful, cute and spunky person. In fact, I must admit that I'm wildly attracted to you. Therefore I would like to explain why I felt the need to bear wrassle you.

First, I'm from the South where wrassling is often done. In a way, it's similar to how Yankees greet each other with a handshake or tip of the hat. But in Kentucky, we just walk up, wrap an arm around our friend's shoulder, and toss 'em to the ground. That is how many a long term and dear friendship begins.

Second, I'm really sorry about your broken collar bone. I understand that they are painful and difficult to brace.

Third, I would be delighted if you would join me for supper on Friday night. My friend Tony is coming up from Florida and he's bringing two or three 'gators so we can watch them fight. I'm probably gonna feed them one of my sheep for dessert. It'll be a grand old time and I certainly hope you can attend.

Fondly,
Bubba

FIGURE 2.8
A sample piece of personal correspondence

FIGURE 2.9
A sample piece of business correspondence

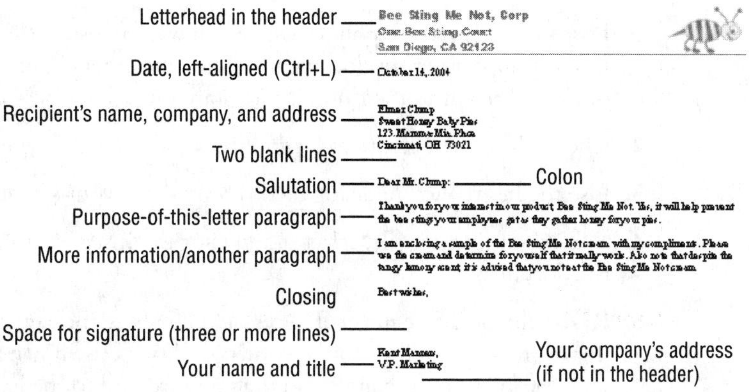

Letterhead in the header
Date, left-aligned (Ctrl+L)
Recipient's name, company, and address
Two blank lines
Salutation
Colon
Purpose-of-this-letter paragraph
More information/another paragraph
Closing
Space for signature (three or more lines)
Your name and title
Your company's address (if not in the header)

How Can I Add My Signature to a Letter?

The easiest way to add a signature to a letter is to print the stinking thing out and sign it. But, no: This is a computer and you must do things electronically.

1. Write your signature a few times on a white piece of paper. Use black ink. In fact, use a fat black marker, like a Sharpie pen. Feel free to write larger than normal or extra fancy. If you sign your signature the same every time, then there's no reason to write it out more than once. Me? I'm different every time, so I have to keep writing until I find a signature I like.
2. Scan the signature you like best. Set your scanner to grab a grayscale (not monochrome) image. Set the pixel depth to 256, but not higher. Scanning at about 150 dpi should do the job.
3. Save the scanned signature to disk as a TIFF image. Save the image in your My Pictures folder, or some other folder where you can easily find it.

NOTE *The signature's size on the screen is not important at this point. In fact, larger is better, since you may have to resize the signature to look best on the page.*

COMMON GREETINGS FOR YOUR CORRESPONDENCE

For familiar recipients, using "Dear" is the proper way to start a letter, as in "Dear Francis." If it's a personal letter, then you can even say "My dearest Christina."

For noncasual relations, "Dear Mr. Manfredi" or "Dear Ms. Johnson" is preferred.

For situations when the person's name is not known, you can use "Dear Sir or Madam," or if you know the title, then use "Dear Product Manager" or something similar.

When you need to stick your signature into a document, then follow these steps in Word:

1. Position the insertion pointer where you want the signature to be plopped down. The signature will appear in your document just like any other chunk of text, so if you want it at the start of a new line, press the Enter key to start a new line.
2. Choose Insert ➤ Picture ➤ From File.
3. Use the Insert Picture dialog box to browse for your signature file.
4. When you find the file, select it and click the Insert button. The signature image appears in the document.
5. Resize the signature image if necessary. To resize the signature, click it once to select it. The image grows "handles" on the corners and sides, as shown in Figure 2.10. Use the mouse to grab the lower-right handle and drag upward and to the left to make the picture smaller, or drag downward and to the right to make it larger.

Inserting a signature like this places that "picture" into the document just like any other character. So if you end up with extra space before or after the signature, simply select and delete those lines. Likewise, because the picture is like any character, you can indent or align it as necessary.

Also see Chapter 3, "Making Your Documents and Reports More Fancy," for more information on playing with images in documents.

FIGURE 2.10
Resizing your signature

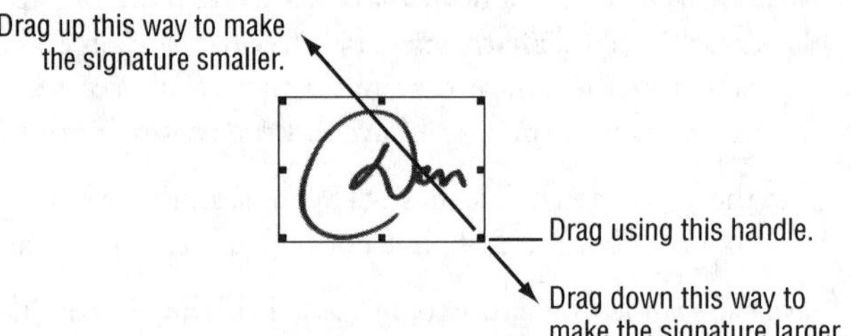

Drag up this way to make the signature smaller.
Drag using this handle.
Drag down this way to make the signature larger.

PROPERLY SIGNING OFF A LETTER

There are many ways to end a business or formal letter, depending on how you feel: "Best wishes," "Sincerely," "Yours truly," and so on. My favorite cold-shoulder ending is "Cordially." For personal letters, you can use "Love," "Fondly," "Cheers," "All my best," and so on, with the closing proper for the recipient.

This closing should be followed by ample space for a signature (I use three lines) and then your full name and, if applicable, company title.

If it's a familiar or casual letter, then writing only your first name is considered fine, but proper etiquette guides recommend against using a casual sign-off such as "Yours" or anything other than those mentioned above.

The only time you don't need to type out your name at the bottom of the letter is if your name already appears as part of the letterhead. You still need to sign the letter, however.

Don't Letters Also Need Envelopes?

After writing your letter, tell Word to print a corresponding envelope. To do that, ensure that the letter document is on the screen, and then open the Envelopes and Labels dialog box:

- In Word 2003/XP, choose Tools ➤ Letters and Mailings ➤ Envelopes and Labels.
- In Word 2000, choose Tools ➤ Envelopes and Labels.

As if by magic, Word picks up the recipient's address and places it into the Envelopes and Labels dialog box, shown in Figure 2.11. If you don't see the proper address there, then Word probably couldn't locate it: Select the address in the document before you open the Envelopes and Labels dialog box. (Or you can always manually type in the address.)

FIGURE 2.11
Adding an envelope

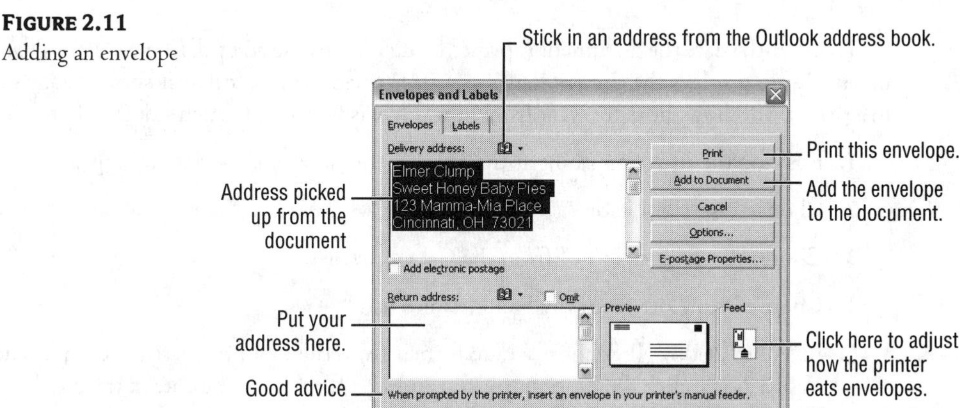

What's the Difference between Inserting Today's Date and the Current Date?

Ah! A logic puzzle: The difference between today's date and the current date is that tomorrow, today's date will be yesterday's date and the current date will again be today's date.

Confused?

Let me put it another way: If you want the document to always have the date it was written, then type in *today's date*: clackity-clack-clack-clack. But if you want to have the document's date change depending on when the document is printed, then use the *current date*.

Oh, bother! This needs more explaining!

To stick today's date into a document, choose Insert ➤ Date and Time. This displays the Date and Time dialog box, shown in Figure 2.12. Pick out a date or time format, and then click the OK button.

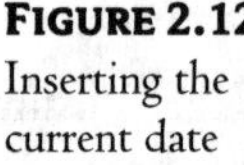

FIGURE 2.12
Inserting the current date

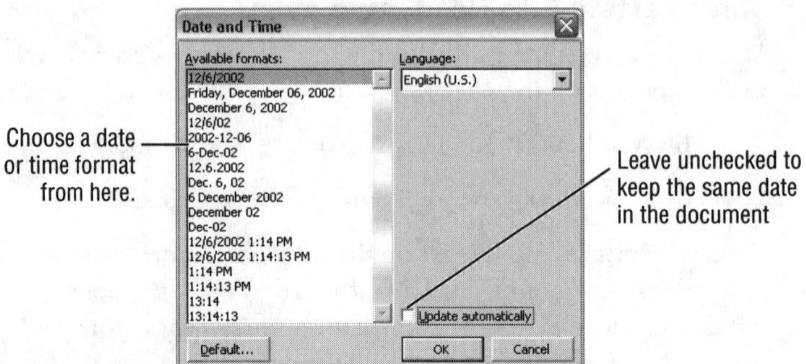

To insert the date the document is printed, you need to use an updating *date field*. That way the document always displays the current date, no matter what. Print it today, it shows today's date. Print it in a year, it will show the date a year from now. Here is how to add such a date field to your document:

1. Position the insertion point at the spot where you want the date to appear.
2. Choose Insert ➤ Field.
3. Choose "Date and Time" from the Categories list.
4. Choose PrintDate from the Field Names list.
5. In Word 2003/XP, choose a date format from the Field Properties column that appears. In Word 2000, click the Options button and set a format for the date in the Field Options dialog box; click the Add to Field button, then click OK.
6. Click the OK button to insert an updating date field.

Don't be alarmed if the date field appears "blank." That's because the date value won't actually be entered until you print the document. Then, when you print, only today's date will be inserted into the document.

To delete the field, you must select it and then press the Delete key.

Also refer to Chapter 7 for more information on fields in Word documents.

What Can I Do If I Have to Send the Same Type of Letter Over and Over?

If you find yourself rewriting the same type of letter, consider creating a document template for the letter. This is covered in Chapter 5.

If the letter merely has small parts that change, such as the recipient's personal information and perhaps a few other items, then you should do a mail merge to produce a stack of similar letters. Alas, this book does not cover mail merge; it's just too radically different for each release of Word.

NOTE *For Word 2003/XP, you can refer to my web page for help on mail merge:* `www.wambooli.com/help/Word/2002.mailmerge/`.

Various Spacing Tricks for Making Your Document Longer or Shorter

I'm sure you've been there. I have. It's the point where some idiot teacher or professor wants a 2,000-word report on how hairstyles influenced political reform in seventeenth-century Mongolia. Or you may be asked to write a five-page dissertation on how hip-hop music affects the mating habits of the North American honeybee. Whatever!

The following sections divulge some of what I think are the sneakiest tricks on getting more crap on the page than you could otherwise do with a typewriter. If you've ever written a two-page report and needed three pages, or needed to whittle down that five-page report to four, then this is the place to look for the best size-changing tricks.

Discover the True Word Count!

Only writers care about word count, and that's because we're often paid by the word. Unlike when you're in school, when you're *paid* by the word you can never seem to find any shortage of them. In school, however, words are as rare as a full set of teeth in a Montana tattoo parlor.

Don't Forget These Simple Resizing Tricks

- The first trick you can pull to change your document's page count is to subtly change the font size. The key is *subtly*, not obnoxiously. Most Word documents use 12-point type. Change it to 11 or 10 if you need fewer pages. To beef up the page count, change it to 13. Forget changing the font size to 14, however, as that's a dead giveaway. (Note that you can type "in between" values directly into the Font Size box.)
- Switch to a smaller or larger font. Not all fonts are the same size. Some are slightly larger or smaller than others. For example, Bookman at 10 points looks about the same size as Times New Roman at 12 points. Reformatting your text to Bookman 12 pt makes the document look longer.
- Adjust your page margins. Use the Page Setup dialog box to squeeze the margins in or out by quarter-inch increments.
- To make a short document longer, select all the text and press Ctrl+5 to change the line spacing to ½.
- Mess with the character spacing. Select the entire document and choose Format ➢ Font. Click the Character Spacing tab. From the Spacing drop-down list choose Expanded to slightly increase the document length, or choose Condensed to tighten things up. Then enter an amount to expand or tighten in the By box. Use the Preview window at the bottom of the dialog box to ensure that you don't go overboard.
- Try using both paragraph-formatting techniques: Start each paragraph with a first-line indent, but also put a space between each paragraph.
- To expand, use a block-quote format for quotations instead of putting the quotations inline. Or vice versa to tighten.
- To make a document longer, break it up with titles. Properly defined title styles include space before and after.

To find out how many words are in your document, choose Tools ➤ Word Count. This displays a dialog box, similar to Figure 2.13, which enlightens you as to a number of document-measuring facts.

If you have Word XP or Word 2003 and become grossly concerned over your document's word count, then you can use the Word Count floating toolbar to keep a constant tab on how your document is faring. To do so, choose View ➤ Toolbars ➤ Word Count. The Word Count floating toolbar appears, which you can move to any part of your document window or "dock" it next to another toolbar or the edge of the window. Figure 2.14 shows how to work the floating toolbar.

FIGURE 2.13
Pulling a word count

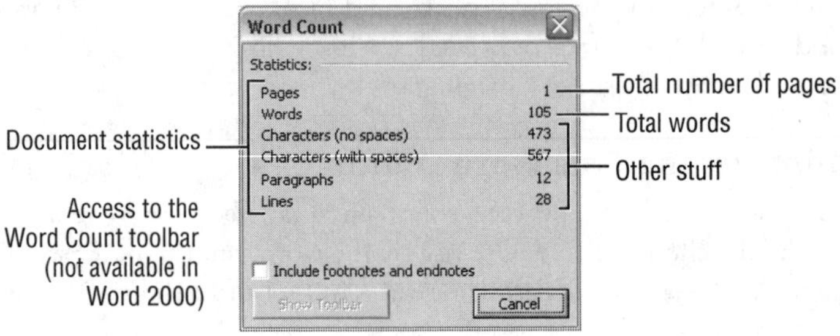

Word Count
Statistics:
Pages 1
Words 105
Characters (no spaces) 473
Characters (with spaces) 567
Paragraphs 12
Lines 28
Include footnotes and endnotes
Show Toolbar
Cancel
Total number of pages
Total words
Other stuff
Document statistics
Access to the Word Count toolbar (not available in Word 2000)

FIGURE 2.14
The handy Word Count floating toolbar

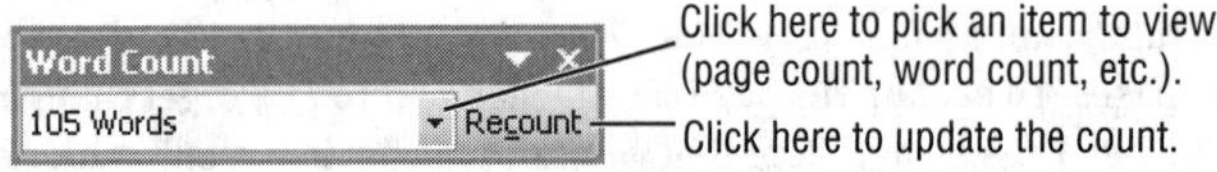
Word Count
105 Words
Recount
Click here to pick an item to view (page count, word count, etc.).
Click here to update the count.

Does Hyphenating Help?

I recommend against using Word to hyphenate your documents. Hyphenation may, on the whole, tighten up a document. However, hyphenated documents are more difficult to read, plus it becomes more of a bother to edit the document, as well as to export the text to another application, should you ever need to do so.

What's the Difference between Adding Spaces between Lines and Adding Spaces between Paragraphs?

There are two ways to "space out" a paragraph. The first is by changing the paragraph's line spacing; the second is by adding space before or after the paragraph proper.

When you change a paragraph's line spacing, you're adding "air" between each line of the paragraph, as well as air between paragraphs. Figure 2.15 illustrates an example of double spacing, where one space is inserted between each line of the paragraph. This is setting is made in the Paragraph dialog box, as shown in Figure 2.16.

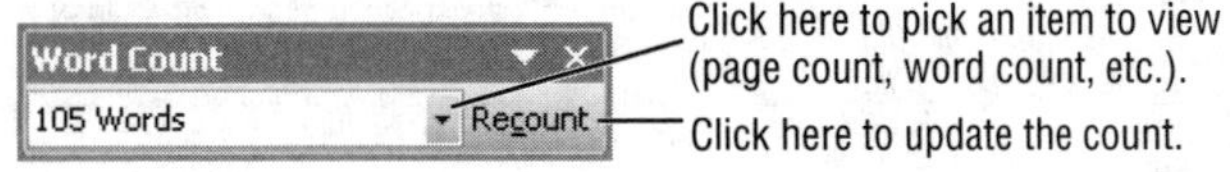

FIGURE 2.15
How double spacing affects a paragraph's look

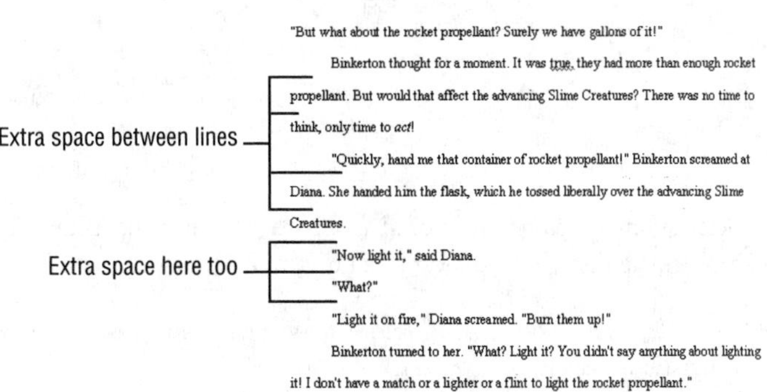

FIGURE 2.16
Spacing options in the Paragraph dialog box

The Line Spacing drop-down list provides several options for changing line spacing, which are listed in Table 2.1.

Also note that Word 2003 sports an interesting Line Spacing toolbar button menu, which you can use to select the line spacing for your document.

Adding line spacing to the start or end of a paragraph merely adds "air" between paragraphs, not in the middle (as line spacing does). Contrast Figure 2.17 with Figure 2.15 to see an example.

TABLE 2.1: VARIOUS LINE SPACING DEFINITIONS

LINE SPACING	KEYBOARD SHORTCUT	DESCRIPTION
Single	Ctrl+1	Each line of text is on a line by itself; no blanks follow the line.
1.5 lines	Ctrl+5	Each line of text is followed by a blank line half the size of the text line.
Double	Ctrl+2	Each line of text is followed by a full-sized blank line.
At least		Specify a point size for spacing between the lines.
Exactly		Specify a point size for spacing between the lines.
Multiple		The At gizmo is used to select the line spacing. For example, choosing 3 from that box sets triple spacing in the document.

FIGURE 2.17
Adding air between paragraphs

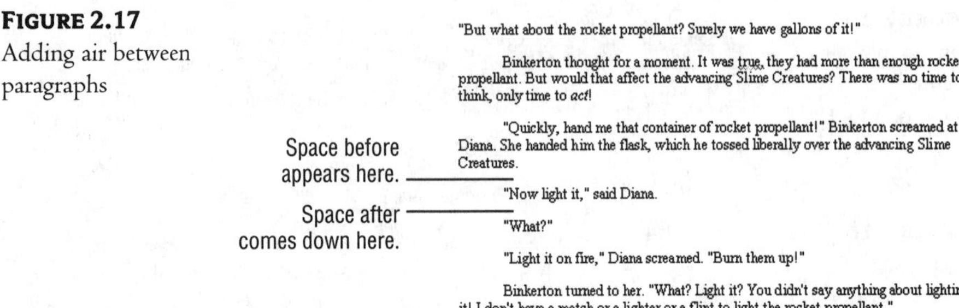

Setting line spacing before or after a paragraph is done using the Spacing: Before or Spacing: After gizmos in the Paragraph dialog box (Figure 2.16).

NOTE *There is no right or wrong choice with space between the lines (line spacing) or space before or after. It's more of an artistic decision on which to go for.*

How Can I Quickly Change My Document from Single to Double Spacing?

The easiest way to change paragraph formatting is by using styles. When you modify a style, you modify all the paragraphs that use that style. Otherwise, you have to adjust your paragraphs manually:

1. Press Ctrl+A to select all the text in your document. Or you can use the mouse or any common selection technique to select the text you want to reformat.
2. Press Ctrl+2 to apply double spacing. Or you can use the Format ➢ Paragraph command and the Paragraph dialog box to change your text's formatting.

What's the Difference between "At Least" and "Exactly" Line Spacing?

The "At Least" option can be fudged a bit when Word needs to, whereas "Exactly" always stays the same. The only time such a difference comes into play is when you have two different fonts or two different type sizes in the same paragraph. In that case, with the "At Least" option, Word may add more space between the lines to accommodate the larger text. However, if you specify "Exactly" instead, then Word will not monkey around with the line spacing.

NOTE *If it ever seems that Word is cutting off the top of your text or, more obviously, the top of a graphic, then it's most likely that the paragraph has been formatted with "Exactly" line spacing. The cure: Switch to any other form of line spacing.*

Which Is Better, Space before a Paragraph or Space After?

I prefer setting extra space *after* a paragraph and not before. After all, that's how the line-spacing function operates in Word.

The only time I specify extra spacing before a paragraph is when the paragraph is a header or contains graphical or other elements that I feel need extra "breathing" room to separate themselves from the rest of the junk on the page.

Why Is There No Shortcut for Adding Space after a Paragraph?

While Word has shortcut keys for line spacing, there is no shortcut key for adding space before or after a paragraph. Sometimes I wish there was. Commonly I add six points between paragraphs. Selecting a paragraph of text and pressing, say, Ctrl+6 to add those six points would be a handy shortcut. In fact, you can create such a shortcut if you follow these steps:

1. Choose Tools ➤ Macro ➤ Record New Macro.

The Record Macro dialog box appears. Alas, I consider macros to be an "advanced" topic, and though they are mentioned in this book, you really need a book on Office Basic or Word Basic or Visual Basic for Applications (or whatever they're calling it this week) to fully understand the bizarre complexity of macros.

1. Type **Add6pt** into the "Macro Name" text box. That means "Add six points after a paragraph."
2. Click the Keyboard button. The Customize Keyboard dialog box appears. This is where you can assign the new command—the shortcut for adding space after a paragraph—to a key combination.
3. Because Ctrl+1, Ctrl+2, and Ctrl+5 each mess with a paragraph's line spacing, why not use Ctrl+6 to add six points after a paragraph? Press Ctrl+6. The shortcut key "Ctrl+6" appears in the "Press New Shortcut Key" box. Note that Ctrl+6 is already assigned to the Unlink-Fields command. That's no big deal; I don't know anyone who places a priority on that obscure command over a paragraph-formatting command.
4. Click the Assign button, then click the Close button.

And now Word is ready to record your actions for the macro. The Stop Recording floating toolbar appears, as shown in Figure 2.18. Also the mouse pointer has grown a cassette tape icon. All this reminds you that your activities in Word are now being recorded. Proceed:

1. Choose Format ➤ Paragraph.
2. In the "Spacing: After" gizmo, choose 6 pt.
3. Click OK.
4. Click the Stop button on the Stop Recording floating toolbar (Figure 2.18).

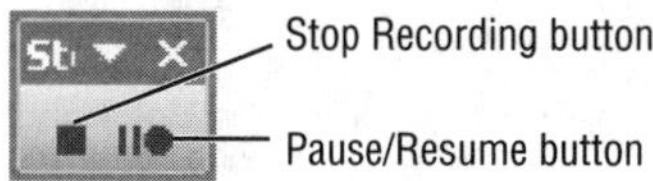

FIGURE 2.18
The Record Macro floating toolbar dealie

Now the macro has been recorded and assigned to shortcut key Ctrl+6. But before leaving it at that, you need to (unfortunately) go in and clean up all the crap Word put into the macro:

1. Choose Tools ➤ Macro ➤ Macros. The Macros dialog box appears with a list of available macros. Unless you've messed with macros before, you should see only one, Add6pt.
2. Select the Add6pt macro.
3. Click the Edit button. Word runs the Microsoft Visual Basic editor, which should shock and appall you, but that's okay; remember this book is not about macros.

The problem with the recorded macro is *too much freaking information*, which is typical of many things Office applications create. (Don't get me started on the excess information that happens when you save a Word document as a web page!)

The idea here is to trim out the unneeded information and leave the macro with only the instructions required to add six points to the butt end of a paragraph. To meet that end:

1. Edit the macro down so that it looks like this and only this:

```
Sub Add6pt()
'
' add6p Macro
' Macro recorded 7/4/05 by Dan Gookin
'
    With Selection.ParagraphFormat
        .SpaceAfter = 6
    End With
End Sub
```

   Just delete all the other crap. If it's not listed above, delete it. (Do note that the line about the macro recorded will be specific for your computer; there's no need to change it.)

2. When you've finished with the changes, choose File ➤ Close and Return to Microsoft Word.

And now you've finished! To demonstrate the macro, click a paragraph or select several paragraphs. Then press Ctrl+6. That changes the paragraph's formatting so that it's followed by six points of space—a great trick to use when trying to provide more breathing room on a page full of paragraphs.

Chapter 3

Making Your Documents and Reports More Fancy

JUST ABOUT ANYONE CAN cobble together a document by using the alphanumeric keys on the keyboard, plus Backspace and Enter. Oh, and the Tab key (if they're clever). But you bought this book because you suspected there was more. And there is!

After reading this chapter, you'll be able to spruce up your boring old report or document with some spiffy new pages, the kind of things that would take those casual word-processing folk *years* to figure out. But you don't need years, only the handy information contained in this chapter!

- Getting the special page thing to happen with sections
- Using sections to control page formatting
- Creating title pages
- Working with page numbers
- Sticking relative page numbers into a document
- Renumbering, un-numbering, and generally becoming numb

How Do You Know a Special Page When You See One?

Special pages are easy to spot *after* they've been created. They give you that sense of "how the heck did they do that?" The answer is "simply." But the reason is, "Because I took some vaguely defined Word commands and put them to use so I could create something unique in my document to make it look better than your document." That's when you go "Oh!" and scurry off to try the trick for yourself.

But don't scurry off just yet! The following sections demonstrate how to create those special pages in any document. They use some obscure or obscurely named Word commands to do it—stuff you may already be familiar with but never knew the full potential of.

Why Do I Need to Know about Sections?

When you scratch Word's formatting abilities just below the surface you'll find boundaries. Character formatting, for example, applies only to text: Font, size, attributes, and all that are applied only to characters.

Beyond character formatting is paragraph formatting. There are certain formatting commands that apply only to paragraphs: Center, Justify, Indent, and so on.

Above paragraph formatting is page formatting, where you set page margins, headers, footers, and other formats applied to the page.

Above the page formatting? Is there anything there?

You bet! It's where you'll find *sections*. By using sections, you can divide up your document's pages by shifting the page format. So if you need a page centered here, you create a new section. If you need a page printed in landscape orientation there, then you apply a section. Sections are the largest chunk you can format in any document.

Figure 3.1 illustrates a document with several sections in it. It's tiny, but still you can see how each section holds its own page formatting. The formatting for the page in one section doesn't affect the formatting in another. Once you know this, then you can take advantage of it to really spice up your documents.

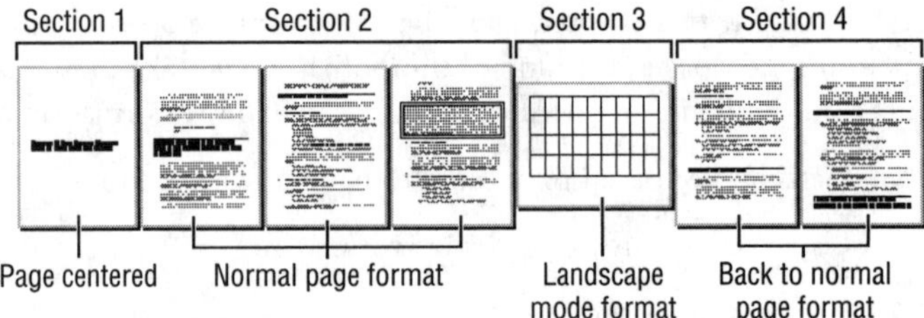

FIGURE 3.1
Various sections in a document

HOW CAN I CREATE A NEW SECTION?

Sections are created using the Break dialog box. It's weird that a computer program would have a Break dialog box. You'd think the idea would be to *not* break things, but no. Or could it be "break" as in break up the text into chunks? Hmmm...

Choose Insert ➤ Break from the menu, and you'll see a dialog box similar to the one shown in Figure 3.2. There you have a choice of page or section breaks, as described in the figure.

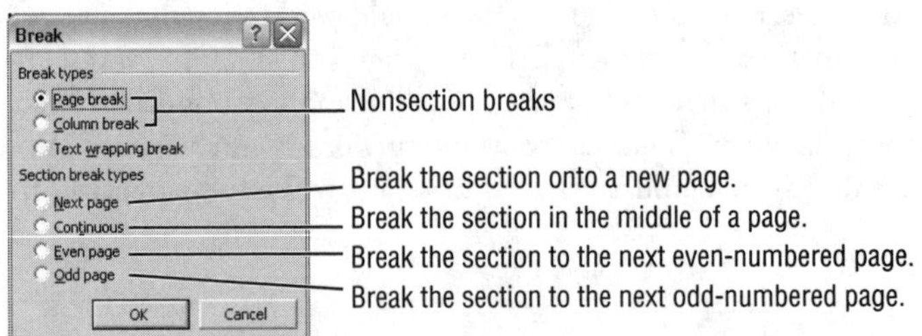

FIGURE 3.2
Sections are created here.

Only the Continuous option doesn't create a hard page break. And the Even and Odd section breaks will insert blank pages to line up the section break properly. (The Even and Odd options are best used when you're creating documents with different even and odd page formats.)

Of course, the key question is "Why bother?" but that's covered over the next few pages of this chapter.

How Can I Tell Which Section I'm In?

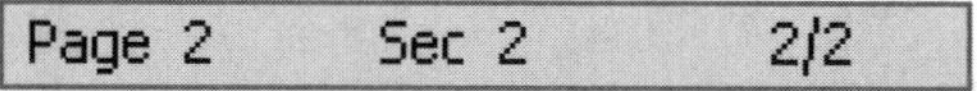

Sections are listed on the status bar with the abbreviation *Sec.* Normally documents have one section, Sec 1. But when you mess with sections, your document can have a bunch of them. That Sec thing on the status bar lets you know which one you're working in.

How Can I Center My Title Page Top to Bottom?

The ideal title page appears as its own section in a document. That way you can use the page-formatting command that centers text from top to bottom on that page and not have it affect other pages in your document. Yes, indeed, a title page is a *special page.*

The typical yet incorrect way to create a title page is to first write the page, insert a hard page break, and then write the rest of the document. The result looks like Figure 3.3, which may be what you want. Alas, many Word users attempt to manually center the text by whacking the Enter key until the title looks more or less centered. In a word processor, that's a "bad thing" to do.

FIGURE 3.3
A typical title page

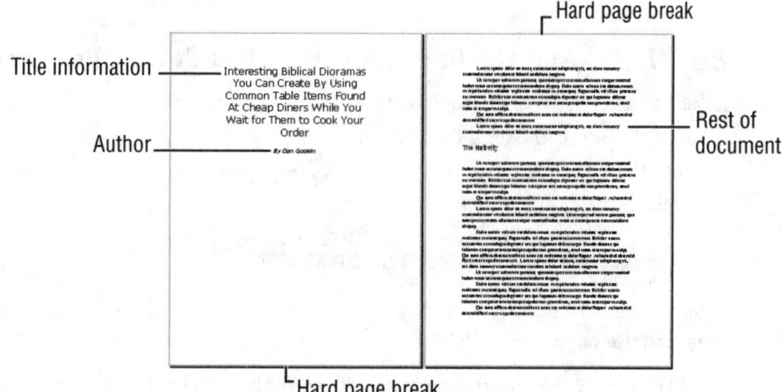

The good thing to do is to use a section break to separate the title page from the rest of the document. This is so close to what most people attempt to do that the difference isn't worth mentioning, but the benefits are huge. Here's how it works:

1. Type the title page.

   Just type the text.

If you've already typed the title page, delete it (and the hard page break, if there). Start over.

NOTE *Most titles are centered. Use the Ctrl+E shortcut to center a paragraph. To double-space the paragraph, use Ctrl+2.*

2. After typing the title, choose Insert ➤ Break.
3. Choose "Next Page" to create a page break and a new section.
4. Click OK.

So far the section break is merely the same as a page break. Only by applying a different page formatting to the title page will the section break really help with formatting.

1. Click the mouse on your title page. You're about to reformat the page attributes for the title page.
2. Choose File ➤ Page Setup.
3. Click the Layout tab.
4. In the Page: Vertical Alignment area, choose Center from the drop-down list. It will likely say Top there now, which is how Word aligns text on the page, from the top down.
5. Click OK. And now the title is centered. You can use Print Preview to confirm this.

Because you built the title page into its own section, its attributes (centered) are not carried over into the next section, which contains the bulk of your document's text.

But I Don't Want a Page Number, Header, or Footer on My Title Page!

Like the ancient word processing nobles they are, page numbers, headers, and footers are wise and respect the section break boundaries. As long as your title page is created as its own section in a document, then you can halt any headers, footers, or page numbers from appearing on that page.

SOME TITLE PAGE KEYBOARD SHORTCUTS

Whether you're heeding my advice or not, here are some of the keyboard shortcuts you can use to help you create a title page:

Ctrl+Enter A "hard page break," this keyboard shortcut forces an immediate new page in the document. (It can be deleted using Backspace or Delete just as any other "character" can be removed in a document.)

Ctrl+E Center a paragraph of text.

Alt+I, B, N, Enter Insert a Next Page section break; better than using Ctrl+Enter when you want to set a title page.

Ctrl+F, U Display the Page Setup dialog box, where most page setting options are made—the options that can affect only one section if you wish them to.

To suppress a page number on the first page, follow these steps:

1. Click the mouse on the first page.
2. Choose Insert ➤ Page Numbers.
3. Remove the check mark by "Show Number on First Page."
4. Click OK.

If that doesn't work, then the page number probably lives on a header or footer, so you'll need to suppress the header and footer for the first page/section. Here's how that works:

1. Choose View ➤ Header and Footer. The Header and Footer floating palette appears over your document (Figure 3.4), and the Header or Footer window appears on your document inside of Word.

   Right now, the header is probably the same for all sections. Which means the header for Section 1 (on the title page) is also used for Section 2.

2. Visit the Section 2 header.

   Click the Show Next button to see "Header - Section 2." If it says, "Same as Previous," then you need to copy the header (and footer) from Section 1 into Section 2. That can be involved, so carefully follow these steps:

   1. Click the Show Previous button to return to Section 1, where the title page lurks.
   2. Select all the text in the header (use Ctrl+A).
   3. Cut the text from the header (with Crtl+X).
   4. Click the Show Next button on the toolbar.
   5. Click the Same as Previous button. This "unlinks" the header text between the two sections.
   6. Press Ctrl+V to paste the header text into Section 2's header.

      The reason these extra steps (above) are required is that otherwise the header is lost when you click the Same as Previous button. Therefore you must cut and paste it before you unlink.

   7. Repeat steps A through E for the footer as well. Click the Switch Between Header and Footer button to do this.

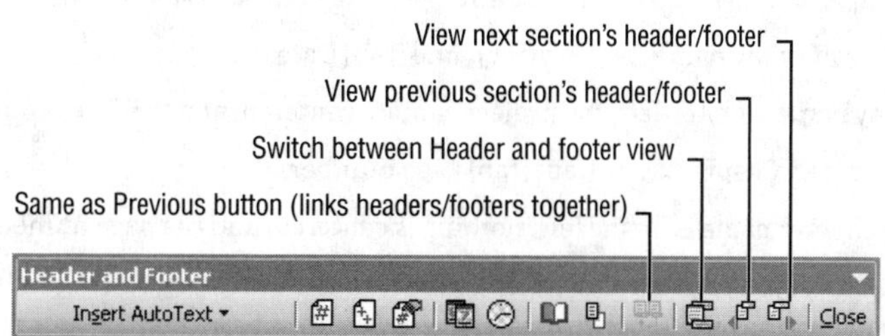

FIGURE 3.4
The Header and Footer floating palette thing

If the Header doesn't say "Same as Previous," then follow these steps:

1. Click the Show Previous button to see Section 1's header.
2. Delete all the text in Section 1's header.
3. Switch to view the footer.
4. Delete any text in the footer.

3. Close the Header and Footer toolbar when you've finished.

I've never seen such a mess as can be created with the Same as Previous button in a header or footer. While that option may seem nice—and it is most of the time—it does create problems when you have to suppress the header and footer for a section and then resume it. In those cases, as outlined above, it's best just to copy the entire header (and footer) from one section to another and avoid using the Same as Previous trick altogether.

How Can I Put a Border around Just the Title?

Want a border around your title to make it look sharp? Try these steps:

1. Select your title text.
2. Choose Format ➤ Borders and Shading. The Borders and Shading dialog box appears, detailed in Figure 3.5.
3. For a quick border, double-click one of the options on the left side of the dialog box: Box, Shadow, or 3-D. Otherwise, you can mess with the settings in the Borders and Shading dialog box to get the kind of effect you want.
4. Click OK and see how it looks.

Don't Load Up Your Headers or Footers with Useless Junk

True, you can put a lot of information into a header or footer—even graphics. I've done that myself when I run out of letterhead, but for complex documents it's best to keep the header or footer information limited.

If you haven't noticed, Word automatically formats each header and footer with left, center, and right tabs. So you can use these tabs to automatically position a page number or other information without having to redo the formatting. Instead, just use the Tab key.

The most complex header/footer arrangement I've used is like this:

Header: My name [tab] Project name [tab] Date

So my name is on the left, the project name is centered, and the date is flush right in the header. And then:

Footer: Chapter name [tab] [tab] Page number

The chapter name is on the left, nothing is centered, and the page number is on the right.

Obviously, you can mix and match this information any way you see fit. Just keep in mind that Word has already set the tabs up for you.

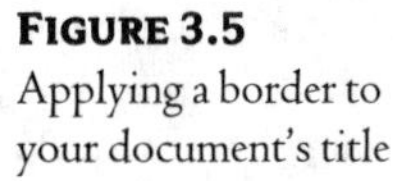

FIGURE 3.5
Applying a border to your document's title

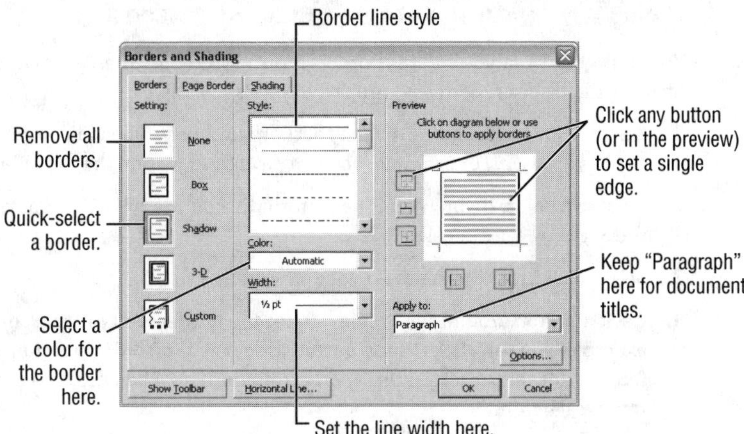

Why Can't I Put a Border around the Entire Page?

The secret to putting a border around a page in Word is to measure the border from the *text* and not the edge of the page. That's where most people screw up.

For example, most people can figure out how to put a border around a page using these steps:

1. Put the insertion pointer thing on the page you want to border. It works best if the page is its own section, though that's not a hard-and-fast rule.
2. Choose Format ➤ Borders and Shading.
3. Click the Page Border tab.
4. Work the dialog box's controls to configure what type, style, and color of border you want on the page. Refer to Figure 3.5 for the details.
5. Click the Options button.
6. Choose Text from the Measure From drop-down list. Ah-ha! This is the secret. If you choose "Edge of Page," then often the page border won't print. (Don't ask me why.)
7. Click OK to close the various dialog boxes.

Now your page has a proper border around it.

NOTE *The Page Border tab in the Borders and Shading dialog box is a close duplicate of Figure 3.5. Note that there is also an Art drop-down list that allows you to create a border out of cutesy little images in addition to boring lines.*

Handy Tips on the Borders and Shading Dialog Box

You can get quite fancy with the borders around your document, providing that you work the Borders and Shading dialog box (Figure 3.5) properly. Here's my advice:

1. Select a line style. There are many of them to choose from, and note that all four sides of the text need not have a style. For example, you can have lines just on the top or bottom.
2. Choose a color, if you wish. The Automatic color is typically black, or whatever color is defined by the Style.
3. Select a width or thickness for your border.
4. Click a button around the Preview to set the border. You can click one or more buttons at a time. For example, you can click the top button to set the top border and then repeat these steps to select a different style for the left, right, and bottom borders. Likewise, you can click a button a second time to remove a border.

Most importantly: Remember that borders need not be on all four sides and that borders can be of different styles, if you wish.

How Can I Paste This Excel Worksheet into Its Own Page?

To make the pasted Excel information, or really any information—an image, table, or what have you—appear on its own page, simply create that page as a section unto itself.

Start the page by choosing Insert ➤ Break and choose "Next Page" as the section break. Then put whatever information you want onto that page.

End the page by choosing Insert ➤ Break, then "Next Page" to create the end of the section and the continuation of the rest of your document.

The section sits by itself, like the Section 3 example shown in Figure 3.1. Any page formatting you change for that section applies only to that single page.

There's a Wacky Landscape Mode Page in the Middle of This Document!

Because each section in a document can contain its own page formatting, you can easily swap page orientation by selecting a Landscape layout from the Page Setup dialog box and applying it to that section only. Refer to the previous section for an explanation of why this is so. To change your page orientation, choose File ➤ Page Setup, and then choose Portrait or Landscape from the Margins or Paper Size tab, depending on your version of Word. Remember to choose "This Section" from the Apply To drop-down list before you click OK!

The Woes of Numbering Pages

One of my most dreadful word processing memories occurred when I saw a friend working painfully on a report. "I thought you were finished with that," I remarked. He said he was, but "I had to change something so I'm going through and renumbering the pages."

ARGH!

Yes, he manually numbered each page at the bottom. When he added text, he had to go through and wiggle every sentence so that the new page numbers fit. What agonizing torture! I'd rather be forced to sit through nine hours of ballet than manually renumber pages in a word processor!

I certainly hope that no one out there is manually numbering pages. Heaven forbid! If there were a Top Ten list of word processing crimes, then manually numbering pages would be in the top three. Fortunately, you know more than the average user, right? If not, then the following sections of page-numbering tips and information will most definitely help.

How Can I Put the Page Number Right Here?

The key to blissful page numbering in Word is the Insert ➢ Page Numbers command, which summons the highly useful Page Numbers dialog box, shown in Figure 3.6.

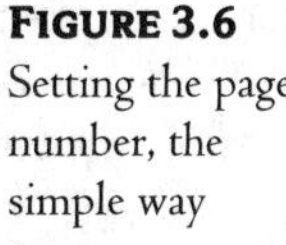

FIGURE 3.6
Setting the page number, the simple way

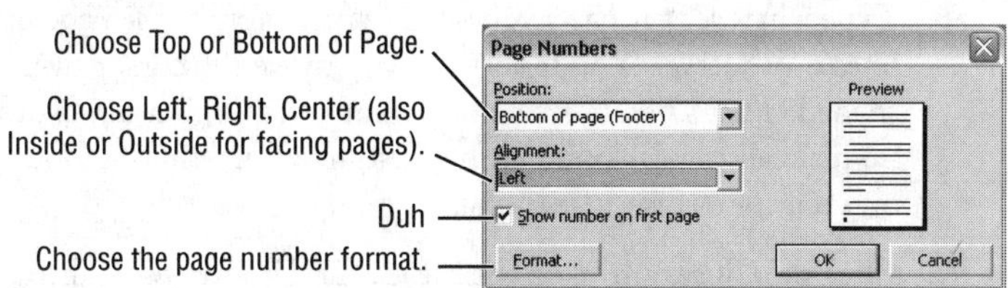

So if you want the page number to be in the bottom center, you choose "Bottom of Page (Footer)" from the Position drop-down list, then Center from the Alignment drop-down list. Click OK and you're finished. Simple.

But I Want the Page Number to Have Little Hyphens on Each Side!

No problem! The Insert ➢ Page Numbers command really—and this is top secret—simply sticks the proper header or footer commands into your document. To "fix" the page number, you merely have to edit the header or footer after you insert the page number (per the previous section's instructions). Here's how:

1. Follow the steps in the previous section. (Even though the steps weren't numbered, they're in there.)
2. Choose View ➢ Header and Footer from the menu. The Header and Footer toolbar appears, you're switched to Print Preview mode (if you weren't in it before), and the header area for the page is highlighted.
3. If the page number is in the footer, then click the Switch between Header and Footer button on the toolbar. The page number appears in the header or footer as you specified it. But note that the page number is not plain text. No, it appears inside a *frame,* which is Word's way of protecting the page number from the rest of the header or footer. It's not a problem, but it helps if you recognize this deception before you get all kooky trying to figure it out on your own.

4. Click on the page number to select its frame. The page number appears within the frame's shaded box, as shown in Figure 3.7.

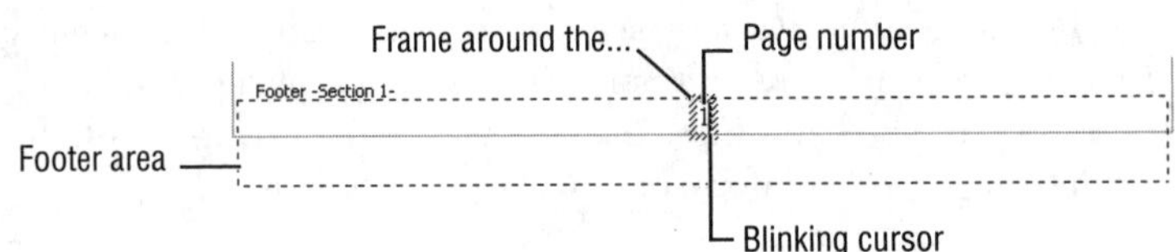

FIGURE 3.7
The page number in the frame in the footer in your document on the screen on your monitor on your desk

5. Click so that the cursor is blinking inside the frame with the page number.
6. Type whatever gewgaws you want before or after the page number, such as hyphens or underlines or whatever. You'll notice if you move the cursor over the page number that it becomes shaded. That's because it's not a number at all, but a *field* designed to show the current page. So it's really a page number in a field in a frame in the footer in your document on the screen on your monitor on your desk.
7. Click the Close button on the Header and Footer toolbar to return to your regularly scheduled document.

For any further fancy page-numbering stuff, I recommend that you simply create a page number in a header or footer. That way you can add whatever text you want around the page number without having to bother with frames and fields and such. Refer to the section later in this chapter titled "How Do You Do the 'Page X out of N Total Pages' Thing in a Document?" for an example.

Is There Any Way I Can Put "This Is Page Number X" in the Middle of a Document?

Page numbers need not be limited to headers or footers. For example, if you want to say, "Here you are, gentle reader, on page 63 and you still haven't fallen asleep!" Then all you need to do is stick a page number field into your document at the proper spot. Obey these steps:

1. Choose Insert ➤ Field. Ah, the secret: fields. Love fields.
2. Choose Numbering from the Categories list.
3. Choose Page from the Field Names list.
4. Click OK.

Because the page number is a field and not just a number you stick into the document, it updates itself as you add or remove text. The page number field *always* reflects the current page number, regardless of what else you do.

I Need to Refer to Something on Another Page by That Page Number, Whatever It Will Be!

Referring to a page number is best done by inserting a field. But in this case, if you're referring to a page other than the current one, you must refer to something interesting on that second page. In this case, that something interesting can be a bookmark.

After setting a bookmark on a page, you can then reference the bookmark's page number with a field. You can stick that field on any other page, which is—in a roundabout and illogical way—exactly what you need!

Okay. It sounds complex, but it's really not—providing you follow these steps:

1. Go to the page that has the text you're referencing.
2. Select the text you're citing. Or if it's a lot of text, just click the mouse so that the insertion point is blinking at the start of the text.
3. Choose Insert ➤ Bookmark.
4. Name the bookmark.

NOTE *No spaces in a bookmark name! So be clever when you name this reference—especially if you have other bookmarks in the document. Be brief and concise.*

5. Click the Add button.
6. Return to the page where you need to reference the bookmark's page.
7. Choose Insert ➤ Field.
8. Choose "Links and References" from the Categories list.
9. Choose PageRef from the Field Names list.
10. In Word 2003/XP, choose the bookmark name from the Bookmark Name list. In Word 2000, click the Options button, and then click the Bookmarks tab; select your bookmark from the list, and click the Add to Field button, then click OK.
11. Click OK.

A page number is inserted into the document, which references the bookmarked text you have elsewhere in the document.

NOTE *When bookmarking in Word, mark the start of the text. So if you're flagging a particularly long section of information, simply place the bookmark where that text starts. The start of the information is typically what a reader is interested in locating, not the middle or end of the text.*

I Need to Restart Page Numbering Here!

Restarting page numbering is simple—providing that you've already inserted page numbers into your document and you create a new section break where you want the page numbering to restart. Observe these steps:

1. Move to the top of the page where numbering is to restart.
2. Choose Insert ➤ Break.
3. Select Next Page.
4. Click OK. This creates a new section break to start your page renumbering. Page renumbering will not work unless you stick a new section in there. And that makes sense because numbering is a page-formatting deal, and sections break up page formatting.

NOTE *You may optionally have to "clean up" after inserting a section break. If so, place the insertion point at the start of the section's text, and then press the Backspace key until the start of the text aligns with the top of the new page/section break.*

5. Choose Insert ➤ Page Numbers.
6. Click the Format button.
7. Click the Start At button.
8. Enter the new page number. For example, if you want to start over with page 1, type a **1** into the box, as shown in Figure 3.8.

FIGURE 3.8
Formatting your page numbers

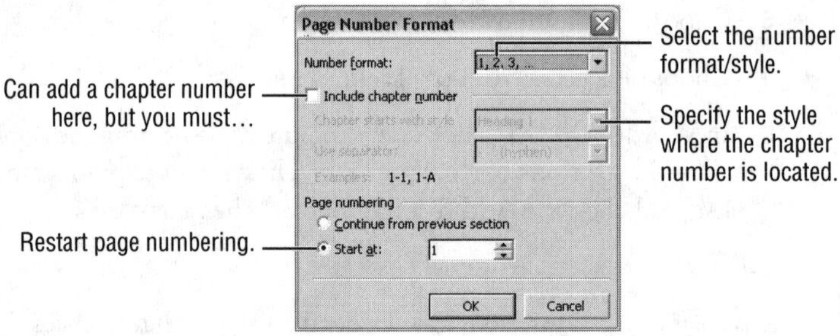

Can add a chapter number here, but you must...

Restart page numbering.

Select the number format/style.

Specify the style where the chapter number is located.

9. Click OK, then OK again to return to your document.

The new page number values appear in the header/footer, or in any page number fields you may have in that section of your document. Do note, however, that the status bar still reflects absolute page numbers from the start of your document.

How Can I Start My Document at Page 72?

Documents can start page numbering at any value. Doing so doesn't even require any sections:

1. Choose Insert ➤ Page Number to place the page numbers in your document's header or footer. This is how it's normally done. But then:
2. Click the Format button.
3. Click the Start At button.
4. Enter the starting page number in the Start At button's box. Type in a number or use the gizmo to select a number with the mouse. (It's quicker to just type in a number, such as 72.)
5. Click OK, then OK again to get back to your document.

Now your entire document starts page numbering at whatever number you chose.

How Can I Number the First Six Pages with Roman Numerals and Then Number the Rest of My Document Normally Starting with Page 1?

It's common to number a document's introduction using Roman numerals and then restart numbering when the "real" text starts. This is easy enough to do in Word, providing you use the Roman numerals in one section and then restart the page numbering with regular numbers in the next section. Easy peasy lemon squeezy:

1. At the start of your document, choose Insert ➤ Page Numbers.
2. Choose the page number's position, alignment, and so on.
3. Click the Format button.
4. Choose the Roman numeral format from the Number Format drop-down list. That would be i, ii, iii in upper- or lowercase.
5. Click OK, then OK again to return to your document. Now the document is being numbered with Roman numerals, which is cute up to a point. (Do you realize that only up until a few hundred years ago that all math was done with Roman numerals?)
6. Move to the point in your document where you want to restart numbering with non-Roman numerals.
7. Insert a section break on the next page. Choose Insert ➤ Break, and choose Next Page as the break's location, then click OK. You'll notice that the new section automatically resets the page numbers back to 1, or "i" in this case.
8. Choose Insert ➤ Page Numbers and click the Format button again.
9. Choose the standard 1, 2, 3 page numbers from the Number Format drop-down list.
10. Click OK, then OK again to return to your document.

And now the second section of your document has standard numbering.

How Do You Do the "Page X out of N Total Pages" Thing in a Document?

I typically show the "page X out of N" thing in a document's footer, as opposed to using the Insert ➤ Page Numbers command. So if you've already started with the Page Numbers command, go back and remove the page numbers, and then follow these steps to stick the page number into a document's footer:

1. Choose View ➤ Header and Footer from the menu. The view switches to Print Layout view, the Header and Footer toolbar shows up (Figure 3.4), and you see the header for your document outlined on the screen.
2. Click the Switch between Header and Footer button to see the document's footer; skip this step if you want to put the page numbering in the header instead.
3. If you want the page number centered, press the Tab key. Or if you want it right-justified, press the Tab key twice.
4. To insert the current page number, click the Insert Page Number button. If you need to type any text before this, then type the text *before* clicking the button, such as **This is page**, followed by a space; then click the Insert Page Number button.
5. Type any text you want to appear between the current page number and last page number—for example, **out of**, as in "This is page X out of N." Or sometimes I just use a slash to separate the values, as in "3/9."
6. Click the Insert Number of Pages button. That inserts the final page number of your document, whatever that number may be.
7. Type any extra text you want.
8. Click the Close button when you've finished.

If you want to include information similar to this in the body of your document, then you merely need to use the NumPages field, which is found in the Document Information category. NumPages is equal to the total number of pages in a document. Combine that with the Page field (from the Numbering category), and you can include the text "This is page X out of N" anywhere in your document.

Chapter 4

Oh the Sacrilege of Drawing in a Word Processor!

It's a left-brain/right-brain thing. On the left side you have logic, calm, and collected. It's words. Colorless, plain, formal, and stiff on the page, the words march relentlessly from sentence to paragraph to page, expressing ideas using cool intelligence expressing rational ideas. It is order. It is peace. It is calm, clear-blue waters.

Then there's the wild party that's taking place in the right brain, just a hemisphere away. It's loud. It's exploding with color. It's a daring psychic rollercoaster with manic highs and accelerated screams, dipping into the dismal darkness of despair painted with the mud-colored ink of the despondent artist. It is chaos. It is insanity. It is the churning, hot frothy blood of passion erupting into a boil.

Obviously, mixing the two sides of the human brain would be like pouring matter into antimatter, yielding the explosive power that hurtles the USS *Enterprise* through the far reaches of space. Or it could just be one of those rare and interesting things that Word does when it attempts to cross the synaptic boundary between the left-brained word processor and the right-brained art program. This chapter shows you how to use those tools to improve the way your stuff looks.

- Breaking up text with boxes, circles, and shapes
- Linking two text boxes through a newsletter
- Carefully wrapping text around an image
- Using captions
- Rotating, cropping, resizing, and relocating images
- Making more interesting document titles

Adding Pizzazz with a Text Box

The text box is one of those cute little things you can stick into a document that just blows people away. They're totally unaware that Word is capable of sticking text into a tidy square container, separate and free from the rest of the document. It's a handy trick to know and one that if used well can really impress your friends and foes alike.

How Can a "Pull Quote" Make My Documents More Interesting?

Figure 4.1 illustrates a *pull-quote*. It's a box of text in the middle of an otherwise boring page of text. It usually contains a quote pulled from somewhere else on the page (get it?), but the quote is larger, bolder, and more prominent than the boring text around it. Pull quotes serve the dual function of breaking up a solid page of text as well as drawing attention to the text from someone who may just be skimming.

FIGURE 4.1

A pull quote in the middle of a page of text

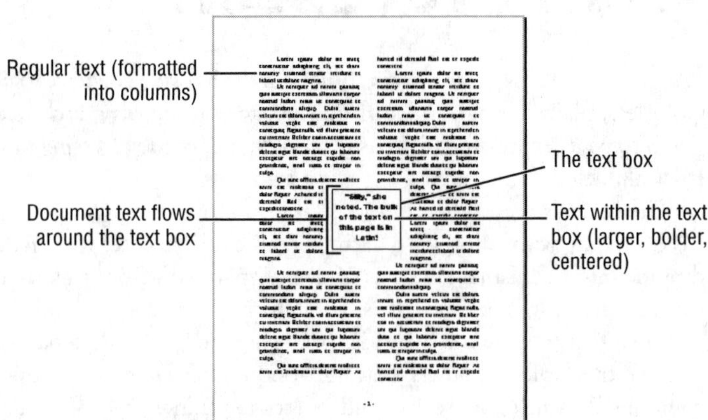

Follow these steps to splash down a text box in your document, similar to what you see in Figure 4.1:

1. Choose Insert ➤ Text Box. The view switches to Print Layout, which is best for dealing with the taboo of nontext items in a document.
2. In Word 2003/XP, press the Delete key to remove the Drawing Canvas. The Drawing Canvas allows you to place several text boxes or other graphical objects into the same area for easy control, but it's unnecessary (and bothersome) for a single text box. Note how the mouse pointer is now a large plus sign.

3. Draw the text box, by using the mouse, to make the text box appear in the size and position you desire. Don't worry about specifics just yet; it can be sloppy. When you release the mouse button, the text box appears right over the top of the text, as shown in Figure 4.2. This is okay.

4. Type and format the text inside the box.

FIGURE 4.2
The text box awaits action in your document.

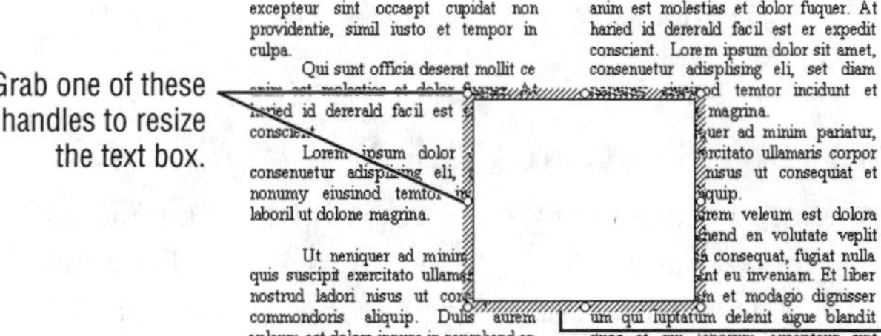
Grab one of these handles to resize the text box.

Point the mouse here to drag/move the text box.

NOTE *Pull quotes are brief, just a few lines. Typically pull quotes are formatted larger, bolder, and centered. If you need to resize the box to make room for more text, do so. But remember that pull quotes are supposed to be short—and enticing. They're a trick designed to get people interested in the details of your text.*

5. Resize the box to better fit your text. Use the top, bottom, left, or right handles to resize the box.

6. Move the box so that it's positioned where you want it. Point the mouse at the text box's fuzzy border. The mouse pointer grows a four-way-arrow thing, which means you can grab and drag the box.

7. Double-click the mouse on the edge of the text box. This brings up the Format Text Box dialog box. (If it doesn't, then try again; double-click when the mouse pointer sports the four-way-arrow thing, shown above.)

8. Click the Layout tab.

9. Choose Tight from the list of dogs.

10. Click OK.

Now the text wraps tightly around your text box, looking a lot like Figure 4.1.

Any Way to Get Rid of This Text Box?

To zap away a text box, click its border with the mouse, and then press the Backspace key. Or the Delete key. Word isn't picky.

The Difference between a Text Box and a Frame

If you want to stick text into a box in Word, then you use the Insert ➤ Text Box command. However there is a command that seems similar, which is the Frames command. Don't confuse them!

Frames are used primarily for formatting web pages in Word, which is something I do not recommend. Therefore, do not mess with the Frames command! If you want text in a box, then use the Text Box command as discussed in this section.

How Can I Do a Sidewards Title?

Unlike text in your document, text in a text box doesn't always have to be right side up. It can also go sideways this way and sideways that way, which makes a text box an interesting tool for adding what I call a "sidewards title" to a document. Figure 4.3 shows what I'm talking about.

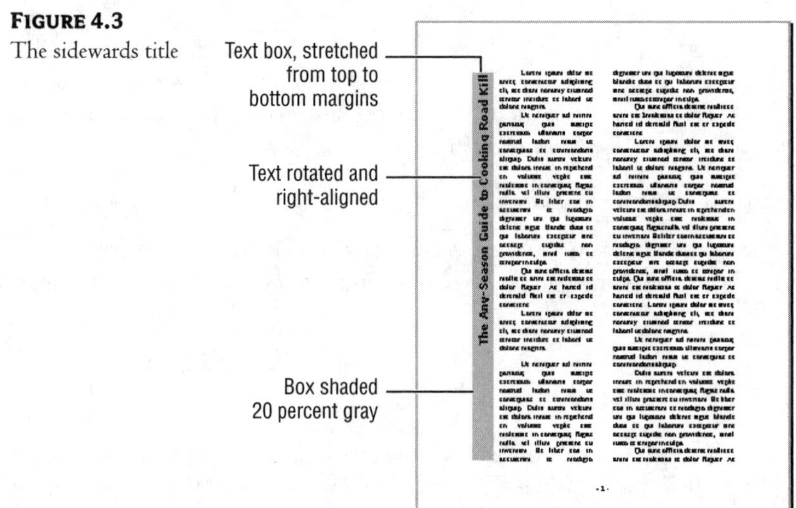

FIGURE 4.3
The sidewards title

To build this type of text box, follow the steps in the section, "How Can a Pull Quote Make My Documents More Interesting?" Then resize and drag the text box so that it stretches the entire length of the document, from the top of the text to the bottom.

Rotate the text by clicking the Change Text Direction button in the Text Box toolbar (Figure 4.4) until the text reads properly.

Optionally add a color background (double-click the text box border to bring up the Format Text Box dialog box, click the Colors and Lines tab, and choose a Fill: Color). Note that in Figure 4.3, the background is set to 25 percent gray and no line is used to outline the box.

FIGURE 4.4
The Text Box toolbar

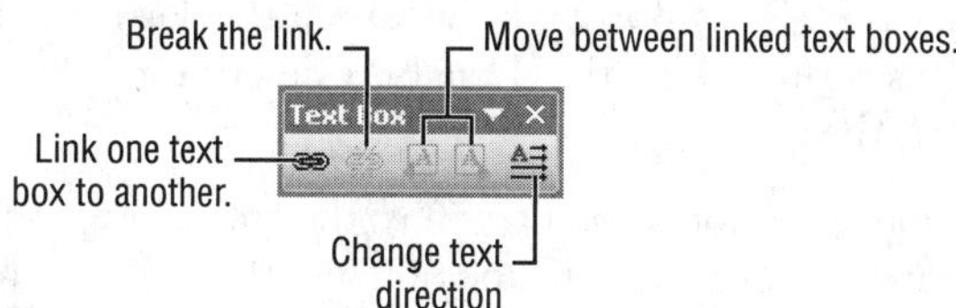

Why Do I Want to Link Text Boxes Together?

By linking text boxes together you can flow text from one into another. Obviously, for small boxes that makes no sense. But with larger boxes, it's possible to create a newspaper column–like effect. In fact, many folks attempt to put together newsletters using text boxes exclusively. Personally I think this is nuts; a desktop publishing program, such as Adobe InDesign or Microsoft Publisher, does a far better job with text boxes. But if you want to attempt such a thing with Word, you can. At your own peril.

Figure 4.5 illustrates how you could use text boxes to snake text through a newsletter. In fact, it seems like you could snake text using text boxes exclusively. The problem with that is Word slows to a crawl when you attempt it. Therefore, I recommend linking only one set of text boxes per document. If you try anything more, be sure to save often!

FIGURE 4.5
Linking text boxes in a newsletter

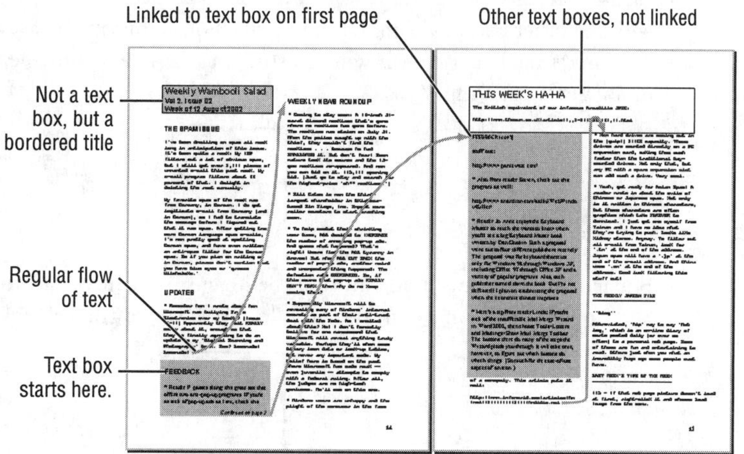

To link two text boxes, heed these loose steps:

1. Create both text boxes, following the instructions earlier in this chapter. Note that the text boxes need not be on the same page.
2. Click to select the first text box. This is the text box that contains the start of your flowing text.

3. Click the Create Text Box Link button on the Text Box toolbar. The mouse pointer changes to a strange thing that I can only describe as a Pyrex measuring cup full of caustic acid. Okay, then.
4. Click the mouse on the second text box, the one the excess text from the first box is to flow into. When you move the mouse pointer into the text box, the cup of acid "spills," displaying the initials of the Microsoft employee who designed the thing.

Now the two text boxes are linked. Text that overflows from the first box will miraculously appear in the second.

You can even add a third or fourth text box, simply by repeating the above steps and linking the second box to the third, and then the third box to the fourth.

NOTE *You can use the Next Text Box and Previous Text Box buttons to move between text boxes. This comes in handy, especially when the two text boxes are several pages apart. (Refer to Figure 4.4.)*

How Can I Wrap Text around Boxes?

Text boxes, pictures, and graphics in your Word document can fit in with the text in a variety of ways. These are controlled by the Layout tab in the object's Format dialog box, where you can set the way text wraps around the image in one of five exciting ways:

Inline In this mode, the graphic behaves just like any other character in the text. It sits "in line" with the other text in a paragraph. I rarely choose this option as, well, it looks dumb on the screen. The only time I've used it is when pasting in a sample text image, such as Chinese characters in the middle of a paragraph.

Square Word puts a box around the image. Text flows around the image from top to bottom and hops over the image in the middle. My favorite choice.

Tight This is similar to Square, but it allows the option of editing the wrapping points around the image to make text wrap even closer or, in some cases, in a shape identical to the image you've placed in your document—whether it's a regular shape such as a circle, for example, or an irregular one like the dog shown on Word's button.

Behind Text The image floats behind the text, making the image or object appear to be printed on the paper before the text was printed.

In Front The image floats atop the text, just as if some wanton four-year-old pasted it on the page right over everything beneath it.

Toss In an Image or Two

Oh, why not? Text is so boring. I mean, consider Dostoevsky. Page after page of text and on and on and everyone has four different names and they all spend several pages internalizing dialog. I mean, KILL THE LANDLADY AND GET IT OVER WITH!

I'm sorry. That was a college flashback.

No doubt if Dostoevsky had used Word instead of a grubby pencil, he probably would have delighted in brightening up his tireless tomes with a few splashy images here or there. It's just too easy.

Saving Images to Disk

There are three important things you must remember when you save a graphic to disk. Whether the image's source was the Internet, a scanner, a digital camera, or something you created with a painting program, know these things:

The File Format Word works best with images saved in these formats: TIF or TIFF, GIF, JPG or JPEG, and BMP. Of these graphic image file types, TIFF is the best one to use. The files are larger than the other formats, but TIFF is very common and produces a good end result.

The Image's Size Images look best when you don't have to enlarge or reduce them. Try to save your images in the exact physical size they will end up on the page.

The Folder or Location on Disk Be sure you save your images in a proper folder on disk. Windows XP tries to save new graphics images to the My Documents ➢ My Pictures folder. However, if you're working on a large project, consider saving the images into the same folder that contains your Word document files. That way you can keep everything together.

The Filename Be sure to give the image file a descriptive or specific name. When I create a document, I usually put in a placeholder for the image until I'm ready to paste it in. So I'll name the placeholder FIGURE1 and the image is named `FIGURE1.TIF` on disk. Or, if the placement isn't important, I'll name the figure relating to its content, such as `DADDY FUNNY HAT.TIF`.

How Do I Get This Image into My Document?

The key to getting any image into Word is to first *save it to disk*. Seriously! No matter where the source, first get the image from wherever it is now to a file on your computer's hard drive. Know the file's name. Know where you saved the file. Once it's there, then the rest is pretty easy:

1. Choose Insert ➤ Picture ➤ From File.
2. Use the Insert Picture dialog box to browse for the picture you saved to disk. (You do remember the picture's name and its location, right?)
3. Select the picture, click the Insert button, and the picture is stuck into your document.

Word sticks pictures into your document as inline text. That means the picture acts basically like any other character in the text, which is probably not what you want. Keep reading in the next section.

How Can I Make the Text Wrap around the Picture?

Your picture can float above, behind, inline with, or inside of your text. The different options are discussed in the earlier section "How Can I Wrap Text around Boxes?" To get at those options, follow these steps:

1. It's much easier to see your document's layout from Print Layout view than Normal view, so switch to Print Layout view, if necessary: Choose View ➤ Print Layout.
2. Right-click the picture you want to format.
3. Choose "Format Picture" from the pop-up menu.
4. In the Format Picture dialog box, click the Layout tab.
5. Choose your layout from the options listed. The one I prefer is Tight.
6. Click OK.
7. If necessary, reposition your picture in the document. Use the mouse to drag the picture around so that the text flows around it the way you want.

Of course, you may discover that you need to resize or even crop the image at this point. If so, keep reading in the appropriate sections that follow.

NOTE *It may help to "zoom out" to get a better idea of how the picture works in with the rest of the text on the page. Use the Zoom drop-down list on the Standard toolbar to zoom out to 75 percent or 50 percent.*

How Can I Wrap This Circle with a Circle?

To make text wrap around an image in a pattern not shown on the Text Wrapping menu, you have to be creative. What you do is choose the Tight option to wrap the image as tightly as you can; then you create your own wrapping image by making, moving, and editing various wrapping points about the image. Here's how it's done:

1. Click the picture to select it.

2. If the Picture toolbar (Figure 4.6) doesn't appear, then choose View ➤ Toolbars ➤ Picture.

FIGURE 4.6
The Picture toolbar helps you edit a picture.

3. Choose Tight from the Text Wrapping button/menu on the toolbar. Click the dog button to see the menu.

4. Choose "Edit Wrap Points" from the Text Wrapping button/menu.

The image is now surrounded by a rectangle with red dashed lines. Four wrapping points appear on the corners.

The red dashed lines demark the boundary to where text will wrap. The wrapping points tell the lines where to go. Figure 4.7 shows you how to set these points so that you can wrap text around an odd-shaped image, such as a circle or oval.

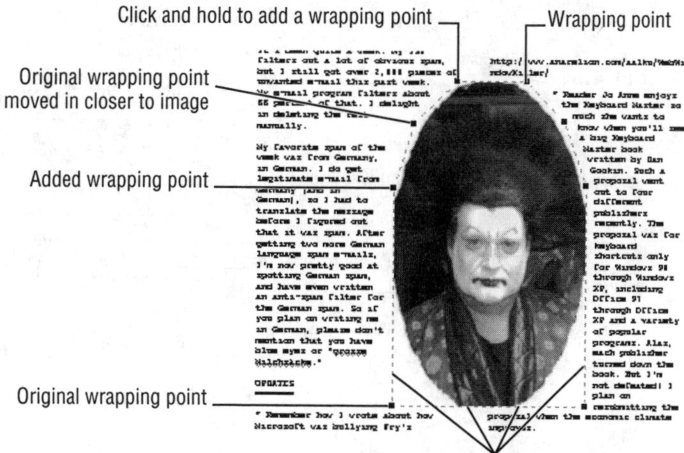

FIGURE 4.7
Editing the wrapping points

1. Click the mouse on the red dashed line to create a new wrapping point. You may have to press and hold the mouse pointer on the red dashed line and then drag the pointer a wee bit to create the new wrapping point. (This takes some practice.)

   When the mouse pointer is in position to create a new wrapping point, it changes to look like a plus symbol.

   When you move a wrapping point, the mouse pointer changes again.

2. Drag the wrapping point to best wrap the red dashed line around your image.

NOTE *You may need to insert more than one wrapping point to properly move the red dashed line around your image.*

3. Keep repeating Steps 5 and 6 until your image is properly wrapped.
4. When you've finished, just click on the image or in your text.

If you need to edit the wrapping points later, repeat these steps and use the mouse to add or move the points.

NOTE *There is no way to delete a wrapping point once it's been added. However, you can change the layout option back to Inline or some other option that "forgets" the wrapping points.*

Any Nifty Way to Add an Image Caption?

Nifty methods abound for slapping a caption onto your figure. The best way is when the picture is placed into your document with the Inline layout—that is, without any text wrapping. In that case, you can add a caption by following these steps:

1. Right-click the image.
2. Choose Caption from the pop-up menu. The Caption dialog box appears, looking similar to Figure 4.8. (The gizmos have different positions in different versions of Word.)

FIGURE 4.8
Slap down a caption on that puppy.

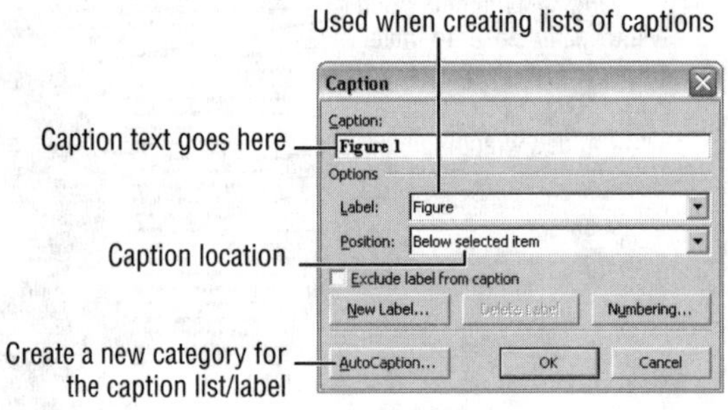

3. Type the caption text.
4. Click OK. The caption text is inserted below the picture.

The chief advantage of inserting a figure caption this way is that Word lets you later create a list or "table" of figures and captions and which pages they're on. This is part of Word's indexing feature, which is covered in Chapter 6, "Writing That Great American Novel or Screenplay."

NOTE *Another way to create a caption is to stick a text box just below the image. That allows you a bit more formatting freedom than using the Caption command.*

Any Way to Make the Image Smaller?

Reducing or enlarging an image is known as *scaling*. It's not "blowing up." No, you do that to old buildings. But to scale an image in Word is cinchy:

1. Click the image once to select it. Note how the image grows "handles," as shown in Figure 4.9? They are the key to scaling the image.

FIGURE 4.9
Selected inline and noninline images

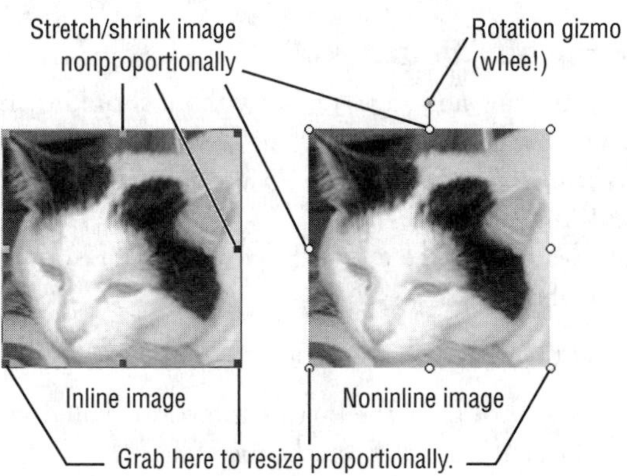

2. Grab the image's lower-right handle.
3. Drag the mouse upward and to the left. The image resizes proportionally as you drag the mouse, scaling it smaller.

NOTE *To stretch in two directions at once, hold down the Ctrl key as you drag a handle with the mouse.*

4. Release the mouse to keep the image at that new size.

You can drag any of the eight handles to resize an image, though the handles on the edges stretch the image nonproportionally.

These changes affect only the image as it appears in your document; they do not alter the original image saved on disk.

NOTE *Working with graphics favors the mouse over the keyboard, so there's only one keyboard shortcut I use frequently: Alt+I, P, F. This is pretty easy to remember for Insert ➤ Picture ➤ From File.*

What If I Need to Rotate the Image?

Rotating the image is done by dragging it with the rotation handle, shown in Figure 4.9. Note that the image cannot be inline; it must have a certain type of wrapping selected other than Inline. After that, you can click the image and you'll see the topmost "green" handle: Point the mouse at that handle, and then drag to the left or right to rotate the image in that direction.

NOTE *You can use the Ctrl or Ctrl+Alt keys while you drag the image to have it pivot around a certain point or rotate around the image's center as you drag the mouse.*

To rotate by specific 90-degree increments, use the Picture toolbar's Rotate Left 90° button.

What Is Cropping All About?

Cropping is a way of resizing an image smaller without shrinking the image. It's like what Aunt Betty does with all her pictures; she whips out a pair of scissors and cuts out the less-meaningful parts. That's one way to bring in the focus on an image, or to eliminate the stuff you don't want others to see, specifically stuff on the edges.

Suppose Marsha really wants to crop exboyfriend Dougie out of that picture of her in the taffeta dress. To do so, she obeys these steps:

1. Click to select the image.
2. Choose the Crop tool from the Picture toolbar. If you don't see the Picture toolbar, choose View ➤ Toolbars ➤ Picture from the menu.
3. Drag one of the picture's eight handles inward to crop the image. To eliminate the top part of the image, for example, grab the top handle and slide the mouse downward. Or to crop in two directions at once, grab a corner handle and drag inward diagonally. (Refer to Figure 4.9 for information on the handles.)

   In Marsha's case, Dougie is standing on the right side of the picture, so she uses the right edge handle, dragging the mouse inward until most of Dougie is gone.
4. Click the Crop tool button again when you've finished cropping.

There is no way to undo cropping errors. Well, there is always the Undo command, Ctrl+Z. However, if you utterly screw things up, remember that you can always delete the image and reload it into the document.

Can I Crop the Image into a Circle?

No. Cropping works only along the edges of an image. If you want the image to be cropped into a different shape, then you'll have to use photo-editing software that sports some type of nonlinear cropping tool.

What about Crop Circles?

Definitely aliens.

Can I Put the Image in the Background?

Setting an image behind the text is done by choosing the Behind Text layout option when the image is selected. This option can be chosen from the Picture toolbar's Text Wrapping button/menu or from the Layout tab in the Format Picture dialog box.

If you do set an image in the background, consider washing it out so that it doesn't detract too much from your text:

1. Click the image to select it.
2. Click the Color button on the Picture toolbar.
3. Choose Washout from the Color button's menu. The image fades sufficiently so as not to detract from the text floating above.

You can undo this option by selecting Automatic from the Color button's drop-down menu.

NOTE *Putting an image behind your text makes it harder to select the image for editing. Cheat a little bit by positioning the image just a hair to the left or right of the text's margin. That way you'll always have a piece of it to grab should you need to edit.*

Why Does Word Slow Down with All These Images?

Hey! Word gets *tired* when you tax it too much! After all, it's a *word* processor, not an all-in-one document-formatting, data-manipulation, number-crunching, figure-editing jack-of-all-trades. (Though it tries to be.)

My best advice is to always add pictures, images, and foo-foo *last*. Save after adding and adjusting each image. And just cross your fingers that Word doesn't crash after you push it too far.

NOTE *The best way to work with words, text boxes, pictures, and artwork is with a desktop publishing program. They're not as well suited to writing as Word is, but if you collect your words in a file and all your images in other files, then desktop publishing software can sew them all together with a minimum of fuss.*

Simple Drawing Stuff

The final thing Word lets you mix into the text salad is *drawing stuff*. This includes lines, shapes, colors, and strange things that you can place into your text like pictures. Word also lets you illustrate your text or create your own figures or what have you. Honestly, I could write an entire book by itself on Word's drawing abilities (which are also shared by Excel). But instead, I'll just wrap up this chapter with some simple drawing basics. It's just enough to entice you without being so much as to overwhelm you.

NOTE *Microsoft has announced a compatibility problem in Office 2003 when using OfficeArt shape drawing objects from previous versions of the software. See their explanation at* `http://support.microsoft.com/?kbid=828041`.

Just Tell Me the Basics about Drawing in Word because I Don't Have a Lot of Time to Waste on This

Let me introduce you to the amazing Drawing toolbar, shown in Figure 4.10, the source of most of the nontext things you can stick into a Word document. And it's so happy to be there, it even has a shortcut button on the Standard toolbar for instant appearances. Otherwise, choose View ➤ Toolbars ➤ Drawing.

FIGURE 4.10

What's what on the Drawing toolbar

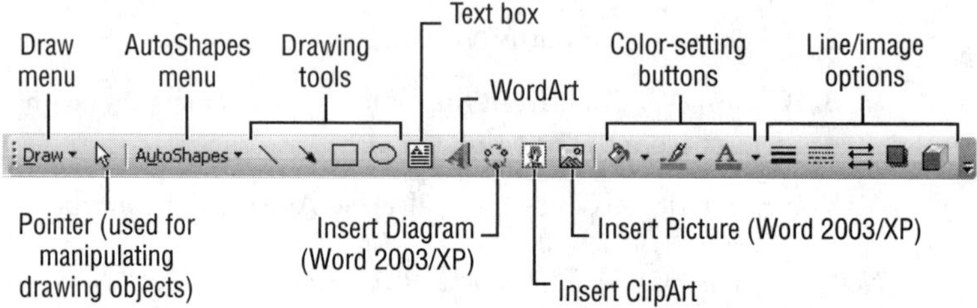

The Drawing toolbar typically appears on the bottom of Word's window, below the document's horizontal scrollbar. (It might already be there; many Word users forget to hide it after they've finished using it.) Also, summoning the Drawing toolbar shifts you into Print Layout view if you're not already in that view.

Drawing works like this:

1. Summon the Drawing toolbar.
2. Click to select the type of object you want to draw. Say you need a circle to illustrate what the sun looks like to people who live only on the dark side of the planet. In that case, you click the Oval tool.

   In Word 2003/XP, a Drawing Canvas appears in your document. You can use this canvas to help group drawings together and to wrap text around the drawings. Otherwise, you can press the Backspace key to delete the canvas.

   In Word 2000, you always draw items on top of the text where they first appear in a document.
3. Drag to draw the object in your document.
4. Optionally select a line style, line color, and fill color for the object.
5. Optionally use the mouse to reposition the object or resize or rotate the object using its various handles. See Figure 4.9.

You can continue to add objects to the document. As you do, be careful to save as you go; the more nontext junk you add to a Word document, the less stable it becomes. So saving often is important.

My best advice: Experiment! Play! Have fun!

NOTE *Don't bother stringing together various lines to create more complex shapes. For example, don't try to link three lines together to make a triangle. Instead, use the AutoShapes pop-up menu and its palettes to select a predefined shape. That will save you some time.*

How Can I Use a Block of Color to Help Spice Things Up?

One great reason to use the Drawing toolbar is to break up a long document or just make it more visually appealing by adding some color or random shapes. For example, suppose you have a page of solid text. Consider adding a blue rectangle in the middle of the page to help break it up:

1. Summon the Drawing toolbar.
2. From the Zoom drop-down list on the Standard toolbar, choose "Whole Page." If you don't see the "Whole Page" option, then choose View ➤ Print Layout. This displays your document's entire page on the screen, allowing you to better place the color block.
3. Choose the Rectangle tool. If the Drawing Canvas appears in your document, press the Backspace key to delete it.

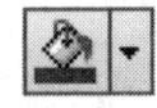

4. Drag to draw the rectangle in the middle of your document.
5. Choose Blue from the Fill Color button's menu.
6. Click the Draw button and choose Text Wrapping ➤ Tight. Or select another wrapping option to match your desire.

   And now there's a blue square in your text. True, that does help break things up. But how about putting the page number in there as well? Continue with these steps:

7. Right-click the blue square.
8. Choose "Add Text" from the pop-up menu.
9. Choose Insert ➤ Field.
10. Choose Numbering from the Categories list, then Page from the Field Names column.
11. Click OK.

    Now the page number sits in the blue square. But it can be better formatted:

12. Choose a fancier font, such as Algerian or something very decorative.
13. Increase the font size to something larger, say 24 or 36.
14. Center the page number. Press Ctrl+E to do this.
15. Adjust the text box's vertical size to more accurately match the page number.

And there you have a custom page number. You can add text to any object you draw by simply repeating the steps above. In that case, the object becomes a specialized form of text box, into which you can place any text or a field, as was done in Step 9.

What About a Few Objects on the Corner of a Dull Page?

Figure 4.11 illustrates how I've placed three color blocks in the corner of a dull page just to help break things up.

FIGURE 4.11
Blocks to break up a dull page

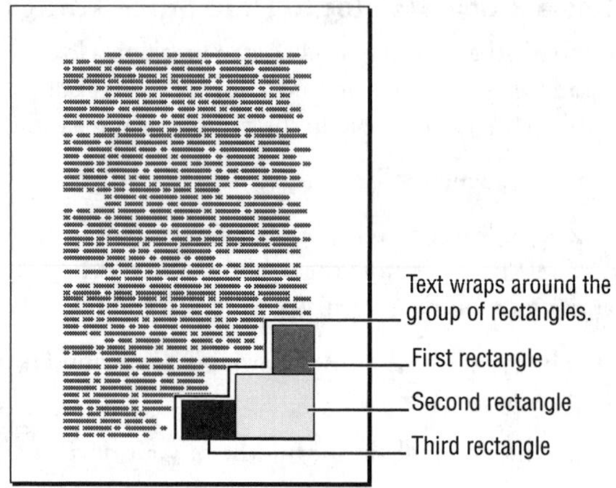

Here's how to do what I did:

1. Summon the Drawing toolbar.
2. Select the Rectangle tool. (In Word 2003/XP, delete the Canvas.)
3. Drag to draw the first rectangle.
4. Color the first rectangle red.
5. Repeat to draw a yellow rectangle.
6. Repeat again to draw a blue rectangle.

To bring the yellow rectangle forward, you'll need to rearrange them:

1. Right-click the yellow rectangle.
2. Choose Order ➤ Bring to Front from the pop-up menu.

Now to treat all three rectangles as a unit, you need to group them:

1. Ctrl+Click all three rectangles to select them. Press and hold the Ctrl key as you subsequently click each rectangle. This selects all of them.
2. Right-click the selected rectangles.
3. Choose Grouping ➤ Group. This allows you to work with all three objects as a single unit.

   Next you need to wrap the text around your group:

4. Click to select the grouped items.

5. Click the Draw menu on the Drawing toolbar.

6. Choose Text Wrapping ➤ Tight.

And the text wraps around the distraction in a nondistracting way, as shown in Figure 4.11.

NOTE *If color blocks seem silly, then consider that you can use the drawing tools to perhaps illustrate something described in the document. For example, the flow-chart tools may help you summarize a character's line of thinking. Or you may be able to draw a crude map or even a stick-figure diagram of the murder scene. Be creative!*

How Can I Point Out a Specific Item in a Picture, Like with an Arrow?

Pictures are great for illustrating text, but often you need to call attention to a specific detail within that picture. That's where the arrow-drawing tool comes in very handy.

1. Insert the picture you want to reference with an arrow. Stick the picture into your document; adjust its size, crop, and so on until it's perfect.

2. Optionally add a text box call-out. You need to label the arrow, after all. Sometimes you can get away without arrows. For example, in the caption or text you could just say, "Arrows point to suspected obscene sculptures." Otherwise, use the text box instructions from earlier in this chapter to create a text box call-out, similar to the one shown in Figure 4.12.

FIGURE 4.12
Using the Arrow tool

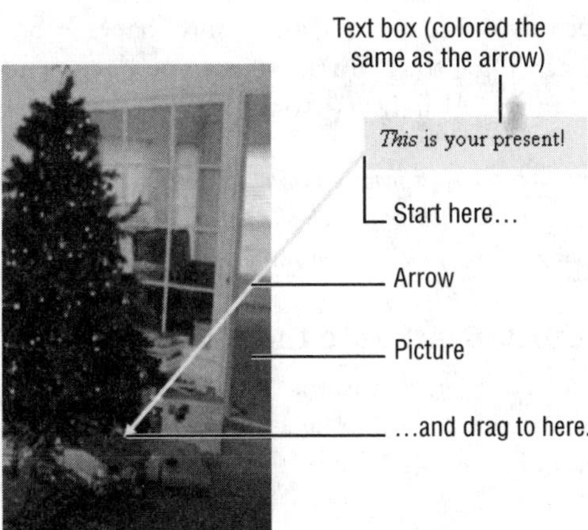

3. Choose the Arrow tool from the Drawing toolbar.

4. Drag to draw the arrow. Keep in mind that the arrowhead appears at the *end* of the line, not the start.

5. Make adjustments as necessary. Move, color, resize, create.

DON'T IGNORE THE TWO DIFFERENT TYPES OF ARROWS

There are two different types of arrows on the Drawing toolbar. The first is the Line tool with an arrowhead attached, known as the "Arrow" tool. You can also use the Arrow style button (on the right end of the Drawing toolbar) to select a specific style for your arrow.

In addition to those line arrows, you'll also find a palette of "block arrows" on the AutoShape button's menu. Unlike line arrows, the block arrows have a width and depth to them and come in a few interesting variations.

I always have to mess with the arrow's color after I've added an arrow. This is to help make the arrow stand out from the image. In Figure 4.12, the arrow is colored yellow, which helps it stand out from the picture as well as show up on the page. (The text box is also colored yellow to match.)

Why Would I Use an AutoShape?

The Drawing toolbar provides you quick access to a few handy drawing tools: the line, square, and oval. But, as anyone beyond the second grade realizes, there are far more shapes than those available to the human imagination. So rather than try to cobble together a triangle, star, or trapezoid, Word gives you those shapes already formed, all neatly categorized on submenus in the AutoShapes menu.

For example, to add a cartoon bubble to that hilarious image of Aunt Courtney getting tackled by the dog, click the AutoShapes button and then choose the appropriate cartoon bubble from the Callouts submenu.

To use a star shape for your text box, choose AutoShapes ➤ Stars and Banners and then pluck out the old five-pointed star. Drag to create the star in you document; then right-click the star shape in your document and choose "Add Text" from the pop-up menu.

NOTE *Avoid choosing the "More AutoShapes" item at the bottom of the AutoShapes pop-up menu. Selecting that item forces Word to venture out onto the Internet to look for more shapes on Microsoft's web page. I've found that more of an exercise in frustration than any handy tool I could really use.*

I Need to Add a Curly Bracket to the Margin

It just so happens that a curly bracket is one of those AutoShapes that the Drawing toolbar provides for you. I've used the curly bracket often when I write a script to indicate that several people are talking at once, as shown in Figure 4.13.

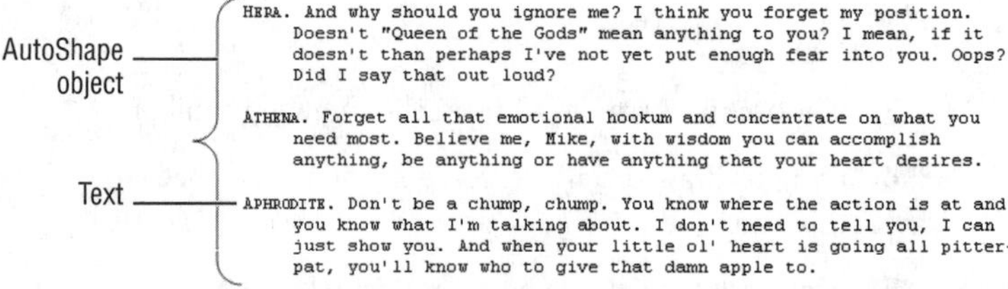

FIGURE 4.13
A curly bracket (or "brace") in the margin

THE BEST DRAWING FRIEND YOU CAN HAVE

If you're into illustrations, then I recommend purchasing a separate drawing program for your computer. Popular applications include Corel Draw and Adobe Illustrator. These are professional-level drawing programs that give you far more control over your drawings than the Drawing toolbar in Windows.

Here's how to add such a thing to your document:

1. Write your text first. After all, you can't bracket what you don't see.
2. Summon the Drawing toolbar.
3. Choose AutoShapes ➤ Basic Shapes ➤ Left Brace from the Drawing toolbar. "Left Brace" is the second-to-last item on the last row of the Basic Shapes menu.
4. Drag to create the brace in your document.
5. Adjust the brace: Resize and reposition as necessary.

What's Better Than a Square for Showing a Part or Chapter Number?

Oh, anyone can be clever with two dimensions. But consider the following steps for putting your chapter number into a three-dimensional doodad:

1. Type your chapter first.
2. Go back to page 1. Press Ctrl+Home to do that.
3. Summon the Drawing toolbar to create your chapter heading.
4. Select the Rectangle tool. In Word 2003/XP, optionally delete the Drawing Canvas.
5. Drag to create the rectangle for your chapter title.
6. From the Draw menu (on the Drawing toolbar) choose Text Wrapping ➤ In Line with Text. This lets Word treat the box like a large character as opposed to an image floating above or below the text.
7. Position the rectangle so that it's on a line by itself. Click the mouse (or use the keyboard arrow keys) to put the toothpick cursor right after the rectangle; then press the Enter key.
8. Click to select the rectangle again.
9. Optionally add color to the rectangle. I use a light gray, say 25 percent.
10. Right-click the rectangle and choose "Add Text" from the pop-up menu.
11. Type the chapter title.
12. Apply a heading style to the chapter title, or format it as you please. It's a good idea to use a heading style on the title, as this helps you organize your document later.

13. Adjust the rectangle so that the chapter title fits nicely within its bounds.
14. And now for the fancy stuff: Choose a 3-D style from the 3-D button's pop-up menu.

This may take some experimenting because the text doesn't warp into three dimensions like the box does. But with practice, you can get it to look like part of the box, as shown in Figure 4.14. What you end up with is more than just a fancy title in a box. It's. . .art!

FIGURE 4.14
A fancy title in a 3-D box

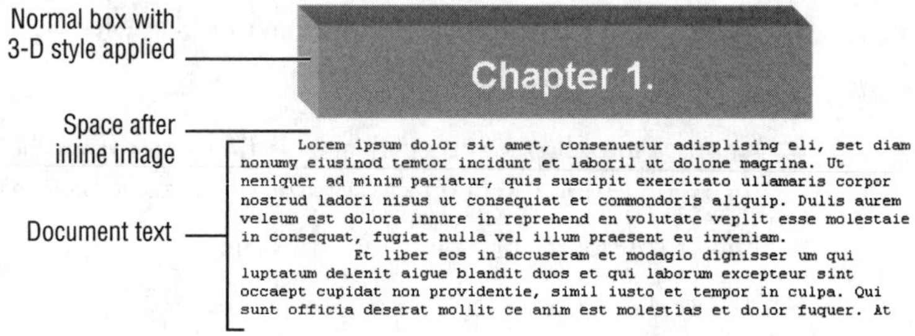

Chapter 5

Using Styles and Templates to Save Oodles of Time

I REMEMBER WHEN STYLES were first introduced to PC word processing, way back in the early 1990s. My reaction to styles was the same as just about any Word user; I freely ignored them. I understood how styles could make formatting a document easier, but like most folks, I found it much easier simply to use the formatting buttons and commands to work with my text. That worked, of course, until I needed to change something. Only then did I discover the true value of using styles and how much time they could save.

For a short document, you don't need styles. But for anything longer than a page, or anything you expect to look professional, you should consider using styles and using them well. They aren't that difficult to understand, so this chapter doesn't concentrate too much on style basics. Instead, I thought I'd dish up about 14 years' worth of style tricks and tips to help you understand and use styles better than anyone else on the block. (Well, at least anyone else who doesn't have this book!)

- Creating a style the easy way
- Automatically applying styles
- Taking advantage of heading styles
- Discovering the power of styles
- Creating a palette of styles
- Working styles into templates

Why Bother with Styles?

A style is nothing more than a collection of formatting commands, all of which can be applied to text in one swift movement. And, honestly, if your document isn't that complex, then you don't need to bother with styles.

NOTE *When it comes to creating or modifying styles, Word 2003/XP and Word 2000 handle styles differently. Word 2000 uses a special Style dialog box. Word 2003/XP uses the Styles and Formatting task pane. Both methods accomplish the same thing. And specific differences will be noted in the text.*

A single style can contain commands that format text in any or all of the following ways:

Font Select typeface, size, text attributes, color, and anything in the Font dialog box.

Paragraph Choose various paragraph-formatting options, as found in the Paragraph dialog box.

Tabs Set tabs.

Borders and Shading Specify any borders or shading or anything else than can be done in the Borders and Shading dialog box.

Language Select a language for the text, to be used for the spell and grammar check.

Frame Stick the text in a frame (for web publishing).

Numbering Apply a bullet or number to the paragraph, per the Bullets and Numbering dialog box.

When Do I Need to Create Styles?

Suppose your document has a simple chapter heading and then a lot of text. If so, you probably don't need styles. (Though if you've used styles before, you'll probably use them even in that case.)

Otherwise, if your document contains any or all of the following, you're better off creating styles:

- A headline or headings to break up sections of text
- A header or footer
- Block-quoted text or any specialized text, such as `computer screen text` or quotations
- Specialized text, such as text in a table or foreign-language text

Essentially, any document that contains anything other than one style of text probably needs a few styles created to help you format.

What's the Best Way to Create a Style?

The best way I've found to create styles is to write your document's text first. Format as you go: If you have a header, format it with a bolder font, centered, bordered, or however you feel it looks right. Just use the formatting tools you have to create the look you want as you go.

The first time you need to reuse a style is when you need to cement the style's attributes and save them as an official Word style.

For example, suppose your document starts out with an A-head, or first-level heading. Then you write a few pages of text and you need another A-head. The first A-head is already formatted as you like. You merely want to copy all that formatting into a style so you can instantly apply it to the second (and any future) A-heads. Here's how:

1. Click the mouse on the paragraph containing the formatting you want to squeeze into a new style.
2. Click the mouse in the Style drop-down list on the Formatting toolbar. This selects the text already there, illustrated in Figure 5.1.

FIGURE 5.1
The Style drop-down list

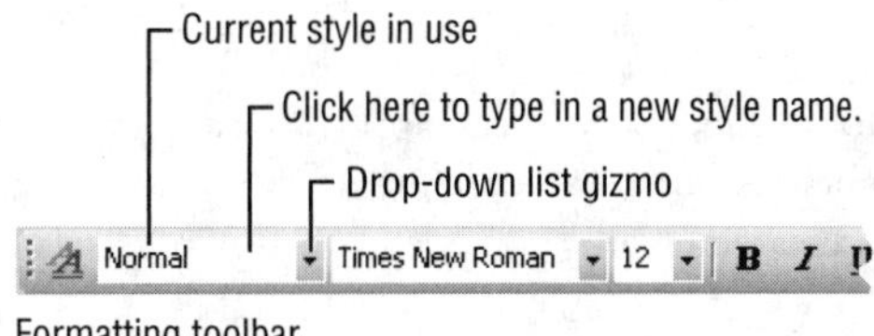

3. Type a name for your style. Use a unique name, such as "A-head" or "First head." Try not to use one of Word's already-created style names, such as "Normal" or "Heading 1."
4. Press the Enter key to lock in that style name. And the style is created.

You can now apply the style to any paragraph of text in your document. So:

1. Scroll down to where the next header can be found. Or go to the spot where you have text that is to be formatted in that same style.
2. Select the text with the mouse.
3. Choose your style from the Style drop-down list on the Formatting toolbar.

And in an instant, that style is applied to the text. The same style, exactly.

Do I Need to Create a Style for Every Bit of Text?

If you don't create a style for every bit of text in your document, then your document uses the Normal style, which in Word is Times New Roman at 12 points, nothing else added or fancy. If that's what you want for your document, grand! Otherwise, create a style based on however you're formatting your text.

What about Plain Text? Does It Need a Style?

I always create a style called "Body" for the body of my document's text. Even though this style is typically just a typeface and a type size, I create it and apply it to the entire document. In fact, I often do it first to all the text and then go back and create other styles as needed.

To create a style for the majority of text in your document, follow these steps:

1. Select a typical paragraph of text, one that is formatted how you want all the text in your document to look: the font, size, typeface, style, paragraph options, and so forth.
2. Click the Style area on the Formatting toolbar (refer to Figure 5.1).
3. Type in a name for the body text style. I use the word "Body." Do not use "Normal" or "Plain Text" as they are predefined styles used by Word.
4. Press Enter.

Now the name is locked in, and you can apply the style to all your document's body text.

If your entire document is Body text, then press Ctrl+A to select the whole thing, and choose Body (or whatever style you created) from the Style drop-down list. That applies that style to all the text in your document.

To apply the style to individual portions of text, select those portions with the mouse, and then choose Body from the Style drop-down list.

NOTE *To reapply formatting to a chunk of text, press the F4 "repeat" key. For example, after applying the Body style to a chunk of selected text, select a new chunk of text and then press the F4 key. This applies that same formatting (style) over again.*

Document Headings and Their Levels

Documents that are divided into sections are organized by using various headings or header levels. This is merely part of the outlining and thought-organization process—the stuff they tried to teach you in school by using 3 x 5 cards that never really sank in. But in real life, when you need to organize your thoughts into a paper, it's best to use various heading levels.

The first heading level is Heading 1, which is also the name of a predefined style in Word. That's the top-level heading or A-head, as it's known in the publishing industry.

Below Heading 1 is Heading 2, which is the second level of organization, or the B-head. Then comes Heading 3, or the C-head, following by Heading 4, or the D-head, and so on. Though, in practice, I've rarely seen a document with anything below Heading 3 used.

The purpose of the headings is purely organizational. Heading 1 defines a broad category. Heading 2 is a specific example of the Heading 1 category. And Heading 3, if needed, is a specific example of what Heading 2 represents. It works kind of like this:

Continued on next page

DOCUMENT HEADINGS AND THEIR LEVELS *(continued)*

Heading 1: Animal

Heading 2: Dog

Heading 2: Cat

Heading 2: Vermicious Knid

Heading 1: Vegetable

Heading 1: Mineral

Heading 2: Sapphire

Heading 3: Red

Heading 3: Blue

Heading 2: Carbon

Tradition holds that you must have at least two headings on each level, though this is debatable. In academic circles, however, they feel that if you have only one header, then there is no need for any header at all. (At least that's what they tell me.)

Why Not Just Use the Normal Style?

You can use the Normal style, if you like. You can even change the Normal style. For example, say that you prefer to have *all* of your documents formatted with the Bookman typeface at 10 points. If so, all you need to do is modify the Normal style:

1. Choose Format ➤ Font to open the Font dialog box.
2. Select the attributes for the Normal style's font. For example, choose a typeface other than Times New Roman, a specific size, and so on. I changed the Normal font on my business correspondence computer so that all my new documents are 12-point Book Antigua font.
3. Click the Default button. This is a special button in most formatting dialog boxes. It takes the changes you've specified and updates the `NORMAL.DOT` template file with those changes, which effectively changes the Normal style.
4. Click the Yes button in the confirmation dialog box.

And the Normal style has been updated. Alas, you cannot update other styles using the Default button; they're keyed into the Normal style specifically. So if you want to use another style in your document, you must create it yourself.

NOTE *When you quit Word, you may be asked to save the updates to the* `NORMAL.DOT` *template. Click the Yes button to do so, which makes your changes permanent.*

Can I Use Information from My A-Level Head Style to Create a B-Level Head Style?

It's possible in Word to base a new style upon the attributes of an existing style. This way the two styles are related. In fact, if you change the attribute of one style, it can affect the attribute of the related style. But before I get into that, here's how to create a B-level head style based on an existing A-level head style in your document:

1. In Word 2003/XP, choose Format ➤ Styles and Formatting; the Styles and Formatting task pane appears. In Word 2000, choose Format ➤ Style; the Style dialog box shows up.
2. Click the New or New Style button; the New Style dialog box appears, as shown in Figure 5.2. (The dialog box looks different between Word XP/2003 and Word 2000; differences are pointed out in the figure.)

FIGURE 5.2
The New Style dialog box

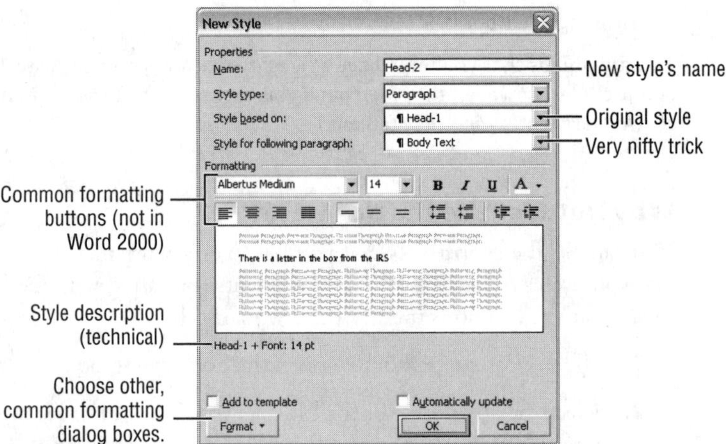

3. Type a name for the new style, such as Head B or B-head. Be descriptive yet brief.
4. Keep Paragraph as the style type. (Character styles are covered later in this chapter.)
5. Choose the original style, the one this style is based on. For example, Head A would be the style that Head B would be based on. Also note in the description area how this style is defined as the original style *plus* whatever options you change.
6. Select whatever body text style you're using as the style for following paragraph. That way, when you press the Enter key after typing your heading style, Word automatically switches to the body text style for the following paragraph. This is a very handy trick.

7. Adjust whatever formatting changes need to be made between the styles. In my documents, heading B is merely a smaller font size than heading A, so I'll just adjust the font size down to 14 from 18. Or sometimes I'll make the B head small caps or italics. Whatever is required to differentiate between an A and B head, make those changes.

8. Click OK to create the style.

Note that the style is *not* automatically applied to any selected text in your document. To apply the style, choose it from the Style drop-down list. Or in Word 2003/XP, select the style from the Styles and Formatting task pane. (Or you can close the task pane if, like me, you feel it's a waste of screen space.)

How Will Changes in One Style Affect a Related Style?

Suppose you have two related styles, such as Head-1 and Head-2. Head-2 is based on Head-1, with the only defined difference being that Head-2 is a smaller font size.

What happens if you change the font for Head-1? How will that affect the document? Try this to find out:

1. Click to place the blinking toothpick cursor inside a paragraph formatted with the original style. It must be the original style, not a style "based on" another style.

2. In Word 2003/XP, choose Format ➤ Styles and Formatting; in Word 2000, choose Format ➤ Style.

3. In Word 2003/XP, locate the style in the scrolling list; in Word 2000, click to select the style in the scrolling list.

4. In Word 2003/XP, point the mouse at the style, click the down-arrow that appears, and then select Modify from the menu; in Word 2000, click the Modify button. For all versions of Word, the Modify Style dialog box appears, which is very similar to the New Style dialog box shown in Figure 5.2.

5. Click the Format button.

6. Choose Font.

7. Select another font or typeface for the style by using the Font dialog box.

8. Click OK.

9. Click OK to close the Modify Style dialog box.

10. In Word 2003/XP, optionally close the Styles and Formatting task pane; in Word 2000, close the Style dialog box.

Observe your document. You'll notice that the typeface has changed for the style you modified. *Plus* the typeface for any styles based on that style also have changed. In the previous section's example, both the Head-1 and Head-2 style's font has changed. That's because Head-2 is based on Head-1, and any changes made in Head-1 are reflected in Head-2.

The only time a change in one style does not appear in another is when that second, based-on style redefines a specific formatting attribute. For example, you could change the point size of Head-1's font to 36, but because the point size for Head-2 is fixed at 14, that wouldn't change.

I Need to Change My Entire Document's Style from 12-Point Text to 10-Point

Again, here is the magic part about using a style: Because all your document's text is defined by a style, all you need to do is change the point size for that style and every bit of text formatting with the style changes.

To modify any style, follow the steps in the previous section. Use the Modify Style dialog box to make your style changes.

(In the previous section, two styles were modified at once because one was based on the other. If no other style is based on the style you're modifying, then the changes you make affect only the current style.)

What's the Point of a Character Style?

Character styles are rarer than paragraph styles but still valuable in the scheme of things. Unlike paragraph styles, character styles affect only character formatting, not paragraphs or tabs. Because of that, there are few types of documents that even need to concern themselves with character formatting.

For example, when I write small computer how-to booklets, I use a special character style for the stuff people are supposed to type into their computer. That text is formatted with the Courier New font, at 10 points, and colored blue.

To make such a style, use the New Style dialog box, shown in Figure 5.2. Follow these steps:

1. Choose Character from the Style type drop-down list. Note that this limits other options in the dialog box to those that specifically cover character formatting.
2. Choose your character-formatting options. In Word 2003/XP, I can do all these with the gizmos present in the dialog box; for Word 2000, I need to click the Format button and choose Font from the menu. In my example, I choose the typeface Courier New, size 10 points, color blue.
3. Name the character style. Don't worry about specifying it as a character style; all character styles show up in lists with the tiny letter *a* by them, whereas paragraph styles appear with the paragraph symbol, the backward *P*.
4. Click OK, and the character style is created.

To apply the character style, select a chunk of text with the mouse, and then choose that style from the Style drop-down list.

Again, the advantage to creating such a style over just formatting text is tremendous. For example, in one of my documents I discovered that the blue-colored text didn't look right when printed. So it was a simple matter to modify the character style and change the text color to red. That one simple change was then reflected on all the text formatting with that style in the document, saving me a lot of time.

Some Style Tricks, Tidbits, and Advice

The beauty of styles is that once you create them, you simply have to use them. That's it! There's no more dinking or re-creating involved, unlike formatting everything manually.

Even though styles are relatively simple things, I've collected a bunch of tidbits, trivia, and other advice to freely dispense, giving you a bit more knowledge on the subject than a cursory tour would do otherwise. So here they are, my style tricks, in no particular order.

Can I Modify a Paragraph That's Already Formatted with a Style?

Any text in a document can be changed. Styles cannot "lock" a paragraph's formatting. For example, if you want *italic* text in the middle of a styled paragraph, you can do that, right? Similarly, you can change the font or color of the text or edit or anything.

If the modifications are common, then consider creating a new style. For example, say you need to change three paragraphs into a bulleted list. If so, then simply create a new style based on the existing one, but a style with bulleted paragraphs.

NOTE *The problem you run into if you don't create a new style based on an old style is that if you modify the old style, you may lose your on-the-fly changes to a paragraph.*

Why Bother with Heading Styles?

If possible, try to let Word identify your heading styles. This is important because Word uses the heading levels for many things, such as creating an outline, a table of contents, or the Document Map. But the key is to identify the heading style as such. Here's how you do that:

1. Modify the style you want to be the first-level heading. Refer to instructions earlier in this chapter for getting to the Modify Style dialog box for your heading style.

2. From the Format button, choose Paragraph. This displays the Paragraph formatting dialog box.

3. Select an Outline Level for the heading style. In the upper-right corner of the dialog box is a drop-down list of Outline Level options, shown in Figure 5.3. For the first heading-level style, choose Level 1. For the second, choose Level 2, and so on.

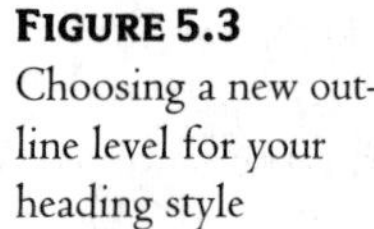

FIGURE 5.3
Choosing a new outline level for your heading style

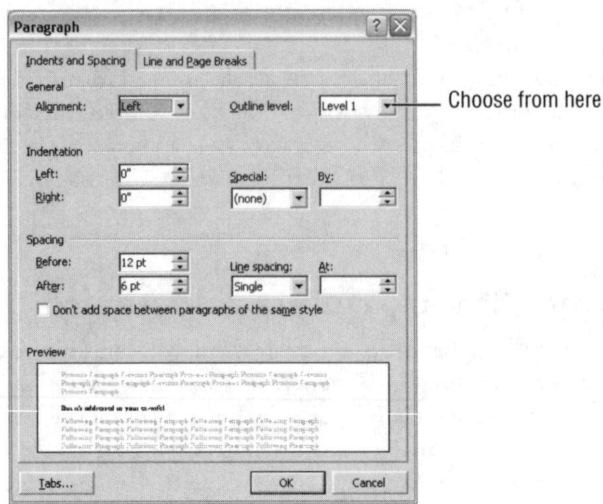

4. Click OK to make the change in the Paragraph dialog box.
5. Repeat this change for other heading styles in your document. Assign to each of them the appropriate outline level value.
6. Close up various dialog boxes and windows when you've finished.

With these changes made, your made-up styles hold the same power over your document as the built-in Heading styles. You can use them to see an overview of the document with the Document Map command, or when switching to Outline mode, or when creating a table of contents.

What's the Benefit to Having One Style Follow Another?

To save time and energy when creating a document, it helps to have one style automatically follow another. For example, as was shown earlier in this book, a heading style should be automatically followed by a body text style. Indeed, the built-in Heading styles all specify that after pressing the Enter key, the following paragraph should be formatted with the Normal style.

This "Style for Following Paragraph" option comes in handy for documents with lots of formatting in specific order. For example, consider a document that starts with a heading, then a subheading, then an initial paragraph that's not indented, followed by paragraphs that are indented. That's *four* styles, but by specifying which style follows which, you can make all the changes take place automatically.

NOTE *A style needs to be created before you can specify it to follow an existing style.*

For example, assume that the first style is Title. That must be followed by the Subhead style, as shown in Figure 5.4. Then the Subhead style is followed by the Body-first style, which is the first paragraph of the document. Finally, the Body style (indented paragraph) automatically follows the Body-first style (unindented paragraph). After that, the Body style simply follows itself.

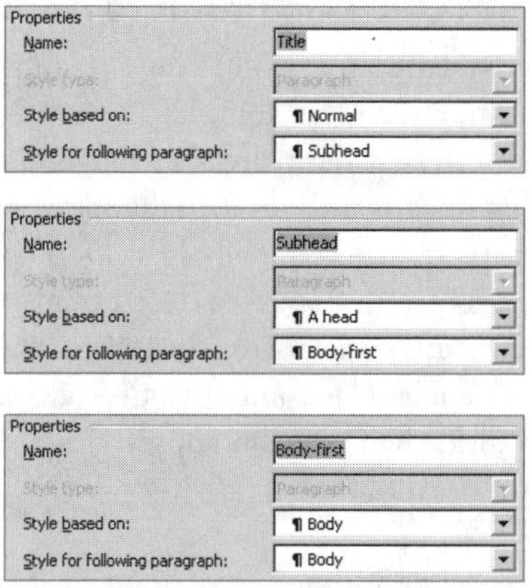

FIGURE 5.4
Styles should be defined in the order you'll use them.

To add a new heading, you must manually select it from the Style drop-down list or Style and Formatting task pane.

How Can I Quickly Restore a Style That's Been Reformatted in the Document?

As long as the style itself hasn't been modified, you can reapply it to any chunk of text. This is easier to do in Word 2003/XP than in Word 2000. In Word 2003/XP, any style that's modified appears as such in the Style drop-down list, as shown in Figure 5.5.

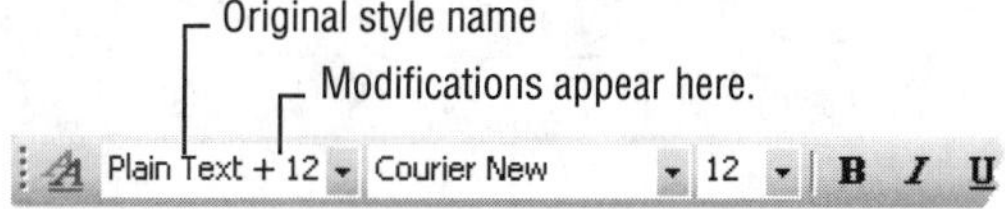

FIGURE 5.5
The style has been messed with, oh no!

In Word 2000 there is no visible way to tell that a style has been messed with. There are, however, a few tricks you can pull in all Word versions to restore a modified chunk of text.

Can I Modify the Standard Styles?

Certainly. Would that be a permanent or temporary modification?

If you merely want to change the styles for a specific document, then feel free to modify them as you would any other style.

To permanently alter the built-in styles, open the `NORMAL.DOT` template file, go into each style, and modify it as you see fit. Save the `NORMAL.DOT` template when you've finished. That way, those styles will be used any time you start a blank document in Word. They'll also be inherited by any other document that uses those styles.

NOTE *A good reason* not *to modify the built-in or standard styles is that some templates do rely on them being of a certain style. Therefore I do insist that you consider creating your own styles as opposed to modifying the built-in ones.*

How Can I Copy Styles from One Document to Another?

The easiest way to share styles is to create a template using the styles. Then you can start any new document with those styles. Or you can attach that template to any document and, presto-chango, that document inherits the styles found in that template. But I'm assuming here that your objective is merely to copy styles between documents and not actually mess with templates. Yes, there is a way. (If you do want to mess with templates, there's a whole section coming up.)

Before you start, it helps to have both files saved to disk. For example, if you're copying styles from `INVASION.DOC` to the current document, then obviously `INVASION.DOC` must be saved to disk. And then, if you haven't yet saved your current document to disk, do so! (Save! Save! Save!)

When both files are saved to disk, then you can copy styles between them, thusly:

1. Choose Tools ➤ Templates and Add-ins.
2. Click the Organizer button. The Organizer dialog box, Styles tab appears, as shown in Figure 5.6. This is where you can copy styles between documents or templates, as described in the figure.

FIGURE 5.6
Copying styles from one document to another

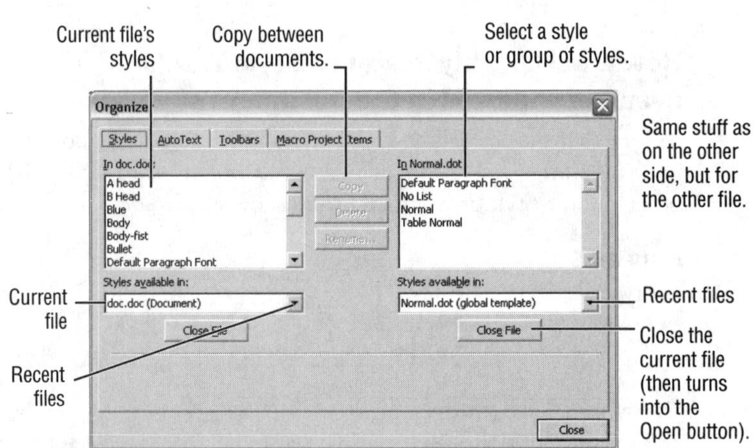

To keep sane, I keep the current document on the left and the document from which I'm copying styles on the right—though this isn't a hard-and-fast rule.

3. Click the Close File button on the left. The only time you don't need to do this is when the open file, such as `NORMAL.DOT`, contains the styles you want. Most of the time, however, that won't be the case.
4. Click the Open File button to locate the file containing the styles you want to thieve, or copy. Or, if you're lucky, the file may be available in the drop-down list above the Open File button.

5. Use the Open dialog box to locate the Word document or template file containing the styles you want. When the file is opened, you'll see a list of its styles appear in the wee li'l scrolling window on the right side of the dialog box.

6. Click to select the styles you want to copy. Or press Ctrl to click, click, click and select more than one style.

7. Click the Copy button, and the styles are copied from that file into the current document. If styles have the same name, you'll be warned about overwriting them, as you would expect.

8. Click the Close button when you've finished.

Ah! Thieving styles! Nothing to be embarrassed about. It's a handy way to move common styles between documents without having to re-create things.

What's a Nifty Way to Keep All These Various Styles Handy?

The Style drop-down list is okay—until you get more than a screen's-height list of styles and scrolling through them is like walking barefoot through a poisonous cactus nursery. And the Styles and Formatting task pane? What a pain!

When I have a project, such as a screenplay, that requires using several styles and manually switching among them, I just give up and create a new toolbar/floating palette full of styles. It's cinchy!

1. Choose Tools ➤ Customize. The Customize dialog box appears. It offers you more power than the mere mortal Word user should be allowed to mess with.

2. Click the Toolbars tab.

3. Click the New button. The New Toolbar dialog box appears, as shown in Figure 5.7.

FIGURE 5.7
Creating a new toolbar

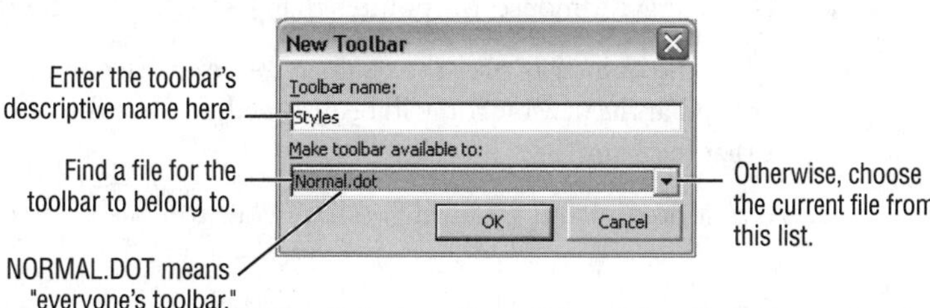

4. Enter **Styles** as the toolbar's name.

5. Choose a place to make the toolbar available. Choose `NORMAL.DOT` if you want the toolbar to belong to all your Word documents, or use the drop-down list to select the current document or its template. (If you can't decide, then select the current document or its template and not `NORMAL.DOT`.)

6. Click OK.

The toolbar appears in two places. First, it shows up in the list of Toolbars in the Customize dialog box. But more importantly, look for its floating palette variation on the screen, similar to what you see in Figure 5.8. Yes, it will grow larger as you attach buttons to the palette.

FIGURE 5.8
Copying styles to the toolbar

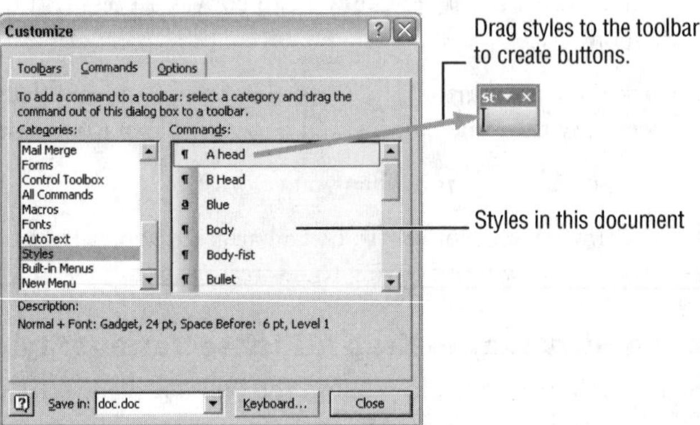

1. Click the Commands tab.
2. Scroll down the list of Categories and select Styles. The styles you've created for your document appear in the scrollable Commands list, as shown in Figure 5.8.
3. Choose a style to place on the toolbar. Make it a common style, one that you use often.
4. Drag that style to the toolbar.

   As you drag the mouse, the pointer changes to the "I'm dragging a style to the toolbar" pointer.

   When the pointer is over the toolbar, a hunky insertion pointer shows you exactly where on the toolbar the new button will be dropped. Release the mouse button to drop the style button at that location.
5. Repeat Steps 9 and 10 until you have your toolbar of styles.

NOTE *You don't need to have all the styles on the toolbar, just the common ones.*

When you've finished, you'll have a toolbar full of text: the blah-blah style and the so-and-so style. And style! Style! Style! It seems like a redundant word, so you can do some editing if you like:

1. Right-click a toolbar button to modify it. A pop-up menu appears.
2. Enter or edit the toolbar button's name using the Name item. 'Click in there with the mouse and either edit the name or type something else that will appear on the toolbar. (I just edit the word "Style" from the name. Or if it's an "A-Head Style," I may just edit it down to "A.")

3. Repeat Steps 12 and 13 for each toolbar button you want to modify.
4. Click the Close button when you've finished. That closes the Customize dialog box, which means the Styles floating palette is now locked into place and can be used to help you format your document.

As with any toolbar in Word, you can drag it to any edge of the window to "attach" it to that window. Or you can resize the toolbar to make the buttons stack vertically instead of horizontally.

You can close the toolbar to make it disappear if you like. To summon it again, choose its name from the View ➤ Toolbars submenu.

Can I Assign a Shortcut Key to a Style?

One of the fastest ways to apply any style is to give it a shortcut key. That way you can instantly apply the style's formatting with the press of a key. Or, actually, several keys because most of the handy Alt and Ctrl keys are already taken by various Word commands.

To slap a shortcut key combination to a style, follow these steps. It is assumed that the style has already been created:

1. In Word 2003/XP, choose Format ➤ Styles and Formatting; in Word 2000, choose Format ➤ Style.
2. Locate the style you want to assign a shortcut key to.
3. In Word 2003/XP, click the style's menu button (to the right) and choose Modify from the menu; in Word 2000, click the Modify button. The Modify Style dialog box appears.
4. In Word 2003/XP, choose Shortcut Key from the Format button's menu; in Word 2000, click the Shortcut Key button. The Customize Keyboard dialog box appears, as shown in Figure 5.9. (In Word 2000 the items are arranged differently.)

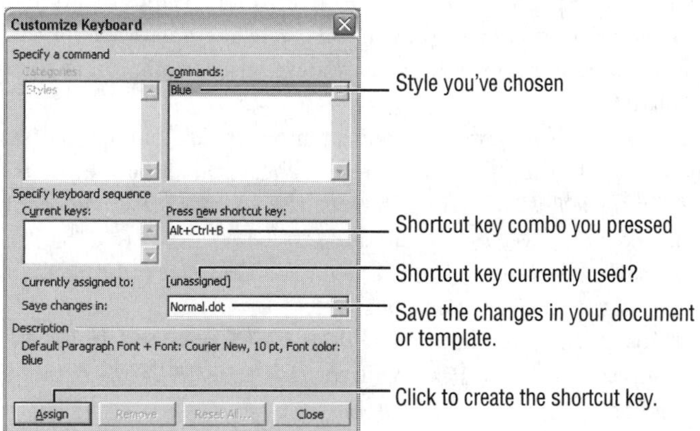

FIGURE 5.9
Assigning a shortcut key to a style

5. Type a key combination for your style. It's best to use the Ctrl and Alt keys together, plus a letter key, such as the first letter of the style, as shown in Figure 5.9.

NOTE *If the key combination is already used by Windows, you'll see the command listed in the dialog box. Try another command in that case.*

6. Click the Assign button to assign that key combination to your style.
7. Choose your document's name or template from the "Save Changes In" drop-down list. Try not to save the changes in `NORMAL.DOT`. If you do, you'll quickly run out of key combinations as you create more styles than can possibly have keyboard equivalents.
8. Click the Close button.

Now to apply that style, use the proper key combination.

NOTE *I prefer using a palette of style buttons over assigning keyboard combinations to styles. That's because when I write I prefer to write first and format second. In that mode, it's easier to use a palette of buttons for formatting than to be messing with the keyboard again.*

Holy Templates, WordMan!

Templates are handy files that let you create similar documents over and over again without having to build (or import) styles or copy and paste common chunks of text.

When it comes to word processing, the subject of templates is really a beginner-level one. Therefore I assembled a set of what I feel are suitable intermediate template topics to round out this chapter.

What Can I Put into a Template?

Templates are prototype documents that contain things that don't change. For example, if you create the same report every month, you can create a template file for that report. Include the headings and styles and headers and footers or whatever else is common to the report every month. Save that as a template file.

Beyond text (and even graphics), templates can contain your styles, toolbars, shortcut keys, and a smattering of other things you create. Those can all be specific to a template. (If not, then they're saved in the `NORMAL.DOT` file, which is why you're occasionally prompted to save `NORMAL.DOT` when it seems like you haven't done anything to it.)

To save a template, choose "Document Template (*.DOT)" from the drop-down list by "Save as Type," in the Save As dialog box.

To use a template, choose the File ➢ New Command. In Word 2003/XP you need to look under the "Other Templates" heading in the task pane. In Word 2000, just pluck a template from the New dialog box.

NOTE *In Word 2003/XP, the "Other Templates" part of the New Document task pane lists any recently used templates. To see the rest of them, click the item that reads "On My Computer." That displays a Templates dialog box (like in the good old days).*

I've Already Made a Document and Need to Make a Template from It

To transform a document into a template, remove everything from the document that is specific. For a letter, keep only the parts that won't change from epistle to epistle. For a report, keep only the headings or whatever else doesn't change. Make the template brief, yet keep those items you know you'll have to type in anyway.

Once the regular Word document is pared down, use File ➤ Save As to save it as a template.

NOTE *I generally create the document first, fumbling through creating styles and whatnot. Then I save that document to disk. Only after that do I open it again, delete most of the unique text, and save it to disk as a template.*

I Need to Reassign This Document's Template!

There, you've done it! You've gone and created a document with a certain template only to find out that you really need to associate it with another template. Oh, drat!

Well, you're not entirely screwed. You can reassociate a document with a given template. You won't get the text from that template, but you will inherit the styles and any other template-y things:

1. Choose Tools ➤ Templates and Add-ins.
2. Click the Attach button.
3. Use the Attach Template dialog box to find the real template you want the document to use, then click the Open button.
4. Be sure to put a check mark by "Automatically Update Document Styles."
5. Click OK.

And your document is now enjoying the benefits and graces of a new template. Changes to a template do affect any documents you've already created with that template. You won't see the changes until you open the document, but they'll be there.

Where the Heck Are the Templates Stored on Disk?

Ah, the sweet mystery of life! Where are those template files anyway? It used to be, back in the bad old days, that Word could hide its templates in any of three different places on the hard drive. It was maddening to determine which location Word was currently using. So if you had the full Microsoft Office installation, the files might be in one folder, but if you just installed Word by itself, the files might be somewhere else entirely.

Fortunately, sanity reigns and the location of the template files on disk depends on your version of Windows more than anything Word or Office is doing.

For Windows XP, templates are a personal thing. You can find them in your account's special area in the Documents and Settings folder:

1. Open Drive C, or wherever Windows is installed.
2. Open the Documents and Settings folder.
3. Open your account's folder.

4. Open the Application Data folder. This is a hidden folder, so you may not see it displayed. (Refer to my book, *Dan Gookin's Naked Windows XP* (Sybex, 2002), for information on displaying hidden files.)
5. Open the Microsoft folder.
6. Open the Templates folder.

NOTE *And if you do have* Dan Gookin's Naked Windows XP, *refer to Chapter 8 on creating a custom palette of programs. You can use those same instructions to create a custom palette of Word document templates—another handy way to start Word!*

For Windows 98 and Windows Me, you can find the templates files here:

1. Open Drive C.
2. Open the Windows folder.
3. Open the Application Data folder.
4. Open the Microsoft folder.
5. Open the Templates folder

And there they are! Normally you don't need to know these "secret" locations for the templates. However, I remember quite a few times when I've tried to manually find this location on disk and was frustrated that it wasn't written down anywhere. Well…now it is!

Chapter 6

Writing That Great American Novel or Screenplay

THE WORD PROCESSOR HAS completely overtaken the typewriter as the ultimate writing tool. After all, a typewriter cared not whether you were typing a school paper, a letter, a novel, or even one of those typing school exercises that, if you typed in all the characters correctly, looked like the Mona Lisa when held at a distance.

As that master of all things written, Word has no preference as to whether you're typing a government grant, a secret diary, or a list of chores for the kids to do while you're away on "business" in Orlando. It's designed to handle small tasks more than adequately, but Word has also been used to write novels, screenplays, and political treaties—heavy-duty stuff.

Where do you draw the line? It depends on what you want to do. For example, if you're writing something creative, such as a novel or screenplay, then you'll probably be using many of the Word tools described in this chapter. If not, then you can get by using a minimal amount of Word. But, for the moment at least, I'll assume that you want more from your word processor than just a letter telling the dentist that his payment will be late this month because alien robots stole your wallet.

- Starting out right with an outline
- Manipulating your outline
- Managing your documents with a master document
- Building a table of contents
- Creating an index
- Cobbling together various creative projects in Word

What the Heck Is Outline Mode?

Outlining is the process of organizing your thoughts before you get them down on paper. For a long project, this is a must. They tried to teach you that in school, but the problem in school is that they don't use a *long* project example. Instead, they try to have you outline a short project, which is a silly waste of time.

Whenever I write anything longer than three pages, or anything that must present issues, ideas, or solutions, I first craft an outline. That way I can ensure that my ideas progress logically and that I cover everything; Outline mode allows you to madly jot down simple ideas or splash words on the page and then rearrange them without worrying about the details.

In the old days, outlining was done on 3×5 cards. Then there was outlining software, such as Acta or the popular GrandView program. About a dozen years ago, Word incorporated an outlining mode into its basic program, so there's nothing more you need to start outlining like a pro.

I Have My Ideas, so How Do I Outline Them?

Outlining is done in the Outline view, yet another of Word's many ways of looking at a document. In this mode, the Heading styles take on special privileges, and certain keyboard and toolbar commands help you manipulate and hide a document's contents—all for the sake of easily organizing your thoughts. Yeah verily, outlining is not only a mode…it's a state of mind.

To begin outlining, choose View ➤ Outline from the menu. Or you can click the Outline button in the lower-left corner of the window. Two things happen: The screen changes to Outline view and the Outlining toolbar shows up, as shown in Figure 6.1.

The next thing to do is to organize your thoughts. You can do so by chapter, as shown in Figure 6.1, or by topic, subtopic, and even sub-subtopic. The idea is to rattle your brain and see what plops out. Then, in Outline mode, you can organize things to flow in whatever fashion you wish.

NOTE *The Outlining toolbar is different between Word versions 2003/XP and Word 2000. Primarily it's missing the useful Outline Level button, though the Style drop-down list works similarly (when you select the Heading styles).*

FIGURE 6.1
Outline mode in full bloom

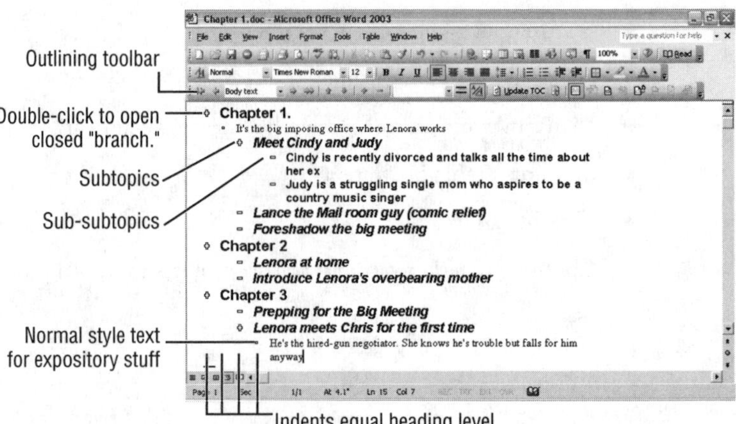

How Do I Create a Topic?

A topic is any high-level heading or subject matter in your document. These are given the Heading 1 attribute in the outline window, and they appear farthest to the left.

To create a topic, type at the – (minus or hyphen) icon in the document. For a main topic, type less information. In fact, in most of my documents the main topic is a chapter title or scene or act from a play.

Remember that main topics are general! Your subtopics can contain more detail. (And for even more detail, I use the Normal style, but more on that in a few paragraphs.)

What's a Subtopic?

A subtopic is a specific aspect or element of the main topic. You create it like this:

1. Press the Enter key. This actually creates a sister topic, but what you want is a subtopic.
2. Press Alt+Shift+right arrow. This key command *demotes* the topic level to a subtopic.
3. Type your subtopic.

Hi-Ho! So Topics Can Be Jiggled Around?

Yes, and this is the beauty of an outline: You can shuffle things around easily. Here's how to move a topic or subtopic:

1. Click the topic's + or – icon. Note that this selects all the subtopics and any text belonging to that topic.
2. Now you can drag the topic up or down (or left or right) with the mouse, but a better way is to use the Outlining toolbar's arrow buttons:

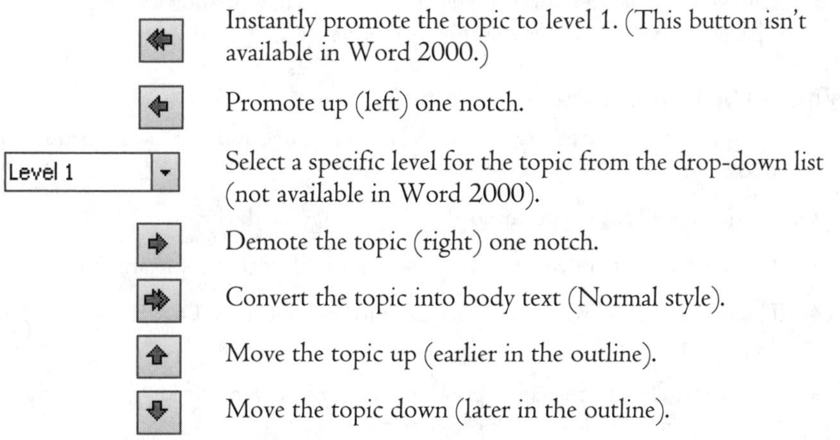

Instantly promote the topic to level 1. (This button isn't available in Word 2000.)

Promote up (left) one notch.

Select a specific level for the topic from the drop-down list (not available in Word 2000).

Demote the topic (right) one notch.

Convert the topic into body text (Normal style).

Move the topic up (earlier in the outline).

Move the topic down (later in the outline).

For example, refer to the quick outline I dished up in Figure 6.2. Suppose you need to move the subtopic "Pablo opens his taco stand amidst much celebration" up, swapping its position with "Maria finally agrees to marry Pablo." Here's how you'd do that:

FIGURE 6.2
A sample outline

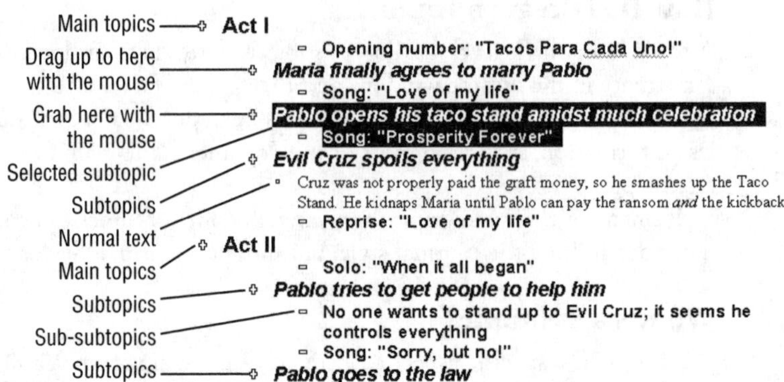

1. Click to select the subtopic "Pablo opens…." This automatically selects any sub-subtopics or text below that subtopic, grouping the entire thing as a block, as shown in Figure 6.2.
2. Drag the subtopic upward. Drag by the + sign. As you drag with the mouse, a horizontal "here" line appears, showing where the moving topic(s) will be reinserted into the outline.

   ——————➤——————————————

3. Release the mouse button to drop the subtopic. In Figure 6.2, it will be positioned just under "Opening number…." (And do note that you can have a sub-subtopic under a main topic.)

   You could also use the buttons on the toolbar to move the topic. In this case, first select the main subtopic so that all its own topics are selected (as shown in Figure 6.2). Then click the Up button twice to move the topic(s) earlier in the outline.

What's the Point of the + or – Icon?

The + and – icons are very handy, serving several purposes in the grand scheme of things. I can think of the following:

- The icon is a handle you can use to drag a topic with the mouse.
- The icon is a button you can double-click to select that topic and all its subtopics.
- The icon indicates whether or not a topic has subtopics. Only a topic with subtopics has the + sign.
- The icons relate to the corresponding keys on the numeric keypad, which can be used to open (expand) or close (collapse) a topic.
- The icons can also be clicked to expand or collapse a topic.

How Can I Split This Topic in Two?

Splitting a topic works like splitting any paragraph or sentence in word: Cleave the topic by clicking the mouse where you want the split and then pressing the Enter key. That creates two sisters where one stood before.

Can I Join Topics?

Yes, just as you would join paragraphs:

1. Put the cursor at the start of the second topic.
2. Press the Backspace key. The topics are now joined, but the words run together, so…
3. Press the spacebar. That sticks air between the last word of the old first topic and the first word of the old second topic.

I Need to Collapse All My Topics: Any Easy Way to Do It All at Once?

To see the Big Picture, you need to tell Word to hide all topic levels except for the first one.

- In Word 2003/XP, choose "Show Level 1" from the drop-down list in the middle of the Outlining toolbar.
- In Word 2000, click the number "1" on the Outlining toolbar.

Doing this is a great way to get a grand overview of your outline—to shove aside the details and concentrate on your major points or elements.

How Can I View Only Level 2 Headings?

I outline my books with the part levels at Level 1 and then the chapter titles at Level 2. So when I want to see all those chapter titles only, I do this:

- In Word 2003/XP, choose "Show Level 2" from the drop-down list in the middle of the Outlining toolbar.
- In Word 2000, click the number "2."

NOTE *Whenever you choose a level to view, Word automatically shows you any levels "above" that level. There is no way to "hide" higher levels.*

It's still possible to view details in this mode. For example, as I started this chapter, I brought up this book's outline and chose to view only the Level 2 headings, which are my chapter titles. Then I double-clicked the + by Chapter 6 to expand it and view the sections and subsections within this chapter.

To see all the levels again: In Word 2003/XP, choose "Show All Levels" from the drop-down list; in Word 2000, click the All button.

FASTER WAYS TO MOVE YOUR TOPICS AROUND

There are a wealth of keyboard equivalents for manipulating your outline. In fact, I use the keyboard more than the mouse when I'm outlining. Here are my favorite keys:

Alt+Shift+arrow The *arrow* can be any one of the four arrow keys on the keyboard: up, down, left, or right. Pressing this key combination moves an individual topic (but not the subtopics) in the direction of the arrow. Very handy.

Numeric Keypad – Pressing the minus key on the numeric keypad collapses a topic, hiding any subtopics from view.

Numeric Keypad + Pressing the + key on the numeric keypad opens a collapsed topic.

Why Bother with the Normal Style in an Outline?

Not everything you want to put into the outline will be a topic. For example, at some point you may want to write a bit of background or, heck, just start writing. In those instances, rather than waste a topic heading, you can just use the body text level to compose your thoughts.

To create a stretch of body-level text, click the Demote to Body Text button.

If you tend to be a little wordy with your body text stuff, and that gets in the way of your Big Picture view, then click the Show First Line Only button on the Outlining toolbar. That "hides" any second (or extra) lines of text in the outline. Click the button again to turn this feature off.

NOTE *Here's the quick way to get Normal: Ctrl+Shift+N. This keyboard shortcut will apply the Normal style to any paragraph of text, or it will demote any outline topic to the body text level.*

Does the Outline Need to Be Saved as a Separate Document?

I always save my outlines as their own document. I typically give them the name `OUTLINE.DOC` or even `TOC.DOC`, where TOC stands for Table of Contents. This file lives in the same folder as other documents for the same project.

For example, for this book there is a separate document called `TOC.DOC` that contains the book's entire outline. But you don't always have to do things that way.

In many cases, if you simply continue fleshing out an outline, then the outline document can eventually become your final document. Simply change the view back to Normal or Print Layout, start formatting, and your document is on its way to completion.

Organizing Your Work (after Outlining)

Some major projects will end up being more than a single document. While Word itself is capable of handing a document of any length, it works better with smaller documents. Plus, I believe you'll find that keeping the files separate reduces the chance that you'll lose information, and it makes it easier on Word (fewer crashes).

Is It Best to Create My Massive Word Project as One Document or as Several Documents?

It depends on how big your massive Word project is. In my travels, most writers put a chapter into each document. So a 42-chapter novel would consist of 42 separate files. Plus there may be separate files for appendixes, a prefix, a foreword, and other elements of a book.

For smaller works, keeping everything in one document makes sense. In fact, I keep screenplays or teleplays, which are from 30 to 120 pages, as their own documents. But for books and novels, I try to put a chapter into each document.

So I suppose the answer to the question is that it all depends on what you find easiest to work with.

NOTE *If you're a professional writer, then check with the publisher to see which format they want. Publishers are very particular about how they want to see text submitted electronically. So ask!*

I recommend you not worry about binding issues: If you're submitting a document to be published, then the publisher makes its own adjustments for binding. Only if you plan on printing out the document yourself should you concern yourself with binding or setting the gutters or using alternating headers and footers on separate pages. This is covered later in this chapter.

NOTE *If you're getting into binding issues, then you're crossing the fuzzy line between desktop publishing and word processing. Consider your needs, and if you do plan on binding your stuff, then get a desktop publishing program and use it instead of Word.*

How Do I Stick Multiple Documents Together?

To compile several smaller documents into a single mammoth document, you need to work with Word's Master Document mode, a kind of hybrid of Outline mode. This is optional, of course. I would bother with this only if you plan on printing your documents and want them all to have uniform page numbers, headers, and footers. Otherwise, you don't really need to mess with Master Document mode.

Assuming that you have all of your separate documents ready to be threaded together, and that you have the guts to go through with this, follow these steps:

1. Start a new, blank document in Word.
2. Switch to Outline View: Choose View ➢ Outline.
3. Click the Master Document button on the Outlining toolbar. This extends the toolbar's length a bit to accommodate the Master Document buttons, as shown in Figure 6.3. (Note that the Master Document part of the toolbar may already be showing, in which case it's not necessary to click the button.)
4. Click the Insert Subdocument button. The Insert Subdocument dialog box appears. It's just an Open dialog box hybrid.
5. Use the Insert Subdocument dialog box to select your first chapter document or the document that you want to be first in your big master document. So if it's front matter, an introduction, a foreword, or a preface, start with that; otherwise start with Chapter 1.

6. Click the Open button to insert the document. The document is inserted into the master document á la a topic in an outline. The chapter appears in a box, complete with all its text and a subdocument doodad icon, as shown in Figure 6.4.
7. You can use the doodad icon to move the entire chapter up or down in the sequence of events. Otherwise, repeat Steps 5 and 6 to continue to add your chapters or other subdocuments to the master document.

The idea here is to glue all the small pieces together into one big document, the master document. Once the pieces are in place, then you can do things like create headers and footers and page numbers for the *entire* document.

NOTE *To prove how the master document works, use Print Preview to observe your entire document as it would be printed.*

Save the master document! Be sure to save it! The thing is just as important as any other document you have. Save after inserting each new subdocument as well.

FIGURE 6.3
The Outlining toolbar, Master Document stuff

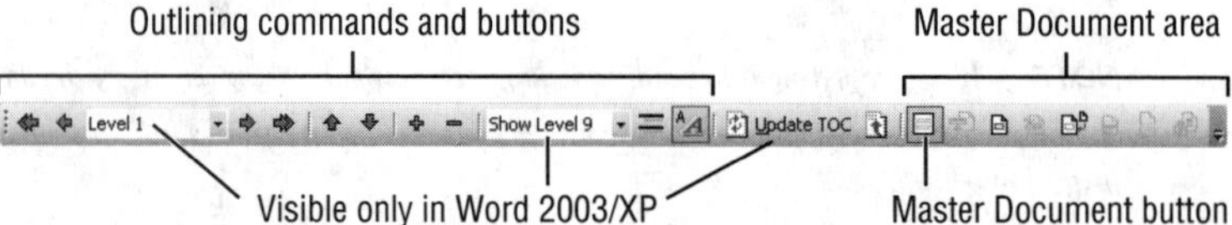

FIGURE 6.4
A subdocument inside a master document

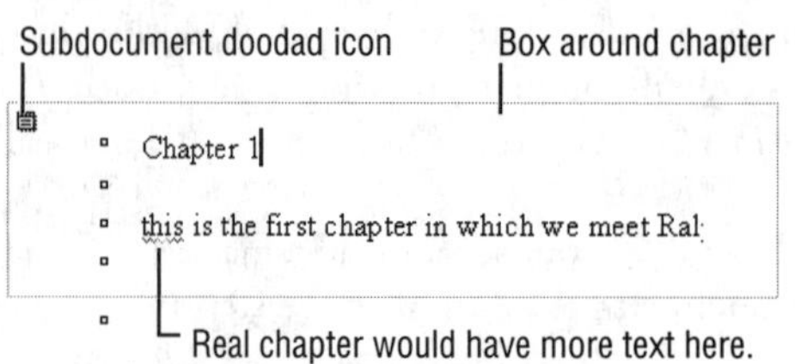

Do I Really Need to See All Those Subdocuments in the Master Document?

No. In fact, you can compress things so that the master document is easier to look at. To do so, click the Collapse Subdocuments button on the Outlining toolbar.

If you haven't saved, you'll be prompted to do so. Afterward, each document is replaced by a hypertext (web page) link to its original file on disk. A little padlock below the subdocument doodad icon tells you that the subdocument is locked and can be edited only in the original file.

To go and visit a subdocument in the compressed state, just Ctrl+click its link. That opens the document in its own window, which is what you're used to in Word.

NOTE *The subdocuments must be expanded before you can view them in Print Preview or print them all off.*

What about Page Numbering across Multiple Documents?

All page numbering can be done in the master document. Just use whatever command you prefer to handle the page numbering.

Each subdocument appears in the master document in its own section. This allows for adjustment of the headers and footers so that, for example, a header doesn't print on a new chapter page. Refer to Chapter 3, "Making Fancy Documents and Reports," for more information on sections.

How Do I Create a Table of Contents?

You don't have to worry about creating a table of contents for any document! Word can do it automatically for you.

A table of contents can be created for any document, from a two-page treatise to a 300-page report. It doesn't have to be a master document or anything fancy. The only requirement for the table of contents is that you use styles, specifically Heading styles, in your document. If so, then Word can easily create a table of contents, complete with accurate page numbers.

To build a table of contents in your document, follow these steps:

1. Go to the place in your document where you want the TOC to appear. If you're working in a master document, place the TOC at the front. For any other type of document, create a page or section break so that the TOC will appear on its own page. (See Chapter 3.)

NOTE *Any document with the proper heading styles used can have its own TOC. Size is not an issue; merely applying the proper heading styles is all that's required.*

2. In Word 2003/XP, choose Insert ➤ Reference ➤ Index and Tables; in Word 2000, choose Insert ➤ Index and Tables. The Index and Tables dialog box pops up.

3. Click the Table of Contents tab. Figure 6.5 shows you what is what, though most of the settings are pretty much the way you want them. There is, however, only one thing you should check:

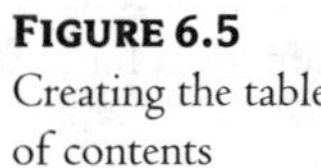

FIGURE 6.5
Creating the table of contents

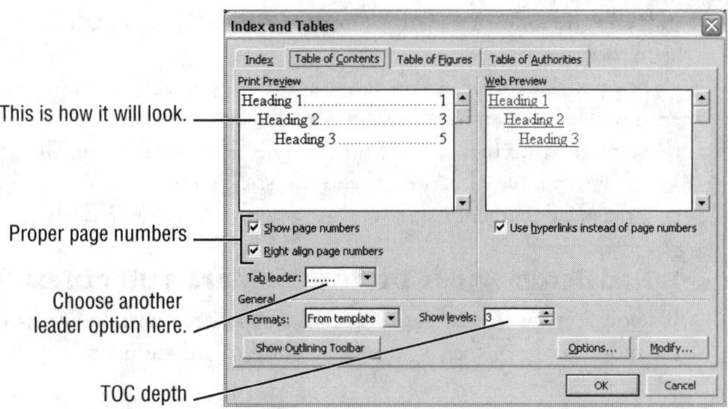

4. Click the Options button.

   Word identifies TOC headings by your document's styles. Up front it assumes that you're using the built-in Heading 1, Heading 2, and Heading 3 styles for your document's headings. If you're using custom styles, such as A-head or Head1 or Title 1 or something unique, the Table of Contents Options dialog box is where you select the difference.

5. Select the proper heading styles for the TOC.

   For example, to have Word use style A Head as the first level in a TOC, scroll through the list to find A Head and assign that to TOC level 1. Assign B Head to TOC level 2, and so on. Or apply the levels to whatever heading levels you're using in your document.

NOTE *If you've already set the proper outline levels for your styles, as described in Chapter 5, "Using Styles and Templates to Save Oodles of Time," then you won't need to go through this extra step.*

6. Click OK.

7. Click OK to create the TOC.

And the TOC is filled in by using the text you formatted with the given styles in your document. Note that it's formatted using a standard body text type of style. You can, if you like, go in and reformat the TOC to look like whatever you want it to. Or you can delete parts of the TOC, edit certain headings, whatever you wish. Treat it like any other text.

Obviously the TOC should be the last thing you create for your document. Use a hard page break or section break to separate its page from the rest of the document. And if you have to update or change things, then simply click the Update TOC button on the Outlining toolbar, or just repeat these steps to rebuild the entire thing.

How Does Indexing Work?

In publishing, it's typically up to the author to index his own work. Even so, there are professional indexers and indexing services that go through books and, for a modest sum, do a far better job than an author can.

For your documents, you can index them yourself providing you remember to create the index entries. That is, you mark text in your document for inclusion in an index. Then Word can take all those marked-up bits of text and compile an index for you, all automatically.

As with a table of contents, you can stick an index into any Word document. It doesn't need to be a master document or, in the case of an index, even have fancy formatting or styles.

It Had Better Not Be Difficult to Mark a Bit of Text for Inclusion in an Index

It's not. It helps if your entire document has been written and polished. Like the table of contents, the index is one of the last things you add to a document.

If everything is ready, then follow these steps:

1. In Word 2003/XP, choose Insert ➤ Reference ➤ Index and Tables; in Word 2000, choose Insert ➤ Index and Tables. The Index and Tables dialog box appears.
2. Click the Index tab.
3. Click the Mark Entry button. The Mark Index Entry dialog box appears, shown in Figure 6.6. It's a "modal" dialog box, which means you can keep it open while you work in your document. So your next task is to collect words and phrases that you want to appear in your document's index.
4. Select a bit of text in your document that you want to appear in the index.
5. Click the mouse in the Mark Index Entry dialog box. The text you selected appears in the Main Entry.
6. Fill in the dialog box as needed.
7. Click the Mark button.
8. Repeat Steps 4 through 7 as needed until you've collected a cache of index entries.

   You can mark as much text as you like. You can even edit the entries you select. For example, if you select the text "Noted legal issues involving the abuse of a spatula," you can edit it down to just "legal issues" if you like.

NOTE *Try to keep in mind what the reader is thinking. Oftentimes they don't use the same terms as you might. For example, in a cookbook consider indexing "Ladle" under "Spoon."*

9. When you're absolutely sick of marking text, click the Cancel or Close button in the Mark Index Entry dialog box. Whew!

Note that marking a document puts special ugly, curly bracket field codes into the document and, well, while you're marking it, the document can look really gross. To make those marks go away when you've done, click the Show/Hide button on the Standard toolbar.

FIGURE 6.6
Creating an index entry

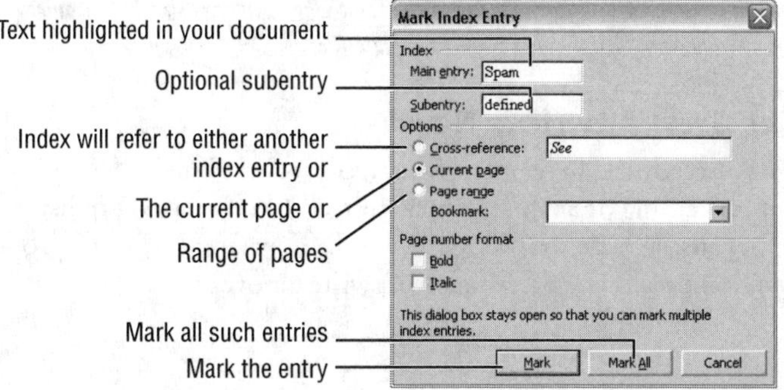

How Do I Put an Index into My Document?

After collecting and marking all the separate index entries, you merely need to order Word to build the index for you. Here's how to do that:

1. Go to the page where you want the index to appear. Yes, typically that's at the end of your document.

NOTE *Don't worry about creating a separate section or page breaks for the index; Word does that automatically.*

2. In Word 2003/XP, choose Insert ➤ Reference ➤ Index and Tables; in Word 2000, choose Insert ➤ Index and Tables.
3. Click the Index tab, if needed.
4. Click OK. Sure, you could mess around in the dialog box, but the settings are pretty standard. By clicking OK, you'll see the index sitting there in your document.

About the only thing you could do in the Index dialog box is to check the box that says "Right Align Page Numbers." That presents the index in a different format, but that's really about the only thing in the dialog box worth changing.

So Now I've Edited My Document and the Index Needs to Be Rebuilt. Help!

The hardest part about doing an index is building it. (Well, in the real world it's getting the stupid page numbers correct, but Word doesn't seem to have a problem with that.) So to rebuild your index, simply select and delete the old one (including the Continuous section breaks), and repeat the steps from the previous section to plop down a new index. Cinchy.

Ideas for Various Creative Projects

The following sections contain some ideas for styles you can put into templates and other tricks you can use when you work on some creative things in Word.

NOTE *Microsoft has a wealth of Word templates you can use or "borrow" from the Internet, although as I said in Chapter 4, searching for and downloading them can be a bit frustrating. In Word 2003/XP, on the New Document task pane, click the link for the Templates Home Page, and you should be connected with a Microsoft web site that has dozens of interesting, handy, and useful template files.*

The Great American Novel

Do you really need a template for the Great American Novel? Nope. Novels are mostly about content, not formatting or anything fancy. In fact, I know of no published author who has ever complained, "They just wouldn't read my stuff until I formatted with the proper heading styles." So rest assured, you don't really need a template to write a novel.

Even so, I do have a template I use for when I go into story mode. It contains the following styles:

Chapter This style has the chapter number or name in bold text, usually centered, with about three blank lines (36 pts) following it. It's automatically followed by the Body style, which is the main style for the document.

Body This paragraph style is usually 12-point Bookman, Palatino, or Book Antiqua, double-spaced with the first line indented one-half inch. No space follows or precedes the paragraph because it's double-spaced. And I use left justification instead of full.

NOTE *Try to avoid making your novel look like a novel. Try not to use columns or full justification. If you plan on submitting the novel for publication, find out from your agent or the publisher in which format the novel should be. With that knowledge, you can easily adjust the style in your document and instantly reformat the entire thing.*

For the template, I typically have it start with the Chapter style ready to go, so that when I open a new document with that template, I can type the chapter number or title and then start writing.

In the header I have my name, the novel's name, and the date. The footer contains the chapter number and the page number. This is all formatted in Arial 10-point bold, but it's part of the template so I don't really create a style for it.

Hurray for Hollywood and the Typical Screenplay

I've written both screenplays and stage plays. (Nothing published, however, mostly because nothing is finished!) Stage plays are easier because they lack the strict style guidelines set down for motion picture screenplays, teleplays, and video plays.

Writing a Typical Stage Play

Stage plays don't have much involved in the way of formatting or style. Aside from the stage directions, the actor's lines make up the bulk of the document. They're formatted sort of like this:

```
Linda: Take off my dress!
Kyle: Yes! At once!
Linda: And don't let me ever catch you wearing my clothes again!
```

Most professionally published scripts have the character name in small caps or often in **bold**. The text is formatted with a hanging indent of about ¼-inch. Stage directions are in either italics or parentheses. There is no hard-and-fast style.

Professionally published plays do have a style, depending on the publisher. Even so, I've worked with local and amateur productions where the script is merely typed out any which way. The idea is merely to make it clear who is speaking which lines.

NOTE *Don't go overboard on your stage directions. Most stage directors look for entrances and exits, plus key business regarding props and physical activity. Overloading your play with too many directions or descriptions merely slows down the reading process, which probably isn't what you want.*

An alternative to the more traditional style is to format the text with the character's name centered above what they say, as in:

```
                      Bert
Molly! Uncle Cedric! What are you doing in that closet?
                      Molly
It's just a little fox trot. The closet is too small to tango.
```

In this case you can take advantage of styles, especially to follow each other:

Actor

This style contains the actor's name. It's centered with the text bold. Single-spaced, no space before or after. Immediately following this style is the Lines style.

`Lines`

This formats the text the actors say. It need not be anything interesting, though I would make it single-spaced with the paragraph followed by 12 points of "air" to separate it from the next bit of text. In fact, this style could automatically be followed by the Actor style in that lines in a play are not broken up into traditional paragraphs of text. (It goes Actor-Lines-Actor-Lines-Actor-Lines, only occasionally broken up by the stage directions.)

NOTE *When writing a script, there is no need to break up what a character says into paragraphs.*

Cobbling Together a Screenplay

Screenplays are strictly formatted. Word can handle it, but most of the "serious" Hollywood writers use a special word processor designed to build screenplays. For the casual writer, however (or until you get your big break), Word does just fine.

I have no idea why screenplays are so exactingly formatted (well, not being in Hollywood, how would I know?). I can guess that it's simply to weed out the less-than-serious from those who really pay attention. After all, if you have a slush pile of 100 scripts, it's easier to toss away something that's formatted improperly than it is to spend time reading the piece.

Figure 6.7 shows a page from a screenplay I worked on when I should have been working on some computer book.

Scene Setting This is the style that introduces a scene, which is an INT (interior) or EXT (exterior), followed by a location and a time of day (the "camera directions" in Figure 6.7). It's also used for camera angles and such, though your script shouldn't contain too many of those. The style is ALL CAPS, right-justified, single-spaced, with a blank line following.

Stage Directions This is the expository style in the script, which explains a setting or situation or a character's mood or internal thoughts (the "directions and descriptions" in Figure 6.7). It's single-spaced, with a blank line following each paragraph.

FIGURE 6.7

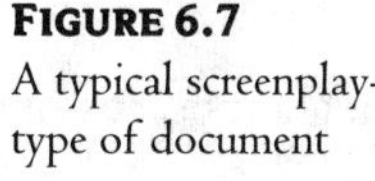

A typical screenplay-type of document

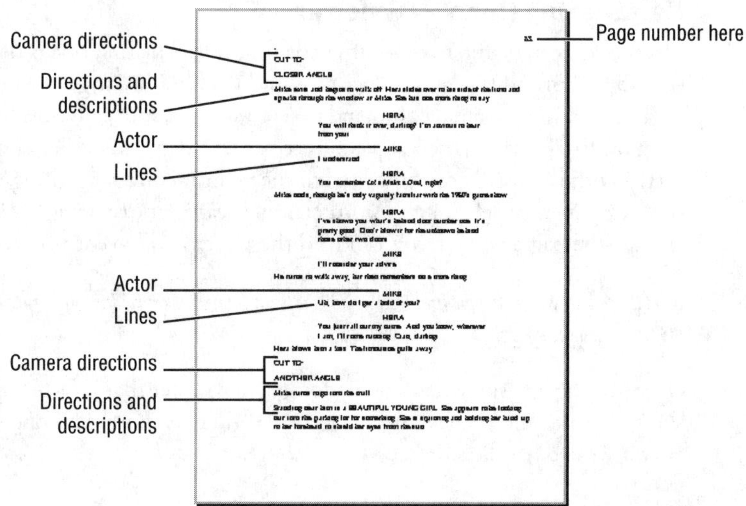

Actor The actor's name is formatted in ALL CAPS. Some scripts have the name centered, but I indent it 2.5 inches. This style is immediately followed by the Lines style.

Lines The Lines style is the format for the lines the actor speaks. It's indented one inch on the left and right (see Figure 6.7). A tab stop is set at position 2.5". It's used to include parenthetical directions in the middle of the line. The paragraph is single-spaced and followed with a blank line. The format for the next style is Actor, since dialog tends to go Actor-Lines-Actor-Lines. That way you can type dialog for a stretch without having to worry about formatting.

NOTE *Unlike a stage play, actors in a screenplay don't talk much. Each block of text for them to speak should be at most five lines long. Longer exposition can be broken up by stage directions, but I would recommend against long exposition for your first screenplay.*

In addition to these styles, the template should contain a page number. It's located in the upper-right corner of the page, and it shows the page number followed by a period. That's it!

The first page of the script should be its own section, without a page number. It contains the film's name and then your name as author, centered in the middle of the page. On the bottom left are your name, address, and phone number. If you have an agent, their name goes bottom center (below the lines containing your name).

NOTE *Scripts are very tricky things to write! I recommend getting a book on screenwriting before you even attempt to submit a script. Most of them will tell you one specific truth: No one makes money by writing scripts for Hollywood. But don't let that stop you!*

Hammering Out a Newsletter

Newsletters can be fun to do—after the first one. The first one is the toughest because it's where you end up making all the layout decisions and deciding what goes where.

The first thing I can recommend is *not* to worry about fancy binding. If you have a printer that can print on 11×17 paper, then you could create a four-page newsletter on one page that folds over. However, Word isn't really equipped to handle printing on such a thing. Ditto for folding over an 8½×11 sheet of paper. Even though Word claims it can print two pages on a sheet of paper, it just can't arrange the pages so that you can fold the paper and have it print out nice and tidy.

NOTE *And where do you find a program that can print out on folded paper nice and tidy? That's right: under the desktop publishing category.*

So, for now, assume that you're doing a newsletter that is to be printed on both sides of a standard sheet of paper and then stapled together (if there is more than one sheet). That's about the best and easiest way to handle things.

Headings First

Start your newsletter with its heading. You can create a giant text block for this or use borders to put lines above and below (or around) the title text. Your title can be a graphic you paste in. But my favorite way to do things is to put the title into a table.

Figure 6.8 shows a table used as the potential header for a newsletter. Further modification can be done, such as removing the grid lines in the table and potentially shading in the different squares of text. And, of course, borders can still be added. (Refer to Chapter 7, "The Tough Stuff: From Labels to Tables," for more information on tables.)

FIGURE 6.8
A sample newsletter heading

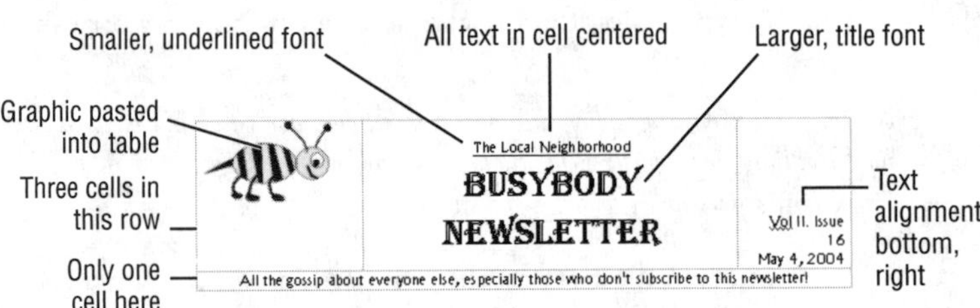

I'd Like to Lay Out Things in Two Columns

After you do the heading, the rest of the newsletter is the *news!* Do you want it in columns or not?

To not use columns requires no skill: Just keep typing.

To use columns, follow these steps:

1. Stick the cursor right after the heading.
2. Choose Insert ➤ Break.

3. The columns need to go into their own section; choose Continuous and click OK.
4. Now you're ready for columns. Choose Format ➢ Columns; the Columns dialog box appears.
5. Choose Two; then click OK.

And your document now has two columns. Write away your content! And spice it up! Refer to Chapter 4 for information on inserting graphics, images, pull quotes, and even random shapes!

NOTE *Columns in newsletters are usually formatted fully justified. Also refer to Chapter 7 for more information on columns.*

How Do I Stop a Column in the Middle of a Page?

Just as there are a page break and a section break, there is also something called a column break. If you want a column to stop at a specific location on the page, simply insert a column break.

To insert a column break, heed this procedure:

1. Position the cursor where you want the column to stop.
2. Choose Insert ➢ Break.
3. Select Column Break and click OK. And the text continues on the next column or page, whichever is closer.

The blank spot where the column used to be? Hey! What a great place for a picture or a text box with more information.

How Can I Start My Text with a Big Letter or Word?

To further draw attention to where text starts, production designers often make the first letter of that paragraph larger than the rest. If they want to get real fancy, they create a *drop cap*, shown in Figure 6.9.

Here's how you, too, can create a drop cap:

1. Click the mouse by the letter you want to drop. Or you can select the letter.
2. Choose Format ➢ Drop Cap. The Drop Cap dialog box contains some interesting options you can mess with later. But the Dropped option is the one pretty much everyone chooses.
3. Select the Dropped option and click OK, and the letter is transformed into a larger version of itself.

In a way, the drop cap is like a text box with the first three lines of the paragraph flowing around it. But don't be fooled: It is *not* a text box.

FIGURE 6.9
A drop cap

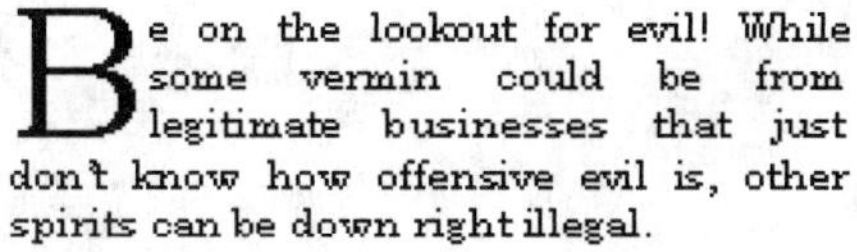

Be on the lookout for evil! While some vermin could be from legitimate businesses that just don't know how offensive evil is, other spirits can be down right illegal.

You can resize the drop cap, though you might just mess it up if you dink too much. To delete the drop cap, click to select it and press the Delete key.

And now, the secret to making a drop *word* instead of a drop cap: After you have the drop cap, click the mouse in the box. You'll notice the flashing cursor appear, which means that you can type. So go ahead and type the rest of the first word of the sentence to create a drop word. (Don't forget to edit the rest of the first word out of the rest of the paragraph, as shown in Figure 6.10.)

NOTE *You can also drop a word by selecting the entire word in Step 1 (above) and then choosing Format ➤ Drop Cap. Same difference.*

FIGURE 6.10
A drop word

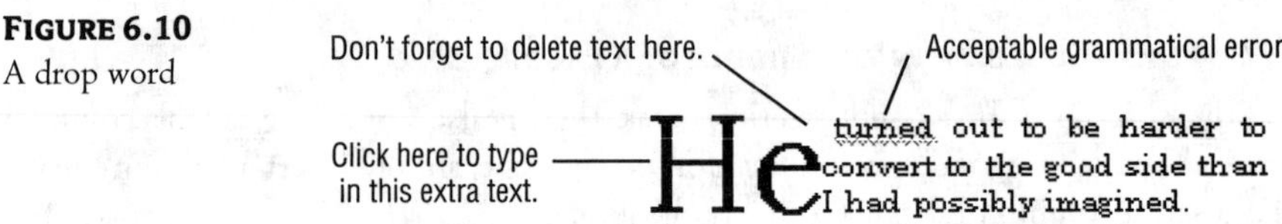

Don't forget to delete text here.
Acceptable grammatical error
Click here to type in this extra text.
He
turned out to be harder to convert to the good side than I had possibly imagined.

Chapter 7

The Tough Stuff: From Labels to Tables

I'M SO HAPPY THAT I wrote the previous chapter on outlining. That way, when I got to this chapter here, I looked up at the title and I said, "Self, you're pretty clever with that rhyme up there. But you really need to teach *tables* before labels." And then I looked at the outline and said, "Self, you really need to teach tabs before tables." And then I realized that my clever rhyming title would no longer represent what was in the chapter. Nevertheless, I rearranged the outline (thanks to the last chapter) so that this chapter would retain its clever title and yet present information in a logical manner.

So with the door closed on my internal thinking process, I can now more properly introduce you to this chapter, which covers some of the esoteric and far-out things that Word attempts to do. About 15 years ago, certain peripheral items crept their way into word processing software. Starting with tabs, and then tables and envelopes and all sorts of not-really-word-processing tools, but yet handy things to have. These features were added to compete with other word processors that lacked such things. But today such competition is moot: Word does everything and, alas, there are no true competing word processors. (Well there are, but don't e-mail me with your pet list.)

This chapter covers the esoteric features with regard to how you can use them to make your documents all the more spiffy.

- Properly setting, adjusting, and abusing tabs
- Lining things up with tabs, left and right
- Discovering the best way to create a table in Word
- Converting from tabbed lists to tables
- Adjusting and formatting the table
- Doing math in tables
- Printing a sheet of labels
- Automating text with fields

Getting the Most from Tabs

Tabs are one of the most powerful features in Word, but sadly one of the most misunderstood. And what's misunderstood is not properly used. Alack! Alack! Alack!

Generally speaking, use a tab any time you really, *really* feel like using more than one space instead. The only time people feel compelled to use more than one space is when they have stuff to "line up." In that case, tabs work far better than spaces.

Also, tabs do not appear at the end of a paragraph. There they would do no good. And there is definitely no point in putting a tab in the middle of a paragraph. Therefore, tabs have a place only at the *start* of a paragraph. That limits their usefulness somewhat.

Hopefully the following sections will help drive all these points home.

TAB STOP BASICS

Tabs appear on the Ruler, along with the paragraph margin gizmos.

To set a tab, first click in the Tab well to select a tab style. Then click on the Ruler where you want the tab to be set. You can drag tab stops to the left or right to reset them. As you drag, a line drops into the document to help you visualize how the text lines up. Dragging a tab stop upward or downward removes it from the Ruler.

Tabs are also set using the Tabs dialog box, which you can get to using the Format ➤ Tabs command. The secret to the Tabs dialog box is to click the Set button to set a tab; clicking the OK button does not set tabs but merely accepts changes and closes the dialog box.

Oh, Come On: I Know All about Tabs! Tell Me Something I Don't Know!

Okay. Try this: Set a tab in the Ruler. No! That's not the trick. Now, point the mouse at the ruler and press *both* the left and right buttons. (Or you can Alt+click.) There you get a graphical distance chart, as shown in Figure 7.1.

Unlike the normal Ruler, the distance measurements tell you how wide your tab and paragraph margin settings are, which can come in handy if your document is constrained by paper size or the size of an image or some other object. It's also easier than calculating widths via subtraction.

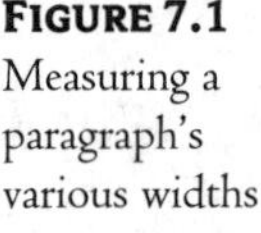

FIGURE 7.1
Measuring a paragraph's various widths

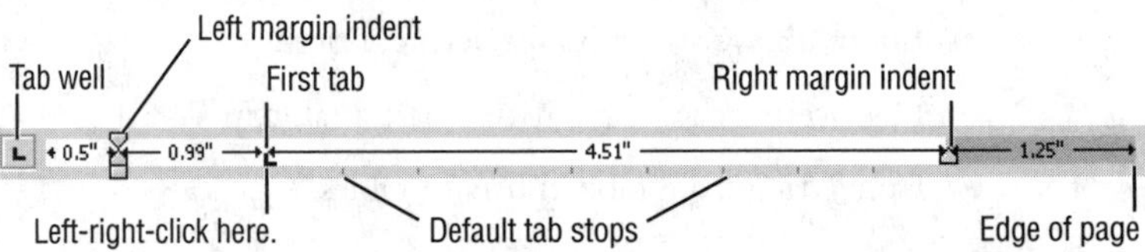

NOTE *You can also drag the mouse left and right with the measurements showing, which may not have a useful purpose, but at least it's fun to do.*

So What's the Advantage to Setting Your Own Tab Stops?

The advantage is that if you set things up right, you need only one tab to line stuff up. That's my rule about tabs. Otherwise, just as with spaces, if you have more than one tab consecutively, you're not properly setting your tab stops.

This rule may not seem obvious right away. Where it saves you time is when you need to edit. Then, having only one tab stop makes realigning and retabbing stuff much easier.

Tabs for All Occasions

Word employs five tab styles. Here they are, along with information on when and how best to use them.

Left tab	Moves text over to the next tab stop, left-aligned at the tab stop.
Center tab	Centers text on the tab stop; used for single-line formatting tricks (see the section "What's the Point of a Center Tab?").
Right tab	Moves text over to the next tab stop, but right-aligns the text.
Decimal tab	Used to line up numbers on the decimal point (see the section "How Can I Line Up Numbers and a Total?").
Bar tab	Inserts a vertical bar into your text (more of a graphical element than a true tab stop).

Where the Hell Are My Tabs?

Tabs are right the hell there on the screen! On the Ruler specifically, as shown in Figure 7.2. Before you get all steamed, however, recognize that tabs are a paragraph-level item. To see the tab stops in a paragraph, you must have that paragraph selected or the cursor must be blinking somewhere within that paragraph.

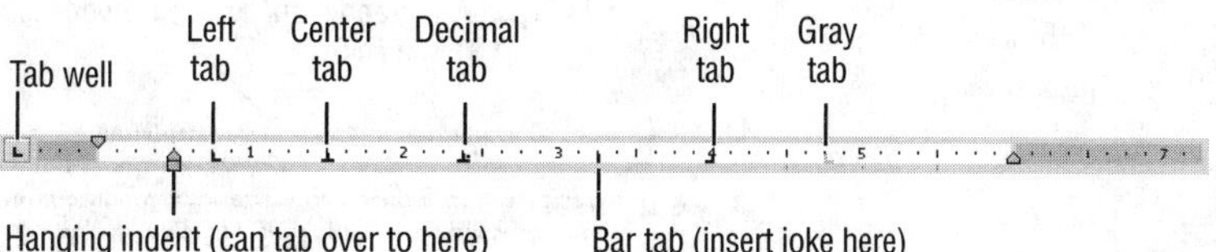

FIGURE 7.2
Tab stops on the Ruler

If a tab stop appears in gray, as shown in Figure 7.2, then that tab exists but not on all of the paragraphs you've selected. It's a rogue tab!

To be specific, of course, you should view your tab settings in the Tabs dialog box. Choose Format ➤ Tabs to see what looks like Figure 7.3 (it's subtly different in Word 2000). I prefer to set tabs visually using the Ruler after I write the text. But sometimes you need to be specific, in which case the Tabs dialog box makes an excellent choice.

FIGURE 7.3
The Tabs dialog box

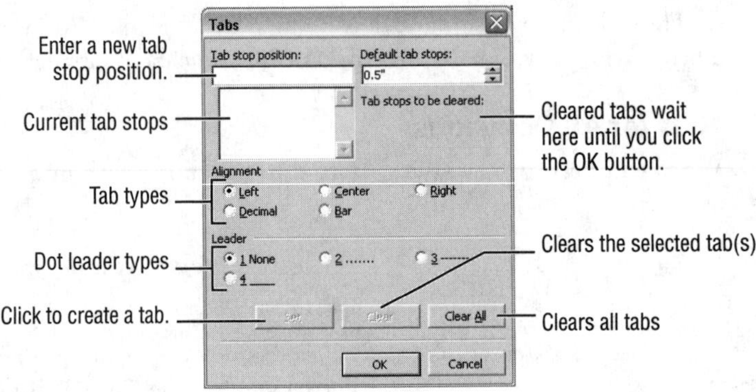

NOTE *The secret to using the Tabs dialog box is to set the tab stop position, and then choose an Alignment option and finally (optionally) a dot leader. Then you click the Set button. Only after clicking Set should you click OK; otherwise, the tabs you picked may not be set properly.*

The final way to find tabs is to reveal them inside your document. This is a great way to track down and fix the jiggly paragraph problem you get with a rogue tab in the middle of a paragraph.

To make tabs visible, click the Show/Hide ¶ button or press Ctrl+Shift+8 (not the 8 on the numeric keypad). This shows hidden codes in your document, as shown in Figure 7.4.

In Figure 7.4, tabs appear as right-pointing arrows. That's the "tab character" produced when you press the Tab key. The type of tab stop you set determines its behavior, but the character itself can easily be removed the same way as any character in a paragraph: with the Backspace or Delete key. In Figure 7.4, pressing Backspace would rid your paragraph of the excess tab.

FIGURE 7.4
Tabs and other junk revealed!

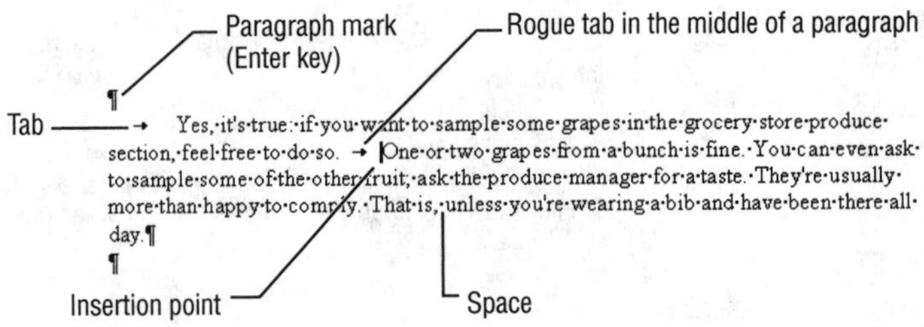

What Is Your Rule about Tabs?

Tabs are great for lining stuff up. In fact, the best use of them was demonstrated in Chapter 2, "Alas, There Is No Such Thing as a 'Simple' Document," inside the long section on indenting paragraphs. That's pretty much the best thing you can do with tabs, though there are other examples later in this chapter.

Outside of indenting paragraphs, tabs can be used to line up lists of items. However, thanks to Word's powerful Table command, even that function for tabs has pretty much gone by the wayside. Otherwise, my main rule remains: As long as you set the tab stops properly, you should never have one tab next to another.

How Can I Line Up Three Columns of Words?

A common use of tabs is to line up various columns of information, as shown in Figure 7.5. Here is the easiest way to format such a beast:

1. Type in the words, pressing Tab between each column. This will look yucky, as shown in Figure 7.5. *Live with it.* Bear with me until you set the tab stops. (You could set them beforehand, but you'd be just duplicating your efforts.)
2. Select your entire list. Very important. Don't forget this, or you'll be setting tab stops for only the current paragraph, not the entire list.
3. Set the first tab stop. Use that drop-down thingy to help line up the tab stop beyond the end of the first column of words, as shown in Figure 7.5.
4. Continue setting tab stops. Set the next stop as you did the first one, dragging it over until the tab clears all the words in the column. Repeat this step for each column in your list.

FIGURE 7.5
Columns of words

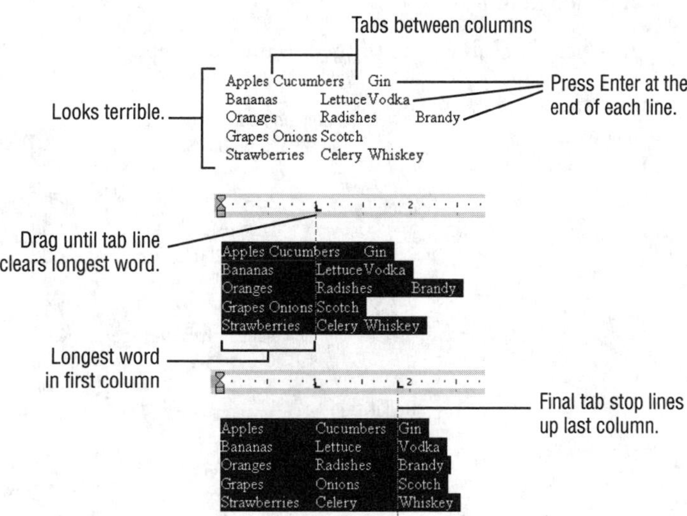

I Must Precisely Position My Tabs!

Suppose you need tab stops at 1″ 2.5″, 3.75″, and 4.25″. You can set those using the Ruler, but because of the precise measurements, you'd be better off setting them in the Tabs dialog box. Follow these steps:

1. Choose Format ➤ Tabs.
2. Enter 1 into the "Tab Stop Position" box.
3. Choose Left from the Alignment area. Unless Left is already chosen, in which case you don't need to click it.
4. Click the Set button. This is the task that actually sets the tab.
5. Repeat Steps 2 through 4 for each of the other values: 2.5, 3.75, and 4.25.
6. Click OK.

The key here is to use the Set button to actually set the tabs; do not just click OK or they won't be set. Only when the tabs are listed in the scrollable list (see Figure 7.3) are they truly set.

How Can I Line Up Numbers and a Total?

Decimal tabs are best used to line up lists of numbers, such as prices or quantities. By aligning the tab stop on the decimal, the Decimal tab creates a nice, even list, as shown in Figure 7.6. Here's how you'd go about setting up such a thing:

1. Type your list. Type the item and then a tab and the amount. All amounts need a decimal point (period) in them.
2. Select your text.

3. Click the Tab well until the Decimal tab appears.

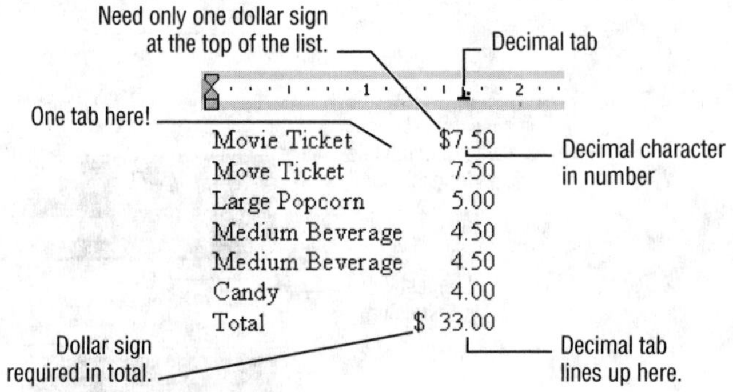

FIGURE 7.6
Lining up numbers with a decimal stop

4. Click to place the Decimal tab on the Ruler.
5. Drag the Decimal tab to the left and right until things line up the way you want them to.

Again, the secret is to use only one tab. As long as you first type in the list (and can hold your breath through the ugly formatting), you can go back and set the proper tab. Then things will look just purty.

NOTE *When you press the Tab key on a Decimal tab stop, the text will right-align itself until you press the period key. After that, the text left-aligns.*

What Is the Right-Tab, Left-Tab Number-Alignment Trick?

Oftentimes when numbering a list, you discover that the numbers become too large and they bump into the text. To solve that problem, you need to right-align the numbers with a Right tab stop and then immediately follow it with a Left tab stop for the rest of your text.

The best way to see how such a thing works is visually. Unlike previous examples, you'll need to set things up in the Tab and Paragraph dialog boxes first and then type your paragraphs to see how this works:

1. Position the cursor at the start of a new paragraph, the one you want to number. Press Enter to do this.
2. Choose Format ➤ Tabs.
3. Create a tab stop at 0.25″, Right alignment; click the Set button.
4. Click OK.
5. Choose Format ➤ Paragraph.
6. Create a Hanging indent at 0.38″; choose Hanging from the Special drop-down list and specify 0.38 in the box.
7. Click OK. The Ruler should now look as it does in Figure 7.7. You're now ready to type your numbered paragraph.

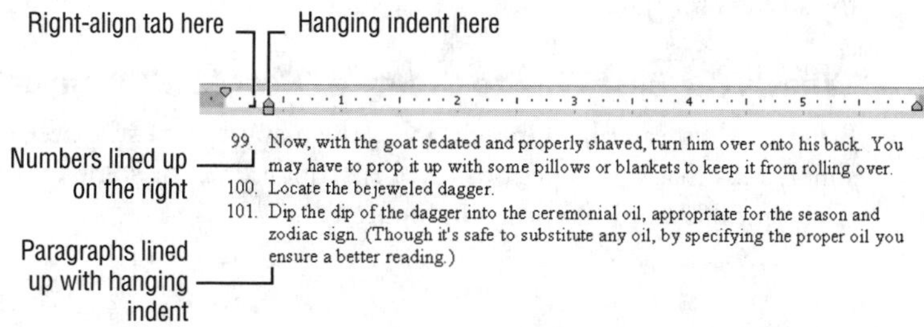

Right-align tab here
Hanging indent here
Numbers lined up on the right
Paragraphs lined up with hanging indent
99. Now, with the goat sedated and properly shaved, turn him over onto his back. You may have to prop it up with some pillows or blankets to keep it from rolling over.
100. Locate the bejeweled dagger.
101. Dip the dip of the dagger into the ceremonial oil, appropriate for the season and zodiac sign. (Though it's safe to substitute any oil, by specifying the proper oil you ensure a better reading.)

FIGURE 7.7
Formatting a tab for a numbered paragraph

8. Press Tab. Start the paragraph with a tab. That moves it over to the 0.25″ tab stop where the number will be right-justified.
9. Type the number. Note how the number slides to the left as you type.
10. Press the Tab key to start typing the paragraph. Thanks to the hanging indent, the paragraph lines up just to the right of the number, as shown in Figure 7.7.

Unlike other ways to number paragraphs, with this style the number is always right-justified, which looks cleaner on a long list than having a left-justified number. This holds true especially if the numbers get rather large.

What's the Point of a Center Tab?

Center tabs have no use in life unless you're formatting something on a single line. That's because anything longer and you might as well just format the entire paragraph centered.

The most common place to find a Center tab is in the header or footer area. There you'll find a paragraph preformatted (by the Normal template) with a Center tab in the middle of the line and a Right tab on the right margin. That way you can type three items on the line, one left-justified, one centered, and one right-justified. Tabs separate each item. Figure 7.8 shows what's up.

FIGURE 7.8
Employing a Center tab

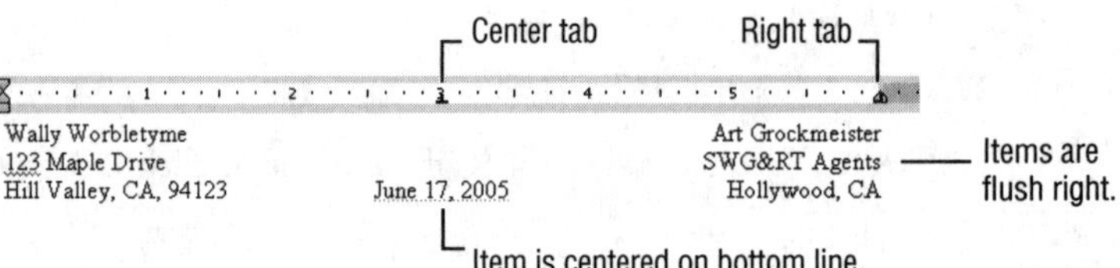

The first two lines in Figure 7.8 sport only one tab, the Right-align tab at position 6″ on the ruler. So to have the two addresses on opposite sides of the page, you type the first name, then press Tab, and then type the second name.

The last line has added a Center tab to place an item between the left and right sides of the page. On that line, I typed the address, pressed Tab, entered the date, pressed Tab again, and then entered the address for the agent.

What's the Best Way to Create a "Cast List" Type of Thing?

Being an old theater ham myself, I've done many a cast list. These employ dot leader tabs, which are simply tabs that shows periods, hyphens, underlines, or some other character instead of just space. The typical example is shown in Figure 7.9.

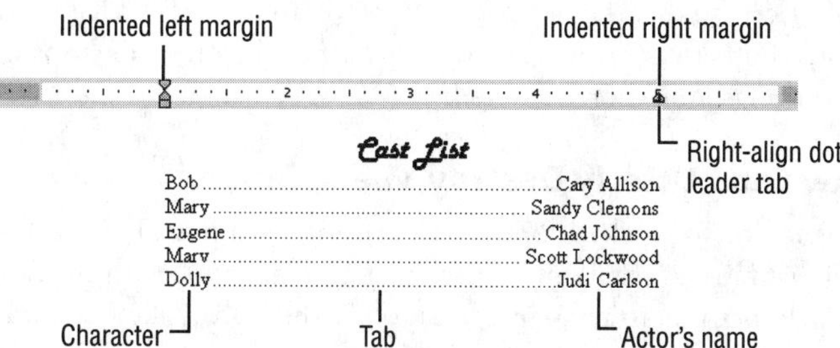

FIGURE 7.9
One of my favorite cast lists

Here's how to format such a thing:

1. Type in the cast list, pressing Tab between the actor's name and the character he plays.
2. Select the entire cast list.
3. Choose Format ➤ Tabs. To do a dot leader tab, you must use the Tabs dialog box.
4. Set the tab at the right margin. You'll notice in Figure 7.9 that I indented the margin 1″ on both sides. My right margin is at 5″.
5. Set a Right-aligned tab.
6. Choose a dot leader style. I like the period myself.
7. Click the Set button.
8. Click OK and the list is formatted as you see in Figure 7.9.

Remember that only *one* tab is required to do all this. Type the list, then format the tabs, and everything lines up nice and neat.

Figure 7.10 shows another alternative for a cast list, also using tabs. In this case the first tab is right-aligned and the second tab is left-aligned. So to type the list, you press Tab, type the actor's name, press Tab again, and then type the character's name. The Right tab and the Left tab (Figure 7.10) keeps things lined up with a wee bit of space in the middle.

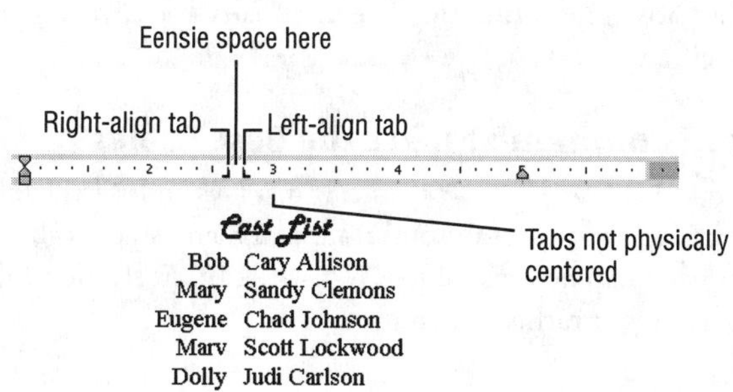

FIGURE 7.10
Yet another way to do the cast list

Notice also that the cast list is off-center for the title. That was a visual decision because it looked lopsided otherwise. It was a simple matter to drag the tab stops on the ruler over to a position that made things look more centered.

How Can I Utterly Destroy These Tabs?

Tabs are fun to pluck off one at a time using the mouse: Point the mouse at the tab on the Ruler, then drag that tab down and into oblivion. You can do this with any tab, even the gray tab (see Figure 7.2).

A cleaner way to remove tabs is to use the Tabs dialog box. Heed these steps:

1. Select the paragraph(s) you wish to cleanse.
2. Choose Format ➤ Tabs.
3. Click the Clear All button.
4. Click OK.

Stumbling over Tables

Oh yes, I scoffed when they introduced the Table feature into Word. What folly, I chortled. But then it dawned on me: tabs and tables. They go together. Organizing things into columns with tabs is really like putting that stuff into a grid. And tables are essentially grids. In fact, I remember manually drawing in the table after I printed a document. Or resorting to using hyphens, underlines, and pipe characters (|) to cobble together a table.

So tables kind of sort of do have a place in Word. Any time you can think of a "grid" of information, slap down a table. You'll find the formatting commands much easier to deal with than trying to mess around with tabs or columns.

When Should I Use a Table?

Well, duh! Use a table any time you need tabular information in your document. You know, such as the results of last week's bedpan snow slide. That fits into a table. I generally move stuff into a table any time I have information in more than three columns. Or when the information in a grid includes not just single words but sentences and other information.

Bottom line: Any time formatting becomes hairy for anything more than two rows and two columns, get yerself a table!

Which Word Command Makes the Best Tables?

The command is Table ➤ Insert ➤ Table. It displays an Insert Table dialog box and does everything described in the following section but in far too many steps to bother with in real life.

The best way to slap down a table is to use the Insert Table tool on the Standard toolbar. That's not really a button, but rather a menu.

Say you need a table that's four rows high by three columns wide. Follow these steps:

1. Click the mouse at the spot in your document where you want the table.
2. Click Insert Table button.
3. Drag down and across until you have a 4 × 3 grid, as shown in Figure 7.11.
4. Release the mouse button to create the table.

The table is then inserted into your document, filling the entire paragraph width, left to right. Figure 7.12 explores what's going on there. To put information into the table, just start typing in a cell.

NOTE *Check your paragraph formatting before you fill in a table. If you have left or right indents or a hanging or first-line indent, the text will be formatted that way in the table and cause you much grief as you type.*

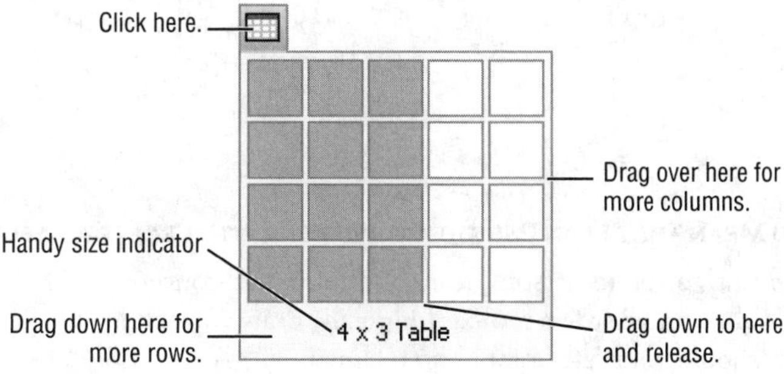

FIGURE 7.11
Creating a 4 × 3 table

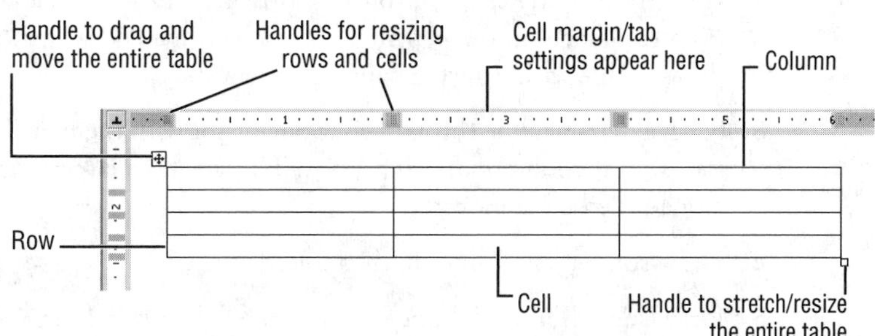

FIGURE 7.12
An empty table in a document

HOW DOES THE TABLE TOOLBAR FIT INTO THIS?

The Table toolbar, along with the Table menu, provides all the handy Table tools you need in Word. In fact, anything you want to do with a table can be found in the menu or on the toolbar, which is one of the reasons working with tables in Word isn't such a pain—no, not like Mail Merge.

To quickly summon the Table toolbar, choose Table ➤ Draw Table from the menu, or you can click the Tables and Borders button on the Standard toolbar. This displays the Tables and Borders toolbar, shown in Figure 7.13. Note that only a few buttons there deal with table-making.

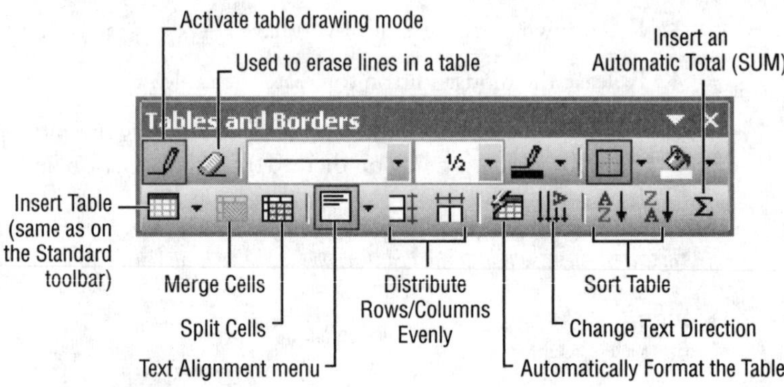

FIGURE 7.13
The Table toolbar is shared with the Borders toolbar.

YOU MEAN THAT I CAN USE THE STUPID PENCIL TO CREATE A TABLE?

Being a right-brain person, I cannot fathom this concept, but yes, you can use the pencil button on the Tables and Borders toolbar to literally draw yourself a table in your document. Here's how to do that, should your left brain be so inclined:

1. Conjure up the Tables and Borders toolbar.
2. Click the Stupid Pencil button. (It's officially the Draw Table button. Like I care.) The mouse pointer changes into a pencil. This is a ham-handed way to let you know that you can now draw a table with it inside your document.
3. Slash a diagonal line through your document with the pencil-shaped mouse pointer. Drag the mouse as if you were drawing a box. This creates a large rectangle in your document, which is a one-celled table monster.
4. Draw some vertical lines in the table.
5. Draw some horizontal lines in the table. The lines don't even have to go all the way across the entire table, as shown in Figure 7.14. And nothing has to be even-steven. Why would anyone want such a contraption? I have no idea. Perhaps you want to shade each cell and create modern art. Who knows?
6. Keep drawing until the table looks like what you want. When you're done, click the Stupid Pencil button to leave Drawing mode and enter normal Word mode.

The eraser tool can be used to further modify your table by removing various lines. Click the button to select the eraser tool, and the mouse pointer turns into a bar of soap (though I suppose it's really an eraser). Click any line in a table to remove that line.

FIGURE 7.14
Penciling in a table

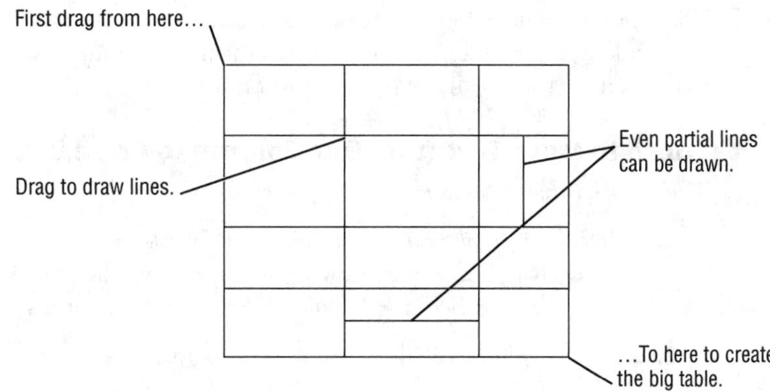

Note that removing lines from a table is not the same thing as deleting rows, cells, or columns. That information is covered later in this chapter.

NOTE *You can use the pencil and eraser tools to modify any table, not merely one created by using the pencil tool.*

I Was Dumb and Created a Table with Tabs, but Now I Want to Copy All That Stuff into a Table

As long as your information is organized with each "column" separated by tabs, you can easily convert it into a table. Follow these incredibly easy steps:

1. Select the text you want to convert into a table. For example, a list of items, as shown in Figure 7.5.
2. Choose Table ➤ Convert ➤ Text to Table. A dialog box appears, though as long as you have tabs in your list, there's nothing to mess with there.
3. Click OK. And your text is now in a table.

You may need to further adjust the table's size or the column widths. To quickly make each column even, click the Distribute Columns Evenly button on the Tables and Borders toolbar, or choose Table ➤ AutoFit ➤ Distribute Columns Evenly from the menu.

NOTE *The opposite of this command is Table ➤ Convert ➤ Table to Text, which takes any selected table in Word and lets you convert it back to plain text, separated by tabs (or some other character). This is useful when sharing Word documents with other applications that may not understand tables.*

How Can I Add or Insert Rows or Columns?

This is cinchy: To add a row to the bottom of a table, put the cursor into the last cell on the right, in the bottom row. Press the Tab key. There's the new row!

To *insert* a row, put the cursor into a row above or below where you want the new row inserted. Then choose Table ➤ Insert ➤ Rows Above or Table ➤ Insert ➤ Rows Below to add your new row.

To add or insert columns, you must use the menu commands, either Table ➤ Insert ➤ Columns to the Left or Table ➤ Insert ➤ Columns on the Right.

I Need to Move Text from One Column to Another

This is easier than it sounds:

1. Select the column you want to move: Point the mouse at the top of the column. The mouse pointer changes to a thick, down-pointing arrow. Click to select the column. Likewise, you can choose Table ➤ Select ➤ Column from the menu, but it's easier to use the mouse.
2. Drag the column to where you want it to go.

If the destination already contains information, then the two columns are swapped. Otherwise, if the column is empty, the information you're dragging fills that empty column.

The same trick works when applied to rows as well: Select the row, then drag it up or down with the mouse to swap that text with any other row.

NOTE *Sometimes with smaller tables it's difficult to swap the last row or column. In this case, it may pay to temporarily add an extra row or column, do the swap, and then delete the extra row or column.*

I Need to Delete Just One Cell and Have the Rows Below Move Up Without Deleting the Entire Current Row

This trick is so easy that I've often converted a list of tabbed items into a table, done this trick, then converted the table back into a list of tabbed items. Here you go:

1. Click the mouse to select the cell you want to delete.
2. Choose Table ➤ Delete ➤ Cells. The Delete Cells dialog box appears, as shown in Figure 7.15.
3. Choose an option. For example, I can choose "Shift Cells Up" to juggle all the cells below up a notch. (The other options are all self-explanatory.)
4. Click OK.

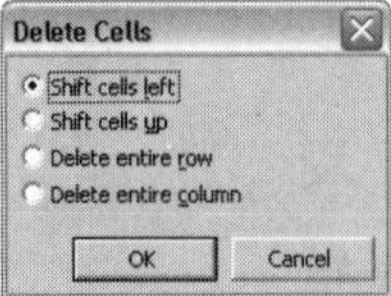

FIGURE 7.15 The handy Delete Cells dialog box

NOTE *If you just need to delete the text in a cell and leave it blank, then simply select the cell and clear out its contents with the Backspace or Delete key.*

How Can I Wrap Text inside a Cell?

Oh, let me count the ways!

Text inside a cell will wrap just as text in any paragraph in Word does. The cell will grow "taller" to accommodate the text. There are a few things you can do with the text in such a cell, as well as the cells in that same row or column.

Making the Cell Accommodate Text with Minimal Wrapping

To avoid a three-foot-tall cell in a table, you can tell Word to adjust the table's column widths to best fit the cells: Choose Table ➤ AutoFit ➤ AutoFit to Contents. That makes columns with narrow text narrow and widens columns with lots of text.

Adjusting Cell Width Manually

You can point the mouse at any column (or row) separator and drag it left or right to increase or decrease that column's width.

NOTE *You can also use the "handles" that appear on the Ruler to adjust a table's column width.*

Changing Text Alignment

A large chunk of text may make other cells in that row look dumb because of their alignment (top, bottom, left, right). You can change a cell's text alignment by using the Align button on the Tables and Borders toolbar. Clicking that button displays a drop-down palette of alignment options, as shown in Figure 7.16.

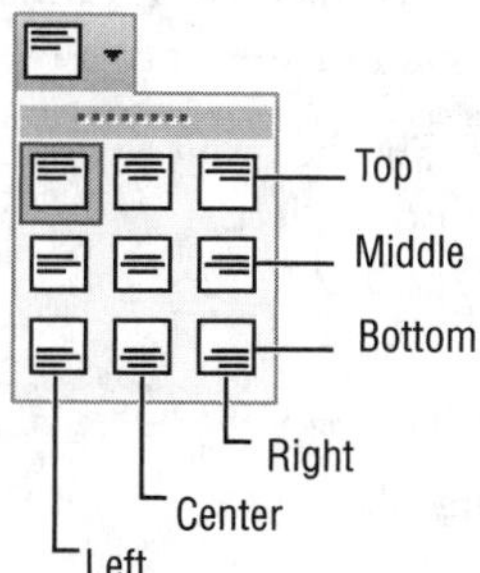

FIGURE 7.16
Select a cell alignment option from here.

Changing Text Orientation

Finally, you can change the text's orientation by using the Change Text Direction button. Clicking this button rotates the orientation of text in the selected cell counter-clockwise 90 degrees each time you click. (Alas, it does not orient the text upside down.)

But I Don't Want the Table's Gridlines to Print!

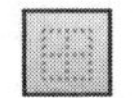

This is easy—and sneaky, too, because by not printing the gridlines, your table just looks like extra-special fancy-formatted text. Fool them all!

To hide the gridlines, obey these enumerated steps:

1. Select the entire table. I just click the table's handle to do this, though you can also choose Table ➤ Select ➤ Table.
2. Choose "No Border" from the Borders button on the toolbar. The "No Border" item is the one that looks like a four-square court without any lines in it.

Ta-da, the table's gridlines are gone. To restore the lines, choose the "All Borders" item from the drop-down list in Step 2.

Why Would I Want to Do Math in a Table?

Tables in Word can incorporate a few handy math functions. For example, to total a column of numbers in a table, do this:

1. Click the mouse in the cell that is to have the total, like in the bottom row of the column.

2. Click the AutoSum button on the Tables and Borders toolbar.

And the total of the numbers in the cells above is put into that cell—cinchy. The AutoSum button sticks a Word *field* into the cell. The field basically says, "Total the sum of all the values in the cells above me." (Sigma, the Greek symbol on the button, is a mathematical doodad for "sum.")

NOTE *The AutoSum button also totals values in a row, providing that there are no values immediately above the AutoSum cell.*

There are a number of functions you can paste into cells for doing limited math. Here are the general steps you'll follow to insert a mathematical function into a table:

1. Click the mouse in the cell where you want the result to appear. For example, say you want the average of the values in the three cells on the left.
2. Choose Insert ➤ Field from the menu.
3. From Categories, choose "Equations and Functions."
4. From "Field Names" choose "= (Formula)."
5. In Word 2003/XP, click the Formula button. Word 2003/XP has a special Formula dialog box where you can paste in formulas. Oh, la-di-da.
6. By the = (equal sign) type **AVERAGE(LEFT)**. The formula name is AVERAGE, and you're finding the average of the numbers on the left.
7. Click OK, and the average of the numbers to the left of the cell is displayed.

Handy Field Codes for Use in Your Tables

Just because I'm a nice guy, here are some field formulas you can plug into a table to get some math happening.

To make the formulas work, put either **LEFT** or **ABOVE** between the parentheses. That tells the formula to operate on the cells either to the left or immediately above the cell where the formula sits.

AVERAGE() Calculates the average of the numbers.

COUNT() Returns the number of cells that contain data.

MAX() Returns the highest value.

MIN() Returns the lowest value.

PRODUCT() Calculates the result of multiplying the values.

SUM() Calculates the total.

These are only a few of the formulas available. There are several more, and they can get quite complex. But remember, at that level you're better off using an embedded Excel worksheet as a table instead of messing with Word's own tables. I'll be getting to that in a minute.

NOTE *This trick works as long as all the cells to the left are filled with numbers. Any blank cells halt the calculation at that cell.*

There are other functions you can use in a table; however, I recommend using Excel instead of learning all the various fields and functions in Word. The only one I use occasionally is the SUM function, which has its own button. The other functions are just too weird to bother with.

I Changed the Table but the Math in the Cell Didn't Change!

Right-click the cell with the SUM (or other field) function and choose "Update Field" from the pop-up menu.

When Is Pasting In an Excel Spreadsheet Better Than Using a Table in Word?

Any time you have more than three or four columns, and especially when the cells need mathematical formulas or fancy formatting, you should consider using Excel as opposed to Word. In fact, it's this easy:

NOTE *Inserting an Excel spreadsheet is also known as embedding.*

1. Position the cursor where you want the Excel spreadsheet/table to appear.
2. Click the Insert Worksheet button on the Standard toolbar. Ah-ha! A select-o-grid drops down, similar to making a table the easy way, as shown in Figure 7.11.
3. Drag to select the size of table/worksheet that you want—say, 3×4.

4. Click the mouse. And an Excel worksheet is secretly screwed into your Word document, as shown in Figure 7.17. Note how the toolbars are now Excel toolbars, not Word. Everything within the *rope of containment* is the domain of Excel.

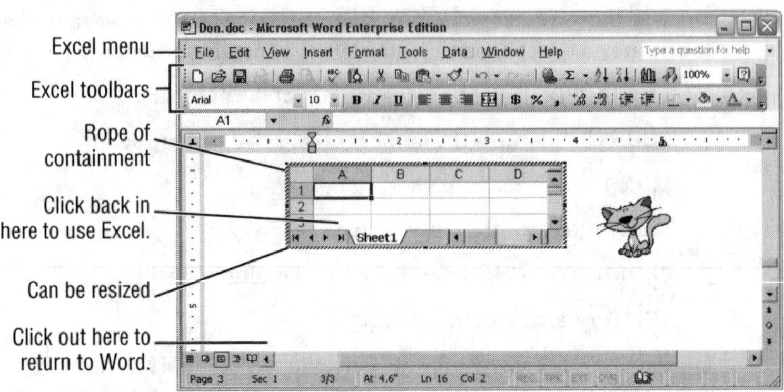

FIGURE 7.17
An Excel spreadsheet lurks in your document.

5. Work the worksheet. And now you're off using Excel, so refer to the later chapters of this book for the details.

6. Click back in your document when you're done: To return to Word, click outside the rope of containment (Figure 7.17). Note that the toolbar and menus change back to Word. To return to Excel, double-click inside the worksheet area.

Despite the wacky appearance of Figure 7.17, the Excel spreadsheet looks like a table in Word, prints like a table, and if it were possible, it would even smell like a table.

Will Sorting the Table Mess Up My Data?

As long as you carefully format your table, there's really nothing you can do to it that cannot be fixed, either by pressing Ctrl+Z (Undo) or just messing around. Consider Figure 7.18.

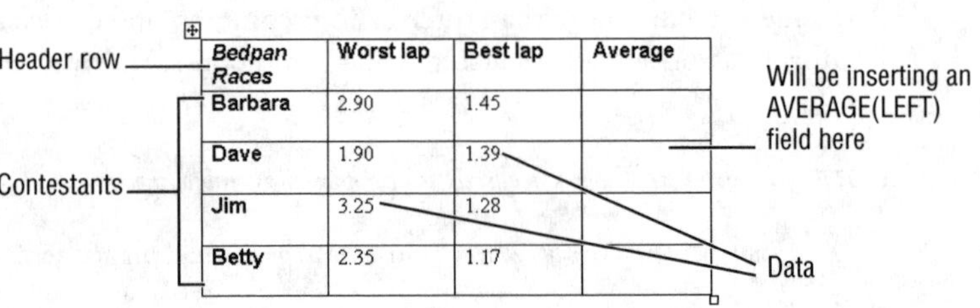

Bedpan Races	Worst lap	Best lap	Average
Barbara	2.90	1.45	
Dave	1.90	1.39	
Jim	3.25	1.28	
Betty	2.35	1.17	

FIGURE 7.18
A table, ready for action

The table shows the preliminary results of this year's bedpan races. The winner is determined by averaging the values of their best and worst laps. Your job is to figure that average (or let Word do it for you) and then sort the results alphabetically because last year they weren't sorted and everyone complained about it.

Gingerly, you follow these steps:

1. Click the mouse in the cell where you want the first AVERAGE(LEFT) field.
2. Choose Insert ➤ Field.
3. Select "Equations and Formulas" from the Category list.
4. Choose "= (Formula)" from the "Field Names" list.
5. Click the Formula button in Word 2003/XP.
6. Type **=AVERAGE(LEFT)** as the formula.
7. Click OK, and the average is calculated and placed into the cell. Time to repeat this action:
8. Click the mouse in the next cell to share that same formula.
9. Press the F4 (repeat) key, and the formula is inserted and calculated instantly.
10. Repeat Steps 8 and 9 for all the cells to share that same formula.

NOTE *The F4 key is not a paste key, it's a repeat formatting key. You're reapplying the Field* format *to the cell, not pasting in a formula.*

11. With all the cells filled, it's time to sort. Click the mouse inside the table to select it. No need to "highlight" the table, just ensure that the insertion point is blinking away happily inside the table.
12. Choose Table ➤ Sort. The Sort dialog box appears, as illustrated in Figure 7.19.

FIGURE 7.19
The Sort dialog box

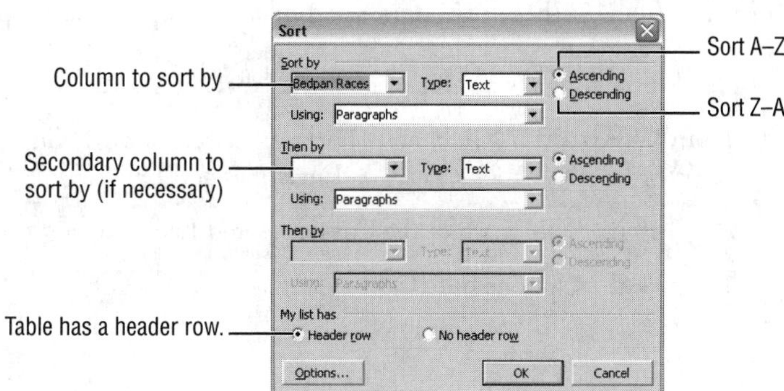

13. Ensure that "Header Row" is selected. This is very important: It tells Word that your table has a header. If so, then Word will *not* sort that row. Also note how the table's header row appears in the "Sort By" drop-down list (as shown in Figure 7.19).

14. Click OK. And the table is sorted by the first column, which is labeled "Bedpan Races," but is actually the contestants' names.

Suppose you wanted to sort the list by who won? In that case, you would be sorting by the *lowest* score that appears in the Average column. Here's how to do that:

1. With the table still selected, choose Table ➤ Sort.
2. Ensure that "Header Row" is selected.
3. Choose Average from the "Sort By" drop-down list.
4. Choose Number from the Type drop-down list. There is a difference between sorting numbers (values) and text. In this case, you need to sort values, so you choose Number from the list.
5. Select Ascending. Lowest scores are best. If highest scores signified the winner, then you'd have to select Descending.
6. Click OK.

And the table is sorted by who won, which is in the Average (last) column. Congratulations, Dave!

Lovely Labels

I've no idea why they added label-making abilities to a word processor. It may be because *labels* rhyme with *tables*. And if you're good with tables, you're good with labels. Because it's possible to fit a table on a document to match labels on a printed page, in which case Word becomes a label printer.

I Need to Make a Whole Sheet of Identical Labels

Every so often, I print myself out a sheet of labels. I use them as my return address on envelopes. It's a "tip" actually: Print yourself out a list of self-addressed labels, and you'll save yourself time over manually filling in the return address part of an envelope. This is especially handy if your handwriting is as lousy as mine.

Here's how to make a sheet of identical labels in Word:

1. In Word 2003/XP, choose Tools ➤ Letters and Mailings ➤ Envelopes and Labels; in Word 2000, choose Tools ➤ Envelopes and Labels.
2. Click the Tables tab in the Envelopes and Labels dialog box, shown in Figure 7.20.
3. Click the Options button.

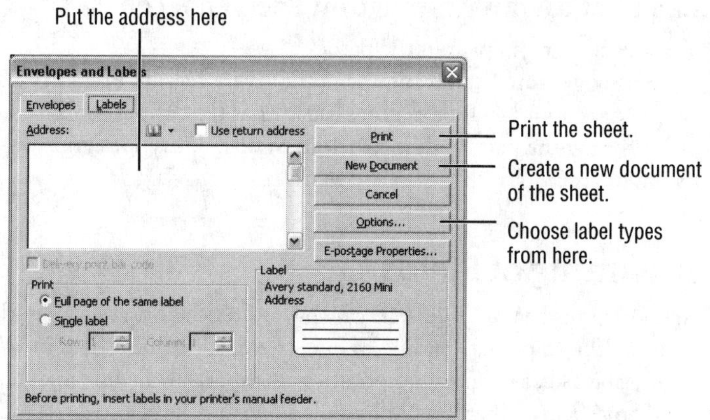

FIGURE 7.20
Making a sheet of labels starts here.

Your first step is to tell Word what type of sheet of labels you have. Word recognizes the common Avery label product numbers, as well as standards from other brands. Remember: You can't print out a sheet of sticky labels unless you have a sheet of sticky labels to print on.

1. Select your label brand and product number. I print my return address on Avery 5160 labels.
2. Click OK.
3. Fill in the Address part of the dialog box. Enter your own address or whatever address you want to fill a sheet with.

NOTE *You can use the Enter key to end a line in the Address text box.*

4. Choose the item "Full Page of the Same Label."
5. Click the New Document button, and a new document is created, full of text that's ready to print on your sheet of labels.

The reason I have you create a document is so you can save it to disk and reuse it later. Save the document in a special Labels folder using a name that will help you remember the contents. After that, whenever you need a sheet of labels printed, conjure up the document and print it.

And now for the special treat: With your document of labels on the screen, choose Table ➤ Show Gridlines.

Ta-da! It's really a table! All the Labels dialog box does is to create a huge, one-page table that has dimensions equal to the sheet of labels you selected. Then it automatically fills in various cells in the table with the same (or different) information. And that's all Word's label printing is about.

Can I Put a Graphic Image on Each Label?

Yes, but it's a royal pain in the patoot.

As a suggestion, I can recommend the Avery Design Pro software for Windows, which is custom-designed to print labels or mailing lists. It has the proper tools for adding graphics to the labels without suffering the pain of doing such in Word. Avery Design Pro is free from the Avery website: `www.avery.com`.

Dreaming of Fields

And now, this chapter's dessert, which should be short and sweet: fields. Force fields. Fields of green pasture. Oh, to be outstanding in one's field. Or to be a field in Word, which means text that magically appears based on some condition or aspect of the document. Yes—that's right! Instead of calling them "fields," they should be called "Magic Text." At least more people would be interested in them that way.

What the Heck Is a Field?

A field is a bit of automatic text in your document. The text is variable; it can change as the document changes. So a field can reflect anything from the current page number to the document's printing date to text that jumps you from one location in the document to another. They're amazingly powerful but not widely used or appreciated.

What Are Some Fields Worth Knowing?

Most of the fields you can really take advantage of involve dates or page numbers. Even so, there are also fields that tell you who worked on a document, the number of times it was saved to disk, the document filename, and lots of other trivial stuff. The following sections explain some of the more useful fields.

Sticking the Document's Print Date into a Field

Some documents I prefer to have dated when they print, as opposed to when I wrote or updated them. To insert the print date field, follow these steps:

1. Choose Insert ➤ Field.
2. Choose the "Date and Time" category.
3. Choose PrintDate from the "Field Name" list.
4. In Word 2003/XP, you can select the date's format from the "Date Format" list.
5. Click OK.

NOTE *In Word 2000, the date may look ugly if the document hasn't yet printed.*

SPECIFYING THE DOCUMENT'S FILENAME

To stick the document's filename into a header or footer, or really anywhere in the document, follow these steps:

1. Choose Insert ➤ Field.
2. Choose the "Document Information" category.
3. Choose FileName from the "Field Name" list.
4. Click OK.

ENTERING HOW LONG IT TOOK TO CREATE THE DOCUMENT

Curious about how long it took you to create your masterpiece? Or does such a thing fill you with anxiety? Here's how to find out:

1. Choose Insert ➤ Field.
2. Choose the "Document Information" category.
3. Choose DocProperty from the "Field Name" list.
4. In Word 2003/XP, choose TotalEditingTime from the Property list; in Word 2000, type TotalEditingTime after DOCPROPERTY in the Field dialog box.
5. Click OK.

The value displayed is in minutes. Scary, huh? But it also grows if you leave your computer on all night and don't bother to close the document's window at the end of the day. So the value can be misleading.

SPECIFYING THE NUMBER OF CHARACTERS/WORDS/PAGES IN THE DOCUMENT

The document actually knows how much work you've done! In fact, budding writers should love this trick. When you're paid by the word, you can insert a field at the end of your document that accurately displays the document's word count. Or you can specify the number of characters or pages in the document. It's all very similar. Here's how:

1. Choose Insert ➤ Field.
2. Choose the "Document Information" category.
3. Choose one of the following from the "Field Name" list:

   NumChars to display the number of characters in the document

   NumPages to list the total number of pages

   NumWords to list the document's word count
4. Click OK.

SPECIFYING YOUR NAME

Word knows who you are—yes you!—sitting there working on a document. In a large office where multiple people may work on a single document, it's possible to list the name of the author by specifying a field, as follows:

1. Choose Insert ➢ Field.
2. Choose the "User Information" category.
3. Choose UserName from the "Field Name" list.
4. Click OK.

Yes, you entered that name when you first installed Word or Office. Now it's stuck there.

The Field Looks Gross!

Yes, fields can look gross. There are two ways to view them: as raw codes and output:

1. Right-click a field in your document.
2. Choose "Toggle Field Codes" from the pop-up menu.

And you now see the field in the raw. It's contained in curly brackets with the field code name followed by any options or settings. The MERGEFORMAT is a flag that prevents Word from messing with the field during certain internal processes.

Note that in the "Field Codes" option, you can edit the field manually, for example, to change a date format as described earlier in this chapter. But mostly you *do not* want to see a field look like this, so repeat the two steps above to get it back to normal.

NOTE *Some fields can have no values, in which case they display "blank" or seemingly useless information. For example, the PrintDate field looks odd until a document is printed. After all, if a document hasn't been printed, what should that field display?*

The Field Is Wrong!

So update it: Right-click the field and choose "Update Field" from the pop-up menu.

Unlike data in some programs, fields are not updated in Word all the time. Some fields update when you print, others when you save or open a document. To force an update, right-click the field and choose "Update Field." Works every time.

How Can I Change a Field?

Alas, only Word 2003/XP has an Edit Field command: If you right-click a field, you can choose "Edit Field" from the pop-up menu. This redisplays the Field dialog box, where you can make adjustments to a field's settings.

In Word 2000, you can right-click and choose "Toggle Field Codes" to update or change a field, but to make any radical changes, you'll have to backspace and delete the field and then reinsert a new field for what you want.

How Do I Format the Date Codes for Word 2000?

If you have Word 2000, then you're not given the opportunity to format the date codes properly. Instead, Word just sticks in the 0/0/00 0:00 AM date format, which is ugly and probably ticks you off. To fix that, you can edit the field's codes to change how the date is formatted:

1. Right-click the PrintDate field.
2. Choose "Toggle Field Codes" from the pop-up menu. You now see the field "in the raw." It may look something like this:

   ```
   {PRINTDATE \* MERGEFORMAT }
   ```

3. Edit the field's text to add the date. Change the text so that it now reads

   ```
   {PRINTDATE \@ "d MMMM yyyy" \* MERGEFORMAT"
   ```

   You're adding the `\@` thing, followed by a date/time format in double quotes.
4. Right-click the field and choose "Toggle Field Codes" from the pop-up menu. The field may still look ugly, but now it will print in format "25 March 2004."

You can build any date field using *d* for the day of the month, *M* for the month name, and *y* for the year. Here are the patterns you can apply between the double quotes. You can also add hyphens, periods, slashes, and commas to the format:

d	The day of the month
dd	The day of the month as a two-digit number (with leading zero, if necessary)
ddd	The three-digit day of the week
dddd	The full name for the day of the week
M	The month's number
MM	The month's number as two digits (with a leading zero, if necessary)
MMM	The month's three-letter abbreviation
MMMM	The full month name
yy	The year as a two-digit number
yyyy	The year as a four-digit number

If you want to specify the time, you can do so using *h* for hours, *m* for minutes, and *s* for seconds. A colon can be used to separate the values:

h	The hour of the day
hh	The hour as a two-digit number (with a leading zero, if necessary)
mm	Minutes
ss	Seconds
am/pm	Append AM or PM to the time

Chapter 8

Sharing Your Work with Others

WRITING IS A SOLITARY and silent art. But few writers have the extreme luxury of writing all their own stuff by themselves. Even published authors have to put up with various stages of editors. There was one publisher I worked for where my document had to pass through five editors. Each of them felt compelled to put at least three marks on the page in their own color. It helped keep them employed, but it did nothing for my manuscript's readability.

So I'll pop the myth: Writing is a group activity that makes lots of noise. Fortunately, if you're the kind of writer who likes their stuff enough to protect it, Word has the tools you can use. Further, Word has tools that let you see who has changed what in your document. Then, if you don't like what they've done, you can change it back swifter than a mere copy editor can say "dangling participle."

- Adding a comment outside of the text
- Reviewing and wantonly deleting comments
- Recording an audio comment
- Finding out what others have changed in your document
- Accepting or rejecting the changes
- Protecting against unwanted changes

Collaboration Tools

Whether you want to or not, someday you're going to work with others on the same document. Oh, joy. The idea is not to sit at the keyboard together and type (though you can do that if you *really* like the person). It's instead a chance to share ideas and provide feedback within the document, all without ticking the other person off. Word has plenty of tools to do that.

I Want to Tell My Collaborator That Something Sucks. How Can I Best Do That?

From a distance. Otherwise, I find the Insert ➤ Comment command works just fine. Here's how I relate such information to a co-author or weary editor:

1. Highlight the text that concerns you. Be specific here, though I've often highlighted an entire paragraph and added the comment "pointless."
2. Choose Insert ➤ Comment. Various things happen here, depending your version of Word and how you have it configured.
   - In Word 2003/XP, the Reviewing toolbar shows up, as shown in Figure 8.1. It's a great tool to use when editing someone else's stuff or when you have to review edits others have made to your stuff.

NOTE *In Word 2000, you can summon the Reviewing toolbar by choosing View ➤ Toolbars ➤ Reviewing from the menu. Note that the Word 2000 toolbar lacks some of the buttons found in Figure 8.1.*

   - If you're in Print Layout view in Word 2003/XP, then a comment balloon appears, as shown in Figure 8.2. That's where you write your comment regarding the highlighted text.
   - Word 2000 has a similar feature: When you insert a comment, the Comment frame opens up, where you can type your comment, as shown in Figure 8.3.
3. Type your comment. Be nice.

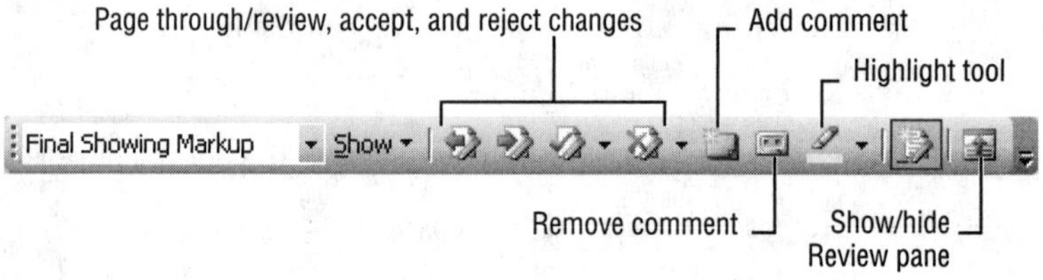

FIGURE 8.1
The Reviewing toolbar

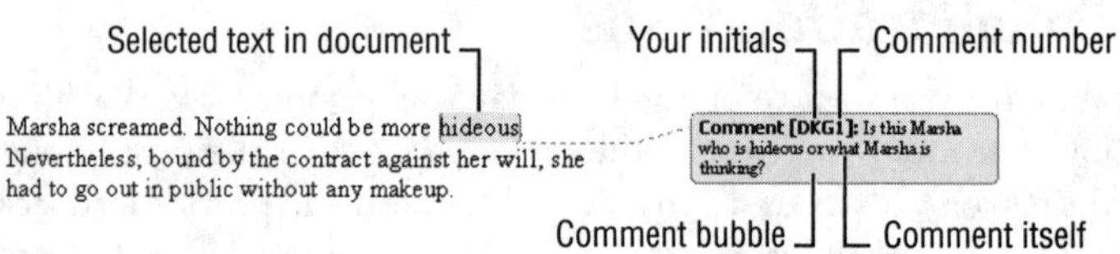

FIGURE 8.2
Using the comment bubble

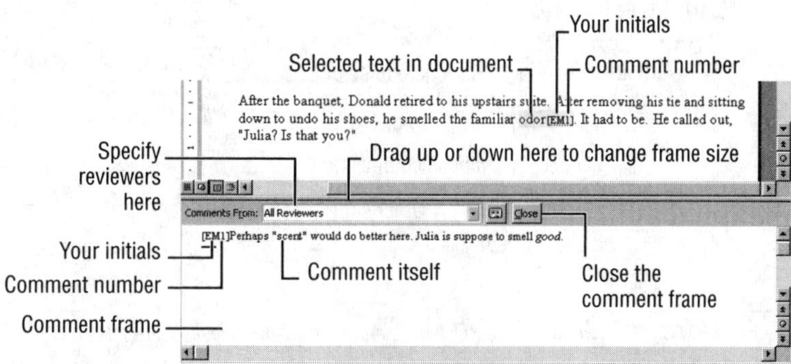

FIGURE 8.3
Adding a comment in Word 2000

Any Way to Hide or Delete the Comments?

What? You fear feedback? Oh, for shame!

- In Word 2003/XP, you can always switch to Normal view to hide the comments: View ➤ Normal. In Print Layout view, you can hide the comment bubbles using the Show menu on the Reviewing toolbar: In Word 2003, choose Show ➤ Balloons ➤ Never Use Balloons; in Word XP choose Show ➤ Comments.
- In Word 2000, click the Close button on the Comment frame to hide your comments.

Note that these steps do not delete the comments. The text is still highlighted on the screen, so you know that there is a comment available.

To delete a comment, right-click the text and choose Delete Comment from the pop-up menu. This removes the comment and renumbers any remaining comments in the document.

Any Way to Rapidly Scan the Comments?

This is my favorite, but it requires the presence of the Reviewing toolbar to work best, so choose View ➤ Toolbars ➤ Reviewing if you haven't already.

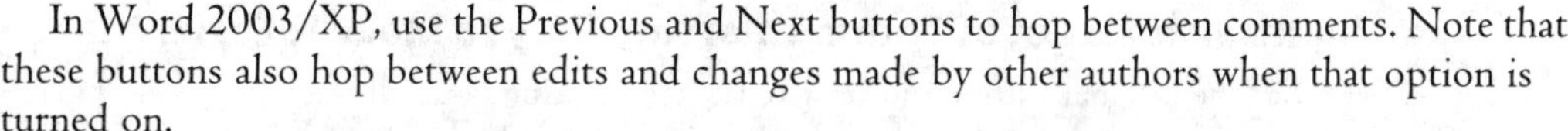

In Word 2003/XP, use the Previous and Next buttons to hop between comments. Note that these buttons also hop between edits and changes made by other authors when that option is turned on.

In Word 2000, there are Previous Comment and Next Comment buttons you can use. These buttons specifically move between comments and not any other gunk in your document.

And, of course, an easy way to review the comments is to open up the Reviewing pane and just read them all, as shown in Figure 8.4.

FIGURE 8.4
Reviewing comments all at once

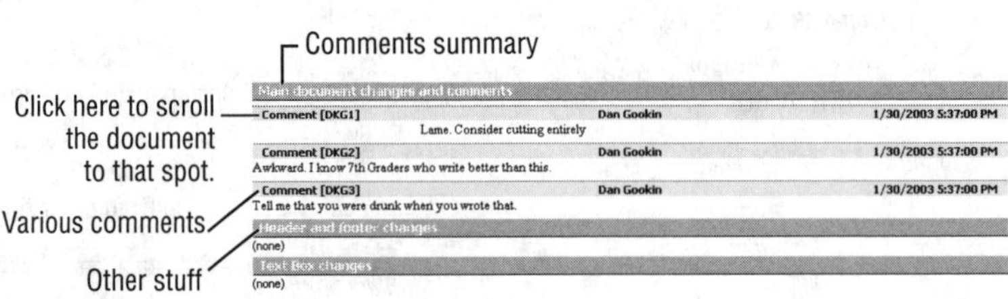

NOTE *Note that Word 2000's Comments frame works similarly, though it lacks the extra information shown in Figure 8.4.*

Can I Review Comments by Collaborators One at a Time?

Certainly. In fact, I find this is a good way to approach things when different collaborators are looking for different things. For example, say Jay is looking only for technical goofs, while Phyllis is looking for gross abominations of English. To view only Jay's comments, from the Reviewing toolbar choose Show ➤ Reviewers ➤ Jay.

Or if you want to see only Phyllis's comments, choose Show ➤ Reviewers ➤ Phyllis.

To see them all, choose Show ➤ Reviewers ➤ All Reviewers.

In Word 2000 you can make similar adjustments. The list of reviewers is found at the top of the Comments frame, as shown in Figure 8.3. Just choose your foe from that drop-down list.

It's Not Enough That I Delete the Comment; I Also Want to Comment Back!

You can comment on a comment simply by clicking the comment and inserting a new comment, as shown earlier in this chapter. Simply type in your remarks.

I've also gone into the Reviewing pane and written my comments after the original jerk's comments: Just click after their comments, press Enter, and then type away. Sometimes I select a new color for my add-on thoughts, such as bright red or hot pink, depending on my mood! Use the Font color button on the Formatting toolbar to set your comment's text color.

I'm Inserting a Lot of Comments. Any Way to Make It Easier?

Yes, fire the original author and rewrite the entire thing yourself.

Now if that is out of the question, then here's what I do:

In Word 2003/XP, I turn off the comment bubbles or switch to Normal view. I find the comment bubbles distracting, especially for text I'm really commenting on.

Next, I open the Reviewing pane (or the Comments frame thing in Word 2000). That way I can click the Insert Comment button (on the Reviewing toolbar) and then type in my comments down at the bottom of the window.

NOTE *To insert a comment much more quickly than any mouse method, press Alt+I, M.*

What's the Tape Recorder Thing For?

The tape recorder is used with the cooperation of Microsoft and the FBI to gather important bowling league information from your computer. Seriously, it allows you to insert audio files into your document—which is something Word does anyway, but in this case it's specifically to create vocal comments. I suppose that's for when your writing just can't blossom with the same expression as your voice. Or perhaps you want to sing your comments—who knows?

NOTE *Adding approximately 10 seconds of audio commentary to your document bulks up the document's file size by at least 200K.*

Because this isn't a PC hardware book, I'm going to assume that you have a microphone properly connected to your computer and that you know how it works. To add a bit of screaming audio as a comment, follow these steps:

1. Access the necessary buttons:
   - In Word 2003, summon the Reviewing toolbar.
   - In Word 2000, display the Comments frame with View ➤ Comments.
   - Word XP, alas, does not have this feature, so you can go to the fridge and get some cookies.
2. Select the text you want to vocally comment.
3. Click the Insert Voice button; look for the tape recorder button, shown in Figure 8.5. This works just like the Insert Comment button/command; however, in addition to adding a comment, it also displays the Windows Sound Recorder program, also shown in Figure 8.5.

   Technically, what you've done is inserted a *Sound object* into Word. In this case, the Sound object was stuck into a comment. But you can also stick a Sound object into any Word document, as covered in the sidebar nearby.
4. Click the Record button.
5. Speak the comment into your microphone. According to the Sound Recorder program, you have up to 60 seconds.

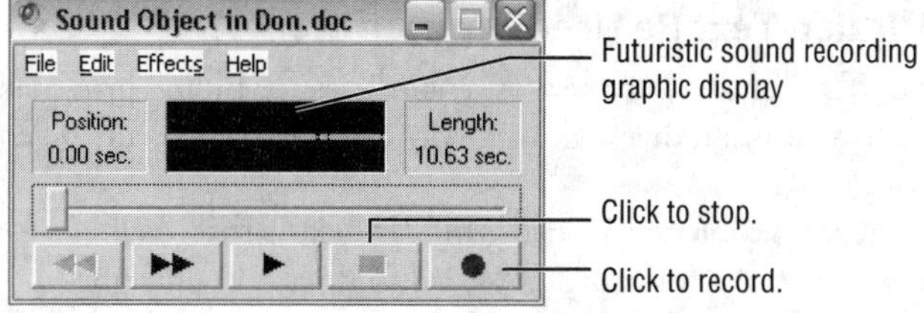

FIGURE 8.5
The Insert Voice button and the Sound Recorder application

6. Click the Stop button to stop recording. You should see a graphic display of your voice as you speak. If not, then you'll need to troubleshoot the microphone. The most common problem is that the microphone has been software muted in the Master Volume Control Panel.

NOTE *Double-click the Volume icon in the System Tray/Notification Area on the taskbar to see the Master Volume Control Panel. There you can unmute the microphone, if necessary.*

7. Close the Sound Recorder program window. A speaker icon appears in your document, telling you that there is an embedded Sound object there.

To hear the sound, double-click the speaker icon. The sound plays back (the Recorder program does not appear). Remark to yourself, "Damn, this is a modern way to communicate updates to my co-author."

INSERTING A SOUND OBJECT

Word gives you the ability to insert just about any type of program "object" into a document. This includes multimedia objects, such as sounds and videos. If you want to insert a sound file—or audio anything—into a document just as you inserted an audio comment, follow these steps:

1. Locate the spot in the document where you want the Sound object to appear.
2. Choose Insert ➤ Object from the menu.
3. Scroll through the list of Objects in the Create New tab until you find "Wave Sound."
4. Click OK.
5. Record the sound; click the Record button on the Sound Recorder application and speak into the microphone.
6. Click the Stop button when you're done.
7. Close the Sound Recorder program.

The speaker icon in your document shows you where the embedded sound lives; double-click it to hear the sound.

Can Hidden Text Be Used for Comments?

No, not effectively. While there are many uses for hiding text, making your comment using the hidden text format is a rather awkward way to do it—especially given the power of the Insert ➤ Comment command.

The biggest problem with using hidden text is that, well, it's *hidden*! To display hidden text, you have to either search for it or tell Word to display it outright:

1. Choose Tools ➤ Options.
2. Click the View tab.

3. Put a check mark by "Hidden Text."
4. Click OK.

Hidden text now appears in the document; it shows up with a dotted underline. That text won't print, and it can be hidden again by repeating the steps above to remove the check mark.

To format hidden text, use the Font dialog box; put a check mark by Hidden, and any selected text in the document is hidden.

Alas, this is just too much work when the Insert ➤ Comment command is so much slicker.

NOTE *To remove all hidden text from a document, select the entire document with Ctrl+A. Press Ctrl+D to bring up the Font dialog box. Clear the check box by Hidden. Click OK.*

My Dumb Co-author Doesn't Know Which Part of the Text I'm Referring To. How Can I Point It Out without Changing the Formatting?

The best way to do that is with the Highlight tool. Like going crazy with a yellow marker, the Highlight tool lets you mark up text that concerns you without having to comment every tidbit. Figure 8.6 gives an illustration.

FIGURE 8.6 Highlighting offensive or questionable text

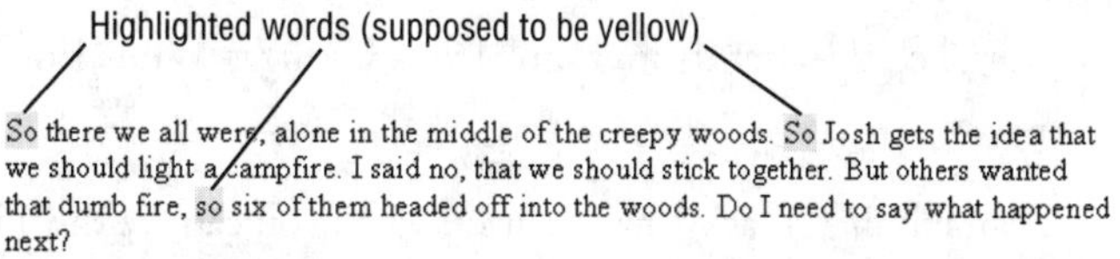

Highlighted words (supposed to be yellow)

So there we all were, alone in the middle of the creepy woods. So Josh gets the idea that we should light a campfire. I said no, that we should stick together. But others wanted that dumb fire, so six of them headed off into the woods. Do I need to say what happened next?

To go nuts and highlight text in your document, use the Highlight tool, which is found on both the Formatting and Reviewing toolbars. Click that tool once, and the mouse pointer turns into the Highlight tool. Then just drag over text to highlight it. Click the tool again to exit this scribbly mode of operation.

If you don't like the Highlight color, click the down arrow by the button and choose from one of 15 exciting colors.

To erase the highlighting, you must select "None" as the color and then use the Highlight tool to drag over the text and erase it. Because highlighting is *not* a part of the font formatting, you cannot use font commands to remove it.

NOTE *Another quick way to remove highlighting is to reselect the highlighted text and just click the button on the toolbar again.*

Will These Offensive Comments and Markups Appear in My Document if I Print It?

Indeed they will—if you tell Word to print them. Deep inside the Print dialog box is an option called "Print What." From that option's drop-down list you can select whether to print the comments or markups or whatever you like. If you want just the document to print, select Document from the list.

Revealing the Offenses of Others

Sadly, you release your document to a friend, coworker, or the most feared individual of any writer: the dreaded *editor*. Who knows what infectious jealousy may possess that person? Will they ruthlessly claw away at your treasured text until nothing of your wit and verve remains? How can you tell? Why, simple! Just review the changes to your document. It's simple. It's easy. And it's the best way to know what was changed and to give it your final thumbs-up or thumbs-down.

I Really Don't Trust My Collaborator and Would Like to Know How to Tell What's Been Changed and What Hasn't

First, give your collaborator a *copy* of your document. Keep the original. That's very important.

Second, before you fork over the copy, turn on the Track Changes option. Now, normally that would be *their* responsibility. But sometimes they forget. Here's how to turn on Track Changes, which depends on your version of Windows:

- In Word 2003/XP, choose Tools ➤ Track Changes.
- In Word 2000, it's slightly more complicated:
  1. Choose Tools ➤ Track Changes ➤ Highlight Changes.
  2. Click to select the option "Track Changes While Editing."
  3. Click OK.

You can tell that Track Changes is on when you can see the TRK on the status bar. That means that all edits to the document from this point on will be marked.

NOTE *A quicker way to activate Track Changes is to merely double-click the TRK thing with the mouse.*

How Are the Changes Marked?

With Track Changes on, go back to your document and delete a word, change some formatting, and then add some text. Here is how such changes are marked, depending on your version of Word:

In Word 2003/XP, in Print Layout view, bubbles appear marking deletions or formatting changes. They describe the changes, and the colors used are specific to different reviewers; to see which reviewer is responsible, simply point the mouse at a bubble, and the reviewer's name will appear along with the date and time of the revision.

New text appears in color as well, double-underlined, as shown in Figure 8.7.

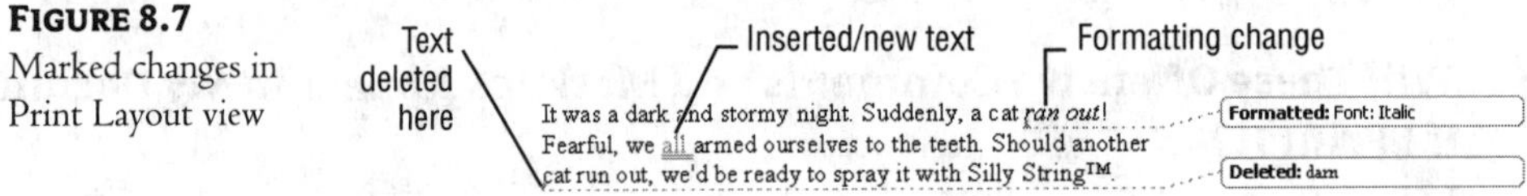

FIGURE 8.7
Marked changes in Print Layout view

In Word 2003/XP Normal view, as well as in Word 2000, no bubbles are displayed. Instead, deleted text appears colored red with the strikethrough attribute. Inserted text is shown as double-underlined in Word 2003/XP and colored in Word 2000. Formatting changes are not specifically marked.

NOTE *The color of the text changes depending on who has reviewed it. Normally, changed text is red. But if a second person edits the document, their changes may show up in blue. Add a third person (annoying, I know), and you get another color, maybe purple or green. These colors are set in the Options dialog box: choose Tools ➤ Options and click the Track Changes tab.*

What's That Annoying Line on the Left Side of the Document?

When you're in Track Changes mode, a vertical line appears on the left side of any modified text. That allows you to quickly locate where changes appear. And under the default settings in Normal view or in Word 2000, it's the only way to tell that text has had its formatting modified (though you still cannot tell specifically what the modifications were).

To remove the line, tell Word not to show you the changes, or simply accept or reject each one. To hide the changes, see the section, "I Just Got My Document Back, but I Cannot See the Changes!"

Will the Changes Print?

Certainly, if you want them to.

In Word 2003/XP, in the Print dialog box there is a drop-down list by "Print What." You need to choose "Document Showing Markup" from that list so that the marked changes appear on the hard copy. (This is similar to printing comments, which was covered earlier in this chapter.)

In Word 2000 go to Tools ➤ Track Changes ➤ Highlight Changes and select "Highlight Changes in Printed Document." The changes will print in color.

I'd Like to Reorient the Document to Landscape Mode for Printing the Comment Bubbles

You can direct Word to print out in Landscape mode to display the comments only—this trick doesn't affect your document's true page layout.

To pull this stunt, and it works only in Word 2003/XP, follow these steps:

1. Choose Tools ➤ Options.
2. Click the Track Changes tab.
3. In the bottom of the dialog box, choose "Force Landscape" from the drop-down list by "Paper Orientation."
4. Click OK.

Oops! I Forgot to Turn on Track Changes!

Man, oh man, are you screwed!

Seriously, if you forget to turn on Track Changes, you still have an ace in the hole: It's your pristine document—the original—still on your hard drive. What you need to do is compare that original with the edited copy. Word will then mark any changes on the screen for you. This isn't as elegant as turning on Track Changes before you hand off a document, but it's the next-best thing.

Comparing Documents in Word 2003/XP

Here's how to compare a document with a modified copy in Word 2003/XP:

1. Open your original document.
2. Choose Tools ➤ Compare and Merge Documents. An Open dialog box, disguised as the Compare and Merge Document dialog box, appears.
3. Locate your document's mangled copy. Find the edited or changed copy using the dialog box.
4. Click Merge.

Word compares the original with the copy on disk. Changes between the two appear in the copy—the document you selected with the Compare and Merge Document dialog box—on the screen.

Now you can see exactly what was done. Your original document is still safe in another window. But the copy has been marked up and presented to you, similar to what you see in Figure 8.8.

Figure 8.8
Changes done on the copy, finally revealed

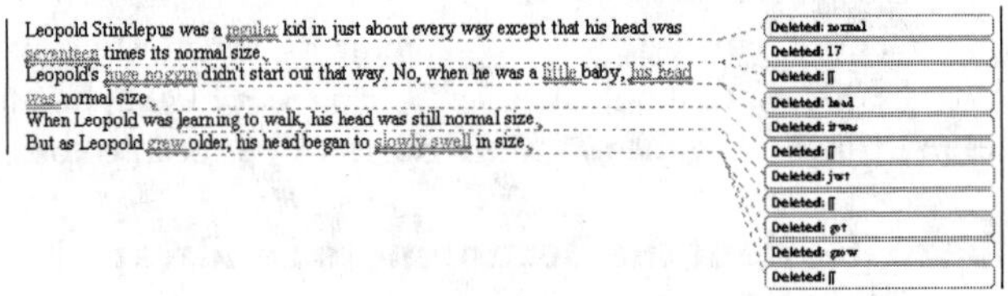

Comparing Documents in Word 2000

Things are different enough with Word 2000 to warrant its own section. Pay attention, as this is different from the Word 2003/XP instructions in a sinister way:

1. Open the *copy* of your original document. You want the edited version on the screen, not your original.
2. Choose Tools ➤ Track Changes ➤ Compare Documents.
3. Use the dialog box to locate and select the original file.
4. Click the Open button.

Word compares the original on disk with the copy on the screen. Any changes are noted in the copy on the screen. The original, still on disk, is left untouched.

The markups appear similar to those shown in Figure 8.8, with the exception of the bubbles off to the right. You can point the mouse at any specific change to read more information about it.

I Just Got My Document Back, but I Cannot See the Changes!

Changes can be hidden, if you like. To make them visible (or to hide them), follow these steps:

Revealing Changes in Word 2003/XP

From the Reviewing toolbar, choose Show ➤ Insertions and Deletions. Optionally, you may also have to choose Show ➤ Formatting. That shows or hides the changes made to your document.

Revealing Changes in Word 2000

Choose Tools ➤ Track Changes ➤ Highlight Changes. In the Highlight Changes dialog box, remove the check mark by "Highlight Changes on Screen." That hides the changes in your document. Or you can repeat these steps to show the changes again.

NOTE *To quickly display the Highlight Changes dialog box, right-click the TRK thing on the Status bar and choose "Highlight Changes" from the pop-up menu.*

Okay, I See the Changes. Now What Do I Do?

As the writer, you always have the final say over what goes into your text. Even if an editor demonstrates flawless English logic, you can still overrule that mini-tyrant with a click of your mouse. It's called Reviewing and Accepting, and Word lets you accomplish this task in a number of ways.

To individually accept or reject a change, point to it and right-click: Choose Accept or Reject from the pop-up menu.

NOTE *It's important that you get the Accept/Reject jargon down: If you Accept a cut, the cut is made. If you Reject a cut, the cut is restored. On the other hand, if you Accept an insert, then the inserted text is kept. To remove the inserted text, you must Reject it. Weird.*

You can also use the buttons on the Reviewing toolbar to hop between changes and then to accept or reject them. Here they are:

Hop to the next change in a document.

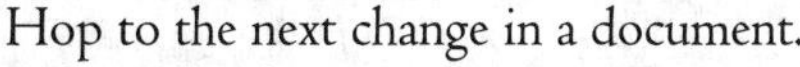

Accept the change.

Reject the change.

NOTE *The buttons look slightly different in Word 2000, but you'll be able to figure them out from these.*

Any Way to Just Accept All the Changes?

Giving up? If you tire of accepting all those wonderful suggestions that the charming editor has made, so much more enhancing your document, then you can blissfully accept them all. Here's how:

ACCEPTING ALL THE CHANGES IN WORD 2003/XP

1. Click the down arrow by the Accept Change button on the Reviewing toolbar.
2. Select "Accept All Changes in Document."

Now if you'd rather reject them all, then just click the down arrow by the Reject Change button and choose "Reject All Changes in Document."

ACCEPTING ALL THE CHANGES IN WORD 2000

Word 2000 has a handy dialog box you can use for reviewing the changes as well as accepting or rejecting everything en masse. To see the dialog box, choose Tools ➤ Track Changes ➤ Accept or Reject Changes. The toolbar appears, as shown in Figure 8.9.

FIGURE 8.9
Reviewing changes in Word 2000

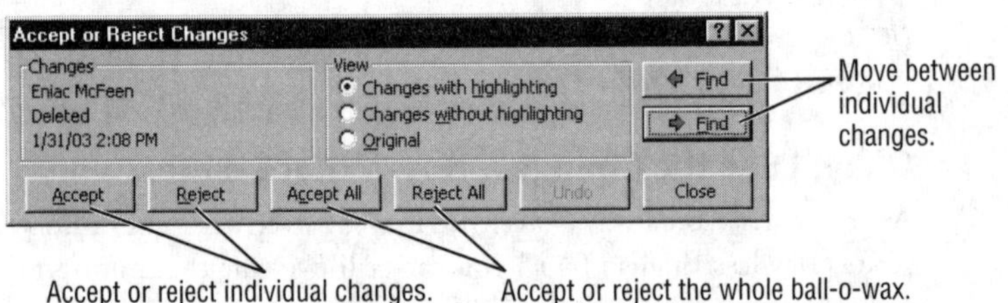

When you elect to accept or reject all the changes, a dialog box appears to confirm your choice. My insiders tell me that Microsoft was forced to put that in there by the United Editors Union.

How Can I More Vigorously Protect My Document against Unwanted Insertions and Deletions?

If you must share, then you must subject yourself to the changes made by others. That's what tracking changes (and the techniques presented in the past few sections) is all about. Even so, there are more drastic steps you can take.

In addition to giving a document an open or read-only password (see Chapter 1, "Life beyond the Basic Word"), you can further protect it by forcing whoever edits the document into Deletion Tracking mode, Comments-Only mode, or whichever options you select. You do this by choosing Tools ➤ Protect Document.

In Word 2003, a Document Protection task pane appears; in Word XP, a Protect Document dialog box shows up. Either way, you can restrict the way the document is edited. For example, to force people into Deletion Tracking mode, choose "Tracked Changes" from the drop-down list in item 2 and put a check mark there. Then click the button "Yes, Start Enforcing Protection." Enter a password twice and the document is protected.

In Word 2000, select an option from the Protect Document dialog box. For example, choosing "Tracked Changes" forces Deletion Tracking on; it cannot be turned off unless an editor knows the password. Enter the password into the box, shown in Figure 8.10. Another dialog box confirms the password, and you're set.

FIGURE 8.10
Adding protection in Word 2000

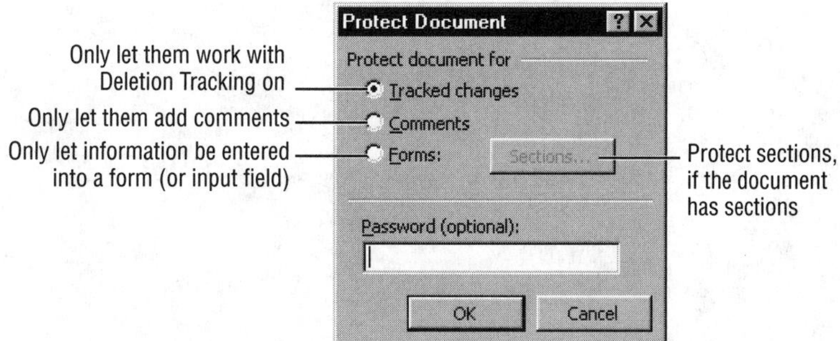

Unlike a password-protected document, anyone can open a document protected in the above manner. However, they'll be forced into Deletion Tracking mode or only be allowed to add comments or whatever restrictions you've set.

To remove this protection, you need to choose Tools ➤ Unprotect or Tools ➤ Unprotect Document. Then you enter the password, and Word behaves as normal.

Chapter 9

Making Your Own Custom Word

YOU SUFFER FROM TOO many choices in Word. I think Microsoft gave you too many options with the idea that you'd be happy. The problem is that you can't realize happiness until you first accept that you're unhappy and then realize that there is a solution or a path to happiness. The situation with Word is that many of its commands, options, and presentation are confusing and overlapping. What you're not being told is that all that junk is optional. You can choose to see it or not. And if you choose to see something, you can always customize it to show what you want to see and hide what you don't.

Yes, Word can be customized beyond your wildest dreams. You are free to do this. It's entirely possible. Cyber storm troopers won't break down your door and accuse you of sedition if you modify or change things from the way Word looked out of the box. So please, by all means, feel free to wrestle Word's interface to the ground, dust it off, and then grow something pleasing and personally useful instead. I encourage it!

- Doing Word full screen!
- Customizing your toolbars
- Creating your own toolbar from scratch
- Making buttons where only text existed before
- Creating new commands with macros
- Removing personal information from a document

To Hell with the Interface!

Love it. Hate it. The remarkable thing about the way Word presents itself on the screen is that it's utterly changeable. You can make Word look like just about anything, from a button-filled hell with only one square inch of writing space, to the pristine and frightening blank page. It's all up to you.

Blank Page? Tell Me More!

Prefer to write staring at a blank page? Then try this: Choose View ➤ Full Screen from the menu. Word abandons its toolbars, menus, doodads, and window gizmos to give you a full screen of nothing but blank paper and text, as shown in Figure 9.1. If you're a traditional, typewriter-style author, you should try this mode for a few days and you'll find it infectiously addicting.

FIGURE 9.1
Word at its most minimal

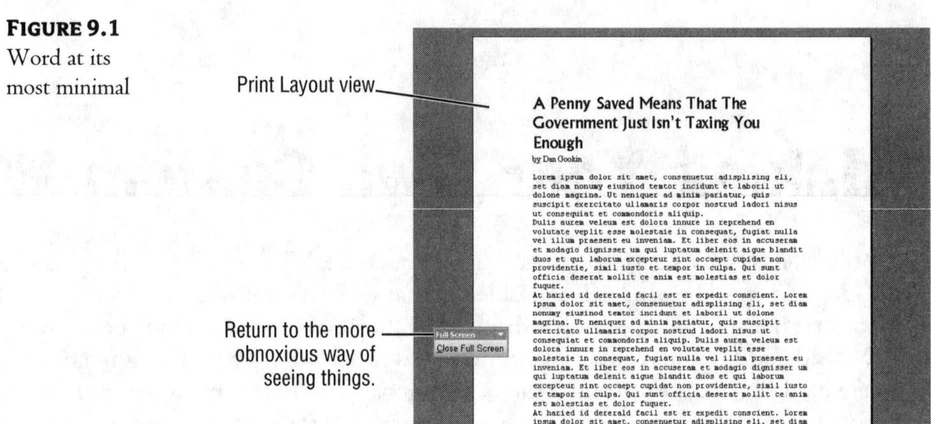

NOTE *Be careful where you drag the Full Screen floating palette. If it gets too close to the edge of the screen (any edge), it turns into a toolbar.*

How Do I Get the Interface Back?

Easy enough: Click the Close Full Screen button, as shown in Figure 9.1. But note that you do not need to do this to use any of Word's commands.

NOTE *With the Close Full Screen button visible, as shown in Figure 9.1, returning to Normal view is only one keystroke away: Alt+C. This command is the same as clicking the Close Full Screen button, when that button is visible on the screen.*

What If I Need to Use the Menus in Full-Screen Mode?

To have the menu bar temporarily displayed in full-screen mode, press the F10 or Alt key on your keyboard. Lo, the menu bar appears, allowing you to select a command. As soon as that command is chosen, the menu bar is hidden again and you're returned to full-screen mode.

For example, if you want to change the view to Normal from Print Layout, press Alt+V, N. To return back, press Alt+V, P.

Press the Esc (escape) key to hide the menu if you don't want to choose a command.

NOTE *The menu also reappears when you slide the mouse pointer to the top of the screen.*

But I Really Need the So-and-Such Toolbar!

To summon any of Word's toolbars, right-click the Close Full Screen button. That displays a pop-up menu of toolbars, as shown in Figure 9.2. Select the toolbar you want from the list.

FIGURE 9.2
Conjuring up another toolbar

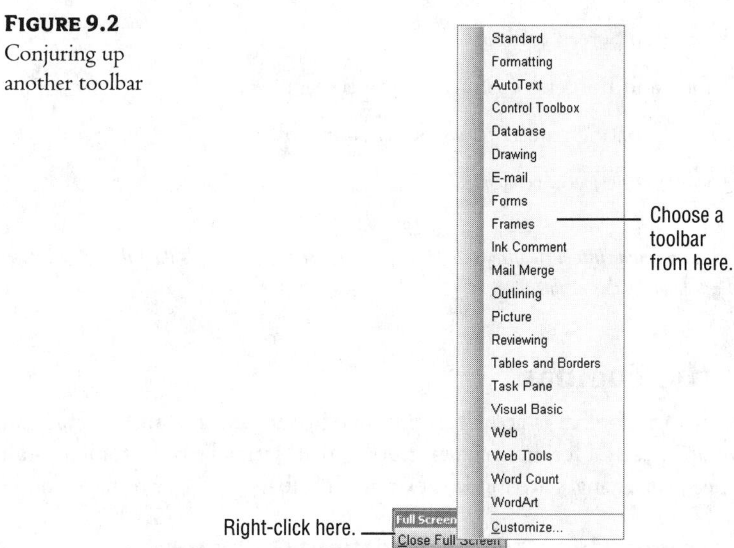

Also refer to the sections later in this chapter on manipulating and moving toolbars, so that you can have more freedom on the display than with a fixed, unmoving toolbar.

NOTE *Actually, the best way to do things is to create a custom toolbar, one that has the Close Full Screen button as well as other buttons for common things you do. This is covered later in this chapter.*

How Can I Get at the Windows Taskbar, the Start Button, or the Scrollbars?

To display the taskbar or Start button—which is part of Windows and not part of Word—press the Windows (Win) key on your PC's keyboard. Or you can press Ctrl+Esc if your keyboard lacks that key.

As for scrollbars: Sorry, can't help you. There are plenty of keyboard equivalents for scrolling your document up or down. If you have a wheel mouse, then you can use the wheel button to scroll up and down.

NOTE *To scroll with the wheel mouse, press the wheel button and drag the mouse up or down to smooth-scroll the document up or down.*

Can I Really Get Work Done in This Mode?

Most certainly! Many of the common Word commands have keyboard equivalents, most of which have been illustrated in the various sidebars and notes throughout this book.

Only a few of the less-common things you do in Word require the presence of the menu bar or specific toolbars. Even in those situations, it's often nicer to view a toolbar while you need it and then dispense with it when you're done.

For example, if you want to draw a table in full-screen mode, follow these steps:

1. Right-click the Full Screen toolbar.
2. Choose "Tables and Borders" from the pop-up menu.
3. Use the toolbar/floating palette to work on your table.
4. Close the toolbar when you're done.

NOTE *Any toolbar can be made into a floating palette. Refer to the section, "What's the Difference between a Toolbar and a Floating Palette?" later in this chapter.*

Belly Up to the Toolbar

It's debatable whether the toolbar is actually a productivity enhancer or merely crap junking up the screen. I vote for crap, myself. I feel no shame for doing that, seeing how the toolbar is ultimately customizable. Whether your changes are mild or extreme, toolbars are eager to have you beat them up.

How Can I Rearrange These Toolbars without Going Insane?

Like anything, toolbars are moveable. You just need to know where to grab them. Figure 9.3 shows the sweet spot.

So point the mouse at the toolbar's handle; then you can drag it up, down, left, or right to rearrange it as you see fit.

NOTE *Dragging toolbars must be done gingerly. Drag them too fast and you will go nuts.*

Be careful of dragging the toolbar away from the edge of the window! If you do, the toolbar becomes a floating palette, as described in the next section.

NOTE *The Standard and Formatting toolbars have a special item on their toolbar menu, "Show Buttons on Two Rows." When this item is chosen, Word automatically arranges the Standard and Formatting toolbars above each other and just under the menu bar.*

FIGURE 9.3
A toolbar, short and stubby

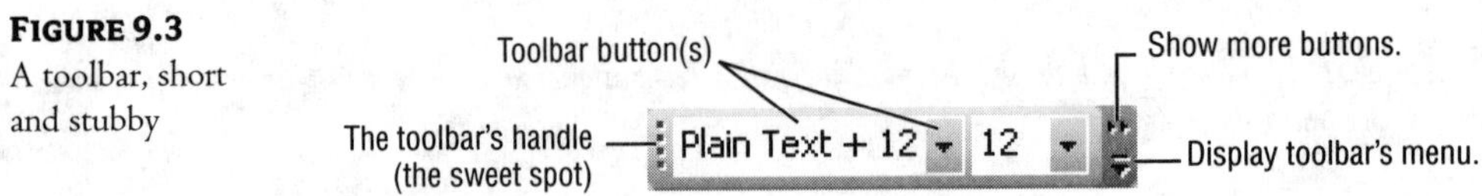

What's the Difference between a Toolbar and a Floating Palette?

Location. Location. Location.

A toolbar is docked to an edge of the window (top, bottom, left, or right). A palette is a little floating window. Just drag any toolbar (by its handle) into the middle of the screen, and it turns into a palette. Figure 9.4 shows the Standard toolbar as a floating palette.

FIGURE 9.4
A floating palette version of the Standard toolbar

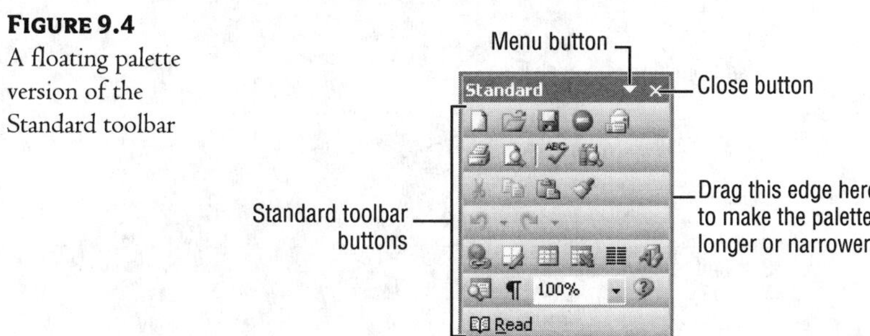

To turn the palette back into a toolbar, drag it back to the edge of the screen, or just close it.

Can I Add a Small Caps Formatting Button?

Certainly. This is easier than you'd think:

1. Click the Menu button on the Formatting toolbar.
2. Point the mouse at the "Add or Remove Buttons" item. You don't have to click it.
3. Choose Formatting. A list of available options is displayed, common Formatting buttons and their functions. If one of them is what you want, then choose it. Alas, "Small Caps" isn't on the list, so you'll have to make a custom modification.
4. Choose Customize. The Customize dialog box appears.
5. Click the Commands tab. This lists all the commands in windows, organized into categories.
6. Choose Format from the list of Categories. ("Small Caps" is a formatting command, found in the Font dialog box, which is part of the Format menu.)
7. Scroll through the list of Commands until you find "Small Caps."
8. Drag the Small Caps icon up and drop it into the Formatting toolbar, as shown in Figure 9.5.
9. Close the Customize dialog box.

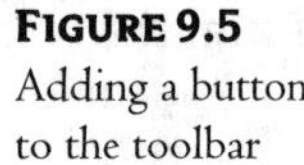

FIGURE 9.5
Adding a button to the toolbar

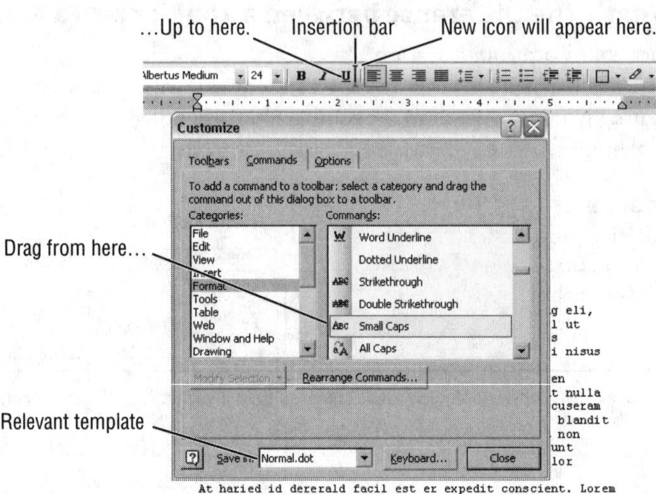

NOTE *While the Customize dialog box is open, you can move, delete, or modify any of the buttons on any visible toolbar. This is done using the mouse. To insert a separator (group) bar, right-click the toolbar and choose "Begin a Group" from the pop-up menu.*

Word must remember these changes, and the place it remembers them is in a template. So you can make these changes specific to a certain template or have them apply to all Word documents by specifying the `NORMAL.DOT` template, as shown in Figure 9.5. (To be specific, choose the current template being used from the drop-down list in the Customize dialog box.)

When you quit your document, you may be asked if you want to update the template. Say Yes; that cements the change so that it appears the next time you start Word.

What's the Point of the [Whatever] Button on the Toolbar When I Never Use It?

You're right! If you don't use that button, then why bother with it! For example, the Hyperlink button! I don't use it. I don't ever plan on using it. I should just send it straight to the fires of perdition by following these ecclesiastical steps:

1. Choose Tools ➤ Customize. There's the holy Customize dialog box, shown in Figure 9.5. When that dialog box is open, every button on every toolbar begs for mercy from the terror of your computer mouse.
2. Point the mouse at the toolbar button that offends ye.
3. Drag it off the toolbar and into damnation. Well, drag it down until the mouse pointer grows an X in a box, in which case you can release the mouse button. The toolbar button is gone.

4. Continue thy wanton ways of destruction.
5. Close the Customize toolbox when ye finisheth.

These changes are saved in the template specified in the Customize dialog box. So if you're asked to save the changes to the template file, click Yes to make your revised toolbar permanent.

NOTE *To make the changes affect all your documents, specify the* `NORMAL.DOT` *toolbar in the Customize dialog box.*

Can I Easily Restore the Toolbar Back to the Way It Originally Was?

Of course:

1. Click the toolbar's menu.
2. Choose "Add or Remove Buttons."
3. In Word 2003/XP, choose Formatting.
4. Choose "Reset Toolbar."

This removes any added buttons and adds back any buttons you removed. The toolbar is restored to its original, out-of-the-box condition.

These steps must be done for each toolbar to restore it to its original look.

Which Toolbar Should I Use for Adding Things?

Try to keep your additions relating to the original function of the toolbar. For example, you add a Small Caps button to the Formatting toolbar, which is logical. Any formatting commands would work best on that toolbar. But, honestly, there are no hard-and-fast rules for any toolbar to add buttons to. In fact, if you plan on adding quite a few buttons, I recommend creating your own toolbar.

Why Would I Want to Create My Own Toolbar?

Simple: Because it would contain the commands you use most often and, therefore, it would be the only toolbar you need. So forget about customizing the other toolbars and create your own toolbar.

Here's how you can create your own toolbar in Word:

1. Summon the Customize dialog box. A quick way to do that is to right-click any toolbar and then choose Customize from the bottom of the pop-up menu.
2. Click the Toolbars tab.
3. Click the New button.
4. Enter a name for your custom toolbar. I named mine Danny's Own, even though it says "Bar None" in Figure 9.6. Other cool names are Unibar, Ultimate Bar, Candy Bar, Ba-Bar, and...you get the idea.

5. Select a template for the toolbar. If you choose NORMAL.DOT, then the toolbar will be available to all Word documents. Otherwise, you can link the toolbar to only the current document or to the current document's template by choosing either item from the drop-down list.
6. Click OK. The new toolbar appears in the list, but also as a floating palette off to the side of the Customize dialog box. Your next task is to fill it with buttons.
7. Click the Commands tab.
8. Select commands to add by choosing an item in the Categories list and then the individual command from the Commands list.
9. Use the mouse to drag that command's button to the toolbar, as shown in Figure 9.6.
10. When you're done, click the Close button.

FIGURE 9.6
Building the toolbar

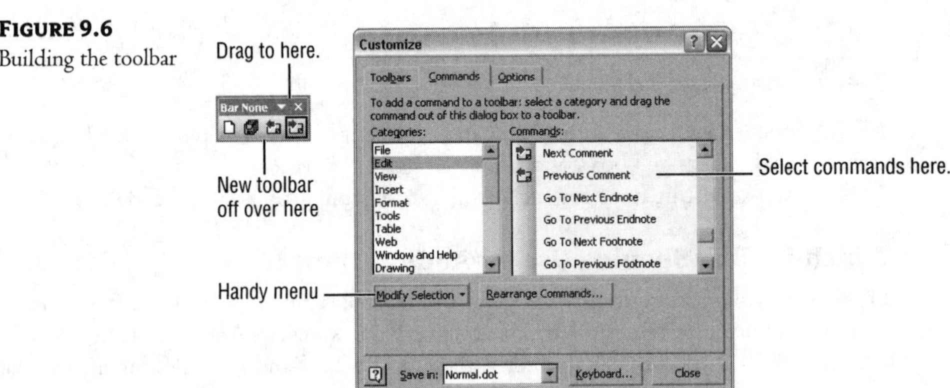

The toolbar can remain floating, or you can dock it on any edge of the screen. It appears as an optional toolbar to display in the View ➤ Toolbars menu, so even if you close it you can summon it back. In fact, it's now a permanent part of whichever template you chose in Step 5. You can show it, hide it, modify it, and so on, all as described in this chapter.

How Can I Make a Separator Bar to Group Commands in My New Toolbar?

Part of the Windows interface involves grouping similar commands on toolbars. You see this on the Standard and Formatting toolbars. On the Standard toolbar, the New, Open, Save, and E-mail buttons are a group. Then comes a separator bar, and then Print and Print Preview and so on. Separator bars visually group similar icons. To do that on your own toolbar, follow these steps:

1. Right-click your toolbar and choose Customize from the pop-up menu. It's the last command on the menu.
2. Click the Commands tab.

3. Click to select the button on your toolbar that starts a new group. Say the first three buttons are file commands and the next three are formatting commands. If so, click to select the fourth button, the first button in the second group.

4. Click the Modify Selection button in the Customize dialog box. The Modify Selection menu appears, as shown in Figure 9.7.

5. Choose "Begin a Group." And the separator bar is inserted *before* the highlighted button.

FIGURE 9.7
The Modify Selection menu

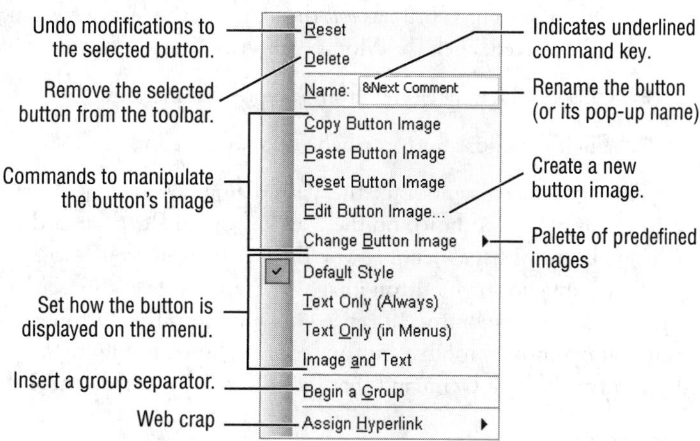

What Can Be Done for Commands That Lack Icons?

Say you're adding a button that lacks a specific icon. For example, in the Format category is a button called Tabs, which is designed to bring up the Tabs dialog box. It lacks an icon, so when you add it to your toolbar you get a text button that reads the name of the command, "Tabs" in this case.

If the text is particularly long, you can edit it. Here's how:

1. Select the text-only button on your toolbar.

2. Click the Modify Selection button in the Customize dialog box.

3. Use the Name command in the menu to rename the button. The Name command contains a text box, as shown in Figure 9.7. You can enter a new name for the button there, something shorter.

   Use an ampersand (&) to identify which letter of the command can be used with the Alt key as a keyboard shortcut. This is also the name of the button that appears if you point the mouse at the button. To display this name as well as the button's icon, also choose Image and Text from the menu.

4. Click the Close button when you're done editing.

Now you might want to dispense with the text and try slapping down your own icon instead. If so, follow these steps to display the icon instead of the text:

1. Click to select the text-only button.
2. Click the Modify Selection button in the Customize dialog box, Commands tab.
3. Choose "Change Button Image."
4. Select an icon from the palette. That is, select an icon if you find one that you like. For example, for the Tab command, the right-pointing arrow might be okay. Choose it.
5. On my screen, Word has *both* the icon and the text. That can be fixed: With the toolbar button still selected, click the Modify Selection button again.
6. Choose "Default Style" from the pop-up menu.
7. Click the Close button when you're done editing.

The right-arrow symbol for the Tabs dialog box is okay. A better symbol, however, would be the arrow/bar, which is shown on the Tab key on all PC keyboards. That symbol doesn't exist on the Change Button Image menu, so you'll have to create your own.

To create your own button image, in Step 3 above, choose the "Edit Button Image" command instead of "Change Button Image." This summons the Button Editor dialog box, which is where you can build your own toolbar button icon, as shown in Figure 9.8. There you can see how I created a button for the Tab command that looks like the icons on the Tab key.

FIGURE 9.8
Creating a new button image

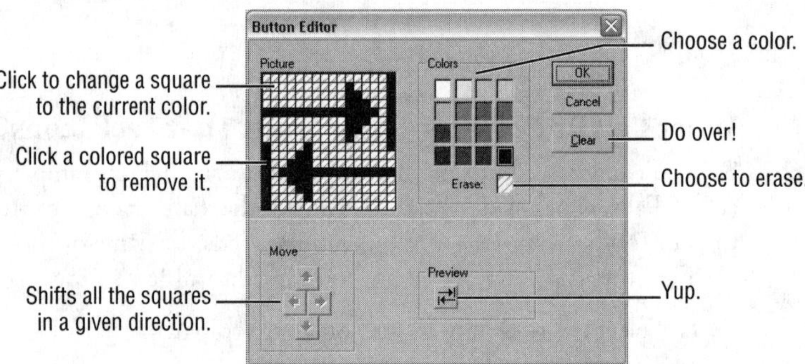

Click OK when you're done creating the button image, and then continue working through the previous set of steps to convert your toolbar button into an image-only button.

How Can I Create a Toolbar Full of Styles?

One special type of toolbar I often create is a formatting toolbar. Ever since Word messed up the Style drop-down list starting with Word 2000, I've enjoyed keeping my most-used styles on a toolbar instead of using the drop-down list. I find that easier for switching styles because each style is a button I can easily click with the mouse.

You can create a style-only toolbar or you can add popular styles to your custom toolbar. It doesn't matter. The key is finding where the styles are hidden in the Customize dialog box. They're in there! You just have to scroll down the Categories list to the bottom, where you'll find Styles listed. Select that category, and the styles associated with the current document and current template are shown in the Commands list.

Simply drag the styles you want on the toolbar over to the toolbar itself, as covered earlier in this chapter.

Generally speaking, I always edit the style names because Word has the habit of tacking on "Style" to each style name. I don't generally apply icons to the styles, though you can do that if you wish; simply follow the instructions presented earlier in this chapter.

NOTE *Remember that styles are associated with a given template, so you'll probably want to create your Style toolbar to belong to a given template only.*

Have fun.

An Introduction to Macros

The more complex the program, the more there has been a need for automation within the program. To meet that end, a program will offer a feature such as macros.

Macros come in two flavors:

The first type of macro is the keyboard recording macro. That's where you can record your keystrokes or mouse commands and then play them back—just like you were watching a video recording of your tasks on the screen. That's one way to automate repetitive tasks.

The second type of macro is more complex. That's where macros are actually programming commands that tell the application what to do. In that aspect, macros can be used to program in new features, add commands, or customize and automate certain operations.

Word sports both type of macros. It will let you record keystrokes and play them back, but it also has richly complex programming abilities. Unlike the simple macro programming languages of yesterday, Word uses a programming language called Word Basic (or Office Basic), which is related to the Visual Basic programming language that Microsoft sells for writing Windows applications.

The following sections cover the use of macros for keyboard recording only. If you want to get into programming macros in Word Basic or Office Basic, then you are better off finding a book or tutorial specific to that subject. It's a pretty vast area and one I don't have time to get into in this book.

NOTE *Alas, I am unable to recommend any advanced macro books for Word.*

Any Way to Automate This Tedious Sequence of Keystrokes?

The problem with automating a tedious sequence of keystrokes is having the tedious sequence in the first place. Word is such a thorough program that there are few things it doesn't do or that aren't automated already. Still, those times do come up when you find yourself pressing the same key sequence over and over. When that happens, it's time to create a keyboard macro to save you some time.

The following is an example of a word-swapping macro. What it does is to take the first word and swap it with the second word. So if you type "brother irritated" and then run the macro, you end up with "irritated brother." Here's how to record that macro:

1. Make sure you have something to manipulate, some text or something to practice on. You need to set up an environment on the screen, in your document, so that you can properly record the macro. Otherwise, you'll have to stop halfway through and start over. It happens.

   In this case, type two words in your document. Put the insertion point at the start of the first word.

2. Choose Tools ➤ Macro ➤ Record New Macro. The Record Macro dialog box appears, as shown in Figure 9.9.

3. Give the macro a descriptive name. No spaces in the name!

4. Choose a location for the macro. If it's in `NORMAL.DOT`, then all your documents can use it. Otherwise, you can put the macro into the current document only or in the document template so that all documents using that template have access to it.

5. This is going to be a keyboard macro, saved to a shortcut key assignment, so click the Keyboard button. The Customize Keyboard dialog box appears, shown in Figure 9.10.

FIGURE 9.9
Creating a new recorded macro

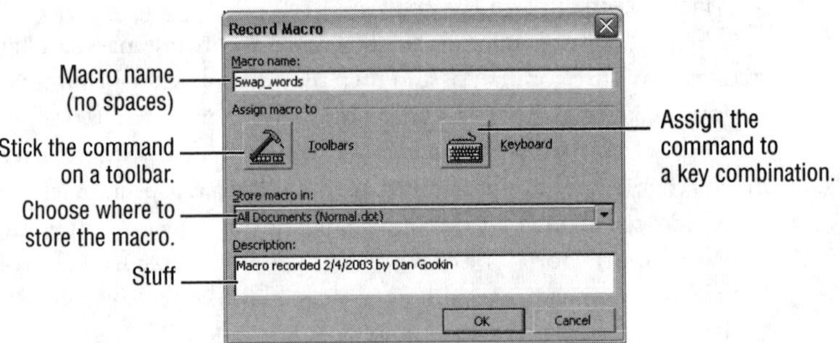

FIGURE 9.10
Assigning the macro to a keyboard shortcut

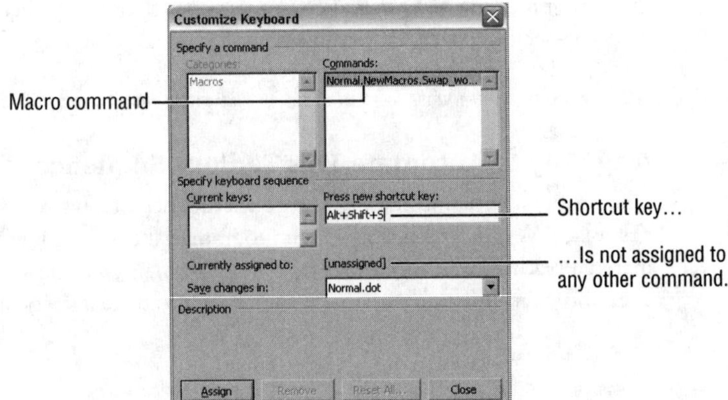

NOTE *If you elect to add this macro as a button on a toolbar, you'll see the Customize dialog box (Figures 9.5, 9.6) with the macro you're recording listed as a command. From there you can drag it to any toolbar in Windows; skip ahead to Step 8.*

6. Press an appropriate shortcut key. Choose a combination not used by any other command. For example, choose Alt+Shift+S for Swap_words.

NOTE *The Alt+Shift+*letter *keyboard combinations are the most open category for you to choose when assigning new keyboard commands.*

7. Click the Assign button.
8. Click Close.

Now you're ready to record. The mouse pointer grows a cassette tape icon, one sign that you're recording. Also the Stop Recording (yes, that's what it says) toolbar floats into existence, shown in Figure 9.11.

1. Start working the commands to go into the macro!

   In this case, you're swapping words. Here are the key commands I would use to swap the words, given that the cursor is blinking before the first word:

   1. Press the F8 key twice. This selects the first word.
   2. Press Ctrl+X. Cut the word.
   3. Press Ctrl+right arrow. Move to the end of the second word.
   4. Press Ctrl+V. Paste in the first word.

   That effectively swaps the words. Time to stop recording.

NOTE *In addition to any keyboard commands, you can also select menu commands or click toolbar buttons. Word records them all.*

2. Click the Stop button on the Stop Recording toolbar.

That's it. The macro has been successfully recorded.

Fortunately making macros to alleviate complex keystrokes is a rare thing. Most of the time what you want might easily be accomplished by the Replace command. For example, I used to have a macro that would find and delete excess spaces at the end of a paragraph. But searching for ^p^w and replacing it with ^p in Word now does the same thing. Still, for those times when the Replace command can't hack it, you can automate your task with a macro.

FIGURE 9.11
Control your macro recording from this toolbar.

How Can I Test My Macro?

Simple: Find a spot in the document where your macro will play out; then issue the macro keyboard command or click the macro toolbar button.

In the case of the Swap_word macro, locate any two words in your document, put the cursor before the first word, and then press Alt+Shift+S.

Yes, of course it works!

Where Are the Macros Kept?

Macros dwell in the Macros dialog box. To get there, choose Tools ➤ Macro ➤ Macros. This shows the list of macros associated with your document or template, as selected in the Macros dialog box and shown in Figure 9.12.

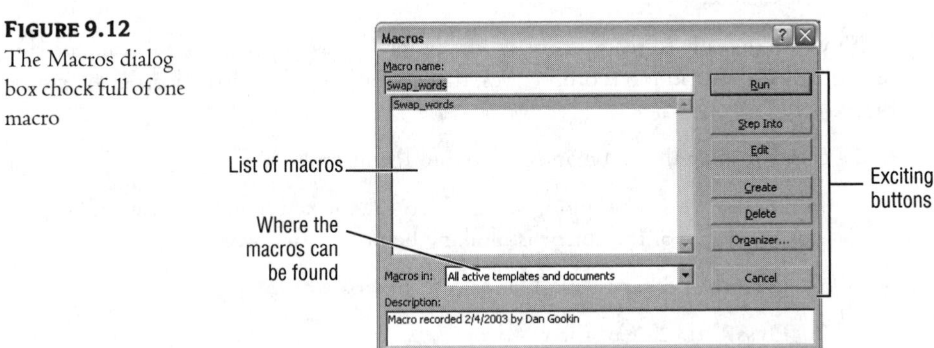

FIGURE 9.12
The Macros dialog box chock full of one macro

You can use the Macro dialog box to run a specific macro, edit a macro, create a new macro, delete macros, and so on, according to the exciting buttons on the side of the dialog box.

The Step Into button is used for debugging purposes. And the Edit button allows you to see the raw macro itself: If you select your macro and click Edit, you can see the Word Basic translation of your recorded keystrokes. It can be pretty complex, so do this only at your own risk. (Press Alt+Q to leave the Visual Basic Editor window and return to Word.)

NOTE *To quickly view the Macros dialog box, use the keyboard shortcut Alt+F8.*

How Can Macros Be a Security Risk?

Word's macros have a lot of power. And, as you know from watching most science fiction television programs, with power comes a lot of responsibility. The problem with Word's macros is that they're powerful enough that the bad guys can write seemingly innocent Word macros that can do devastating things to your entire computer.

For example, Word macros can be written to delete documents on disk, to send out bogus e-mail, or to have vital information from your computer sent out to other computers elsewhere via the Internet.

Occasionally when you open a document with a macro, you may see a dialog box displayed explaining that there are unknown macros in the document. The dialog box gives you the option to disable the macros. Especially if it's a document you downloaded from the Internet, click that Disable button! You don't know what the macros could be or how they could affect your document. Better to be safe than sorry.

Peeling Personal Information from a Document

Whether you like it or not, Word (as well as other Office applications) saves personal information in each document you create. It's possible for someone to find out who created the document, how much time you've spent working on it, and other information that some of us would consider to be personal and private. Yet, all versions of Word save this information to disk with each document you create.

In some cases the data saved in Word documents has been used by law enforcement to track down criminals. For example, the doofus who created the famous Melissa virus a few years back didn't realize that such personal information was included with each infected Word file; once the FBI knew this, it was a simple thing for them to look into an infected document and locate the guy's name and also which company he worked for.

Where the Secret Information Lurks

The information your Word document stores about can be found in the document's Properties sheet. You can see that information by using the File ➤ Properties command in Word. This displays the Properties dialog box where you can see the document's title, the author, perhaps a company name, and other information—even available in an utterly blank document.

Don't for a minute believe that Word is being clairvoyant; the Author and Company information was input when you registered your copy of Word, or perhaps when your organization registered or installed Word.

In the Properties dialog box, Statistics tab, you can find information about the document, including the exact date and time work was started, how long you've been working on the document, when it was last printed (if ever), and so on. In some organizations, with network-installed versions of Word, there may be even more information included with the document, maybe even your hat size!

Getting Rid of the Information in Word XP/2003

If you'd rather not have your personal information floating around in your Word documents then follow these steps:

1. Choose Tools ➤ Options.
2. Click the Security tab in the Options dialog box.
3. Put a check mark by the item, "Remove Personal Information from File Properties on Save."
4. Click OK.

Now the information will not be saved to disk with your document.

To make the change permanent for all documents, it's necessary to modify Word's standard template, the NORMAL.DOT file. This can be tricky:

1. Open the NORMAL.DOT template. Do this as you would edit any template file on disk.
2. Make the changes listed above (steps 1 through 4) inside the NORMAL.DOT template.
3. Save the modified NORMAL.DOT template to disk as NORMALA.DOT. Remember that name!
4. Quit Word.
5. Venture out to disk and find the Templates folder where Word stores your template files. A cinchy way to do this is to search for the file named NORMALA.DOT with the Windows Find File or Search command. When you find the file, open that folder. It should list all your Word templates, including the original NORMAL.DOT.
6. Delete the original NORMAL.DOT file.
7. Rename the NORMALA.DOT file as NORMAL.DOT.

These steps have to be complex because Word has internal mechanisms that prevent NORMAL.DOT from being modified this way from inside of Word. So what you did above (in steps 1 through 7) was make the changes in an alternative template, then switch templates behind Word's back. That's the best way to make the change permanent and keep that personal information out of your documents.

Getting Rid of the Information in Antique Versions of Word

If you have an earlier version of Word, then you're pretty much stuck with the personal information embedded in your document; there really is no straightforward way to eliminate it. Despite the lack of an official off switch, you're not completely stuck out in the cold.

One way to remove the information from the Word document is to save your text in a neutral format, then reopen that format in Word. Because the format isn't a native Word document, the information isn't saved with it. Of course, this may seem bothersome, but if security is important to you, it's worth a shot.

Another way is to copy all your text from Word and then paste it into WordPad, which is the less-than-capable word processing program included with Windows. Sadly, this doesn't save a lot of the formatting and special features that make Word worthy. Otherwise, follow these steps to export your document into a neutral format:

1. Choose File ➤ Save As.
2. In the Save As dialog box, put double quotes around the filename. This ensures that Word saves the file using the .DOC extension and does not create a new file on disk. (This is a tricky step, so you may have to work it a few times to get things right.)

3. From the "Save as Type" drop-down list, choose either "Text Only (*.txt)" or "WordPerfect 5.x for Windows (*.doc)". Choose the Text Only option if your document doesn't need to be formatted; otherwise, to retain most of your formatting, choose the WordPerfect option. Avoid the RTF or HTML formats as they still retain the personal information like standard Word documents do.

NOTE *If the WordPerfect format isn't installed on your computer then you'll need the original Office or Word CD to install that feature. Word will prompt you for the CD when that's the case.*

4. You may see a warning about saving in the alternative file format. If you do, then click the Yes button.

The document is then saved on disk in the other file format without the personal information.

You're not out of the woods here: if you open that supposedly clean document in Word again, then your personal information is added back. My advice here is that if security is truly an issue for you, then upgrade to Office 2003, where this feature can be more easily disabled.

Chapter 10

Why the Hell Would Anyone Other than an Accountant Use Excel?

I LOVE SPREADSHEETS FOR three reasons and only one of them is that I'm a nerd. The other two are that I hate paying taxes and, most importantly, I understand the whole *grid* concept thing.

You see, Excel isn't about numbers. It's about tables. It's the grid thing! Any information you can stick into a table is probably best handled by Excel. That's the way it works. So where Word gives you the blank page to fill as your creative juices desire, Excel presents you with a massive grid full of thousands of cells. Anything you can picture in a grid—names and dates, city blocks, prisoners, quilting patterns, team rosters, or even (yes) financial data—goes into Excel.

Even though this book is intermediate in nature, I'm going to assume that you probably don't use Excel too much. Most people don't. They avoid it for reasons mathematical in nature. But if you study this chapter (and those that follow), you'll soon discover the secret most Excel mavens know: It's not just for accountants.

- Introducing Excel
- Finding your way around the worksheet quickly
- Wrestling with formulas
- Referencing other cells directly, by name, or absolutely
- Decoding the various common and annoying error messages
- Busting an Excel table into a Word document

Some Information for Excel Newbies

The first spreadsheet software was called VisiCalc, short for Visible Calculator. The program's designer envisioned a calculator that had many different windows or locations, similar to an accountant's general ledger form. Because such a thing was made on a computer, the numbers on the form could be "live" and relate to one another, updating and changing as new information was entered. Oh, and those accountants went nuts over the thing.

While a spreadsheet has its foundation in numbers, the truth is that any information that goes into rows and columns can be more easily manipulated in a spreadsheet than in most other types of software. The key to your understanding of Excel is to stop thinking of numbers and switch your brain over to a mode where you see information presented in rows and columns. Once you see those rows and columns, you're ready to start using a spreadsheet.

The Cheap-Ass Tour of Your Basic Excel Window

Like all Office programs, Excel shares a common look and feel with its sisters and cousins and aunts. Figure 10.1 illustrates the basic big-picture things you see when you gawk at Excel after starting it the first time.

How Many Rows and Columns Are There?

More than you'll ever use! Keep in mind that information doesn't need to fill every cell, however.

To find out the exact answer, locate the Select All button on the grid; see Figure 10.1. If you click that button once with the mouse, you select the entire worksheet. But if you click and *hold* the button, you'll see the worksheet's maximum size displayed in the Name box.

On my screen it says that the worksheet is 65,536 rows tall by 256 columns wide. That may seem like enough for anything, but rumor has it that there are massive worksheets in major corporations that are many times that size.

NOTE *The larger a worksheet is, the more memory it consumes. Very large worksheets can bring a computer system to its knees.*

Most of the worksheets you create will fit on a single screen or a printed page of text. Some may be longer, such as worksheets that track information over time, but only rarely will you see a worksheet that comes close to using every single cell.

FIGURE 10.1
Excel, naked and exposed

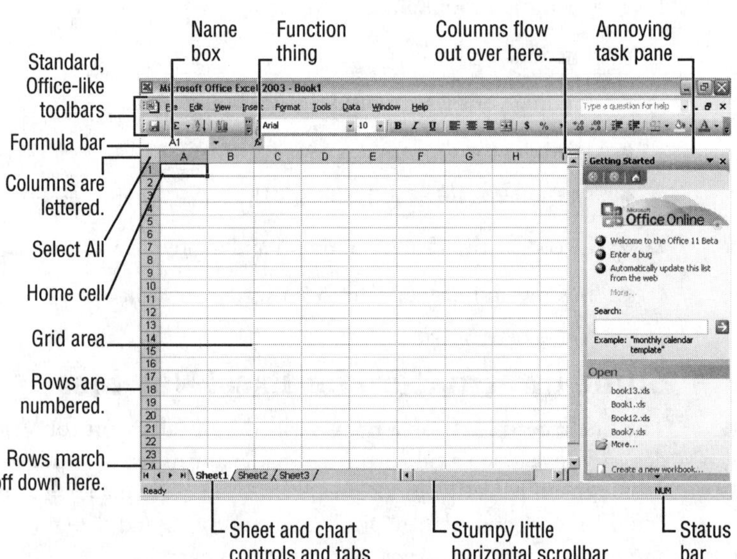

I Want to Go Visit the Last Cell!

The first cell, or home cell, in the worksheet is named cell A1. That's from the A column and the first row. The very last possible cell in a worksheet is cell IV65536, which reads like some perverse Roman numeral combination, but it's not. It's column IV and row 65536.

To visit the last cell, type **IV65536** into the Name box and press the Enter key. There's nothing there, but it's a curious spot to look at.

To zoom back to the home cell, press Ctrl+Home.

(No, Ctrl+End does not go to the last cell in the worksheet; it goes to the last cell in your work area on the worksheet, which probably won't be that far down and to the right.)

Can I Get My Dumb Toolbars on Two Rows, Please?

For some reason, Office programs like to display the two usual toolbars, Standard and Formatting, on one row. To fix that, you must grab the second toolbar (on the right), which is usually the Formatting toolbar, and carefully drag it down and to the left, below the Standard toolbar.

In Office 2003/XP, you can click the down arrow at the end of the toolbar and choose "Show Buttons on Two Rows" from the menu. That fixes the problem without making you wrestle the toolbars with the mouse.

Where the Heck Is the Office Assistant?

If you feel the urge to use the annoying, animated Office Assistant with Excel, then summon it from its locked vault: Choose Help ➤ Show the Office Assistant. Or if you tire of that dumb thing, choose Help ➤ Kill the Office Assistant. This command may not be found on all versions of Excel, so instead you'll have to settle for the Help ➤ Hide the Office Assistant command.

Do You Have Any Other Immediate Helpful Information That Will Soothe My Frayed Nerves?

Though it's stated in this book's introduction, again I'd like to remind you to turn off the Personalized Menu feature of Excel. That is, remove the options that keep "recently used items" at the top of the menu and occasionally shuffle menu items depending on how you use them.

To ensure that these options are properly set, follow these steps:

1. Choose Tools ➤ Customize.
2. Click the Options tab.
3. Here's where things get weird because Excel 2003/XP is utterly opposite of Excel 2000:
   - In Excel 2003/XP, the top two items in the dialog box must be checked.
   - In Excel 2000, the top two items in the dialog box must be unchecked.
4. Click OK.

Now Excel is set up to behave in a sane and predictable manner.

The Difference between a Spreadsheet, Worksheet, and Workbook

There are three general terms you need to know to use Excel:

Spreadsheet This is the type of software Excel is; just as Word is a word processor, Excel is a spreadsheet.

Worksheet This is the thing that Excel displays in its window. It's the grid full of cells, from A1 to IV65536.

Workbook This is a collection of worksheets saved to disk, the equivalent of a document in Word. In Excel, you save a *workbook* to disk. You open a *workbook* previously saved on disk. You do not open a spreadsheet nor do you open a worksheet, though the terms may be improperly used that way.

How Do You Best Deal with the Task Pane?

The best way to deal with the task pane is to close it: Press Ctrl+F1 and it goes away in Excel 2003, or you can choose View ➤ Task Pane to banish it (in both Excel 2003 and Excel XP).

A more important question to ask might be, "How do I get the task pane *not* to show up when Excel starts?" The answer is to use the Options dialog box:

1. Choose Tools ➤ Options.
2. Click the View tab.
3. Uncheck the box by "Startup Task Pane."
4. Click OK.

Note that Excel 2000 does not use the task pane. Blessed be Excel 2000!

Do I Have to Start at Cell A1?

Heavens, no! Unlike a word processing document (where elements are all in sequence, so there's always a first and a last character), there is no "first" cell. The first cell is literally A1, but the first cell into which you sling data can be any cell in the worksheet.

Logically, it makes sense to use a cell you can see on the screen. But the cell doesn't have to be at any specific location in the worksheet.

For example, when I start a new table of data in Excel, I typically start it at cell D5 or C3, as shown in Figure 10.2. There are no rules or traditions here; start wherever you like, even cell A1 if you need to.

What Goes into a Cell?

Cells can contain three things: text, values, or formulas.

In addition, cells can be formatted and shaded, and their size can be changed at a whim.

Also, as with other Office applications, you can draw objects on top of the worksheet to help illustrate things.

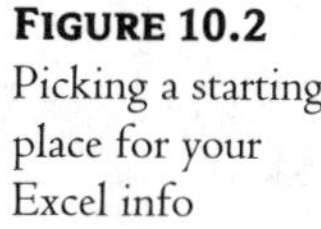

FIGURE 10.2
Picking a starting place for your Excel info

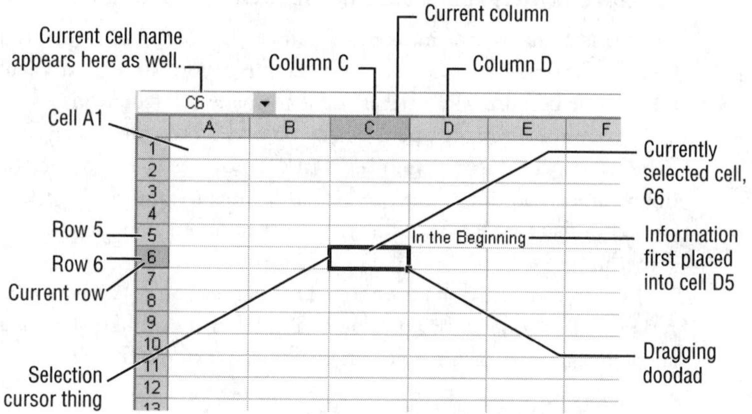

TYPING IN A WORKSHEET? NO, IT JUST DOESN'T SOUND RIGHT TO ME.

Text has just as much of a right to exist in a worksheet as information. I suppose they figured this out early when the pioneer spreadsheet users discovered that numbers should often be *labeled* so that you know what they mean.

In Excel, of course, you can use text as titles to your worksheet, to add information and explain things. In fact, if you wanted to, you could put a lot of text into a single cell. Do remember, however, that Excel is a grid thing. Writing should be done in Word.

NOTE *See Chapter 12, "Some Formatting Tricks," for information on formatting the text in a cell.*

Something you may not know: All text you type is assumed to be text. Yeah, that seems dumb. But there is a prefix character you can type to ensure that Excel interprets what you type as text and not a label or anything else. That is the apostrophe key. Follow these steps:

1. Click cell C3.
2. Type **Pugsly School of Wart Removal.**
3. Press the Enter key. This moves you down to cell C4.
4. Type **'LaWanda Ridgeway, Chief Artist.**
5. Press Enter. And you're at cell C5.

Notice that the single tick before the text in cell C4 isn't displayed? That's because the tick is a prefix character that tells Excel to assume the cell's content is text. This is optional, of course; Excel is generally smart enough to know text when it sees it.

WHAT'S THE DIFFERENCE BETWEEN A VALUE AND A NUMBER?

A value is a quantity or measure of something. Normally I would just call it a number, but in Excel there is also a numeric nonvalue. For example, your street address may be 4140. That's a number. It's not a value because you'll never use it to make a calculation.

For example, what happens when you add 15 to your Social Security number? Well, you get someone else's Social Security number, but the point is that the Social Security number is just a number, not a value. You don't ever need to add, subtract, multiply, or find the square root of that number.

So numbers are like text, but values are numbers you can play with and treat like they're measuring something.

As with text, you don't have to tell Excel that you're typing a value into a cell; Excel is smart enough to know. But you can flag a value as a number if you like. That's done by prefixing the value with a single quote mark, the secret text prefix tick. Follow these steps:

1. Click cell G1.
2. Type **1234**.
3. Press Enter. That's a value. Note how Excel automatically right-justifies a value in a cell?
4. In cell G2, type **'9876**.
5. Press Enter. That's a number. Actually it's text; note how it's left-justified.

   In Excel 2003/XP, a green diamond appears in the cell's upper-left corner. That's the "This Cell Is Weird" warning that Excel gives. In this case, you're being alerted to the fact that you deliberately put in a number as text, and Excel thinks you're a dodo for doing that.

   1. Click the mouse in cell G2. A warning icon appears next to the cell.
   2. Point the mouse at the warning icon. A menu button appears!
   3. Click the menu button. A drop-down menu appears!
   4. Choose "Ignore Error." That gets rid of the green diamond.

   Meanwhile, back in cell G3…

6. Type =5.
7. Press Enter.

Like the tick, the equal sign can also be used as a prefix. In this case, when followed by a number, it means the contents of that cell equal that value. Dumb. Redundant. But it's an option, and I'm required by the Computer Book Author's Code to demonstrate it to you.

Like the tick mark for text, the equal sign for values is optional. Excel is smart enough to know a value when it sees one. Unlike the tick mark, however, the equal sign cannot be used with text. If you do use it, you'll confuse Excel. And that makes sense because there is no numerical equivalent for "Brian's Bitchin' Tax Avoidance Scheme."

NOTE *If you try to type = followed by text, Excel displays a #NAME? error. It believes the text to be the name of a specific cell or range of cells, which it's not. You'll have to edit the cell and remove the equal sign, promising yourself not to be so impertinent in the future.*

Formulas? I Hate Chemistry Worse than Math!

No, not that kind of formula! In Excel, a formula is a mathematical or logical operation that takes place within a cell. This can involve numbers and symbols, as well as any of Excel's powerful and scary built-in functions. The formula's equation sits inside a single cell all alone, or it can reference other cells in the worksheet—or even cells in other worksheets or information on the Internet. It's very powerful. And scary.

Unlike with text or values, you *must* prefix a function in a cell with the equal sign. No options or cop-outs here. In fact, from the previous section, typing **=5** is the simplest form of Excel function. The function is basically the value 5. It "equals five."

Wander through these steps, which assume that you have values in cells G1 and G3 per the previous section's instructions:

1. Click cell G5 to select it.
2. Type **=2+2**. Just like in the old Password game, imagine an offstage voice whispering, "The formula is two plus two." Or you could say, "The contents of this cell are equal to two plus two."
3. Press Enter. Good! Two plus two still equals four. It's a simple formula, but Excel can handle it.
4. Into cell G6 type **=G1+G3-G5**. Now that's a formula! It reads "The contents of this cell are equal to the value of cell G1 plus the value of cell G3 minus the value of cell G5.

NOTE *You don't have to type in G1 or G3 or G5; simply click the mouse on a cell, and it's address is automatically entered into the formula.*

5. Press Enter. On my screen it shows 6543 as the result. Just kidding! It's 1235.

Of course, the most interesting thing about formulas is that they're *live* and change as information elsewhere in the worksheet changes.

1. Click cell G1.
2. Type 99.
3. Press Enter. Not only does cell G1 change its value, but also the formula in cell G6 updates to reflect the updated information. Nifty.

Beyond simple math, formulas also contain functions that let you manipulate values in incredible and often brain-numbing ways. But don't ever fuss over this: It's *the computer* that does the calculations. All you need to know is which function to use, which is where this book helps a lot.

What's the Trick to Editing a Cell?

You may notice that, unlike a word processor, the cursor keys move the cell selector and do not let you edit the contents of a cell—no matter how hard you stare at it.

There are two ways to edit a cell. The first is to select the cell and then use the Formula bar to change the cell's contents. The Formula bar always shows a cell's inner workings, whereas the cell itself merely displays the results (see Figure 10.3).

A better way to edit a cell is to select it and press the F2 key, shown in Figure 10.4. This does the same thing as clicking the mouse in the Formula bar: It expands the cell to reflect its true contents (or formula), which you can then edit using the mouse or cursor keys.

NOTE *To refer to another cell while you're editing, either type in that cell's name directly or use the mouse to click the cell (or select a range of cells), which inserts the cell(s) reference into your formula.*

Also notice that when you edit a formula, any cells referred to are highlighted in color on the screen. This is pretty cool, unless you're colorblind.

You can use the Cancel button on the Formula bar (the X) to weasel out of your edits. Use the Enter button on the Formula bar (the check mark) if your arm is too heavy to lift and you can't press the Enter key on the keyboard instead.

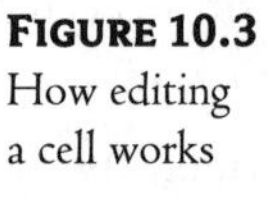

FIGURE 10.3
How editing a cell works

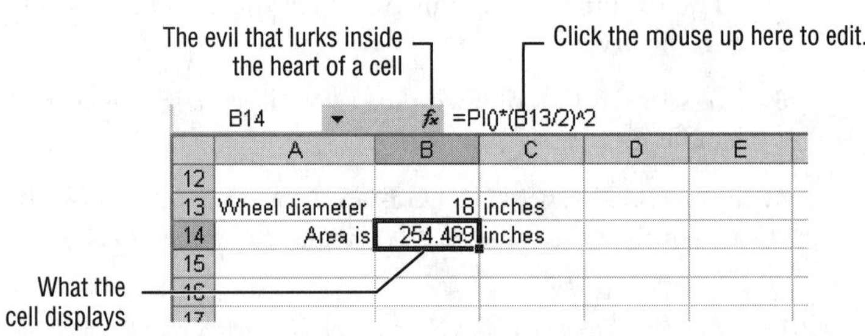

FIGURE 10.4
Editing a cell

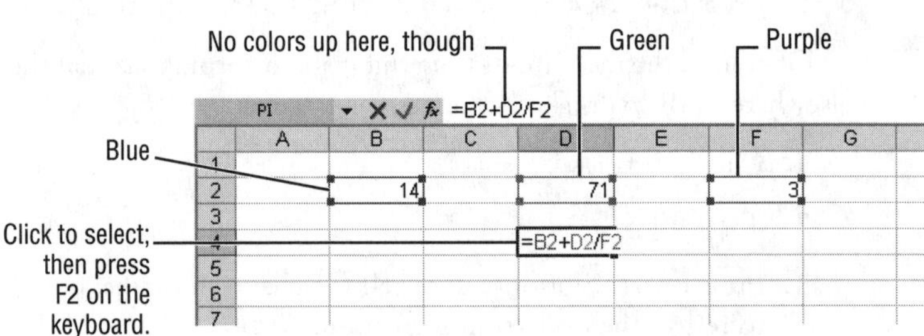

EDITING A CELL

While you can edit a cell using the Formula bar, I'm stuck in the old-fashioned keyboard-bound method of doing things, which includes using these keys:

F2 Press the F2 key to edit the cell's contents.

Esc Cancel editing.

Ctrl+Z Undo any editing changes.

Worksheet Tricks, Stunts, and Tomfoolery

The casual or briefly exposed Excel user may benefit from many of the following tips and suggestions. I've listed them in a somewhat random order to keep them interesting. Hopefully you'll find one or two that you didn't already know!

Where Am I in My Worksheet?

All worksheets are the same size: a gazillion cells by a zillion cells. The actual numbers are listed near the start of this chapter, but what you really want to know is how big your *data region* is. That's the part of the spreadsheet that's populated with information.

- To go to the southeast corner of your data region, press Ctrl+End. That selects the cell that is equal to the rightmost column and bottom-most row that's filled with something in your worksheet. Yes, it can be (and often is) an empty cell.
- To hop to the last occupied cell in the current row, press Ctrl+right arrow.
- To hop to the last occupied cell in the current column, press Ctrl+down arrow.
- And, of course, Ctrl+Home always moves you to the A1 cell on the worksheet.

It's possible to scroll around and view a worksheet and lose where the cell selection thing is. The quick way to find it is *not* to scroll around madly, but rather press Ctrl+Backspace. That refocuses Excel's window on the location of the highlighted cell.

Any Spiffy Way to Jump to a Specific Cell off in the Yonder?

If you know the cell's address, just type it into the Name box on the Formula bar (see Figure 10.1). Press the Enter key and there you are.

To jump to a *named* cell, choose the cell name from the drop-down list on the Name box. You can also use the Go To command, Ctrl+G, which displays the Go To dialog box from which you can choose any of several recently visited places in your workbook, as shown in Figure 10.5.

FIGURE 10.5
Going to a specific location

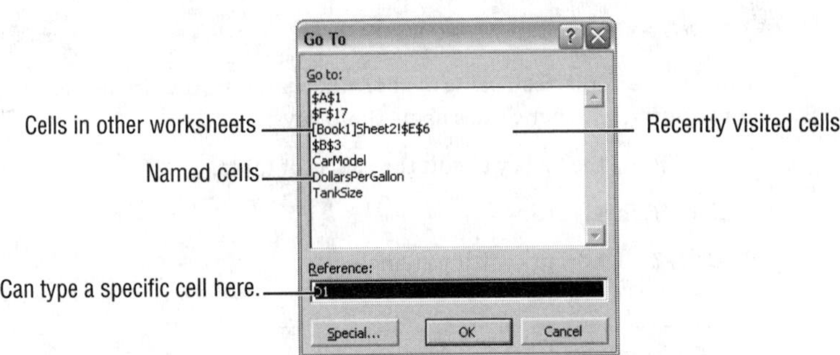

How Can I Better Remember Cell H34?

I find that I often remember specific cells if I keep on referencing them. However, that doesn't help if you insert or delete some rows or move portions of the worksheet around with Copy and Paste. Therefore, to be certain that you'll remember a specific cell or a range of cells, name it (or them).

To name a cell, follow these steps:

1. Click to select the cell you want to name.
2. Choose Insert ➤ Name ➤ Define. The Define Name dialog box appears, as shown in Figure 10.6.
3. Type a name for the cell. Be descriptive of the cell's contents. Also avoid using spaces.

NOTE *The more descriptive you are, the more your formulas can make sense. For example: =DollarsPerGallon*TankSize is obvious as a formula to calculate how much it may cost to fill up on gas. That's more apparent than =H21*G15.*

4. Click OK, and the cell is given that name.

   The name sticks so well that you'll see it displayed instead of the cell's address in the Name box on the Formula bar. In fact, there's your shortcut: To quickly name a cell, click the cell and type the name into the Name box. That saves a few steps.

FIGURE 10.6
Naming a cell

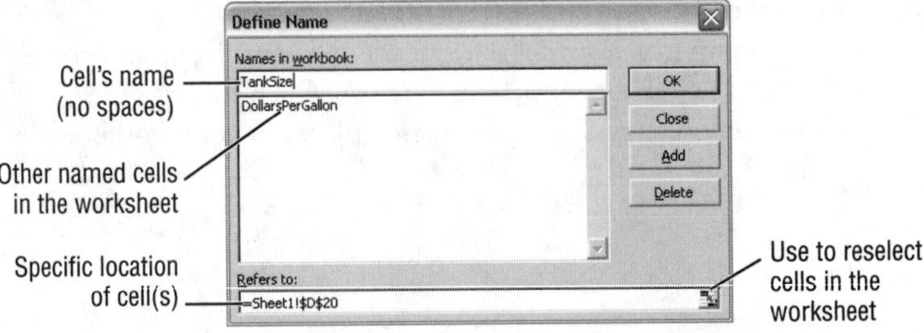

NOTE *You can also name a range of cells or any cluster of selected cells. Simply select the cells, and then assign a name to them using any of the techniques covered in this section. The single name treats all the cells as a unit and can also be used in functions.*

I'm in the Middle of a Function and Need to Recall a Name That I Forgot!

After you type that = sign, the Formula bar switches over to Function mode and the Name box disappears. So it's really difficult to recall the specific wording of the labels in your document. Fear not! There is an easy way:

1. Select a cell.
2. Press = to start entering the function.
3. Press the F3 key. This is the same thing as choosing Insert ➢ Name ➢ Paste. It brings up the Paste Name dialog box, shown in Figure 10.7, from which you can select any of the labels specified in your workbook.
4. Choose a name from the list.
5. Click OK. And that name (the cell it refers to) is slapped into your function.

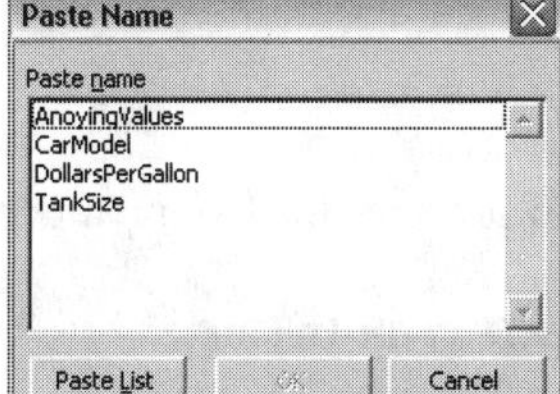

FIGURE 10.7
The Paste Name dialog box

MOVING AROUND THE SPREADSHEET

Hopefully, your worksheets won't be that huge or busy. Even if they are, you'll find these keyboard shortcuts handy for navigating regions near and far inside Excel:

Arrow keys Move the selector one cell in the given direction.

Ctrl+arrow key Hop to the end of the data region or to the far edge of the worksheet (depending on how many times you press the keys).

PgDn Move down one screen.

PgUp Move up one screen.

Alt+PgDn Move left one screen.

Alt+PgUp Move right one screen.

Ctrl+PgDn Display the next sheet in the workbook.

Ctrl+PgUp Display the previous sheet in the workbook.

You Mean I Can Finally Use the Scroll Lock Key?

Spreadsheets are perhaps the only program in the universe for which your computer keyboard's Scroll Lock key comes into play. With the Scroll Lock key pressed, and its wee little light on, the four arrow keys actually slide the worksheet left, right, up, or down, depending on which key you press.

The cell selector does not move when Scroll Lock mode is on.

Pressing Scroll Lock again leaves Scroll Lock mode and returns the cursor keys back to normal. And the wee little light goes off as well.

Why Does the Text Get Lopped Off?

Text in a cell stretches out as far to the right as possible—until it bumps into something. So if there is nothing to the east of the cell, then the text goes on and on. But the first occupied cell "in the way" halts the meandering text in its tracks. Figure 10.8 kind of shows how this works.

FIGURE 10.8
Various stages of text lopping-off-ness

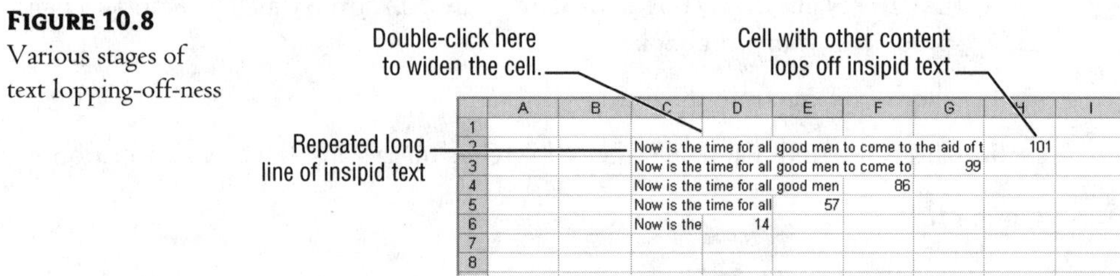

There are a few tricks you can pull to prevent this from happening.

The Old Enlarge-the-Cell-with-the-Text-in-It Trick

You can resize a cell so that it's wide enough to contain the long strand of text. The easiest way to do this is to double-click the mouse on the line separating the cell's column from the next column, such as between columns C and D shown in Figure 10.8. Double-click there, and the cell is automatically resized to fix the text length.

NOTE *You can also choose Format ➤ Column ➤ AutoFit Selection to do the same thing as the double-click trick.*

A drawback to this approach is that it widens all cells in the column. If that's a drawback.

The Old Format-the-Cell-So-That-the-Text-Wraps-in-It Trick

Think about it: When is it necessary for the text to march all the way across several cells in a worksheet? Probably only for titles and such. So as long as the text is what's important and not its position across the screen, you can format the text so that the cell consumes it all without crashing into other cells. Here's how:

1. Click the cell containing the long, winding text.
2. Press Ctrl+1 to format the cell.

3. Click the Alignment tab, as shown in Figure 10.9.
4. Check "Wrap Text."
5. Click OK.

Now the text wraps within the cell's left and right boundaries, but the cell gets incredibly tall; the cell's new height affects the entire row. That may be livable. Of course, you can always adjust the cell's width at this point as a sort of trade-off.

NOTE *Wrapping text in a cell does not permanently alter the row height. If you delete or edit the cell, then the row's height changes accordingly.*

FIGURE 10.9
Various ways to mess with text in a cell

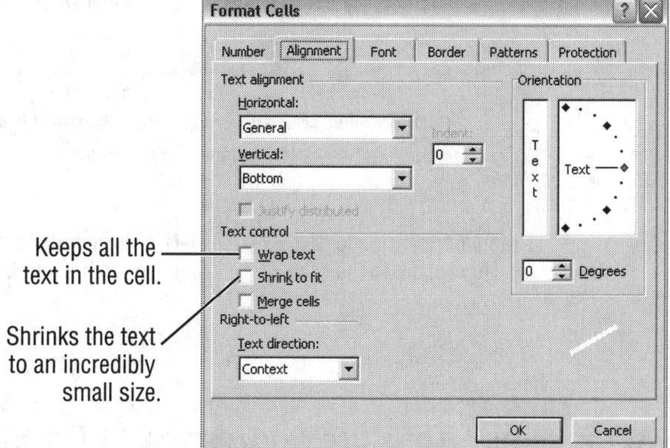

FORGET THE CELL AND PUT THE TEXT INTO A DAMN BOX

The final way to stick a long bit of text into a document is to forgo putting it into a cell altogether. Instead, just use the Text Box drawing tool and put your text into there. Here are the details:

1. Click the Drawing button to bring up the Drawing toolbar.
2. Click the Text Box button on the Drawing toolbar.
3. Drag the mouse over your worksheet to create a rectangle for your text. Start at the upper-left corner and drag down and to the left to create the rectangle.
4. Type your text into the box.
5. Drag the mouse over your text to select it.
6. Format the text. Choose a font, size, attributes, and alignment from the Formatting toolbar. Or you can press Ctrl+1 to summon up a special Format Text dialog box that contains only the Font tab.

7. Drag the text box by its edge to the location where you want it. Refer to Figure 10.10.
8. Finally, you can use the Fill Color or Line Color icon on the Drawing toolbar to change the line or fill color of the text box.

Note that the text box floats over cells in the worksheet. Unless you want those cells hidden on purpose, try not to fill them in.

NOTE *To remove the text box's border, choose "No Line" from the Line Color pop-up menu palette.*

Be sure to close the Drawing toolbar when you're done with it.

FIGURE 10.10
Using a text box for text

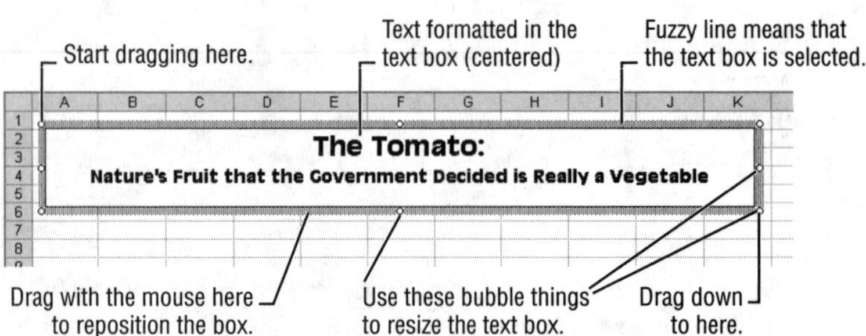

Relative Addressing? Absolute Addressing? Why Should I Care?

When you refer to a cell in your worksheet, the reference is considered relative. Consider the worksheet snippet in Figure 10.11.

Follow along by creating a similar worksheet in Excel. Enter the values shown in Figure 10.11 using the same cell locations by following these steps:

1. Into cell C2 type **Tipping Percent.**
2. Into cell B3 type **Meal Cost.**
3. Into cell C3 type **.05.**

FIGURE 10.11
Making a tip sheet

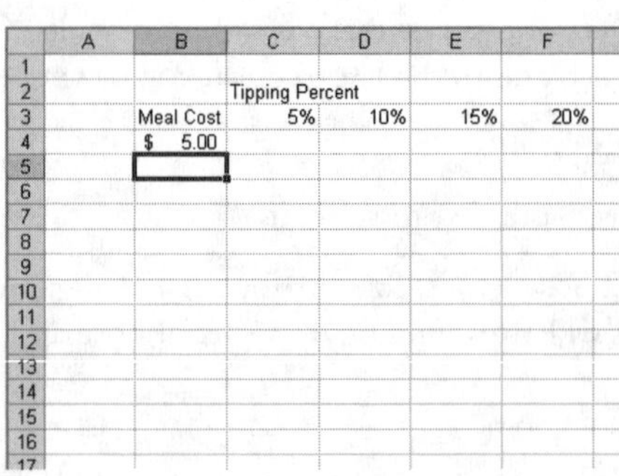

NOTE *Instead of pressing the Enter key after typing the number, press the right arrow key.*

4. Into cell D3 type .1.
5. Into cell E3 type .15.
6. Into cell F3 type .2.
7. Select cells C3 through F3 and click the Percent Style button on the Formatting toolbar. This formats the values into percentages, which is why you entered them as decimals in the first place: .05 is really 5% when formatted as a percentage. Had you entered 5 instead, then when you formatted it as a percent you would have gotten 500%, which is your first and most visual clue that you've screwed up something—or you're a really good tipper!
8. In this case you want 5, which represents the cost of the meal in dollars. Into cell B4, type **5**.
9. Select cell B4 again and click the Currency Style button on the Formatting toolbar.
10. Click cell B5. Now the screen should look similar to Figure 10.11. You're ready to use relative addressing to fill in the Meal Cost column. Relative addressing means that a cell refers to another cell in a nonspecific manner. For example:
11. Into cell B5 type **=B4+2.5** and press Enter.

NOTE *You don't have to type B4 into the formula; use the mouse to click the B4 cell, and that address (B4) is automatically inserted.*

This formula reads, "The contents of this cell equal the contents of cell B4 plus 2.5 (two dollars and fifty cents)." Pressing the Enter key yields the result, $7.50.

The formula you just entered uses relative addressing. The "B4" in the formula doesn't specifically mean "cell B4" but rather "the cell above the current cell." That's the way Excel normally does things, and it enables you to do fancy tricks, such as the following:

12. Select cell B5.
13. Fill down 15 cells. Here's how to fill down if you're unfamiliar with it:
    1. Point the mouse at the square on the cell selector's lower-right corner, shown in Figure 10.12. The mouse changes to a solid + when you've found the sweet spot.
    2. Drag the mouse down 15 cells, to cell B20. When you release the mouse button, the cells fill with the appropriate series. In this case, the series is "Add 2.5 to the number above"—relative addressing.

Now you have your tipping percentages in a row and various meal prices in a column. Time to fill in the rest of the sheet.

FIGURE 10.12
How to drag a cell into a series

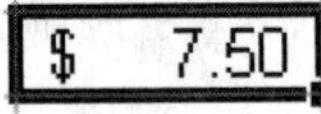

14. Select cell C4.

15. Type =B4+(C3*B4).

The formula for the tip is equal to the price of the meal (B4) plus the tip. The tip is calculated as the percentage (C3) times the meal (B4). You should see $5.25 listed in cell C4, which is proper—for a 5 percent tip.

16. Use the mouse to drag and fill down from cell C4 to cell C20.

Theoretically, this should give you the 5 percent tip total for all those different meal costs. Alas, the result is, well—wrong!

The #### things means that the value is too large (wide) to display in the cell. But if you gander at cell C6, you'll see that it's the waiter's dream of a tip, nearly 50 times the meal cost! How did that happen?

Blame relative addressing! Click cell C5 and read the Formula bar. The formula reads =B5+(C4*B5). The B5 part is correct; that's the cost of the meal. But the C4 part is incorrect; that isn't the tipping percentage but rather the tip total for the previous line. Oops!

The solution is to use absolute addressing so that the tip value always refers to cell C3.

17. Click cell C4.

18. Press the F2 key to edit the formula.

19. Place a dollar sign ($) before the 3 so that the formula reads =B4+(C$3*B4).

The dollar sign tells Excel to focus on a specific cell—absolute addressing. In this case, it's not a specific cell but rather a specific row. The $3 means, "Always look in cell 3 for the value, no matter which row this is."

I could have written it as $C$3, which means, "Always look in cell C3, column C, row 3." But the $3 thing will come in handy as the formulas are copied off to the left into other columns.

20. Refill from cell C4 down through cell C20, and the tip values should fill in rather nicely.

21. With cells C4 through C20 selected, grab the Fill gizmo and drag to the right to fill cells F4 through F20.

22. That should complete the table, but alas, things still don't add up right. The problem again is relative addressing. Click cell D10.

As an avid restaurant goer, I know that the 10 percent tip on $20 is $2, for a total of $22. But the value in cell D10 shows $23.10. Look at the Formula bar and you'll see the cause:

=C10+(D$3*C10)

Relative addressing works with D$3 because it zeros in on the third row in the current column, accurately giving you the 10 percent value. But C10 is not the cost of the meal; the cost of the meal is in B10. The value $23.10 is the accurately calculated 10 percent tip on a $21 meal, not a $20 meal.

Time to fix relative addressing one more time!

1. Click cell C4.
2. Press the F2 key to edit the function.
3. You know that C$3 means to address row 3 in the current column. Likewise, $B4 means to always look in column B in the current row: Add two dollar signs into the function so that it now reads =$B4+(C$3+$B4).

   This reads (and follow closely), "Take the value from column B in this row and add it to the value in row 3 plus the value from column B again." That's absolute addressing: specific rows and columns. You'll notice that pressing Enter doesn't change the value displayed in cell C4, also that adding the dollar signs doesn't move the color highlights from the proper cells.

   Now the tricky part:

4. Drag and fill from cell C4 down and right to cell F20. Drag down to cell C20 first, and then drag over to cell F20 to fill in the entire table. The values will now be correct for each entry in the table, thanks to absolute addressing.

If you're still having trouble with the concept, then click any cell in the table. For example, click cell E14, which shows a value of $34.50. Look at the Formula bar. You'll see = $B14+(E$3*$B14). If you mentally remove the dollar signs, you'll see the same raw formula as introduced at the start of this section. What the dollar sign does is keep the cells specific for drag-and-fill operations. That way, in this case, values are always referred to from column $B and row $3 no matter which cell is accessed in the grid.

Finally, if you need to access a specific cell, then you use two dollar signs, as in $C$3, which always refers to cell C3 from anywhere else in the worksheet. I could have used such an absolute reference in the tipping chart, but then I would have had to create new formulas for each column. So instead, I used a dollar sign.

ABSOLUTE ADDRESSING SHORTCUTS WITH F4

You can use the F4 key in the Formula bar to "toggle" various absolute addressing options and shift the dollar sign ($) around inside a cell reference. With a cell address, such as B4, selected inside the Formula bar, pressing the F4 key toggles the address to an absolute address ($B$4). Pressing F4 again toggles it to an absolute row address (B$4); pressing it again toggles it to an absolute column address ($B4); and finally, pressing F4 a fourth time toggles it back to a relative address (B4).

I Don't Want My Data to Just Sit There! Any Way to Make Cells Do Things to Each Other?

Excel's reason for being is to have the cells and their contents interact with each other. It's not only math but also built-in functions that do so many calculations that your typical desktop calculator would hide in a drawer out of pure jealousy.

Why Bother with Parentheses?

Parentheses serve two purposes in a formula. The first is to contain the values required by a function; the second is to tell Excel in which order to make calculations. Calculations within the parentheses take place first. That way you can ensure that the answer is calculated properly.

For calculations, it never helps to be too precise. For example:

1. In your worksheet, find a cell and type in **=24-4*3**.
2. In the next cell below type **=24-(4*3)**.
3. In the next cell below type **=(24-4)*3**.

The results in the first two cells are the same, 12. In the last cell, the result is 60, despite the same numbers being used. That's because the parentheses changed the order of the computation.

Excel normally evaluates equations from left to right, reading along as it goes. However, multiplication and division are higher priorities for Excel than addition and subtraction. So in the first example, =24-4*3, the 4*3 calculation is done first.

Now I probably explained that well and accurately, but my point here is that even I forget which things come first. I normally force the operation by using parentheses as shown in examples 2 and 3. So even though I know that examples 1 and 2 are identical, I'll still use the parentheses to force the issue.

Bottom line: To ensure that the equations evaluate as you want, make liberal use of parentheses. What you put in the parentheses happens first.

I Need Help with a Long, Complex, Boring Formula!

My best advice is to keep your formulas as small as possible. The more you can separate things and keep from having a formula that wraps itself twice in the Formula bar, the more you can split everything off into smaller bits.

Example 1: This Could Work Better in a Table Elsewhere!

I once had a formula in a travel expense report that had me input all my receipts into one cell, on one line. The formula looked like this:

=6.22+3.90+1.25+6.5+12.5+1.98+12.50+3.75+10.25+2.88+9.66

Don't ever do this yourself! It is *not* a formula. No, that looks like a list to me, and lists belong in separate cells, arranged either horizontally or, more often, vertically.

The solution here was to create elsewhere on the worksheet the same numbers but in a column with each value in its own cell, as shown in Figure 10.13. That way, the thing can be looked at "from a distance," and improper values can be replaced by editing a single cell instead of a foot-long formula sentence.

The total from those cells can then be used in whatever other formula you want or displayed in a single cell.

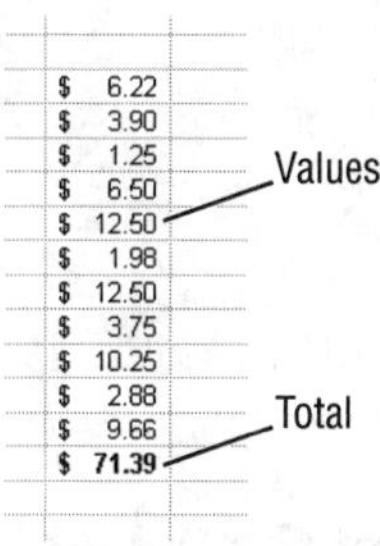

FIGURE 10.13
A small table elsewhere instead of a long formula

EXAMPLE 2: THE FORMULA IS JUST LONG AND THERE'S NOTHING I CAN DO ABOUT IT!

Wrong! Formulas can *always* be broken up. Consider the following:

=A15+A22-(C3+C4+C7)

Granted, this formula isn't that long. Even so, it can be made shorter.

First, consider creating a cell where you add the contents of A15 and A22.

Second, create a cell where C3, C4, and C7 are added.

Finally, build the formula based on those two cells instead of the five original cells: =E14-E15.

If you name the cells properly (as covered earlier in this chapter), you'll end up with not only a smaller, more manageable function but a readable one as well: =Income-Expenses.

Where Are the Functions, Because I Can't Remember Them?

The easiest way to get at the numerous functions is to click the Function (Fx) button, located on the Formula bar in Excel 2003/XP or found on the Standard toolbar in Excel 2000. This displays the Insert Function dialog box in Excel 2003/XP (shown in Figure 10.14) or the Paste Function dialog box in Excel 2000. Regardless of the visual differences, the dialog boxes do essentially the same thing: Stick a function into the current cell.

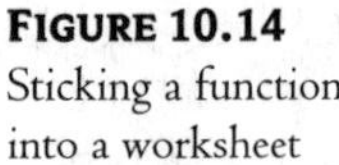

FIGURE 10.14
Sticking a function into a worksheet

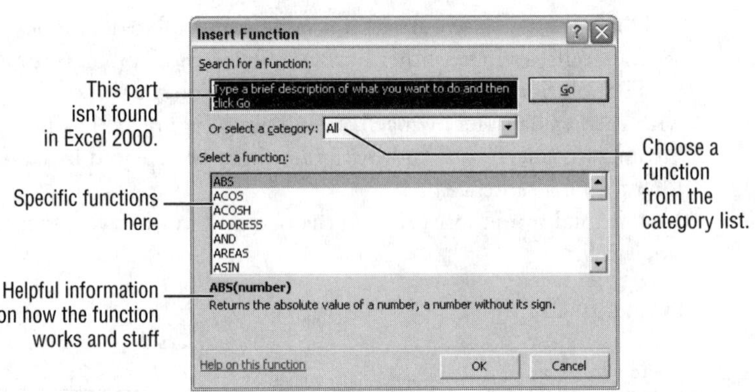

NOTE *Recently used functions are kept in the Formula bar's Name box. After you press = in a cell, the Name box lists the most recently used functions. To see the list, click the down arrow to the right of the Name box.*

I Can Remember the Formulas but Not the Dajoobies That Go in the Parentheses.

Ooo! Me too! I can never remember in the ROUND statement whether the value or the number of digits comes first. Very annoying. In Excel 2003/XP, the program will prompt you; but for Excel 2000 users, here's a solution:

1. Select the cell into which you plan on burying the formula.
2. Click the Formula bar. This trick works only if you type the function's name into the Formula bar, not into the cell directly.
3. Type = and the function's name, such as =ROUND.
4. Press Ctrl+Shift+A.

   Imagine in your head that Ctrl+Shift+A is the keyboard shortcut for "Automatically give me the guts!" You'll see the formula's secret bits displayed, as shown in Figure 10.15.
5. Enter the function's dajoobies. You can manually type them in or click a cell or range of cells to place their references into the function. Do whatever is necessary to complete the function.

Remember that this trick works only when you're entering the function directly into the Formula bar.

Excel 2003/XP users don't really need to bother with this trick; as you enter the function into a cell, a "hint" bubble appears below the function to remind you of the dajoobies.

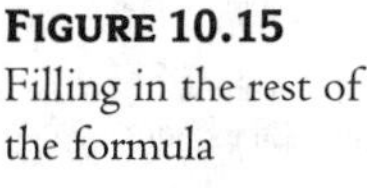

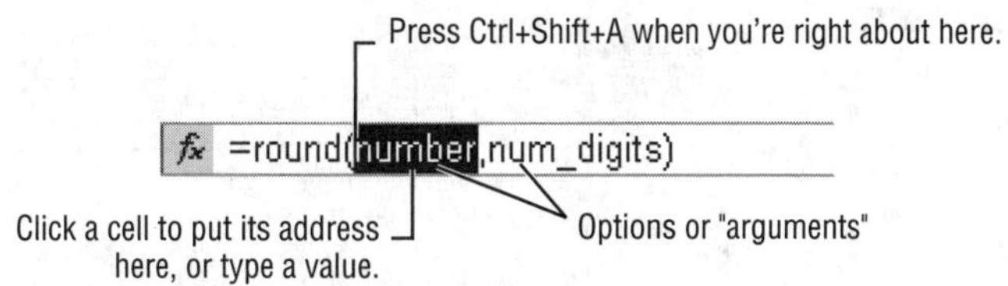

Press Ctrl+Shift+A when you're right about here.
=round(number,num_digits)
Click a cell to put its address here, or type a value.
Options or "arguments"

FIGURE 10.15
Filling in the rest of the formula

What Does the F9 Key Do in a Formula?

If you press the F9 key while the cursor is blinking in the Formula bar, then Excel translates the function displayed there to show the result. Now that's kind of a silly thing to do, since the cell in the worksheet already displays the result. But you can use the F9 key to evaluate portions of a formula or function to help you troubleshoot.

For example, suppose you have the following formula in the Formula bar:

=D4+D5+E4+E5+E6

To find out what the value of cells D5 and E4 calculates out to, follow these steps:

1. Select the portion of the Formula bar you want to evaluate. So you would select D5+E4.
2. Press F9. The text D5+E4 in the Formula bar will change to represent the total of those two cells—say, 42.
3. Press Esc to return to your formula. If you don't press Esc, then the 42 becomes part of the equation and not D5+E4.

This is a great trick to check on the values in various cells, especially when the worksheet is large and you cannot see the entire thing at once.

How Can I Get the Function Calculation Thing Back?

One of the joys of choosing functions from the Insert Function or Paste Function dialog box is that Excel presents you with one of those handy function input dialog boxy things, such as the one shown in Figure 10.16. These are useful for entering values or cells into a function—a wonderful tool.

So if you're lingering in the middle of a function and need the helper dialog box, click the Function button. You must have a function name in the cell for this to work. The cell must start with =, then a function name, and then whatever. Once that minimum is met, you can click the Function button and you'll see the dialog box displayed, similar to Figure 10.16 but specific to your function.

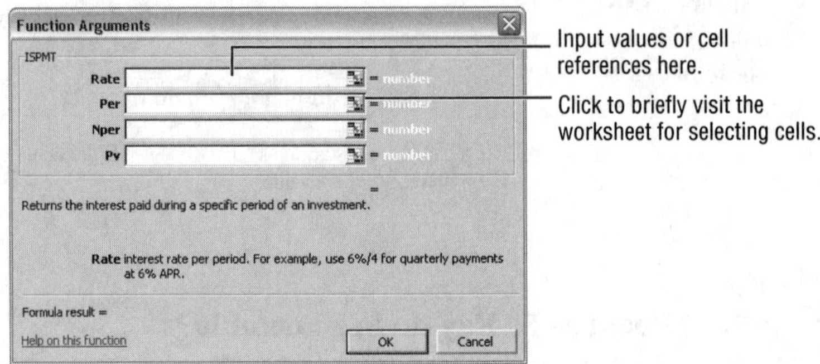

FIGURE 10.16
The calculation thing

The Common "I Am Stupid" List of Excel Error Messages

Anyone using Excel for any length of time should be familiar with the common Excel error messages. I've written them down below mostly for their amusement value.

How Can I Fix the ###### Error?

This is the easiest Excel error to fix, mostly because it's not really an error. The ### (nah-nah) things appear to indicate that the value for the cell is just too dern wide to display.

The immediate solution is to make the cell wider, which is the same thing as making the entire column wider: Position the mouse between the current column heading and the next, such as between the C and D column headings, as shown back in Figure 10.8, then double-click. That widens the column (C in the figure) to be as wide as the widest cell needs to be.

Another solution is to display the number in a different format—if that works. By removing the $ or the trailing .00, you can often squeeze a number into a cell without resizing:

1. Click to select the cell.
2. Press Ctrl+1 to bring up the Format Cells dialog box.
3. In the Number tab, choose General.
4. Click OK.

Sometimes this may render the number in *scientific notation,* that is, some monster like 1.23E+10. That's the way scientists fill in their tax forms, and while it amusingly drives the IRS bonkers, it's just not the way humans are used to seeing numbers portrayed.

What Does #REF! Mean?

The referee has obviously made a bad call: One team is full of anger and resentment, while the other is walking around innocently trying not to give away that they agree it was a bad call.

In Excel, #REF! in a cell means that you've referred to a cell that doesn't exist or has been deleted. This usually crops up after a copy or cut-and-paste operation, so be on the lookout. If you get a #REF!, then immediately undo the operation with Ctrl+Z and rethink your strategy.

Where Do You Get Off Calling Me That #NAME?

This is a simple error to fix: For some reason you typed in a word that is not the name of a cell, the cell's address, or the name of a function. No, it's a #NAME? name.

Most often you see #NAME? when you mistype a function's name. For example, instead of typing in SQRT to do the square root, you type in SQR (which is the name of the square root command in the BASIC language). So

=SQR(4)

gets you a #NAME? error, whereas:

=SQRT(4)

gets you 2.

Or it could be that you're referring to a named cell and mistyped the name. Use the Insert ➤ Name ➤ Paste command in that case, so that you are inserting a properly named cell or series of cells.

How Can I Fix a #VALUE! Error?

Typically the #VALUE! thing happens because you've attempted to do math on a cell that contains text.

But I Really Do Need to Divide by Zero!

Computers just cannot abide to divide anything by zero. I know that in algebra class, you (just like me) probably thought that dividing by zero was no big deal. After all, if you take 3 and divide it by nothing, you get 3, right? In my brain, dividing by zero is the same thing as not dividing at all. But in Excel's brain, it's the ugly #DIV/0! error.

There are two ways to handle #DIV/0! The first is to ensure that the denominator (the value on the bottom) is never zero. The second is to create an exception for the case when the value ends up being zero anyway.

For example, suppose you're tabulating results from a survey. You get the answers to questions and then determine the percentages. Say a number of people answer the question, "Do you like chocolate ice cream?" You present the results in a worksheet, as shown in Figure 10.17.

FIGURE 10.17
The sample survey where a dreadful and potential #DIV/0! error lurks in waiting

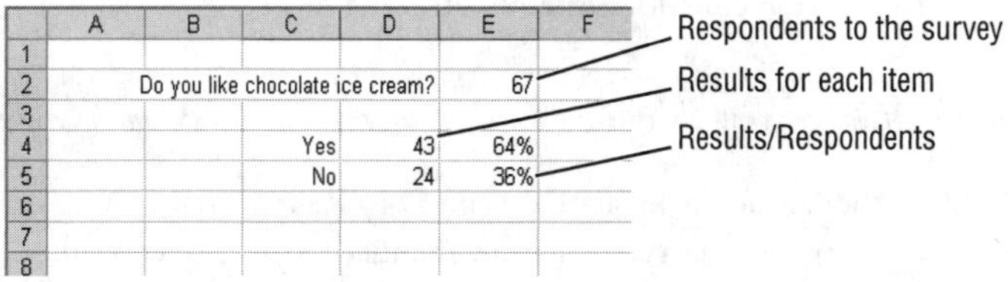

	A	B	C	D	E	F
1						
2		Do you like chocolate ice cream?			67	
3						
4			Yes	43	64%	
5			No	24	36%	
6						
7						
8						

Respondents to the survey
Results for each item
Results/Respondents

Here's how to create such a worksheet, complete with a safety check for dividing by zero:

1. Into cell D2 type **Do you like chocolate ice cream?**
2. Click the Right Align button on the Formatting toolbar to right-align the cell's text contents.
3. Name cell E2 "Respondents." The quickest way to do this is to select cell E2 and then type **Respondents** into the Name box on the Formula bar.
4. Into cell C4 type **Yes**.
5. Into cell C5 type **No**.

The number of respondents to the survey will go in cell E2. The number answering Yes goes into cell D4; the No response goes into cell D5. The formula to calculate the percentages goes into cells E4 and E5.

A percentage is calculated using the old "is over of" formula. In this case, what percentage *is* cell D4 *of* cell E2? Or use D4/E2 to calculate the percentage:

1. Into cell E4, type **=D4/E2** and press Enter.

   Oh, crap. There's the #DIV/0! thing. Now the way to avoid it, obviously, is to input some values. But it looks ugly without values, like something is wrong. To avoid some snoopy, non-spreadsheet person from thinking you've screwed up, you can fix the formula so that #DIV/0! doesn't show up.
2. Into cell E4 type **=IF(**. Don't forget that first paren!
3. Click the Function button. Now you can use the dajoobie to fill in the complex and often-confusing IF function's arguments. The Logical_test is, "What if the value of cell E2 is zero?" Yes, that's a logical test!
4. At the end of the Logical_test line, click the Go to Worksheet button. The dajoobie reduces in size to a Function Arguments dialog box.
5. Click cell E2. The word *Respondents* appears in the Function Arguments dialog box. Good. That's the name of the cell.
6. Type **=0**. So the Logical_test is "Respondents equals zero" or Respondents=0.
7. Click the Return to Dajoobie button.
8. In the Value_if_true box type **No Respondents Yet!**. This is okay: You can put text in an IF function. Remember, the result is the *contents of the cell*, not some math function.

NOTE *If you're manually entering the IF statement, then the text must be in double quotes.*

9. In the Value_if_false box, type **D4/Respondents**. You can use the buttons to select those cells, or you can type them in manually if you're careful.

So the whole logical IF statement reads, "If the value of the cell Respondents is equal to zero, then display the text 'No Respondents Yet!' in this cell. Otherwise, display the value of cell D4 divided by the value of cell Respondents."

1. Click OK, and you'll see "No Respondents Yet!" displayed because there is no data in the worksheet at cell E2.
2. Drag to fill cell E5 with cell E4. Drag the cell selector by its lower-right corner, down just one notch. That copies the same IF formula into cell E5. (Also, because the cell reference is relative to D4, the new formula in cell E5 properly references cell D5. However because cell E2 is named, it remains constant in both functions.)
3. Now fill in the data: Put 67 into cell E2. And you see that with a value there, both cells E4 and E5 fill in with values (not errors).
4. Put 43 into cell D4.
5. Put 24 into cell D5. And now your worksheet should look like Figure 10.17.

Plopping an Excel Thing into a Word Thing

Ah, the big trick you've been waiting for! Because Excel is so good at putting information into tables, you've probably been dying to do just that: Slap an Excel worksheet—or at least the good part of one—right there into a Word document. It's not that hard, but as you might suspect, there are several ways to do it.

At What Point Do I Give Up and Use Excel instead of Word's Table Feature?

One-word answer: math. Any time the table in Word requires math, switch over to Excel and do the table in there. For tables of text or smaller tables, using Word's table feature is fine. But also keep in mind that for tables of text, Excel has more powerful sorting features than Word does.

Another key thing people forget is simply that this trick is possible. I don't know how many meetings I've sat through where they handed out two sets of sheets, one the written report in Word and the other a random stapling of Excel worksheets. I ended up flipping back and forth between the two sets of sheets, agonizing that if only the poor slob would have bought this book, he would have saved everyone in the meeting a lot of time and paper-shuffling noise.

If I Need to Put a Worksheet into Word, Do I Start in Word or Excel?

Either way works fine. If you're clever, you'll start in Word and stay there. Otherwise, you can move data back and forth between the programs at any time. The following sections explain the details.

Building an Excel Worksheet from within Word

The secret to building an Excel worksheet in Word was covered in Chapter 7, "The Tough Stuff: From Labels to Tables." The secret is to click the Insert Worksheet button, which creates a worksheet of a given size inside the Word document. An example of that is shown in Figure 7.17.

Note that although you began in Word, since you inserted the Excel worksheet, the toolbars and keyboard commands all reflect Excel and not Word. Clicking inside or outside the Excel worksheet area is what switches you back and forth between the two programs.

Nerdily speaking, the Excel worksheet inside a Word document is *embedded.*

You can also insert an Excel worksheet by using the Insert ➤ Object command and then choosing "Microsoft Excel Worksheet" from the Object dialog box.

Copying Part of a Worksheet from Excel into Word

The other way to get an Excel thing into a Word thing is to start Excel by itself as opposed to starting Excel in Word. (In fact, it's not very common to use the embedded type of worksheet covered in the previous section.) Supposing that you have a table in Excel that you want to shove into a Word document, here's how it's done:

1. Select the cells you want to copy. If the table has row and column headings, be sure to select them as well.
2. Press Ctrl+C to copy. Or you can use any of the other, numerous Copy commands.
3. Switch to Word. Or start Word if it's not started already.
4. Paste. And there's the table.

This variation, where the simple table is copied and pasted, basically creates a table in Word and copies the information from Excel into that Word table.

You'll notice that only data is copied; formulas and functions do not survive the simple copy/paste operation. So where your table may have originally contained complex formulas or relationships between the various cells, only the visible contents of the cells are copied into Word. If you want to retain the relationships, you have to do more than a simple copy and paste.

Copying a Live Worksheet from Excel into Word

Pasting a live table from Excel into Word is actually Word's responsibility. Instead of the standard Paste command, you have to use SuperPaste. Here's how:

1. Copy the table in Excel.
2. Switch to Word.

NOTE *Press Alt+Tab to switch between two running programs in Windows.*

3. Choose File ➤ Paste Special. The Paste Special dialog box appears, as shown in Figure 10.18.
4. Choose "Microsoft Excel Worksheet Object" from the list.

NOTE *If this doesn't work at first, then return to Excel and reselect the table, copy it, and then return to Word.*

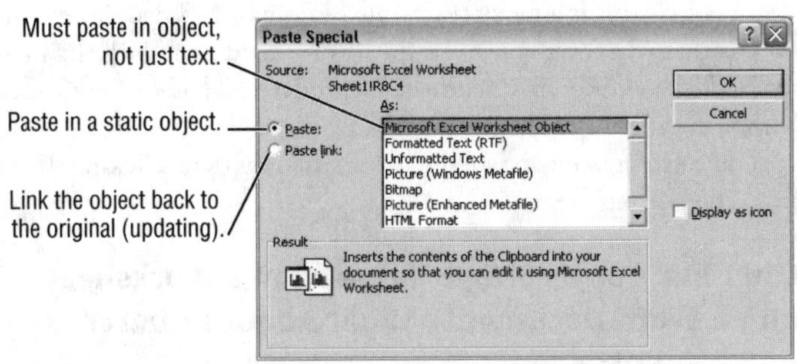

FIGURE 10.18 More than just pasting, it's special pasting.

And the table appears, but it is in fact an embedded Excel object, just as you would have gotten had you clicked the Insert Excel Worksheet button: Click inside the object to visit Excel; click outside to revisit Word.

The difference between this and regular pasting is, first, that you end up with a real Excel object and not a simple Word table. Second, the cells retain all their Excel formulas and functions and formatting. If you double-click inside the embedded worksheet, you can edit and modify the table just as if you were in Excel.

WHAT'S "PASTE LINK"?

You may notice the "Paste Link" option in the Paste Special dialog box. That's yet another way to paste in an Excel worksheet object. In this case, the embedded worksheet is actually *the same thing* as the original document you copied from. Here's how that works:

1. Copy a table from your Excel worksheet. For example, copy the Chocolate Ice Cream survey table.
2. Switch to Word and choose Edit ➤ Paste Special.
3. Select "Microsoft Excel Worksheet Object" from the list.
4. Click to select "Paste Link."
5. Click OK.

So far, things look as you would expect; you've pasted in an Excel worksheet object that is really like a tiny copy of the original worksheet. Because you selected "Paste Link," however, it is not a copy: It is the original.

1. Return to Excel.
2. Change the Yes responses in cell D4 to 1.
3. Change the No responses in cell D5 to 66.
4. Return to Word. And the results have changed there as well. This wouldn't happen otherwise, but you embedded a *linked* worksheet. So the information from it will always be reflected in both the Word and original Excel documents.

Of course this is a fancy trick, but I know of few people who actually use it. One potential drawback is that whenever you open the Word document with the link in it, it will ask you if you want to check the workbook document for updates. That's a minor inconvenience to some and a major bother to others.

You can manually update the linked item by right-clicking the table and choosing "Update Link" from the pop-up menu.

Can I Just Copy a Single Value from a Worksheet into a Word Document? What About a Chart?

Sure. It works the same as copying a whole table of cells, as discussed in the previous sections. You're just copying a single-cell table in this case.

Charts copy over from Excel into Word just as portions of a worksheet do, as described in the previous sections. The only difference for pasting in chart objects is that you'll choose "Microsoft Excel Chart Object" from the Paste Special dialog box instead of choosing the worksheet object.

Chapter 11

It's Super Dooper Grid Time!

LOOK! UP IN THE sky! It's a cell! It's a row! It's a column! It's a grid!

No, it's *super grid.* And it's the ability of Excel to do wondrous and strange things with the grid, beyond the normal cell-block approach to listing numbers and labeling them as "expenses this" and "income that." Yawn!

Beyond basic worksheet manipulation, this chapter explains a bit more about how to use Excel as a database. It's not as primitive as you might think. Excel can do amazing things with lists and tables (and without any math). Rounding that out is a visit to Bizarreland and the topic of the PivotTable, which most beginner books avoid the way Yuppies dodge trick-or-treaters. It's not that terrible, but not really that useful either.

All of it is covered here under the general guise of Super Dooper Grid tricks—more than what you would expect from your parents' spreadsheet.

- Managing worksheets in a workbook
- Moving data and worksheets between workbooks
- Exploring some automatic and automated things Excel can do
- Working with lists and tables
- Moving information between Excel, Word, and Outlook
- Sorting out the various database finding and sorting functions for tables
- Exploring the confusing PivotTable

Why Bother with the Extra Worksheets?

Bringing up the notion of "extra worksheets" summons the awful word combination "extra work." But it doesn't have to be that way. Multiple sheets are what makes a workbook document a workbook and not a single-worksheet document. Consider the extra sheets as bonuses, handy things to have, optional—or just ignore them.

Do you need them? Of course not! If all your stuff fits on one worksheet, great. If it all fits on the visible screen, even better. Worksheets are huge, so it seems tough to justify using more than one. However, I often find myself putting stuff into the extra worksheets.

For example, I may put all the main information or a summary on Sheet1, but then I use the other sheets to show raw data and how it was manipulated. That way, Sheet1 is kept clean and, if you plan things right, will all print on one sheet of paper.

Another example is keeping separate but related reports on each sheet. For instance, inflows on Sheet2, checks written on Sheet3, details on Sheet4.

Worksheets can also help add a third dimension to your tables. For example, Sheet1 could be data from 2001, Sheet2 from 2002, Sheet3 from 2003, and so on. Each worksheet is the same but contains data from different years.

Oh, the possibilities are endless! Just be thankful that there are extra worksheets. The following sections tell you how to mess with them.

Do I Have to Put Up with Sheet1 As a Name?

Absolutely not! Sheet1 is a dull, insipid name implying all that is bad with socialism. You can name your sheets anything! To wit:

1. Right-click a sheet's tab. Refer to Figure 11.1, not because it's necessary to do so, but just because I like the figure and need to put it on this page somewhere.
2. Choose Rename from the pop-up menu.
3. Type in a new name. Be short. Brief. Descriptive. Spaces are okay, but it's best not to use them as that can complicate formulas that cross between the sheets. (That sounds funky, but keep reading and you'll find out what I mean.)
4. Press Enter.

And you can always rename the sheets back.

I like to keep financial data and several reports all in one workbook with each worksheet labeled as a year. For the first year, I renamed Sheet1 to 2001. Then Sheet2 was renamed to 2002. Now I'm inserting new sheets and naming them for each year as it comes—yet another way to use the basic worksheet motif in Excel to help organize data.

The only problem you may run into when renaming sheets is external references to your sheets. For example, if another workbook or even a Word document references your worksheet, then changing the name may break the link. Therefore, if you're going to rename the sheets, do it first, before you enter any information.

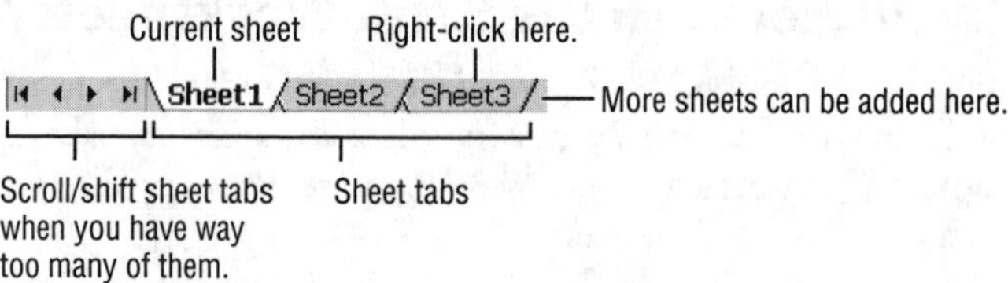

FIGURE 11.1
All the sheet you need to know

Quick Sheet Tricks

I'm not certain how nifty-keen-o these tricks are, though I do use them. After right-clicking a sheet tab, you get the pop-up menu shown nearby. At that point, pressing the first letter of any command immediately selects that command. To wit:

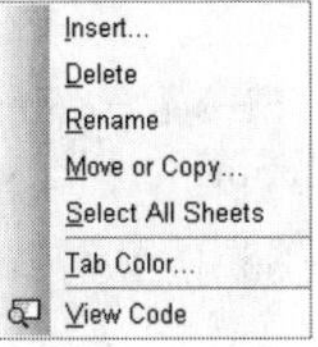

I Insert a new sheet, chart, macro, or whatever.

D Delete the current sheet.

R Rename the current sheet.

M Move or copy sheets to another workbook.

S Select all the sheets (for moving, copying, deleting).

T Change the sheet(s) tab color (Excel 2003/XP only).

V View the code for a Macro tab.

Must a Sheet Have a Name?

Yes, but the name could be a single space or a set of underlines. That way, for example, if you wanted the sheet tabs to be colors instead of looking like text, you can do this:

1. Right-click the tab you want to un-name.
2. Choose Rename from the pop-up menu.
3. Type a space for the new name. Or a single underline or a period—some unobtrusive character.
4. Press Enter to lock in the new name.
5. In Excel 2003/XP, right-click the tab and choose "Tab Color" from the pop-up menu. (Yes, Excel 2000 lacks this feature. Boo-hoo.)
6. Pick a color and click OK. The tab changes to that color—but only the bottom part. To see the tab filled with a color, you have to switch to the other sheet.

So, bottom line: Sheets must have names, but because you can rename a sheet with "space" as the name, it looks like they're not named. Also be aware that each tab needs a unique name; you cannot rename all the tabs to "space."

I Want My Sheet Color to Match the Tab's Color.

Okay. Say you have a light pink tab (created in the previous section) and want the entire sheet to be light pink. You can do that by selecting all the cells in the data region and filling them with the same color:

1. Press Ctrl+Home.
2. Press Shift+Ctrl+End. This selects all the cells in your worksheet's data region. If you want to select more than that, continue dragging the selector down and to the right.
3. Click the Fill Color icon on the Formatting toolbar.
4. Choose a color to fill all those cells, preferably the same background color as the sheet's tab.

Another way to do this would be to create a graphics file on disk the same color as the tab color. Then use the Format ➤ Sheet ➤ Background command to fill the worksheet's background with that color. Unlike using the Fill Color icon, that retains the worksheet's grid.

I Need Only One Worksheet, so Can I Kill Off the Excess?

Certainly:

1. Right-click the tab of the worksheet that offends you.
2. Choose Delete from the pop-up menu. Excel stupidly asks if you really want to delete the sheet, which somehow may contain data even though you know darn well that the thing is empty.
3. Click the Delete button, and the sheet is gone!

NOTE *You can use the Ctrl key to click and select multiple sheets for group deletion: Press and hold the keyboard's Ctrl key as you click, click, click several sheets. Then right-click any selected sheet and continue with Step 2 above.*

The Edit ➤ Delete Sheet command also does the job of zapping a worksheet to kingdom come.

I Don't Want Anyone Else to See the Sheet So That My Dumb Employees Won't Mess with the Data There

You can hide any sheet in the workbook. In fact, I recommend first renaming the sheet with another reference, which further helps throw naïve Excel users off the trail. Then to hide the worksheet:

1. Click to select the worksheet you want to conceal. It cannot be the only sheet in the workbook; the workbook must have at least two sheets and you must keep one sheet unhidden.
2. Choose Format ➤ Sheet Hide, and it's gone!

Actually, the sheet is still there and data on the sheet can still be referenced. But it's not visible, and unsuspecting Excel users will never know.

To get all the hidden sheets back, choose Format ➤ Sheet ➤ Unhide. An Unhide dialog box appears, and you can choose which sheet to unhide. Click the OK button, and the sheet falls back into the room like a drunken party guest stumbling out of a coat closet.

Must. Have. More. Sheets.

To add another sheet, choose Insert ➤ Worksheet or press Shift+F11. Thwoop! There it is! You can also quickly add a chart by choosing Insert ➤ Chart or pressing the F11 key.

If you need to use a template or macro, then you have to summon the Insert dialog box. Follow these steps:

1. Right-click any sheet tab.
2. Choose Insert from the pop-up menu. The Insert dialog box appears, with icons for inserting generic worksheets and charts, but also listing any templates you may have created.
3. Select what you want to add.
4. Click the OK button.

You'll notice that the sheets (or tabs) seem to be inserted in a rather haphazard manner. That's no problem. You can use the mouse to drag any tab to any position. Or you can Ctrl+click to select a group of tabs and move them as a cluster.

Adding a New Worksheet or Chart, and Changing the Sheets

Bringing in the sheets, bringing in the sheets. For some reason, if you need a new sheet or tab in Excel, the F11 key is the one to drool over. And I'll throw in a quickie on how to move from worksheet to worksheet.

F11 Stick a new chart into the workbook.

Shift+F11 Add a new worksheet into the workbook.

Alt+F11 Prepare to build a dialog in the ominous and scary Microsoft Visual Basic Editor.

Ctrl+F11 Add a new macro worksheet.

Ctrl+PgUp and Ctrl+PgDn Use these to shuffle between the sheets.

Why Would I Want to Share This Sheet with Another Workbook?

Sometimes sheets are just so brilliant that they must be shared. For example, I copy a sheet from my tracking workbook into a year-end financial workbook. It's much easier than copying and pasting the entire worksheet—or even that copy-paste-link embedding nonsense. Here's how:

1. Open the other workbook, the one into which you want to copy a sheet (or chart).
2. Right-click the tab of your most beloved worksheet, the one you want to share with another workbook.
3. Choose Move or Copy from the pop-up menu. The Move or Copy dialog box appears.

4. Select the destination workbook from the "To Book" drop-down list.
5. Choose "(Move to End)" from the Before sheet list.
6. Click to put a check mark by "Create a Copy."
7. Click OK, and the sheet is copied over to the other workbook.

The worksheet retains the same tab name, so if there is a duplicate you'll see something dumb like "Sheet1(2)" displayed. Refer elsewhere in this chapter for information on renaming the sheet to something less insipid.

Any Way to Get Data from Another Worksheet into This One?

You can reference data in other sheets in a workbook just as you can reference cells in the same worksheet. It looks something like this:

```
='Sheet2'!$A$1
```

This refers to cell A1 over on Sheet2. If the worksheet was named Prince Harry, then you'd see

```
='Prince Harry'!$A$1
```

The nifty thing here is that all that's required of you is to recognize the format: sheet name in single quotes, exclamation point, cell reference. You never really have to type that exact thing in, just copy and paste the cells. To keep the reference linked to the other cell, use Edit ➤ Paste Special and be sure to choose the Link option. Or in Excel 2003/XP, click the Paste Options button and choose "Link Cells" from the pop-up menu.

There's one more doohickey that can appear here: If you're linking to a cell in another worksheet, then the format is

```
=[book1.xls]Sheet1!$A$1
```

The filename appears first, in square brackets. That links the cell back to the original worksheet in the original workbook document.

Okay. Enough of that nonsense for now.

Letting Excel Do the Work for You

Obviously, Excel is going to do the work for you; otherwise, you would have saved a few hundred dollars and bought an abacus instead of a computer. In addition to doing math, Excel recognizes that many elements in a worksheet are often the same: perhaps not the contents or values of the worksheet as much as common conventions, such as the days of the week or months of the year. These and other things appear in most common worksheets, and Excel has a bushel of tricks to help you enter such common things.

If I Have to Type Monday, Tuesday, Wednesday Again, I'm Going to Pull Out My Hair!

Save your hair and follow these steps:

1. Type a day of the week into a cell. It can be any day. And you can type the full day, such as **Monday**, or type the abbreviation **Mon**.
2. Reselect that cell.
3. Drag down or to the right to fill in a series of days. Figure 11.2 shows the sweet spot.

FIGURE 11.2 The sweet spot for dragging a series

4. Release the mouse button when you're done.

Yes, you can drag in any direction, though down or to the right is most common. And you can drag more than seven cells.

In Excel 2003/XP, after you drag to fill a series, the AutoFill Options icon appears in the worksheet. Pointing the mouse at this icon produces a menu button that produces a menu with some options. One of them is "Fill Weekdays," which allows you to fill only Monday through Friday in your worksheet.

Can the Same Trick Work with Months or Quarters?

Yes: Start with any month, January through December, or use the month's three-letter abbreviation, Jan through Dec. Or for quarters, start with Q1 and then drag away; Excel automatically does the Q2, Q3, Q4 thing for you, repeating it if necessary.

How Can I Do a Series of Years?

Alas, there is no way to tell Excel which value is a year and which is just a number. So the best way to create such a row or column of years is simply to fill a series. Here's how:

1. Type the first value into a cell—say, **1990**.
2. Use the right mouse button to drag that value to the right or down. If you use the left (normal) mouse button, then "1990" fills the series. But if you use the right mouse button, you get a pop-up menu when the button is released.
3. Choose "Fill Series" from the pop-up menu.

And the values in the selected row or column are all incremented by 1, giving you a series of years.

How about a Series That Skips by Threes?

There are two ways to do this. The first is automatic using a built-in Excel function. The second is a devious way I think you may prefer, especially if you're using the series as a basis for a table.

The Boring Excel Way

Here's how to create a series that skips by different values between the cells:

1. Select the starting cell.
2. Enter a starting value.
3. Reselect the starting cell.
4. Drag to the right or down to create a series. Use the sweet spot (Figure 11.2) to drag. The series will contain all the same number, but you're about to change that.
5. Choose Edit ➤ Fill ➤ Series. The charming and inviting Series dialog box appears, shown in Figure 11.3.
6. Choose Rows or Columns, depending on how your cells are selected.
7. Choose Linear.
8. Enter **3** into the "Step Value" box.
9. Click OK, and the cells are filled with values that bump up by three each time.

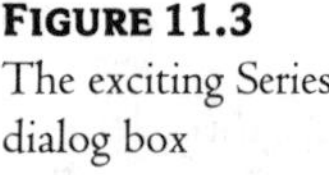

Figure 11.3
The exciting Series dialog box

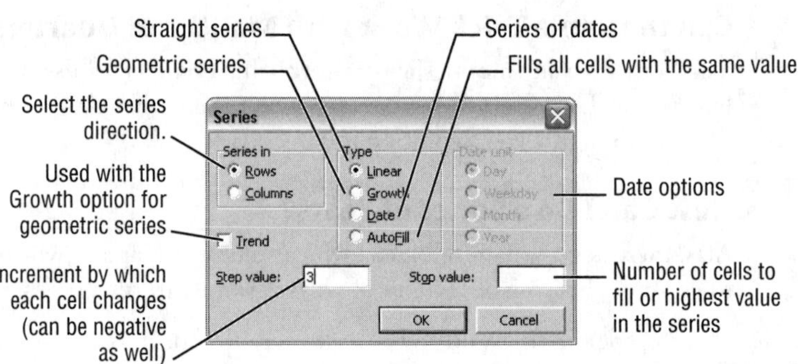

Dan's Dirty yet Completely Ethical Way to Do the Same Thing

I prefer to have a wee bit more control over my tables when I build a series. And, let's be honest, what the series represents is one of two axes in a table. So suppose you want to build a table for your movie theater that shows ticket prices versus patronage, as shown in Figure 11.4. Here's one way to do that:

1. Into cell A2 type **Patrons.**
2. Into cell B1 type **Ticket Prices.**

FIGURE 11.4
A sample table with weird incrementing axes

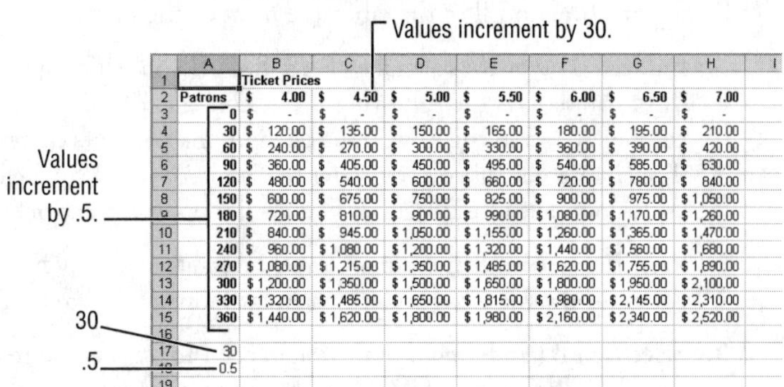

	A	B	C	D	E	F	G	H	I
1		**Ticket Prices**							
2	**Patrons**	**$ 4.00**	**$ 4.50**	**$ 5.00**	**$ 5.50**	**$ 6.00**	**$ 6.50**	**$ 7.00**	
3	**0**	$ -	$ -	$ -	$ -	$ -	$ -	$ -	
4	**30**	$ 120.00	$ 135.00	$ 150.00	$ 165.00	$ 180.00	$ 195.00	$ 210.00	
5	**60**	$ 240.00	$ 270.00	$ 300.00	$ 330.00	$ 360.00	$ 390.00	$ 420.00	
6	**90**	$ 360.00	$ 405.00	$ 450.00	$ 495.00	$ 540.00	$ 585.00	$ 630.00	
7	**120**	$ 480.00	$ 540.00	$ 600.00	$ 660.00	$ 720.00	$ 780.00	$ 840.00	
8	**150**	$ 600.00	$ 675.00	$ 750.00	$ 825.00	$ 900.00	$ 975.00	$ 1,050.00	
9	**180**	$ 720.00	$ 810.00	$ 900.00	$ 990.00	$ 1,080.00	$ 1,170.00	$ 1,260.00	
10	**210**	$ 840.00	$ 945.00	$ 1,050.00	$ 1,155.00	$ 1,260.00	$ 1,365.00	$ 1,470.00	
11	**240**	$ 960.00	$ 1,080.00	$ 1,200.00	$ 1,320.00	$ 1,440.00	$ 1,560.00	$ 1,680.00	
12	**270**	$ 1,080.00	$ 1,215.00	$ 1,350.00	$ 1,485.00	$ 1,620.00	$ 1,755.00	$ 1,890.00	
13	**300**	$ 1,200.00	$ 1,350.00	$ 1,500.00	$ 1,650.00	$ 1,800.00	$ 1,950.00	$ 2,100.00	
14	**330**	$ 1,320.00	$ 1,485.00	$ 1,650.00	$ 1,815.00	$ 1,980.00	$ 2,145.00	$ 2,310.00	
15	**360**	$ 1,440.00	$ 1,620.00	$ 1,800.00	$ 1,980.00	$ 2,160.00	$ 2,340.00	$ 2,520.00	
16									
17	30								
18	0.5								
19									

3. Into cell A3 type **0**. That's zero, not O.
4. Into cell B2 type **4**.

Now you're going to build a series of incrementing patron numbers and incrementing dollar signs to complete the two axes of the table. You'll be using Excel's formulas to create the series.

1. Into cell A4 type **=A3+30**. The formula reads, "The contents of this cell equal the contents of the above cell plus 30."
2. Press Enter.
3. Reselect cell A4 and drag down to cell A15. There is no need to fill a series here; AutoFill is in action and it automatically copies the [cell above]+30 formula down through cell A15.

Time to do the same thing with the ticket prices.

1. Select cell C2.
2. Type **=B2+.5**. That reads, "The contents of this cell equal the contents of the cell on the left plus point five." And point five is 50 cents here.
3. As you did with the column of patron numbers, drag-fill right with the ticket prices from cell C2 through cell H2. As you drag and fill, the formula [cell left]+.5 is copied to each cell, creating the series.

After creating the two series, some formatting is needed:

1. Select cells A2 through A15 and format them as bold.
2. Select cell B1 and format it as bold.
3. Select cells B2 through H2 and format them as bold and with the Currency style.

Finally, it's time to fill in the table, the meat of the matter:

1. Into cell B3 type the formula **=$A3*B$2**. If you're not familiar with absolute addressing, then this formula says the following, "The contents of this cell are equal to the value of the cell in column A and in this row, multiplied by the contents of cell 2 in this column." The $ keeps the cell reference absolute. (Refer to Chapter 10, "Why the Hell Would Anyone Other Than an Accountant Use Excel?" if you need more information.)
2. Press Enter. Notice how smart Excel is to automatically format the cell as a dollar amount. Of course, the value is zero: Zero patrons at any price is zero. Prove it:
3. Select cell B3 and drag it out through cell H3. Again you're filling a series, but in this case it's an AutoFill; the same formula is copied to each cell. Thanks to absolute referencing, the formula works out just fine.
4. With cells B3 through H3 selected, drag down to fill the entire table, from cell B3 down through cell H15. Again, the absolute reference keeps all the values properly referenced and calculated.

NOTE *If you see excessive ####s in your table, select the table (if you need to) and choose Format ➤ Column ➤ AutoFit Selection.*

At this point your table should look just like Figure 11.4, but with two minor exceptions: the values in cells A17 and A18. Those are my incrementing updating values. You see, the table you created is in a beautiful number-crunching program called Excel. There's no reason to think the table is done or even static. Now you're going to find out how flexible this system can really be:

1. Select cell A17.
2. Name the cell Pincrement; type **Pincrement** into the Name box. That's *P,* as in *Patrons, increment.*
3. Put the value **30** into cell A17.
4. Select cell A18.
5. Name the cell **Tincrement**. That's *T,* as in *Ticket prices, increment.*
6. Put the value **.5** into cell A18.

Now you're ready to modify the table, though the results will still be the same (for now):

1. Edit cell A4 so that the formula reads **=A3+Pincrement**. Replace the 30 by clicking cell A17, which inserts the name Pincrement into the formula.
2. Select cell A4 and drag-fill down through cell A15. Nothing visible should change, though the formulas are all now linked to cell A17. More on that in a few steps.

3. Edit cell C2 to read **=B2+Tincrement**. Again, replace the .5 by clicking cell A18, which inserts the name Pincrement into the formula.

4. Select cell C2 and drag-fill right through cell H2. Still there is no visible change to the table or axis. Until you:

5. Put the value **1** into cell A18. Ta-da! The table instantly updates with a new series of ticket prices. Similarly:

6. Put the value **25** into cell A17.

This goes along with some of my Excel philosophy presented in the previous chapter: As long as you can keep the values in functions separate, you'll find it easier to update and examine your worksheets. New results are easier to calculate when the values in a function can be adjusted without having to edit a formula and then refill that formula through a table.

NOTE *To quickly select a table, click to select any cell in the table and then use the key combination Ctrl+Shift+8.*

You Know, the Rows Are Numbered—Why Can't I Just Use the Row Numbers in My Worksheet?

In the Page Setup dialog box, Sheet tab, there is a setting that tells Excel to print the row and column headings, 1 through whatever and A through whatever. But it's ugly, as shown in Figure 11.5.

A better solution is to just incorporate row numbers into your worksheet's cells. The key here is the ROW function, which returns the number of the current row. At one time I thought this was a silly function, but then I did something like this:

1. Click cell B3.

2. Type =ROW(). That's the ROW() function, which returns the current row.

3. Press Enter. The value 3 appears in the cell.

FIGURE 11.5
How a worksheet prints with row and column headings

	A	B	C	D	E	F	G	H
1		**Ticket Prices**						
2	**Patrons**	**$ 4.00**	**$ 5.00**	**$ 6.00**	**$ 7.00**	**$ 8.00**	**$ 9.00**	**$ 10.00**
3	**0**	$ -	$ -	$ -	$ -	$ -	$ -	$ -
4	**25**	$ 100.00	$ 125.00	$ 150.00	$ 175.00	$ 200.00	$ 225.00	$ 250.00
5	**50**	$ 200.00	$ 250.00	$ 300.00	$ 350.00	$ 400.00	$ 450.00	$ 500.00
6	**75**	$ 300.00	$ 375.00	$ 450.00	$ 525.00	$ 600.00	$ 675.00	$ 750.00
7	**100**	$ 400.00	$ 500.00	$ 600.00	$ 700.00	$ 800.00	$ 900.00	$1,000.00
8	**125**	$ 500.00	$ 625.00	$ 750.00	$ 875.00	$1,000.00	$1,125.00	$1,250.00
9	**150**	$ 600.00	$ 750.00	$ 900.00	$1,050.00	$1,200.00	$1,350.00	$1,500.00
10	**175**	$ 700.00	$ 875.00	$1,050.00	$1,225.00	$1,400.00	$1,575.00	$1,750.00
11	**200**	$ 800.00	$1,000.00	$1,200.00	$1,400.00	$1,600.00	$1,800.00	$2,000.00
12	**225**	$ 900.00	$1,125.00	$1,350.00	$1,575.00	$1,800.00	$2,025.00	$2,250.00
13	**250**	$1,000.00	$1,250.00	$1,500.00	$1,750.00	$2,000.00	$2,250.00	$2,500.00
14	**275**	$1,100.00	$1,375.00	$1,650.00	$1,925.00	$2,200.00	$2,475.00	$2,750.00
15	**300**	$1,200.00	$1,500.00	$1,800.00	$2,100.00	$2,400.00	$2,700.00	$3,000.00
16								
17	25							
18	1							

Now, most people who build worksheets don't typically start the worksheet at cell A1. No, you want room up there for headings and titles and other fancy foof. So if you wanted to show cell B3 as row 1 instead of 3, you would do this:

1. Select cell B3.
2. Press F2 and edit the function to read **=ROW()-2**. So the function now reads, "The value of this cell is equal to the current row number, minus 2." If the row is 3, then 3 minus 2 is 1.
3. Drag to fill the cell down through cell B12. And you have a series of numbers, 1 through 10 based on the rows.

The only time this can goof up is if you insert any rows above your ROW() function cells:

1. Select cell B2.
2. Choose Insert ➤ Rows. Oops! Now the table is numbered 2 through 11. You'll need to re-edit the function to **=ROW()-3** and then drag-fill in the rest of the cells to update them as well.

So I suppose the moral of the story is not to use the ROW() function unless you're dang sure you're not going to be inserting any new rows.

NOTE *There is also a corresponding COLUMN() function that returns a numeric value representing the column the cell lives in. Column A is 1, Column B is 2, and so on.*

What's a Great Tip for Entering a Whole Range of Cells with the Same Value?

It's the miraculous Ctrl+Enter key combination. And it works like this:

1. Select a range of cells. It can be a row. It can be a column. It can be a whole swath of cells.
2. Type something into the first cell: Text. Value. Function.
3. Press Ctrl+Enter, and every selected cell is filled with that text or value or function.

Is There Any Easy Way to Stick the Current Date into a Cell?

Yes, but I'd rather ramble on about dates for a few pages.

There is a problem with the date in Excel. Do you mean the current date or today's date? So do you want the worksheet to always say "May 5, 2005" or to say whatever date it is today? Big choice.

Unlike other programs, the date in Excel is a function. That function returns a number, not a date. The number can be formatted to look like a date, but otherwise all dates in Excel are really numbers. It's grossly complex how it works, so, like for gravity and time theory, just nod your head and hope that you're talented enough to fool others into believing that you understand this crap.

Here goes:

1. Select a cell where you want the date to be displayed.
2. Type =DATE(2002,4,15). The format for the DATE formula is year, month, date.

3. Press Enter. Excel is smart enough to show the date in a date-like format, 4/15/2002, which happens to be the date my first divorce was final. The worksheet will always show that date because it's fixed. It's a number…
4. With the same cell selected, press Ctrl+1.
5. Click the Number tab.
6. Choose General from the list and click OK. 37361. That's the real date. It's a number. Scary, huh? Try this:
7. Type **100** into a cell. It can be the same cell.
8. Press Ctrl+1 and format the cell as a date. It's April 9, 1900, back when a spreadsheet was something Grandma would quilt.

Did you notice that the DATE() function disappeared, by the way? The only purpose of the DATE() function is to insert that magic number into a document. There is no record of the date kept, just the secret number. On the other hand, the NOW() function always returns the current date, no matter what day it is:

1. Edit the same cell so that its contents are **=NOW()**. And there is today's date, but…
2. Select the cell. Look in the Formula bar. It's still the NOW() function, which means that cell will always reflect the current date. Or time:
3. Press Ctrl+1.
4. Choose Time from the Category list and click OK.

And now the cell shows the current time. Or, actually, the time when you updated the cell's format. The time doesn't update automatically. You must change a cell or edit something in the worksheet to see the time updated.

NOTE *There are two keyboard shortcuts you can use to instantly input the current date and time: Ctrl+; inserts the current date as a value, and Ctrl+Shift+: inserts the current time as a value.*

Why Do I Need to Know about Goal Seek?

Goal Seek is one of those weird descriptions of something you've probably wanted to use in the past but said something like, "I wish I knew how to juggle these numbers to get the result I want." That's Goal Seek.

For example, how much would you have to earn an hour to make $51 million dollars this year? Hmmm.

1. Create a worksheet similar to the one you see in Figure 11.6. The only formula is in cell F4, which is =B4*C4*D4*E4. That's shown in Figure 11.6, in the Formula bar. Also format cells B4 and F4 for Currency.
2. Choose Tools ➤ Goal Seek. The Goal Seek dialog box appears, as shown in Figure 11.6.

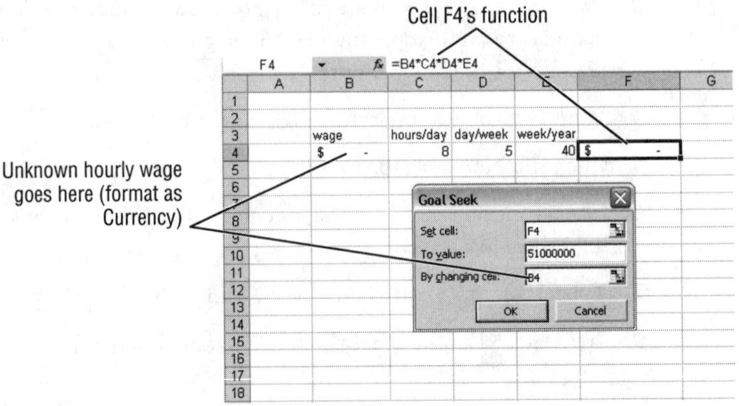

FIGURE 11.6
Working the Goal Seek thing

3. Enter **F4** into the "Set Cell" box.
4. Enter **51000000** (51 million) into the "To Value" box.
5. Enter **B4** into the "By Changing Cell" box.
6. Click OK. The values are filled in, but alas they're a little wide, so you'll have to make some adjustments.
7. Click OK to close the Goal Seek Status dialog box. Occasionally Goal Seek comes up with multiple solutions, which is possible in some situations. The Goal Seek Status dialog box helps you to weed through various solutions, should they be available.
8. Adjust the widths of columns B and F to see how much you need to make an hour. Boldly go forth and ask your manager for a raise.

I enjoy using Goal Seek because I often don't know how to phrase the mathematical question properly. Even in this example, if you take $51 million and just do division instead of multiplication, you get the results. So Goal Seek is there to help those of us who are not adept at seeing the mathematical possibilities all at once.

And thank goodness for that!

Letting Excel Be a Database of Sorts

Remember the grid thing? Excel isn't only numbers but also anything you put into a grid or table. For example, your vintage vinyl record collection or just your current CD collection. Or an inventory of all that paint in the basement, or your video discs, or video tape library. For my fellow Idahoans, it could be a list of the guns we own. Or maybe people you feel should die twisted, horrible deaths. In fact, there need not be any math associated with the thing at all. It can be just any old list.

Any Way to Import My Playlists into Excel from the Windows Media Player?

Yes, but not without extra software. As it stands, Excel cannot read the ASX file format that Media Player uses with its File ➤ Export command. The resulting file is a text file, but Excel can't make sense of it (nor should you).

The solution is to go to the Microsoft website and search for the Windows Powertoys. There is a Windows Media Player Powertoy "wizard" that converts the playlist ASX file into something that Excel can read and then display as a list database.

The address for the Windows Media Player Powertoys is

`http://www.microsoft.com/windows/windowsmedia/download/bppowertoys.aspx`

This address is current as this book goes to press.

Can I Use My Word Mail Merge List in Excel?

Absolutely. In fact, Excel is a better place to manipulate those lists because of all its fancy list features. The only weirdness here is that Excel 2000 lacks an easy way to import Word's mail merge *data source* (which is the official name).

Grabbing a Data Source in Excel 2003/XP

To grab a mail merge list you've already created in Word and stick it into Excel, follow these steps:

1. Choose Data ➤ Import External Data ➤ Import Data. The Select Data Source dialog box appears. It's focused on the My Data Sources folder, which is where Word 2003 or Word XPstores the data files created when you mail merge.
2. Choose the file from the list and click the Open button. And the Import Data dialog box appears.
3. Choose "New Worksheet." You can choose the "Existing Worksheet" option to stick the data source information into the current worksheet, though I like putting it into a new worksheet myself. (And that's work*sheet*, not work*book*.)
4. Click OK, and your imported data list appears in the worksheet.

The mail merge fields appear in the top row, in bold. In the rows below appear the data. Hey! It's a list! Now you can use Excel's powerful list management controls to work with the list. (These are covered later in this chapter.)

The Not-So-Slick Excel 2000 Way to Do This

Excel 2000 lacks the Import External Data command, so you'll have to rely on old-fashioned copy and paste to get the data source into Excel. Here's how:

1. In Word, open the data source file: Use the standard File ➤ Open command. The data source file is merely a table saved in a Word document. So the file appears in the Open dialog box like any other Word document.
2. Select the data source table: Click the mouse in the table and choose Table ➤ Select ➤ Table from the menu.

3. Copy the table: Press Ctrl+C to copy, or use any of the numerous Copy command equivalents.
4. Close Word and switch to Excel. Save the data source file, if you're asked to do so.
5. Select the cell that will be the upper-left corner of the table. I'll use cell A1 in a new worksheet.
6. Paste the table: Use Ctrl+V or any Paste command; there is no need to Paste Special here—unless you want the tables linked.

Now you can use Excel's powerful list management toys to manipulate the table. Doing so is covered later in this chapter.

How Do I Save the Data Source Back to Disk?

You cannot save it back to disk as a data source; once the Word mail merge data source has been imported into Excel, it becomes a list or table in a worksheet. At this point, you should save it to disk as a workbook with a new workbooky name and everything.

If you want to use a table or list in the worksheet as a data source, then that is possible. I recommend saving the workbook to disk in the My Data Sources folder, which is where Word will look for it the next time you do a mail merge. This discussion continues in the next section.

NOTE *The data source file in Word 2000 is nothing more than a Word document with a table, the table containing the data source. In Word 2003/XP, the data source file is an actual database file.*

How Can I Create a List in Excel and Then Use It As a Word Mail Merge Data Source?

There is no direct way to export a list in Excel into the format used by Word as a mail merge data source. While you can create a list in Excel and save it to disk, the burden then falls upon Word to properly import that data for use in a merge operation.

Start by creating the list in Excel. It can be any sheet in a workbook, such as the one shown in Figure 11.7. Note that the list must have headers, as shown in the figure. This file must be saved to disk. It doesn't have to be closed, but it must be saved to disk.

NOTE *To save yourself time, save the file in the My Data Sources folder so that Word 2003/XP can easily locate it. For Word 2000, just save the workbook in a known location.*

FIGURE 11.7
A list in a worksheet

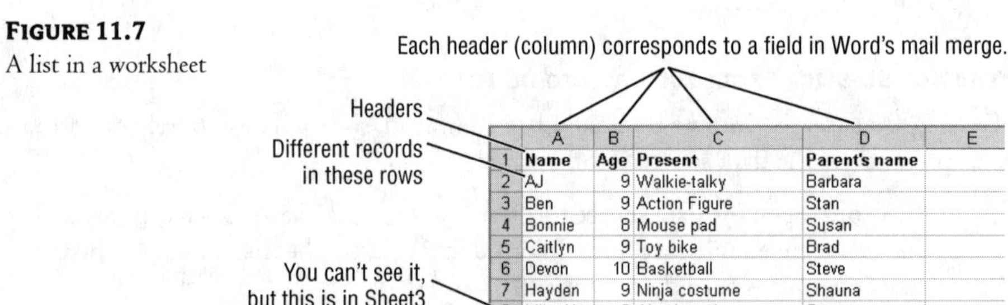

Each header (column) corresponds to a field in Word's mail merge.
Headers
Different records in these rows
You can't see it, but this is in Sheet3 of the workbook.
A
B
C
D
E
1 Name Age Present Parent's name
2 AJ 9 Walkie-talky Barbara
3 Ben 9 Action Figure Stan
4 Bonnie 8 Mouse pad Susan
5 Caitlyn 9 Toy bike Brad
6 Devon 10 Basketball Steve
7 Hayden 9 Ninja costume Shauna
8 Mike H 9 Aluminum bat Steven

Now you're ready to use the list with Word in a mail merge.

When it comes time to select the data source for the mail merge, take these steps:

1. 1 .In Word 2003/XP, Step 3 of 6 in the Mail Merge task pane, choose Browse to use an existing list. In Word 2000, Section 2 of the Mail Merge Helper, from the Get Data button menu choose "Open Data Source;" an Open/Select dialog box appears.
2. Choose "Excel Files" or "MS Excel Worksheets" from the "Files of Type" drop-down list. That narrows the selection in the dialog box to only Excel worksheets.
3. Browse to the folder containing the worksheet.
4. Select the worksheet and click the Open button.
5. If necessary, choose the sheet or the location on the sheet where the list is located, as shown in Figure 11.8. If there is no doubt, then only one item appears in the dialog box.
6. Click OK. In Word 2003/XP, you'll see the "List of Recipients" displayed in a dialog box, as shown in Figure 11.9 (which you can contrast with Figure 11.7).
7. Continue with the Mail Merge process.

   Remember that the key here is to create the merge names as the list's "header" in Excel. Then use the rows beneath to fill in the list items. Save that file to disk; then you can use it as an external source for Word's mail merging.

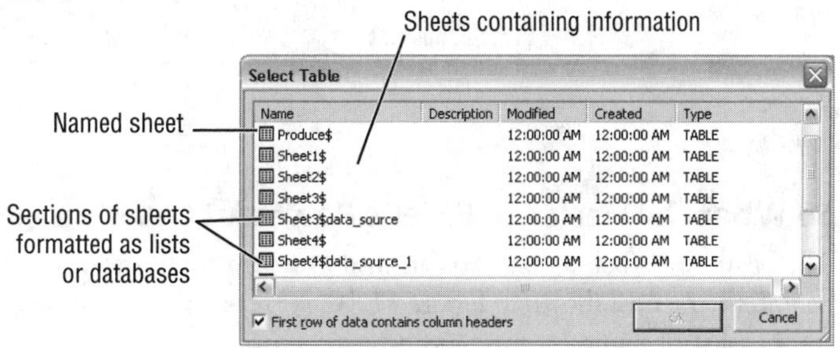

FIGURE 11.8
Word wants to know where the data can be found in the workbook.

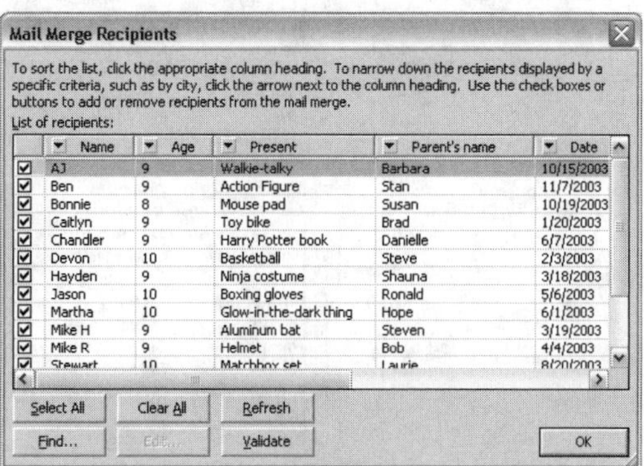

FIGURE 11.9
The final result for the data source (in Word)

What's the Difference between a Table and a List?

The most important thing is first having the list; taking the time to write down information into rows and columns, and storing that information in the computer. In Excel, that stuff becomes a list, which you can manipulate—especially if you convert the table over into a list officially. Here's how:

1. Select the table. Click any cell in the table, and then press the forgettable key combination Ctrl+Shift+8.
2. Choose Data ➤ Filter ➤ AutoFilter.

The table is now modified slightly (contrast Figure 11.7 with Figure 11.10). Each header has grown a drop-down menu button, which can be used to control the table in relation to the contents of that column.

FIGURE 11.10
The list-ified table

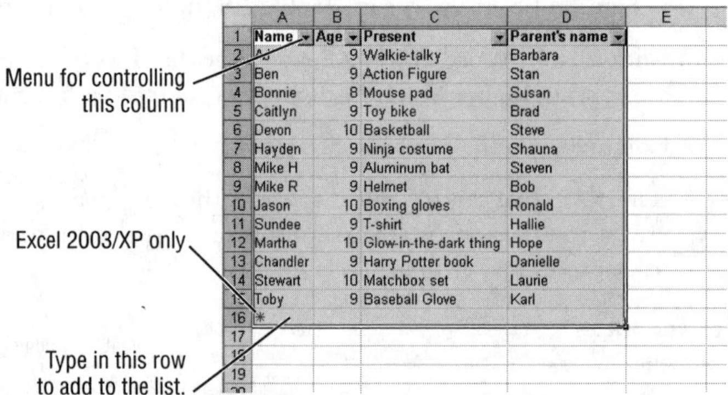

So What the Heck Are Excel's Powerful List Management Controls?

The beauty of a list is that you can easily sort through it to get to the data you want. That's the key behind the menus, shown in Figure 11.10. A better example of this can be seen in Figure 11.11, which shows a list of names, teams, and bowling scores.

FIGURE 11.11
The infamous bowling team list

	A	B	C	D	E
1	Name	Team	Average	High Game	
2	Abdulla	Rolling Rollas	167	290	
3	Ayatollah	Rolling Rollas	175	255	
4	Bill Clinton	Expresses	126	157	
5	Che	Los Locos	155	220	
6	Danny Ortega	Los Locos	167	296	
7	Fidel Castro	Los Locos	156	210	
8	Gerald Ford	Expresses	162	267	
9	Gomez Addams	Jokers	202	300	
10	Herman Munster	Jokers	162	300	
11	Jimmy Carter	Expresses	145	198	
12	Madonna	Chix with Balls	145	208	
13	Mike Brady	Jokers	175	269	
14	Mullah	Rolling Rollas	182	260	
15	Patton	Old Faders	160	240	
16	Romell	Old Faders	157	229	
17	Roseanne	Chix with Balls	155	240	
18	Wynona	Chix with Balls	157	206	
19	Yamamoto	Old Faders	161	209	
20	*				
21					

Say you want to view only the Jokers team members. To do so, click the menu button by the Team heading. The menu lists many options, as shown in Figure 11.12. Choosing the Jokers option limits the list to showing only those matching rows, as shown in Figure 11.13.

After the list is narrowed down, as shown in Figure 11.13, you can further manipulate things. For example, to find the Jokers team bowler with the highest average score, choose "Sort Descending" from the Average header's menu. (Though in this example it's easy enough to eyeball the highest score, imagine a table with hundreds of values.)

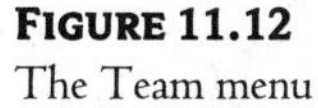

FIGURE 11.12
The Team menu

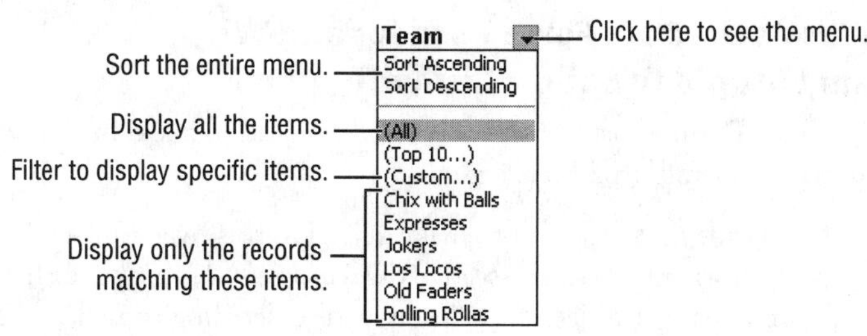

FIGURE 11.13
Manipulating the list

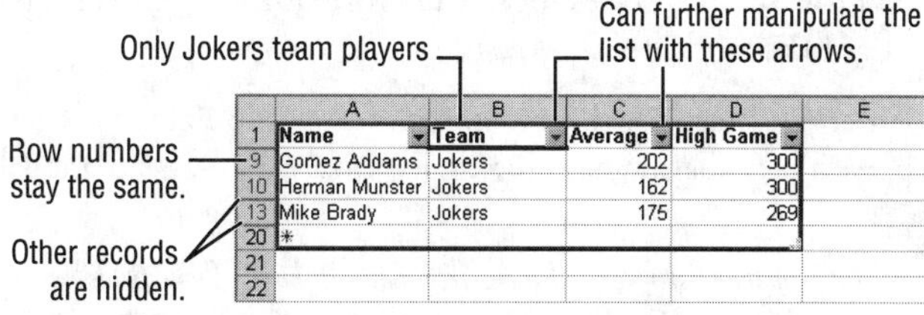

How Can I Find Duplicates in a List?

After spending all weekend entering your CD collection into an Excel database, you may wonder if you spent any time reentering the same albums. Or maybe you have two copies of one album and you *know* that you input it twice. Here's how to find out:

1. Select any cell in the table.
2. Choose Data ➤ Filter ➤ Advanced Filter. The Advanced Filter dialog box appears, plus it automatically selects your table. How nice.
3. Click to check "Unique Records Only."
4. Click OK.

Now the hard part: Any duplicate records have been hidden from view. The row the record is on isn't shown. You'll have to look carefully on the left side of the window for any missing rows (the line is thicker between the row labels).

Hiding the duplicate rows does not delete the items on those rows. To do so, you'll need to make a note of the hidden rows, then unhide the rows (choose Data ➤ Filter ➤ Show All). Finally, go back and manually delete the duplicates.

How Do I Convert the List Back into a Normal Table?

Playtime is over! Time to return to normal tablehood in Excel: Choose Data ➤ Filter ➤ AutoFilter and it's turned off.

What's the Data Form Used for and Why Am I Stupid to Build a List without It?

The Data Form is just a handy way to edit or add to a list. In fact, if you're making a list, it's just best to use the Data Form. Here's how:

1. Decide that you want to make a list. Do this over coffee and pastry, preferably at a downtown spot where you can be seen in the window. Combine your facial expressions and body language in a manner to let others know you're deciding to make a list. Do it in such an obvious way that even casual passersby would recognize your intent, despite your wearing dark glasses.
2. Create the labels at the top of each column. You must do this first. The labels must be created in a row by themselves. I typically format them bold and put them in the very tippy-top row (1) of the worksheet.
3. Enter the first record. I recommend this step because otherwise Excel gets confused and displays a bewildering warning dialog box. So go ahead and fill in the first record for your list.

NOTE *Filling in the first record also ensures that you have all the fields you want; it's amazing what new fields you may think you need as you build the table.*

4. Choose Data ➤ Form. And the input form, custom-designed for your list, appears. Shown in Figure 11.14, it makes it easy to add, remove, modify, and review all the junk in your list.

FIGURE 11.14
Using the Data Form

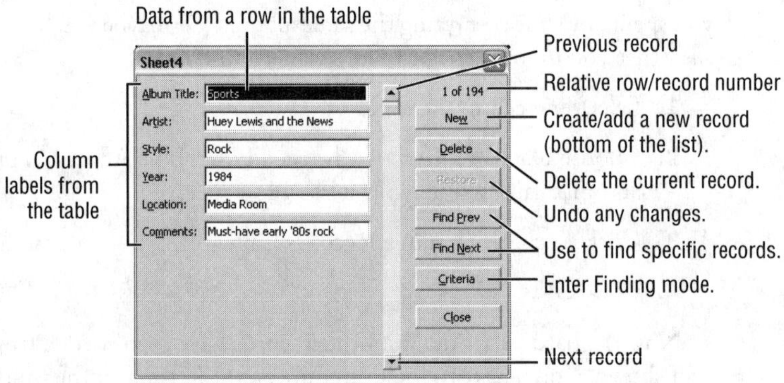

When modifying an existing record, use the New button to record the changes. Or use Restore to undo them. (The Tab key moves you between the fields.)

For information on using the Data Form to search through the records, see the next section.

I Can't Get the Data Form to Search; What's the Deal?

The secret to searching for information in a table with the Data Form is to click the Criteria button (Figure 11.14). That blanks out all the fields, allowing you to input information to match.

Say, for example, you had a table that listed record albums and you wanted to find all the albums from 1984. Here's what you would do:

1. Choose Data ➤ Form to display the data form for your table.
2. Click the Criteria button.
3. Type **1984** into the Year field.
4. Click the Find Next button.

Remember that you can also use the List mode's AutoFilter to have the list display only those records matching 1984. Refer to the section "So What the Heck Are Excel's Powerful List Management Controls?" earlier in this chapter.

Can I Select a Random Person from a List?

I use this function every time I hold a contest on my website. The list is an array of e-mail addresses. My job is to draw one name from the list on a random basis. This involves four functions and a named array of names. Sounds odd, but here's how to work it:

1. Select the entire range of names. They'll probably be in a column, for example, from cell B2 through cell B24. This range is known in Excel as an *array*.
2. Name the cells names. Click the mouse in the Name box and type a name for the array of cells. I chose the name "names" for this example.
3. Click to select some cell, such as D3. This is a calculation scratchpad cell, so it need not be on the visible part of your worksheet. I'm using D3 as an example.
4. Enter the formula =ROWS(**names**). The function returns the number of rows in the array represented by "names."
5. Press Enter.
6. Into cell D4 enter the formula =INT(RAND()*D3)+1. Ah! A lovely complex formula. I'll start in the middle and work outward:

   RAND() This generates a random number between 0 and 1—a small fraction, so it must be multiplied by a larger number, in this case:

   *D3 The random number is multiplied by the number of names in the list.

INT The resulting number needs to be rounded to its integer portion only, which (in English) lops off the fractional/decimal part of the number. So instead of 7.8121216 you get 7.

+1 This adds 1 to the number so that the random value is between 1 and the number of rows. Otherwise, the value 0 could be returned as a result.

Of course, it could be best just to carefully copy the function and understand that this is a universal way in Excel to get a random number between 1 and whatever value is held in cell D3.

Now the value displayed in cell D4 is a row number, which might be enough to determine the random person in the list. But Excel is trickier than that. Keep moving along:

1. Into cell D5 enter the formula **= INDEX(names,D4,1)**. Here we go again: The INDEX function returns the contents of a cell in a table. In this case, it's the "names" array, or list of names, not a table. The second item, D4, is the cell containing the row number, randomly drawn. And the third item is 1, because the "names" array is only one column wide.
2. Press Enter, and as if by magic, the winner's name—randomly selected—appears in cell D5. A nifty payoff for some bizarre labor.

The RAND() function is an updating function, like the NOW() function. Any time anything changes on the worksheet, the function returns a new value. So if you type **1** into a cell and press the Enter key, you'll get a new RAND() random value, a new row number, and therefore a new result from the INDEX function. Be aware of this! Remember that when you save the worksheet and open it up again, a different name appears in the cell.

What's the Best Way to Sort a Table without Converting It into a List Thing?

Choose Data ➤ Sort. This command displays the Sort dialog box, but it's also smart enough to instantly select a table in your document. If the table has headings, then the Sort dialog box uses them, as shown in Figure 11.15.

FIGURE 11.15
Sorting with the Sort dialog box

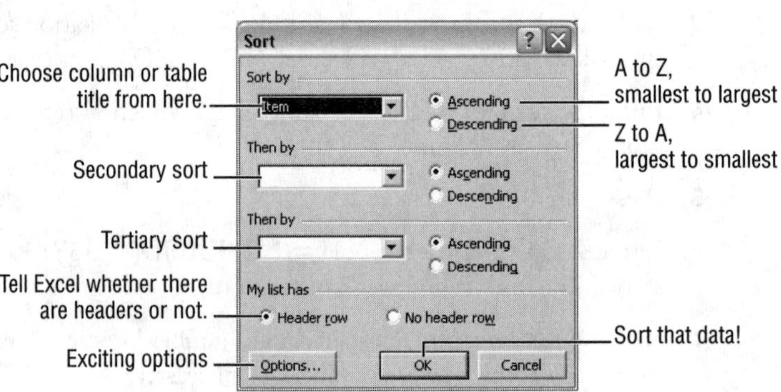

Because Excel is wise enough to see the whole table, items are sorted while the integrity of each record in the table is maintained. In other words, despite selecting only one column to sort, Excel sifts the entire table's data, not just the single column.

But I Need to Sort Only a Column

If the column is all by itself, then simply use the Data ➤ Sort command on it. Otherwise, Excel feels bound to the table the column lives in. To sort that column away from the table, simply select the column, and then copy and paste it elsewhere in the worksheet. Then use Data ➤ Sort on that column.

PivotTable Is Designed to Make Me Go Insane, Right?

PivotTable is an ugly term for simply giving yourself a more flexible way to view information in a table. It would be wholly unnecessary if it weren't for Excel's last, great spreadsheet competition, a program called Improv.

Improv was created by Lotus (the 1-2-3 spreadsheet people) for the brand-new NeXT computer back in 1989. Improv wasn't like the traditional spreadsheet program. It was more of a build-your-own grid, but not just a grid, more like a cube that could be twisted and turned to see data in three dimensions. (Yes, I was a fervent Improv fan.)

It was the insane jealousy over Improv that caused Excel's designers to create this wild PivotTable utility for Excel. I'll run over the basics of this advanced feature in the next few sections. Yes, there is a point to it all. Don't give up on it yet.

What's the Key to Understanding the PivotTable?

Simple enough: The key to using the PivotTable is to have a table in your document that has more than one dimension to it. Keep in mind that PivotTables were inspired by the old Improv worksheet, which wasn't really a worksheet but rather a way to manipulate information in many directions.

DON'T FORGET THE QUICK SORT BUTTONS ON THE TOOLBAR!

You can always rely on the Sort Ascending and Sort Descending buttons on the toolbar to do a quick sort in your worksheet.

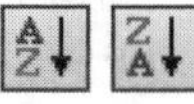

If you have a table, then the Sort buttons sort by whichever column is selected in the table (or whichever column the cell selector is in).

For sorting a single column, just click to select any cell in the column. Excel is smart enough to find the top and bottom of the column, and Sort Ascending or Sort Descending does its job and sorts the column accordingly.

FIGURE 11.16
A multidimensional table

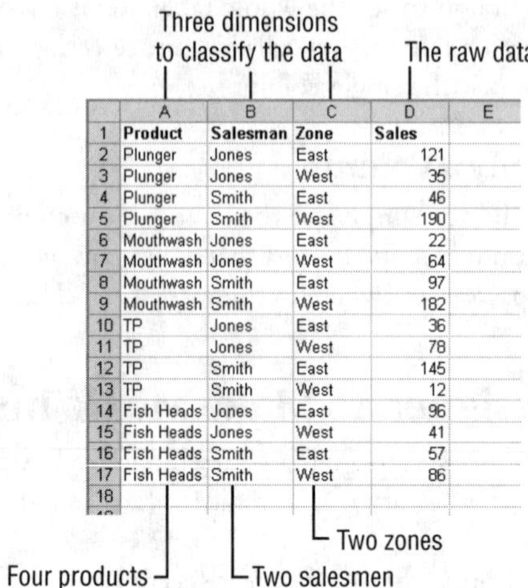

	A	B	C	D	E
1	**Product**	**Salesman**	**Zone**	**Sales**	
2	Plunger	Jones	East	121	
3	Plunger	Jones	West	35	
4	Plunger	Smith	East	46	
5	Plunger	Smith	West	190	
6	Mouthwash	Jones	East	22	
7	Mouthwash	Jones	West	64	
8	Mouthwash	Smith	East	97	
9	Mouthwash	Smith	West	182	
10	TP	Jones	East	36	
11	TP	Jones	West	78	
12	TP	Smith	East	145	
13	TP	Smith	West	12	
14	Fish Heads	Jones	East	96	
15	Fish Heads	Jones	West	41	
16	Fish Heads	Smith	East	57	
17	Fish Heads	Smith	West	86	
18					

Consider the table in Figure 11.16. This is actually a four-dimensional table, which is fine for a PivotTable. Here's how to look at it:

- The Sales column contains the data.
- Sales are divided between the East and West zones in the Zone column.
- Sales are further divided by salesman in the Salesman column.
- Finally, sales are broken down by the product sold, listed in the Product column.

The table may look like it contains a lot of repeated information, but it doesn't. It's just highly classified into different things, different *dimensions*.

So Then, How Does One Make a PivotTable?

A multidimensional table is the key to making and using a pivot table. Once you've determined that you have such table, building the PivotTable is a cinch. Witness:

1. Choose Data ➤ PivotTable and PivotChart Report. A funky dialog box appears.
2. Click the Next button.
3. Ensure that your multidimensional table is selected in the worksheet. If it isn't, then select the table now; drag over it with the mouse.
4. Click the Next button.
5. Click the Finish button.

And the PivotTable is created in a new worksheet, as shown in Figure 11.17. Isn't it pretty? Well, actually not. It needs to be filled in and messed with. That's done by dragging and dropping field names (column headings) from the list and into the PivotTable itself. The next section discusses this.

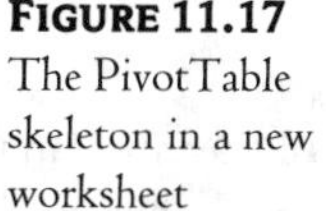

FIGURE 11.17
The PivotTable skeleton in a new worksheet

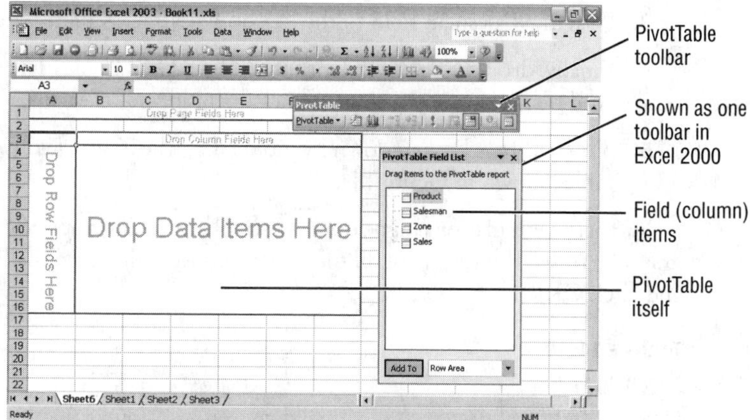

Any Necessary Rules about Dragging and Dropping Stuff into a PivotTable?

The key is to know what *data* is. You'll notice that the PivotTable (Figure 11.17) has a large central area called "Drop Data Items Here." That's the meat of the matter and the key to using the PivotTable and dragging and dropping.

PivotTables answer questions. The questions are composed of the column headings or field names. For example, "How many plungers did each salesman sell in each zone?" Here's how to answer that question:

1. The table is about plunger sales. Plunger is a product, so drag the Product field up to the "Drop Page Fields Here" item.

2. Choose Plunger from the Product heading's drop-down list, as shown in Figure 11.18; click OK.

FIGURE 11.18
Setting up the PivotTable

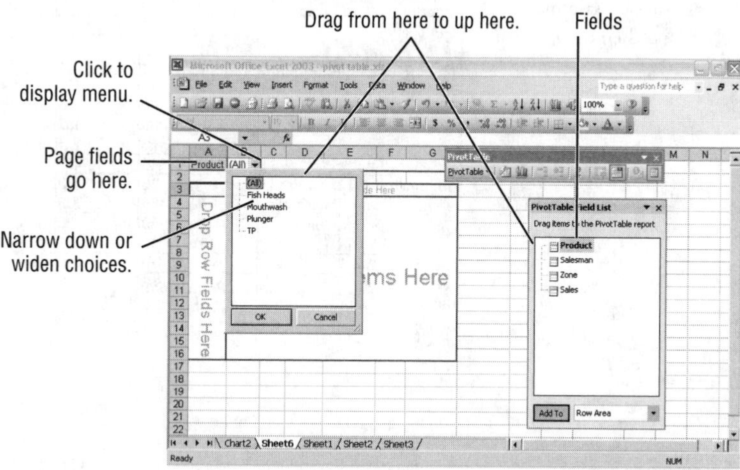

3. Drag the Salesman field to the "Drop Row Fields Here" area.
4. Finally, drop the Sales field into the "Drop Data Items Here" part of the table (in the middle). And there you see the sum of sales for plungers by each salesman, as shown in Figure 11.19.
5. To see things broken down by Zone, drag the Zone field to the "Column Field" area in the table (shown in Figure 11.19).

Further manipulation can be done by simply choosing a specific item from each field's menu. For example, to see about sales of all the items, choose (All) from the Product field's drop-down menu, and click OK.

FIGURE 11.19
Summing up the sales of plungers

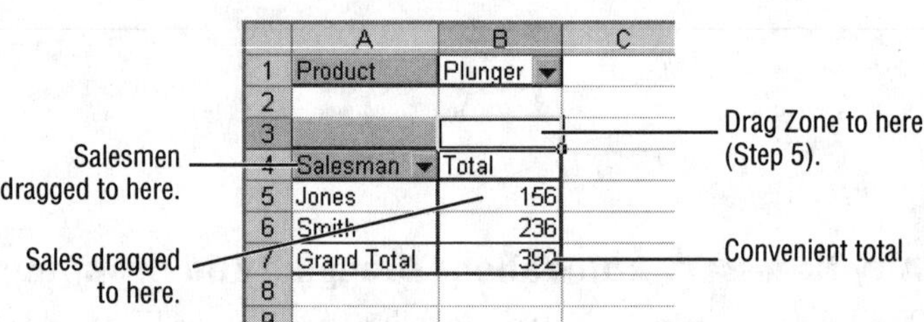

So What's So Magic about the PivotTable?

Continuing from the previous example (which you must have in order to get this magic stuff): Drag the Product field down from the top of the table and drop it right on top of the Salesman field. (As you drop, a fuzzy I-beam appears to the right or left of the Salesman field; ensure that the fuzzy I-beam is to the left of the salesman.)

FIGURE 11.20
Sales by salesman and then by product

	A	B	C	D	E
1	Drop Page Fields Here				
2					
3			Zone		
4	Salesman	Product	East	West	Grand Total
5	Jones	Fish Heads	96	41	137
6		Mouthwash	22	64	86
7		Plunger	121	35	156
8		TP	36	78	114
9	Jones Total		275	218	493
10	Smith	Fish Heads	57	86	143
11		Mouthwash	97	182	279
12		Plunger	46	190	236
13		TP	145	12	157
14	Smith Total		345	470	815
15	Grand Total		620	688	1308
16					
17					
18					

Now you have something that looks like Figure 11.20, with sales broken down by salesman and then by product.

Drag the Product field to the left of the Salesman field, and you get something like Figure 11.21. Or drag the Salesman field up next to the Zone field to get something like Figure 11.22.

FIGURE 11.21
Sales by product and then by salesman

Drop Page Fields Here

		Zone		
Product	Salesman	East	West	Grand Total
Fish Heads	Jones	96	41	137
	Smith	57	86	143
Fish Heads Total		153	127	280
Mouthwash	Jones	22	64	86
	Smith	97	182	279
Mouthwash Total		119	246	365
Plunger	Jones	121	35	156
	Smith	46	190	236
Plunger Total		167	225	392
TP	Jones	36	78	114
	Smith	145	12	157
TP Total		181	90	271
Grand Total		620	688	1308

FIGURE 11.22
Product sales by salesman and then by zone

Drop Page Fields Here

	Salesman	Zone					
	Jones		Jones Total	Smith		Smith Total	Grand Total
Product	East	West		East	West		
Fish Heads	96	41	137	57	86	143	280
Mouthwash	22	64	86	97	182	279	365
Plunger	121	35	156	46	190	236	392
TP	36	78	114	145	12	157	271
Grand Total	275	218	493	345	470	815	1308

How Can I Delete a Field from the Table?

Just drag the field down and off the table, until the mouse pointer grows a red *X* (meaning delete). Then release the mouse button, and the field is off the table.

Remember that you can always add the field back by dragging it over from the palette.

Does the PivotTable Update When I Change Data Elsewhere in the Worksheet?

No, you must manually update the PivotTable: Click the exclamation point button (Refresh External Data) on the PivotTable toolbar.

Chapter 12

Some Excellent Formatting Tricks

A WELL-FORMATTED worksheet is the sign of refinement. Not only are the numbers properly formatted, but perhaps there is some playfulness with the fonts or a dash of color. Maybe there's a line here or there or a box. This chapter covers a few of the elements of formatting: arranging cells, formatting them directly, and then working with the final, printed result. The idea is to get something on paper that looks better than it does now. The tricks are subtle, the hints are robust, and the tips are sublime.

- Adjusting column and row width and height
- Properly fitting information into cells
- Splitting and merging cells
- Creating and using styles
- Arranging text inside a cell
- Applying color
- Adjusting the way the pages print
- Fixing the document's headers and footers

The Narrow and Wide of Things

Don't be afraid to adjust the size of the cells in your worksheet! Instead, bask in the glory of the ability Excel has to change its cell size. Older worksheets had fixed cell sizes, which meant information might be only partially displayed or that you'd have to go through the agony of figuring a house payment displayed using scientific notation.

So relax! Take it easy. And understand that a cell can be any size you want!

How Can I Make All These Columns Wide Enough?

Oh, those narrow column blues....

Not all columns need to be the same width; some columns can be very wide, others very narrow or even nonexistent. To set the column width to be as wide as the widest item in all of the column's rows, follow these steps:

1. Select the columns you want to adjust. To select a column, point the mouse at the column header. The mouse pointer changes to a down arrow. You can then drag to the left or right to select a swath of columns.

2. Choose Format ➤ Column ➤ AutoFit Selection. Thwoop, and everything fits.

You can also instantly adjust any individual column's width by dragging the right edge of the column header, as shown in Figure 12.1. Or you can double-click that spot to resize the column to hold its widest cell.

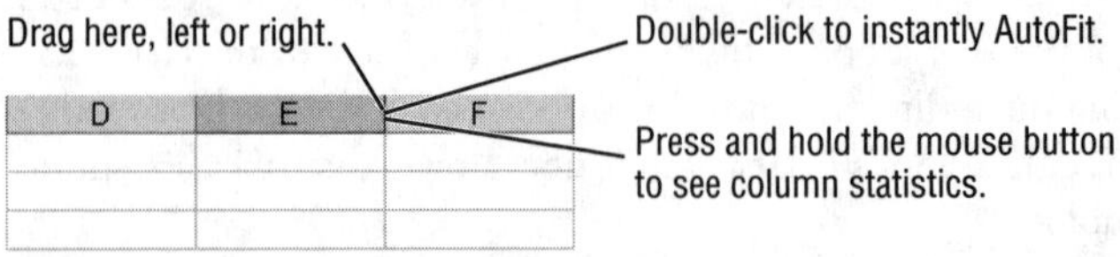

FIGURE 12.1
How to resize a column

Drag here, left or right.
Double-click to instantly AutoFit.
D
E
F
Press and hold the mouse button to see column statistics.

NOTE *Shift+spacebar selects the whole current row; Ctrl+spacebar selects the whole current column.*

Any Easy Way to Make This Column's Width Match That Column's Width?

Without getting a ruler and measuring—or using the mouse to determine the exact column width, you can copy and paste column width values. Here's how:

1. Click to select the original column. Click in the column header; this is the column that has the width you want.

2. Press Ctrl+C to copy. Or choose Edit ➤ Copy.

3. Click to select the destination column.

4. Choose Edit ➤ Paste Special. Note that this is a special Paste Special dialog box, designed to paste column-width information, not specific values.

5. Choose "Column Widths" from the Paste Special dialog box.

6. Click OK, and the two column widths will match.

I'd Like the Column to Be Wide Enough to Display $1 Million, but Not Wider. How Can I Set That Up?

Column width values are measured by how many digits you can cram into a cell. Assuming that you're not messing with the standard font size (Arial 10), the column width required to hold 1000000 is 7. Go ahead and try this: Type **1000000** into a column, and then drag the column heading's right edge over until the width value equals 7. You'll find that 1000000 fits snugly in that space.

Of course, people don't write one million as 1000000; they use commas. That adds two digits to the column width, so you'll have to widen the column to 9: Drag the column heading's right edge over until 9.00 is shown for the width. Then click the Comma Style button on the Formatting toolbar to stick commas into the number: 1,000,000.

Ooops! Doesn't work, does it? That's because the Comma style button also adds a period and two zeros after the decimal place. So you really need a column that is 12 characters wide: Manually adjust the column width to 12. And it fits.

Adding the dollar sign? Widen the column to 13, one more place to hold that $ character.

And there you go.

How Can I Shrink My Column into Oblivion?

You can drag the column heading's right edge over to the left until the column shrinks into nothingness. When you try this, however, it often messes with the width of the column on the left. To prevent that, simply select the column you want to vanish, then choose Format ➤ Column ➤ Hide.

To resize the column back into the visible realm, choose Format ➤ Column ➤ Unhide.

Painfully Detailed Information on Column Widths

When you squeeze the mouse on the right edge of a column's heading, you see a pop-up bubble that gives the column's width in both column width and pixel values.

Shown here, you see that the column has a width of 8.43 with a pixel size of 64—common for Excel.

Width: 8.43 (64 pixels)

The column width value is the left-right measurement of how many digits of the standard font will fit into a cell. The standard font is Arial 10 points. A digit is a number from 0 through 9. So the value 8.43 means that the column is wide enough to hold almost 8 and a half digits from the Arial font at 10 points. (If you change the default font, then the column width values change accordingly, but the cell size remains fixed at a certain number of pixels).

The pixel size is a hardware measurement. It's how many graphic dots (picture elements, or pixels) wide the cell is on the screen. This measurement is very consistent from PC to PC, where the monitor typically displays 72 pixels per inch.

When adjusting the column width manually (by dragging the column heading's right edge), you see the width and pixel values adjust accordingly. However the dialog boxes that control column width all use the width (character size) values.

Can Rows Be Adjusted, Grown, Shrunk, or Hidden Just Like Columns?

Yep. Row height, like column width, has two measurements: The first is points, which is relative to the height of the standard font (Arial 10), plus a few more points for wiggle room, things like commas and other items that float above or below the text. The second value is pixels, just as it is with column width.

You adjust the row height by dragging the row heading's lower border.

NOTE *Standard row height is 12.75, or 17 pixels.*

However, you rarely need to adjust row height. Most of the time, things you do in the cells automatically affect the row height. For example, if you choose a larger font, that automatically adjusts the row height to accommodate the bigger text.

Or say you wrap text within a cell. If so, the row height grows tall enough to accommodate all the text in that cell.

I Need My Rows to Be "Yea" High

As with formatting column width, to automatically adjust a row's height, double-click the row heading's bottom border.

If you need the row to be a specific height, choose Format ➢ Row ➢ Height and enter the character height value.

I Tried Wrapping Text in a Cell, but It Makes the Row Height Too Tall and Screws Up the Rest of the Worksheet. Anything Else I Can Do?

This is where the Merge Cells command comes in handy: It allows you to temporarily discard the boundaries between cells so that you can fit more information into a tight area without affecting the rows to the left or right of the cells.

It's really best to see this in action, so take these steps:

1. Select cells F3, F4, and F5.
2. Press Ctrl+1 to format the cells.
3. Click the Alignment tab.
4. Click to check "Merge Cells." This groups the cells into one, but it won't wrap the text in the cells. For that, you have to:
5. Click to check "Wrap Text."
6. Click OK, and now you have one big cell where you had three before.

Figure 12.2 shows how the merged cells form a single cell. Note the absence of grid lines.

The group of merged cells is referred to by the topmost cell in the group. In the case of Figure 12.2, all three of the merged cells are now cell F3.

You can also merge a group of cells, say a block of four by five cells. This doesn't affect any other cells, rows, or columns in the worksheet. The unit of merged cells is referred to by the cell in the upper-left corner.

FIGURE 12.2
Merged and wrapped cells

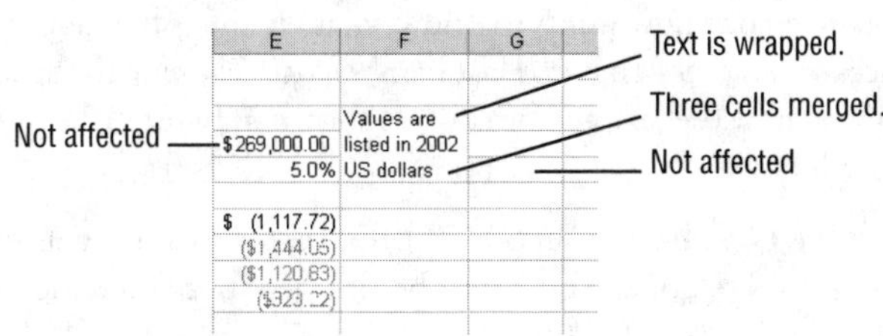

Any Quick Way to Merge Cells?

You can glue two or more cells together, eliminating the line between them, by merging the cells. To quickly merge a group of selected cells, click the Merge and Center button on the Formatting toolbar. This does not, however, wrap the text in the cells.

How Can I Unmerge the Cell(s)?

Unmerging cells is a snap: Click to select the massive cell, and then click the Merge and Center button. That undoes things rather nicely.

The contents of the merged cells are shoved into the top (or top-left) cell. The other cells are free again. Free! Free! Free!

Any Way to Split Cells?

No. But you can split up text across cells. This can be rather silly; for example, you wouldn't want to split a title, "Pan Dimensional Accounting," but you may want to split a list where the first and last names appear in one cell. That way the names could be split into two cells. Here's how to do that:

1. Type a list of names in cells A1 through A6. For example, U.S. presidents' names:

```
George Washington
John Adams
Thomas Jefferson
James Madison
James Monroe
John Adams
Andrew Jackson
```

2. Select cells A1 through A6, the cells you want to split.
3. Choose Data ➤ Text to Columns. A wizard dialog box appears.
4. Select Delimited (if it isn't selected already). Choose the "Fixed Width" option only if all the text in every row has the same number of characters.
5. Click the Next button.

6. The dialog box now wants to know what separates the items in your text. Click to check Space; spaces separate the first and last names. After clicking the space, you'll see a vertical line drawn, showing how the text will be split, as shown in Figure 12.3. (You may uncheck the Tab option if you like.)
7. Click the Next button. In Step 3 of 3, the wizard lets you format each column, but for this exercise you're done. You could be finished, but you're done.
8. Click the Finish button.

First names in column A. Last names in column B.

NOTE *If the cells to the right of the cells you're splitting contain data, a warning dialog box is displayed. The cells cannot be split without destroying any data in the cells to the right. Remember that before you set things up so you can move those cells out of the way.*

FIGURE 12.3
Splitting text between columns

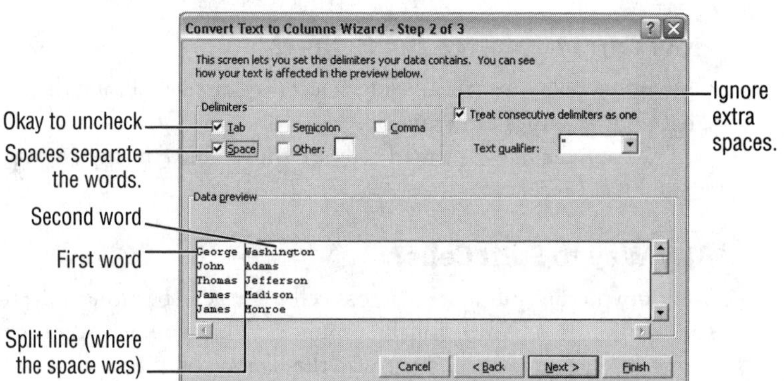

Beyond Simple Formatting

Formatting your worksheet is fairly easy. Anyone who is familiar with Word—or even anyone who's bothered to format an e-mail—can manage to format text in a worksheet. There are, however, a few finer points I'd like to go over before you win your intermediate-level Excel scholarship.

How Can I Format All the Cells with the Same Style of Text?

This is an easy one: First select all the cells in the worksheet that you've messed with. A quick way to do this is to press Ctrl+End to move to the "end" of the worksheet (or merely the part that you're using). Then press Shift+Ctrl+Home to select all those cells as a unit.

With all the cells selected, choose your formatting commands. This can handily be done from the Formatting toolbar, or you can use the Font tab in the Format Cells dialog box: Press Ctrl+1 to see that dialog box, shown in Figure 12.4.

A STYLE COVERS MORE THAN JUST THE CELL'S FONT

Styles include information on all aspects of formatting a cell. From Figure 12.4, you see that each of the check mark items relates to a tab in the Format Cells dialog box. A style can use (or control) any setting from any of those tabs in the Format Cells dialog box. In addition to the font, that means you can have a specific number style with a certain alignment or perhaps a border. It can be any combination.

FIGURE 12.4
Formatting fonts

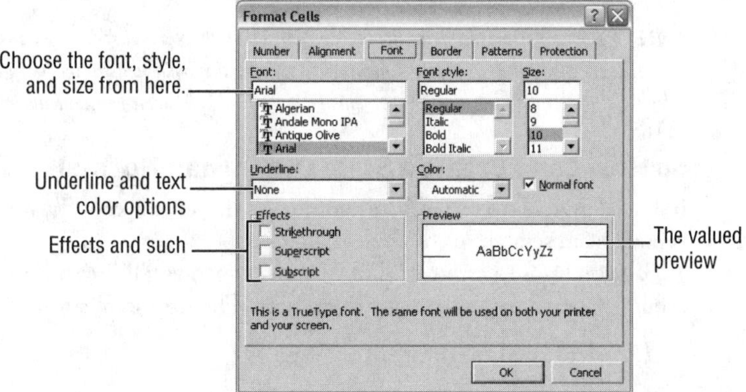

Why Should I Bother Selecting a Style? Can't I Just Change the Normal Style?

The Normal style in Excel defines how cells are formatted automatically for every sheet in the workbook. You can change this style if you like, but keep in mind that it does affect every worksheet.

To change the Normal style, mind these steps:

1. Choose Format ➤ Style. The Style dialog box appears, as shown in Figure 12.5.
2. Click the Modify button. The Format Cells dialog box appears.
3. Click the Font tab.

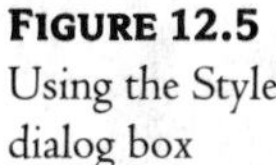

FIGURE 12.5
Using the Style dialog box

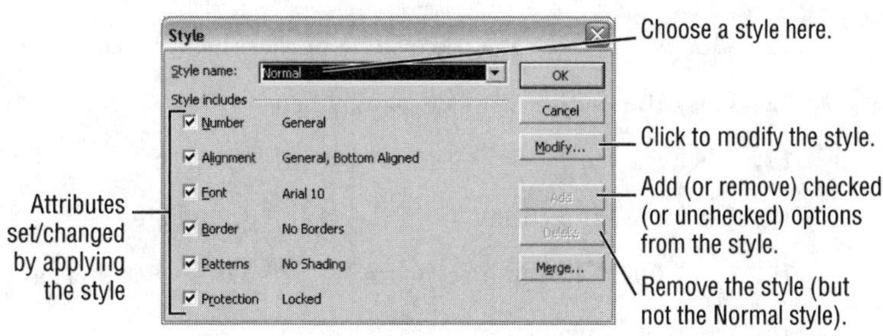

4. Select the attributes for the new font you want to use for the entire workbook. Set the typeface, style, size, and other options.
5. Click OK.
6. Click OK to close the Style dialog box.

And the new font is used as the Normal font for all worksheets. You'll notice that the cells may adjust their size if you've chosen a larger font.

NOTE *I do not recommend modifying the Normal style. Normal serves as a base—a plain, boring, nondescript format for a cell. By modifying it, you're removing a chance to unformat cells in the worksheet. Now that may be livable, but consider reading through the next few sections before you decide upon permanently altering the Normal style.*

So How Can I Create a Style Other than Normal?

In Excel, Styles are created by example. While you can modify a style after it's created, no style itself is built from scratch in the Style dialog box.

Say you want to create a "Total" style, which you'll use to bring out the various cells that display totals (or grand totals) in your worksheet. The first step is to format the cell how you like it:

1. Select a cell to format as a Total.
2. Press Ctrl+1 to bring up the Format Cells dialog box.
3. Click the Number tab.
4. Choose Currency from the Category list. The total is always a dollar amount.
5. Click the Alignment tab. Looks good.
6. Click the Font tab.
7. Make the style Bold.
8. Change the point size to 12.
9. Click the Border tab.
10. Click that Outline button.
11. Ooops! Maybe make the outline border thicker: Select a thick, solid line from the Style area.
12. Click the Outline button again. There.
13. Click the Patterns tab. Nothing worthy there.
14. Click the Protection tab. Nope, nothing fun here.
15. Click OK. The cell is formatted as you like, but no style is created yet. Keep that cell selected.
16. Choose Format ➢ Style.

17. Type a name for the style, such as **Total**. Notice how when you start typing, you see your text replace "Normal" and your settings appear by the check marks in the dialog box, as shown in Figure 12.6.
18. Click OK.

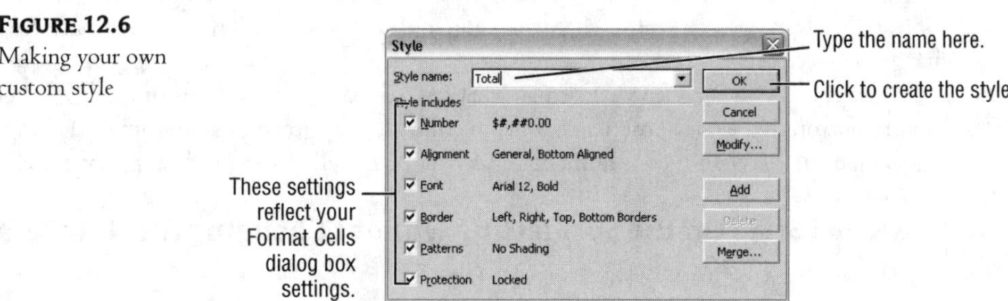

FIGURE 12.6
Making your own custom style

Now you could just click Add if you wanted to stay in the dialog box, but you don't. You want to apply the style.

1. Select the cells in your document that you want to apply the style to. You can use the Ctrl key and click the mouse to select several noncontiguous cells at once.
2. Choose Format ➤ Style.
3. Select your style from the "Style Name" drop-down list.
4. Click OK, and the style is applied.

NOTE *Ctrl+Tab moves between the tabs in any dialog box; Shift+Ctrl+Tab moves "backward" between the tabs.*

I Just Want to Copy the Formatting from One Cell to Another. Do I Need to Create a Style?

No, just use the Format Painter instead. Here's how:

1. Click the cell that has the style you want to copy.
2. Click to select the Format Painter button. The mouse pointer changes to a large + with a paintbrush by its side.
3. Click a cell to "paint" the original cell's format.

And the original cell's formatting—all of it—is copied to the cell you clicked. If the original cell was formatted with a style, then the new cell also shares that formatting style.

You can also drag the mouse to paint a swath of cells with the Format Painter.

To undo the painting, press Ctrl+Z right away. If you're too late, then just click a normal, non-formatted cell in Step 1 and repeat the process to paint a cell Normal.

NOTE *To continue painting after clicking a cell, double-click the Format Painter button on the toolbar. That keeps the Format Painter active so that you can paint/format many cells. Press the Esc key to end this mode of operation.*

What's the Point of Creating a Style When I Can Just Use the Format Painter?

If you can remember from Chapter 5 on Word, "Using Styles and Templates to Save Oodles of Time," the advantage of a style is that when you modify the style, all the cells formatted with that style change at once.

For example, you can choose Format ➤ Styles. Choose your style from the list. Then click the Modify button to change some aspect, say, to color the text green or something. Clicking the OK button changes that style but also immediately changes all cells formatted with that style.

How Can I Strip Off the Formatting without Changing the Numbers?

The easiest way is to reapply the Normal style:

1. Select the cells you want to strip of formatting.
2. Choose Format ➤ Style.
3. Select the Normal style from the drop-down list.
4. Click OK, and the cells are blandly formatted once again.

NOTE *To repeat the last formatting command given, just select a cell and press the F4 key. This saves time from having to choose a style or use the Format Cells dialog box.*

And Now for Some Basic, yet Common Formatting Q&A

Here is a smattering of other formatting questions I've received over the years. Keep in mind that there are no right or wrong ways to format things; there are only opinions as to what looks or works best.

How Can I Run My Text from Bottom to Top?

The Alignment tab in the Format Cells dialog box is where you can set your text direction, as shown in Figure 12.7. Text can appear tilted 90 degrees either clockwise or counterclockwise as set by the Orientation gizmo.

Figure 12.8 shows a worksheet with various text-alignment tricks, as explained in the figure.

NOTE *Alignment works not only on text but on cells containing numbers as well.*

Any Way to Do Upside-Down Text?

Nope.

Well, there is, but it's not a totally Excel solution: To create upside-down text, enter the text in a drawing program, such as the Paint program that comes with Windows. Use the text tool to create your text. Then use the painting program's drawing tools to rotate the text until it is upside down.

Save the upside-down text in a graphics file, or copy it from the painting program. Then place it into the worksheet as an image. That's the only way you can get upside-down text in a worksheet.

FIGURE 12.7
Aligning information in a cell

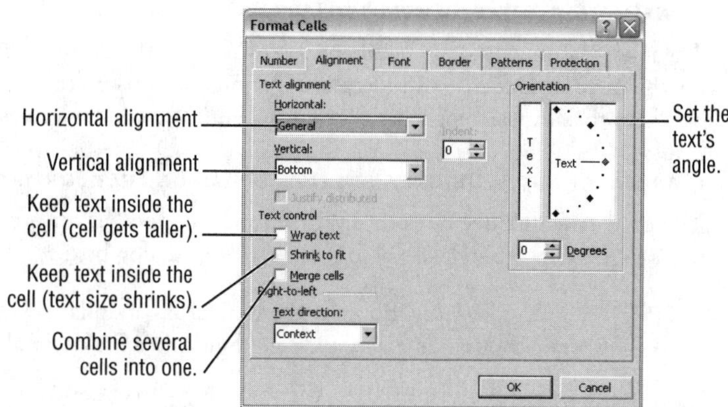

FIGURE 12.8
Various alignment tricks

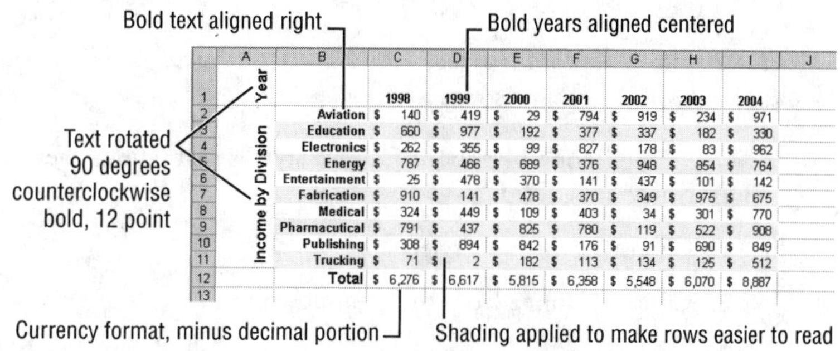

Income by Division / Year	1998	1999	2000	2001	2002	2003	2004
Aviation	$ 140	$ 419	$ 29	$ 794	$ 919	$ 234	$ 971
Education	$ 660	$ 977	$ 192	$ 377	$ 337	$ 182	$ 330
Electronics	$ 262	$ 355	$ 99	$ 827	$ 178	$ 83	$ 962
Energy	$ 787	$ 466	$ 689	$ 376	$ 948	$ 854	$ 764
Entertainment	$ 25	$ 478	$ 370	$ 141	$ 437	$ 101	$ 142
Fabrication	$ 910	$ 141	$ 478	$ 370	$ 349	$ 975	$ 675
Medical	$ 324	$ 449	$ 109	$ 403	$ 34	$ 301	$ 770
Pharmacutical	$ 791	$ 437	$ 825	$ 780	$ 119	$ 522	$ 908
Publishing	$ 308	$ 894	$ 842	$ 176	$ 91	$ 690	$ 849
Trucking	$ 71	$ 2	$ 182	$ 113	$ 134	$ 125	$ 512
Total	$ 6,276	$ 6,617	$ 5,815	$ 6,358	$ 5,548	$ 6,070	$ 8,887

WHAT'S THE BEST WAY TO ALIGN A DATE?

Dates are generally hard to line up when the digits are not consistent. For example:

```
3/6/05
12/19/05
```

Obviously, those two dates will look ugly whether aligned left, right, or center.

For lining up days and months, I use the "6-Mar" format, right-aligned, as shown in the first column of Figure 12.9. The "6-Mar-2005" format (column 2) also works right-aligned, as does "March 6, 2005" in the third column. These patterns are chosen in the Number tab of the Format Cells dialog box.

FIGURE 12.9
Good formats for lining up dates

6-Mar	6-Mar-2005	March 6, 2005
12-Mar	12-Mar-2005	March 12, 2005
24-Mar	24-Mar-2005	March 24, 2005
31-Mar	31-Mar-2005	March 31, 2005
1-Apr	1-Apr-2005	April 1, 2005
4-Apr	4-Apr-2005	April 4, 2005
8-Apr	8-Apr-2005	April 8, 2005
13-Apr	13-Apr-2005	April 13, 2005
1-May	1-May-2005	May 1, 2005

How Can I Get These Numbers to Line Up?

The main reason why some numbers don't line up is the decimal place. To adjust the decimal place, use the Increase Decimal and Decrease Decimal buttons on the formatting toolbar: Select the numbers, and then experiment with the buttons until you get the values lined up as you like.

I Can Make $ and % Quickly, but How Do I Undo That Format?

There are actually three buttons on the Formatting toolbar for quickly formatting numbers in three styles—yes, they are styles as defined in the Style dialog box:

Currency style: Formats the value using a dollar sign, with commas at the thousands place, and two digits after the decimal.

Percent style: Formats the value as a percent.

Comma style: Same as Currency style, but without the dollar sign.

NOTE *Remember that 1 is actually 100 percent. Percent values less than 100 percent are less than 1: .5 is 50 percent; .02 is 2 percent. This always goofs people up.*

One thing I don't like about Comma style is that it adds the decimal point and two digits. Of course, this can be fixed:

1. Choose Format ➤ Style.
2. Choose Comma from the drop-down list.
3. Click the Modify button. In the Format Cells dialog box, Number tab, reduce the number of decimal places to zero.
4. Click OK.
5. Click OK to close the Style dialog box, and the Comma style is changed for the entire workbook.

How Come Some Numbers Line Up Differently than Others?

What you're probably describing are numbers formatted in the Accounting format. That format uses parentheses to display negative values. Because of that, all the positive numbers are given a little extra space on the right, so that positive and negative numbers line up, as shown in Figure 12.10.

So if you have a column of numbers, and one of the cells is formatted with the Accounting style and the others are in some other style, then yes, they will not line up properly. The solution is to use the same type of format for all numbers.

NOTE *The Currency Style button on the Formatting toolbar actually applies the* Accounting *style format. Weird, huh?*

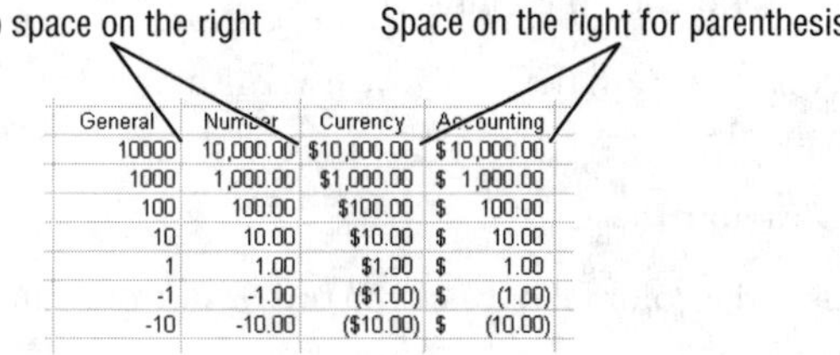

General	Number	Currency	Accounting
10000	10,000.00	$10,000.00	$ 10,000.00
1000	1,000.00	$1,000.00	$ 1,000.00
100	100.00	$100.00	$ 100.00
10	10.00	$10.00	$ 10.00
1	1.00	$1.00	$ 1.00
-1	-1.00	($1.00)	$ (1.00)
-10	-10.00	($10.00)	$ (10.00)

FIGURE 12.10
Numbers line up differently depending on the format.

COMMON NUMBER FORMAT MISCONCEPTIONS

In addition to giving a little space on the right for the parenthesis, there are other subtle differences between the number formats.

For example, in Figure 12.10, notice how the Currency and Accounting formats display the currency symbol ($)? Accountants like the dollar sign off to the left of a cell, whereas the Currency format keeps it snug against the number.

WHY DO ACCOUNTANTS SOMETIMES PUT A DOLLAR SIGN AT THE TOP OF A COLUMN OF VALUES BUT NOT FOR EVERY VALUE?

I don't know. I suppose it's because they're trained or beaten that way. For example, in Figure 12.11 you see a column of dollar values formatted the way your typical accountant would format things: dollar values on the top and bottom, other values in the middle.

Here's how to format such a column:

1. Type in all the numbers first.
2. In the final, Total cell, click the AutoSum button on the Standard toolbar (the Greek letter *sigma*[Σ]), and then press Enter. This automatically inserts the column's sum or total into the bottom box.
3. Drag to select the entire column, including the total.

FIGURE 12.11
Formatting numbers like a real accountant would

$ 1,233.95
27.00
63.50
99.56
35.23
19.17
52.65
$ 1,531.06

Accounting format
Accounting format minus currency symbol
Total (AutoSum), formatting bold

4. Press Ctrl+1 and click the Number tab.
5. Select Accounting from the Category list. Ensure that two decimal places are selected, as well as the $ symbol.
6. Click OK. Almost there.
7. Now reselect the column, but not the top or bottom value.
8. Press Ctrl+1 again.
9. From the Symbol drop-down list choose None.
10. Click OK.

And your list is formatted in a manner that would make an accounting teacher weep bitter tears of joy.

NOTE *In Figure 12.11, the total was also formatted in bold, so that it's more apparent it's a total and not just some burp in the column formatting.*

How Can I Effectively Use Color?

Color can be used in many ways, but most importantly color can provide handy mental links to certain areas in the worksheet. For example, many of the number formats can display negative values in red text. That's one great way to draw attention to a certain part of a worksheet—even better if you have a color printer.

The Font Color button on the Formatting toolbar is used to color text fonts. One example of effectively using color would be to color similar items in a worksheet with similar text colors. For example, color code values by region or salesperson.

The use of color fonts is especially effective if they're scattered in a table. In Figure 12.12, the regions with the best results for the quarter are colored in red; the worst results are colored in blue (pretend you can see this on the grayscale figure).

Fill Color can be used to shade cells in the worksheet. This can be done for design purposes. For example, jump ahead to Figure 12.20, and you'll see how color is used to highlight design elements in the invoice. Better still, way back in Figure 12.8, color is used to help identify rows in a table.

NOTE *Unless you just want a blob of color, be sure to choose a light shade to fill your cells. Darker shades make the cell contents harder to see.*

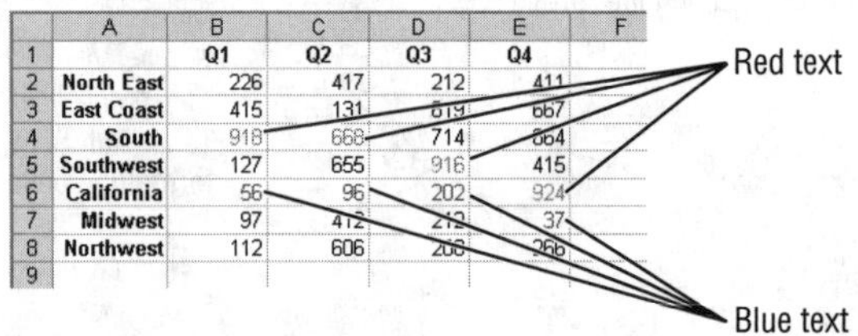

	A	B	C	D	E	F
1		Q1	Q2	Q3	Q4	
2	North East	226	417	212	411	
3	East Coast	415	131	619	667	
4	South	918	668	714	864	
5	Southwest	127	655	916	415	
6	California	56	96	202	924	
7	Midwest	97	412	212	37	
8	Northwest	112	606	206	266	
9						

FIGURE 12.12 Using color to highlight elements in a table

How Do I Apply the Color?

Whether you're coloring text or filling a cell, the color is applied the same way:

1. Select the cell(s) to color.
2. Click the proper button on the toolbar: Fill Color to shade a cell's background or Font Color merely to color the font.

If you want to choose a new color, click the menu button by the icon to display a drop-down color palette. That shows 40 predefined colors you can use, or you can select the No Fill or Automatic option to remove the color.

NOTE *Automatic merely resets the cell's text color to whatever color the current style defines.*

What's the Difference between a Pattern and a Color?

You want to use colors; you want to avoid patterns.

Well, not all the time; patterns can be used as design elements. But as the background "color" for any cells with information, patterns tend to be too annoying to be useful.

Patterns are doled out in the Format Cells dialog box, Patterns tab, shown in Figure 12.13. But to set the patterns, you have to click the drop-down button, which displays the menu shown in Figure 12.14.

FIGURE 12.13
The evil Patterns tab

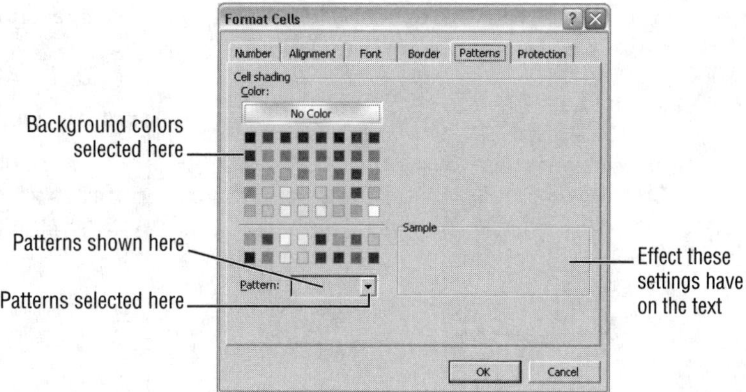

FIGURE 12.14
Selecting a pattern

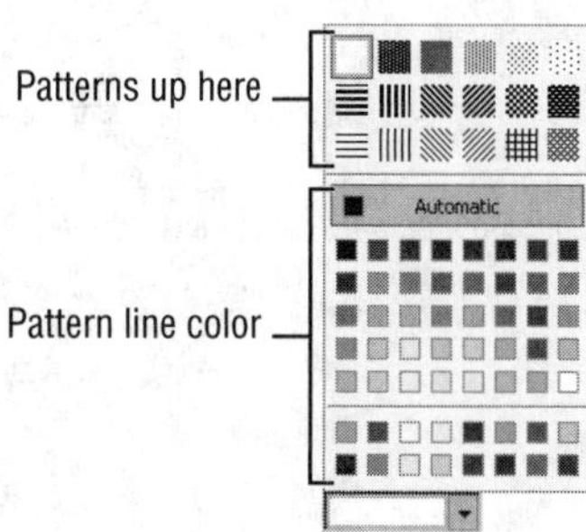

Selecting a pattern is a two-step process. First, select the pattern from the top part of the pop-up menu (Figure 12.14). Then select a color from the bottom part. The color affects only the pattern. If you want to set a color for the cell's background, you have to do that from the main part of the dialog box (Figure 12.13).

NOTE *Again, most people find the use of patterns to shade cells extremely annoying. Try to use them as design elements only.*

Printing Woes and Worries

Despite this section's heading, it has nothing to do with the anxiety you can get over printing bad news. Ideally, you want the worksheet to be accurate and informative, regardless of the negative news it may feature. But that's not the point here: The point is printing the worksheet, which is actually quite painless—if it weren't for the minor quirks and worries solved in the following sections.

Unlike other programs, worksheets don't rely on the paper's page size to create apparent printing boundaries. So you can never really tell how close you are to the edge of a page when you're working on a worksheet—which is okay, I suppose.

The trick I used to pull was using Print Preview. By choosing File ➤ Print Preview or clicking the Print Preview button, you can see how your document prints, one page at a time. But more important than that, when you return to the document, you can see dotted lines representing the page boundary (Figure 12.15) and then use those lines to help you keep a report or such all on one page.

Alas, this is not the best way to deal with things.

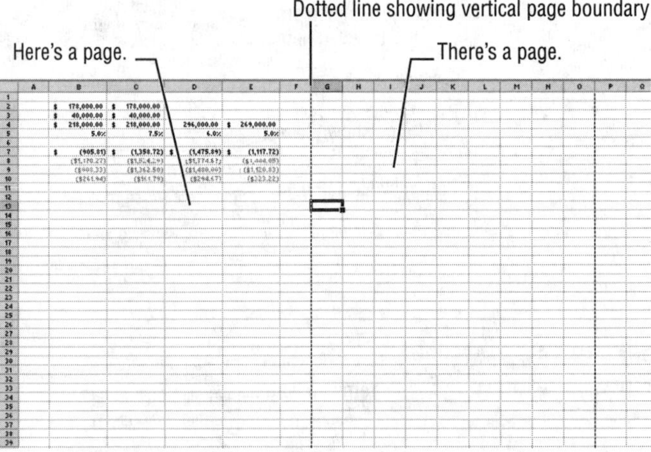

FIGURE 12.15 Dotted lines appear in the worksheet after using Print Preview.

WHAT ABOUT DRAWING LINES AND BOXES AND STUFF?

Excel shares the same Drawing toolbar as Word. For information on drawing various objects in Excel, refer to Chapter 4 on Word, "Oh the Sacrilege of Drawing in a Word Processor!" The instructions there apply to both Excel and Word.

Is There Any Other Way to See Where the Page Breaks Fall?

Of course! It's called Page Break Preview, a command that shows how there is an obvious need to know where page breaks are in a worksheet.

To view your entire worksheet and see its page breaks, choose View ➤ Page Break Preview. Instantly, or longer if you bought your computer locally, the screen shows a seriously scrunched up version of your worksheet with page breaks appearing as dotted blue lines, similar to what's shown in Figure 12.16.

Now you can see how the document can print—the big picture, if you will. But the best part is that you can manipulate the pages by dragging the page breaks or even adding new ones. Keep reading.

NOTE *Do not try to edit your worksheet in Page Break Preview mode. You will go insane.*

FIGURE 12.16
Page Break Preview in action

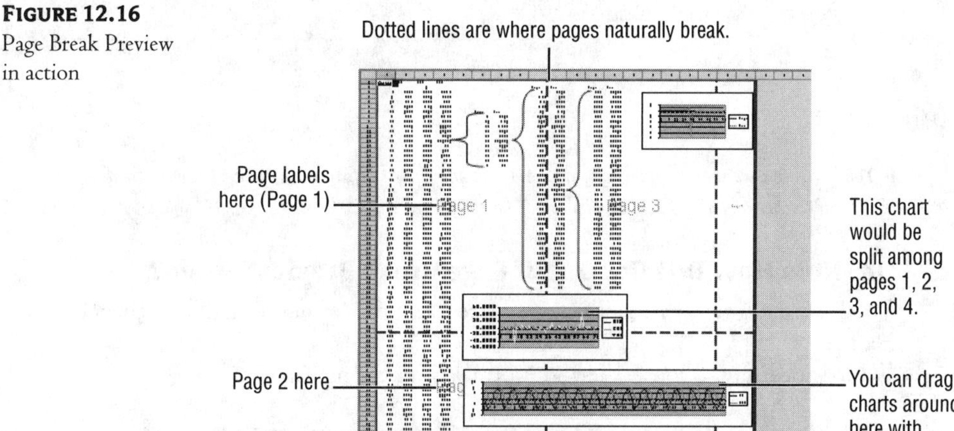

When Do I Need to Move a Page Break?

First, before you decide you need to move a page break, determine whether the entire sheet can't print better in Landscape mode.

For example, in Figure 12.17 you see the Page Break Preview, but the paper is still printing in a Portrait representation. If you choose File ➤ Page Setup, choose Landscape orientation, and then click OK, the worksheet fits, as seen in Figure 12.18. There's no need to mess with the page breaks in that case.

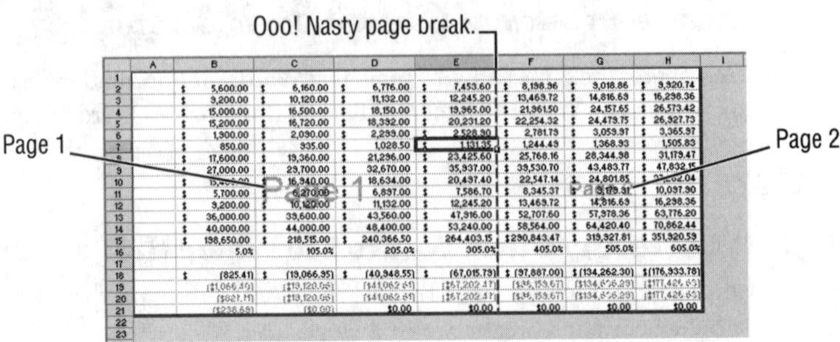

FIGURE 12.17
A nasty page break due to Portrait orientation

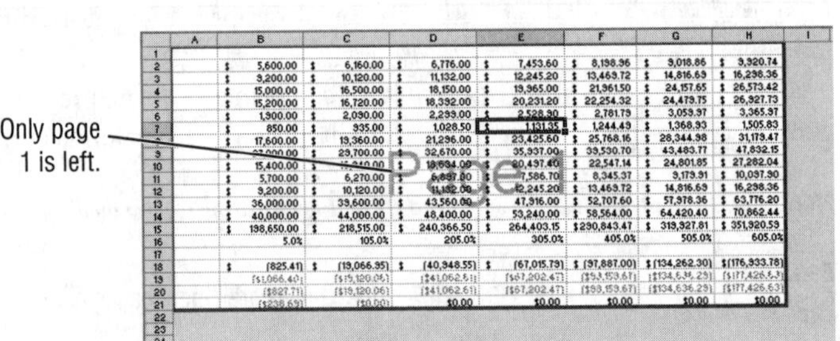

FIGURE 12.18
Page break is gone in Landscape orientation!

NOTE *If you see that stupid Welcome dialog box displayed before Page Break Preview mode appears, be sure to click the "Do Not Show This Dialog Again" check box before you click OK.*

Uh, Now How Do I Get Out of Page Break Preview Mode?

You can't. You've permanently altered Excel and the program cannot be changed back. Sucker! Ha-ha!

No, not really. Choose View ➤ Normal from the menu.

Printing in Landscape Mode Doesn't Help, So I'd Like to Know How to Move a Page Break

Occasionally, despite your best efforts, the stuff you want printed on one page spreads into two, as shown in Figure 12.19. The solution is to drag the page break over until all your stuff fits on a single page, as shown in Figure 12.20.

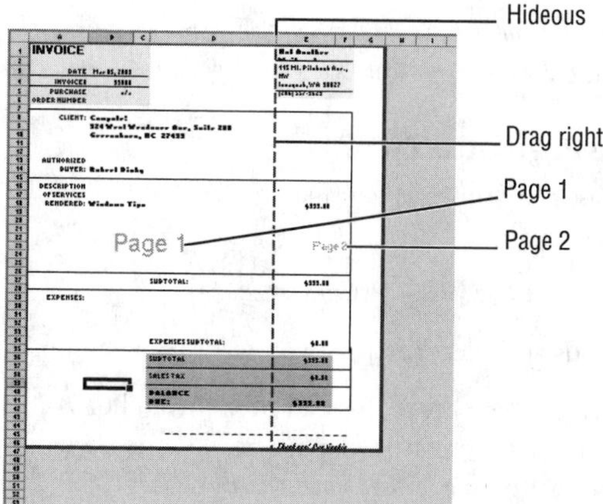

FIGURE 12.19
Ugly page break

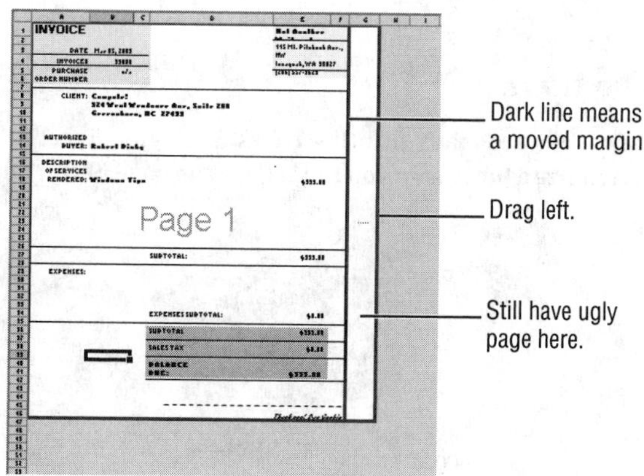

FIGURE 12.20
Ugly page break moved over!

Here is how you can do that:

1. Choose View ➤ Page Break Preview.
2. Point the mouse at the dashed, blue page break. The mouse pointer changes to a left- and right-pointing arrow, meaning that's the direction you can drag the page break.
3. Drag the vertical page break to the right, just outside column F on the screen. Refer to Figure 12.19. This still, unfortunately, leaves you with an extra blank page that prints, shown in Figure 12.20.
4. Drag the right edge of the page over one cell. Yes, you can drag the page edge. The final result is all set to print on one page.

NOTE *In Figures 12.19 and 12.20, a better solution would most likely be to resize column D, which looks rather wide. Upon first glance, it doesn't appear that there's anything in the worksheet that requires that column to be so wide.*

Can I Split One Page into Two?

Pages can be split as many times as you like, thanks to the handy Insert ➤ Page Break command. Here's how to work it:

1. Choose View ➤ Page Break Preview.
2. Click the mouse to select the page you want to break up.
3. Choose Insert ➤ Page Break. Instead of splitting horizontally, as Word would, your single page is split into fourths with two page breaks, one horizontal and the other vertical. Note that this does affect other page breaks in the document.
4. Move the page breaks to where you want them.

Drag the page breaks around until your document looks as peachy and as keen as you like.

How Does It Do That?

These page break tricks are really printing tricks. Basically, Excel just scrunches up the worksheet, reducing its printed size a bit to help you fit it all on one page. (After all, it's not the paper that's changing size here.)

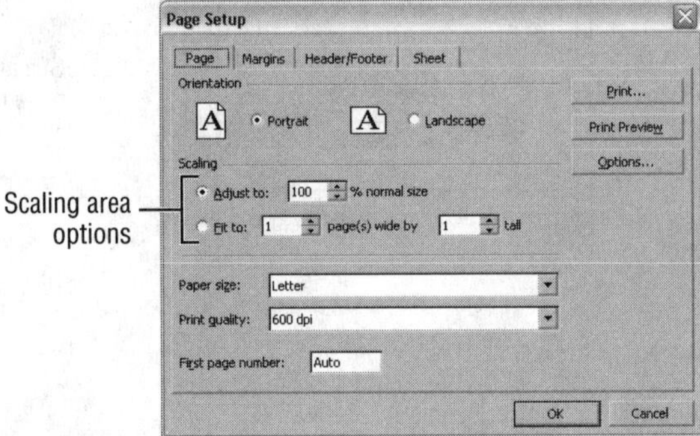

If you choose File ➤ Page Setup, you'll see a Scaling area in the Page tab, shown above. There are two options. The first, "Adjust To," is used to scale the entire document, reducing its printed size so that it fits on the page according to how you broke things up in Page Break Preview.

The second option, "Fit to," allows you to select how many sheets you want the entire worksheet to print on, regardless of size. So you could force the thing all onto one page if you like. Or choose two pages wide by one page tall to see it on two pages.

How Can I Remove a Page Break? Or All Page Breaks?

There are two ways to delete a page break: First, you can drag the page break off the page.

Second, you can click the page break and choose Insert ➤ Remove Page Break from the menu—though oftentimes this command doesn't seem to show up.

If you get all screwed up with page breaks and would like to see things restored to the way they originally were, just right-click in the print area and choose "Reset All Page Breaks" from the pop-up menu.

How Can I Get Rid of This Blank Page?

Suppose you have a setup such as the one shown in Figure 12.21. After adjusting the margins and moving a few of the charts around, you discover a blank page in the middle of the worksheet. According to Figure 12.21, it's page 4.

The secret here is to use the Print dialog box and direct it *not* to print page 4:

1. Choose View ➤ Page Break Preview, and you'll see something like Figure 12.21.
2. Use the mouse to select a large chunk of the area you want to print. Yes, you can use the mouse to select things in Page Break Preview; just be careful that you select all of the text on the page and don't miss any rows.
3. Choose File ➤ Print Area ➤ Set Print Area. This defines the area you selected as printable. Nothing else will print.

Now if you have a weird shape, as shown in Figure 12.21, then you'll need to add to the print area.

1. Select the next chunk of the worksheet you want to print.
2. Right-click the selection and choose "Add to Print Area" from the pop-up menu.
3. Repeat Steps 4 and 5 until all the pages you want printed are selected. You'll end up with something like Figure 12.22, where the blank page is simply not selected as part of the print area.

FIGURE 12.21
An ugly blank page in the middle of a workbook

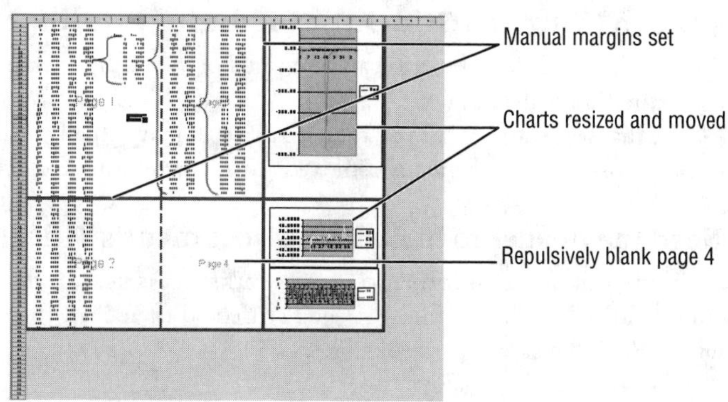

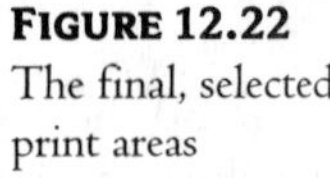

FIGURE 12.22
The final, selected print areas

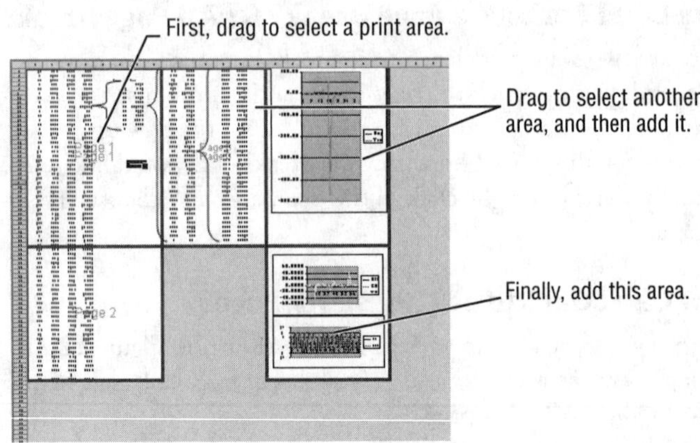

First, drag to select a print area.
Drag to select another area, and then add it.
Finally, add this area.

Now you can go ahead and print and not have to worry about printing the blank page.

NOTE *To restore the document so that the original print area is seen, choose File ➤ Print Area ➤ Clear Print Area.*

Can't I Also Use the Ctrl Key to Select Multiple Parts of the Worksheet?

Yes. You can hold down the Ctrl key while you use the mouse to select several cells or groups of cells at once. Then you can choose File ➤ Print Area ➤ Set Print Area to set the multiple portions of your document as a single print area, all at once.

Can I Change the Order of When Things Print?

Not really. In the Page Setup dialog box, Sheet tab, there is a section on "Page Order," as shown in Figure 12.23. Your only two options are listed in the figure. (Choose File ➤ Page Setup to see this dialog box.)

How Can I Turn the Grid On or Off during Printing?

Refer to Figure 12.23: The grid can be turned on or off by clicking the Gridlines check box in the Page Setup/Sheet dialog box.

Note that sometimes what you may see as a grid may actually be borders or lines drawn in the document. Those must be manually removed (lines) or reformatted (borders).

I Need the Header to Include the Document's Title, Not the Filename

The header and footer information for a worksheet is kept in the Header/Footer tab of the Page Setup dialog box. Choose File ➤ Page Setup, and then click the Header/Footer tab to get there. Figure 12.24 shows what it looks like.

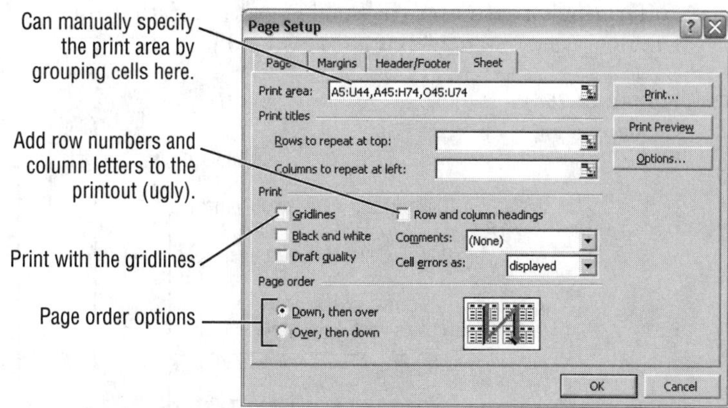

FIGURE 12.23
Various goodies in the Page Setup dialog box

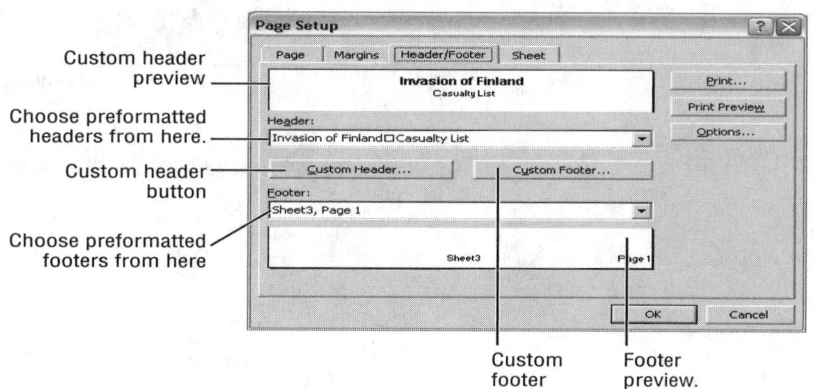

FIGURE 12.24
Setting headers and footers in the Page Setup dialog box

The drop-down lists by Header and Footer contain common information usually found in worksheet printouts, such as the sheet name, workbook filename, and other various and sundry things.

To create a custom header or footer, click the Custom Header or Footer button. You'll see a dialog box such as the one shown in Figure 12.25. As you can see, there are some buttons for automatically inserting information, plus formatting your text. And you have three positions in which to place things: Left (flush left), Center (centered), and Right (flush right), according to the figure.

To include a document's title in the header, click the Custom button and type the document's title into the "Center Section" box, as shown in Figure 12.25.

FIGURE 12.25
Creating a custom header

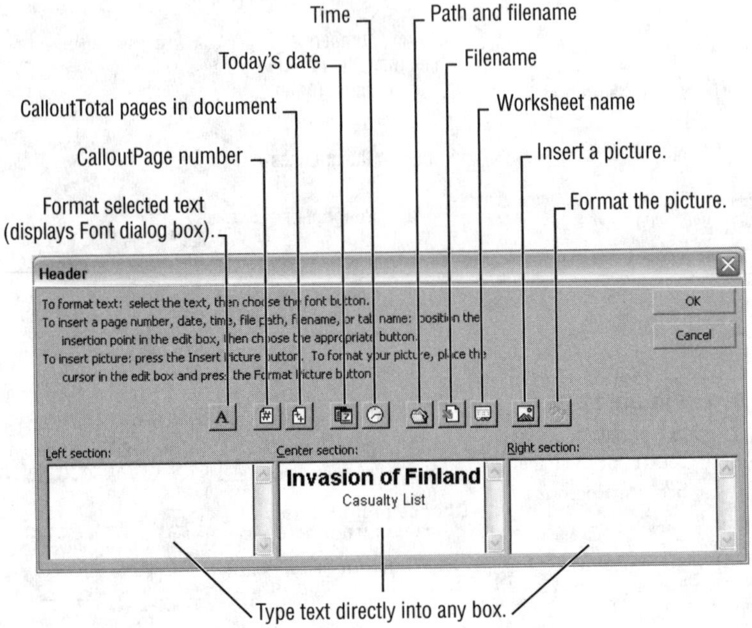

Chapter 13

Oh No! The Horrible Math Chapter!

WHAT BETTER NUMBER FOR a math chapter than 13, huh?

Here's the whole deal with math on a computer. This is very simple, so you can rest your furrowed brow and release the tension in your shoulders. Ready? Good. The truth is that it's the *computer* that does the math, not you. Whew!

Of course, *you* are not off the hook. While it's the computer that does the math, it's your job to translate whatever it is you want into a language the computer understands. Fortunately, Excel is very forgiving and helpful to the point of being annoying. Combine that with the genteel way this chapter presents mathematical concepts necessary, useful, and obscure, and you're bound to actually enjoy doing math in Excel. Promise!

- Properly using math symbols in Excel
- Raising to power and lowering to roots
- Going positive
- Finding the remainder
- Getting the total of a column, row, or chunk
- Finding uses for the COUNT function
- Mixing text with addition

Basic, Annoying Math

One day, should I live long enough, I am going to re-create the basic math primer for all humans in the galaxy. That's because it's almost universally accepted that math is one of the worst things you can force your brain to do (beyond, of course, trying to understand avant-garde art). There's a reason for this (see the sidebar nearby), and I won't dwell on any of that here. Just let me start out with the simple and you can take it from there.

Why Isn't the ÷ Symbol Used in Excel?

Quick answer: Because it's not on your keyboard.

Rather than make the keyboard this colossal, imposing, button-filled monster, the computer designers were forced to choose only a few limited keys. Because the / (slash) key can also be used to separate items, and it's used to set up a fraction, it was determined that it could double as the division symbol for a computer—just as * doubles for the × in multiplication.

The key to remembering the computer's mathematical symbols is your keyboard's numeric keypad. Clutching the edges of the keypad like barnacles on a hull are the four basic computer math symbols, also used in Excel:

+	Addition
–	Subtraction
*	Multiplication
/	Division

Officially these are known as *operators*, because they perform a mathematical operation on two or more numbers. Excel's pantheon also includes the following symbols:

%	Calculate (display) the value as a percentage.
^	Express exponentiation, such as 2^3, which is the same as 2^3.
–	Negation; makes positive numbers negative and negative numbers positive.

How Is the % Sign an Operator?

The % symbol serves both to format a value and input that value as a percent. For example, type 20% into a cell and you see 20% displayed. But the value entered into the cell is 0.2 (two tenths).

This can also happen when you're inputting a long formula. Say you need to calculate a price plus 8.2% sales tax. Here is the formula:

```
=10.99+(10.99*8.2%)
```

That is, the original price of the item, 10.99, plus the sales tax, which is the price of the item times 8.2 percent.

Remember that the parentheses specify order but also organize the items. Here you are talking about two different prices: the price of the item and the price of the sales tax. The price of the sales tax *is not* 8.2% (or 0.082). A percentage must be calculated on a value for it to work; otherwise it's not a percentage, just a value.

Also remember that I prefer to keep numbers listed in cells and have the formulas operate on cells instead of the numbers directly. In that case, consider Figure 13.1 as another potential solution to the sales tax problem.

FIGURE 13.1
Breaking out the sales tax percentage formula

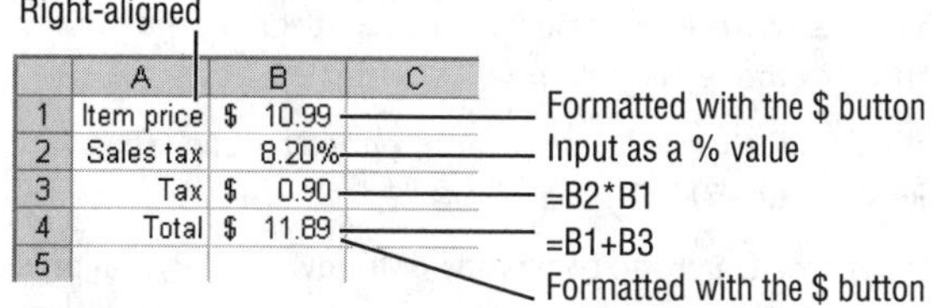

Create such a thing to play with:

1. Fill in column A as shown in Figure 13.1. All items are right-aligned.
2. Type a value into cell B1, such as **10.99**; format the value by clicking the Currency button on the Formatting toolbar.
3. Into cell B2, type **8.2%**. You do not need to use the equal sign, nor do you need to click the % format button. Entering the % operator automatically make the value a percent *and* formats the cell.
4. Into cell B3 type the formula **=B2*B1**. The added tax value is the sales tax percentage times the original price.
5. Into cell B4 type the formula = **B1+B3**. Or, the total purchase cost is the original price plus the added tax.
6. Select cells B3 and B4 and format them with the Currency button.

If you want a homework assignment, consider naming the cells:

- Name cell B1 **ItemPrice.**
- Name cell B2 **SalesTaxRate.**
- Name cell B3 **SalesTax.**

Now the formulas will read a little better. In cell B3 you'll have

```
=SalesTaxRate*ItemPrice
```

And in cell B4 you'll have the logical

```
=ItemPrice+SalesTax
```

WHY MATH IS MADE TO DRIVE YOU NUTS

The first math book was written over 2,500 years ago by Euclid. Or it could have been someone else who was also named Euclid, seeing how Euclid was a common name back then and how others wrote books and often attributed the authorship to some great (and potentially dead) person.

There are several odd things about that first math book.

First, almost every textbook written today that purports to teach math is based on the same organization as that original book, written over 2,500 years ago.

Second, the book was written in ancient Greek, and some argue that it was never fully translated from ancient Greek into any modern tongue.

Third, and most curious, the book was *never* intended to teach the average human being how to do math. (Does it all make sense now?)

Euclid was a Pythagorean, a group consisting of followers of Pythagoras. You remember him? Pythagoras brought us the famous theorem about triangles, the Pythagorean theorem—which I'm not getting into here. Pythagoras was the first mathematician, and the Pythagoreans were those who followed him, that is, other *mathematicians*.

The Pythagoreans flourished in Egypt, principally in Alexandria. They were Greeks, not Egyptians, remnants of Alexander the Great's conquest of the world around 500 B.C. Euclid was a member of this group but was also the librarian of the great library that Alexander established on that Mediterranean coastal city. That's where the link between Euclid the Pythagorean and Euclid the author comes into play.

While you might think of the Pythagoreans as noble, philosophy-spouting Greeks, and that may have been true, when it came to math they mostly kept their mouths shut. That's because the Pythagoreans were pretty much a secret society, almost like a cult. Their purpose was to practice math and produce interesting mathematical things for others—like accountants do today. They did not exist to teach math to the unwashed masses. Far from it, their goal was to express math in some of the most cryptic manners possible, specifically to keep it from the masses and further solidify their position in society.

And there you have the problem: Today's math is being taught from a book written 2,500 years ago, a book whose author believed that no one outside a select group should ever learn math. Why does learning math hurt? Because Euclid wanted it to hurt! It's supposed to be awkward and cryptic and difficult to learn. The Pythagoreans didn't want it any other way!

So the next time you sit down and puzzle over some mathematical problem, accept the fact that clever Greeks two thousand years ago set you up for a fall. Now you can feel good when it comes to "not getting it" regarding math.

Why Does the % Formatting Button on the Toolbar Often Give a Wrong Amount in a Cell?

It, in fact, does not; you've entered the wrong value.

If you want to input a value as a percent, use the % operator. Otherwise, if you click the % button on the Formatting toolbar, you get the percent equivalent of whatever value is in the cell—which is usually wrong; the value 100 formats out to 10000%, which is true. The value 1 formats to 100%.

How Do You Do That "Raised-to-the-Power" Thing?

The raised-to-the-power thing—known as *exponentiation* in mathematician coffee klatches—is done with the caret symbol, Shift+6 on the keyboard, which produces the ^ thing.

If you ever need this doohickey, then it works like this: Suppose you're creating a table of holy computer numbers:

1. Enter the values **0** through **10** into column E.

   If you're clever, you'll remember how to fill a series so that this takes only one step. Otherwise, if you forgot how to fill a series—which happens—you'll happily take these substeps:

   A. Enter the value **0** into a cell.

   B. Select that cell.

   C. Drag the cell (by its lower-right corner) with the mouse's right button; drag down 10 cells. That's to cell E11.

   D. Choose "Fill Series" from the pop-up menu.

   And there is your column, 0 through 10.

2. Into cell F1, type **=2^E1**. This reads, "The value of this cell is equal to 2 'raised to the power' of the value in cell E1 (on the left)." Ah, yes: a *relative* reference.

3. Drag to fill cell F1 down through cell F11.

And the end result looks like Figure 13.2, with power values in column E and holy computer numbers in column F.

FIGURE 13.2
A handy holy computer number table

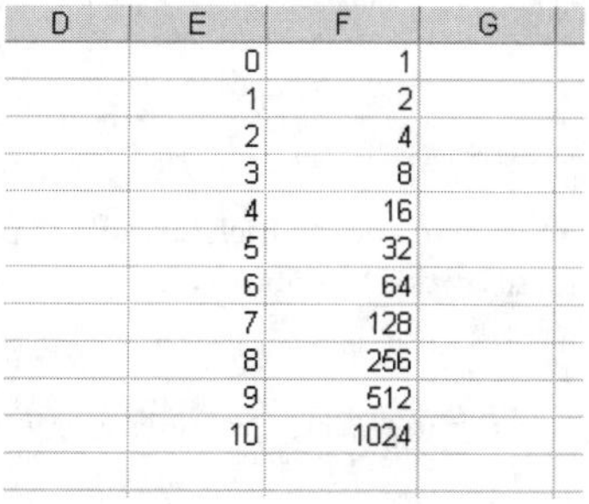

D	E	F	G
	0	1	
	1	2	
	2	4	
	3	8	
	4	16	
	5	32	
	6	64	
	7	128	
	8	256	
	9	512	
	10	1024	

Excel also uses the POWER function to raise a value to specific power. It works just like the ^, but as a function. So to modify column F in Figure 13.2, you could change the formula in cell F1 (Step 2) to be:

```
=POWER(2,E1)
```

Then drag-fill down to get the same results.

Is There an Opposite for the Raised-to-the-Power Thing?

Yes: The LOG function is essentially a backward raised-to-the-power thing. I realize how much logarithms pained you back in school, but they're essentially variations on the raised-to-the-power theme.

Continuing from the example in the previous section:

4. Into cell G1 type =LOG(F1,2). This reads, "The contents of this cell equal the value of cell F1 'unraised' to the power of 2."
5. Fill-copy the formula down through cell G11.

The results are the same as column E; the original number is raised to the power of 2 in column F. But in column G it's "lowered" back to the original value. So here are the two formulas as they stand opposed to each other:

```
value=base^number OR value=POWER(base,number)
```

That's like saying *value*=*base*^{number}, or raising number *base* to the power *number* gives you a *value*. That clever little twisty can be undone by

```
number=LOG(value,base)
```

Or to put it another way (and close your eyes here if you're utterly confoosed):

```
number=LOG(POWER(base,number),base)
```

This silly function reads that the same number will be returned when you raise it to the same power as you lower it with the LOG function. I assume there is some cosmic significance to this and that the first person who discovered it was probably called a "genius." For a while, at least.

Okay. Time for a beverage!

VARIOUS POWER AND RAISING-TO FUNCTIONS

Again: Excel does the math, but it's up to you to know which formula to plug in. The raising-to-the-power-of function, or exponentiation, is handled by the ^ symbol:

=value^power

The cell's contents equal the *value* raised to the *power*. Lord only knows when you'll need something like that in a financial statement.

There are four other power functions in Excel: EXP, LN, LOG, and LOG10.

EXP is the base e logarithm. So =EXP(1) displays the value of e, or 2.718282. Only geeky scientists will know how best to use that number (though it comes up all the time in many common calculations).

LN is the natural logarithm. It's the inverse of the EXP function—if that helps.

LOG returns the logarithm of a number in whatever base you specify.

LOG10 returns the base 10 logarithm of a number. (It's the same as =LOG(*value*,10).

Where Does the SQRT Function Figure into All of This?

SQRT is simply the square root function, not the "squirt" function. It returns the square root value of a number, or whatever value multiplied by itself equals another value.

NOTE *The SQRT function has nothing to do with exponentiation; it is a multiplication function.*

Is There a "Cube Root" Function?

Thankfully, no.

But because this is math, and you suffered through math just as I did, you know that there's always *something* going on. In this case, although there isn't a cube root companion to the SQRT function, there is still the POWER function.

You may recall from math (or probably not) that the square root of a value is the same thing as raising that value to the 1/2 power:

$$4^{1/2} = 2$$

Now they probably have a SQRT function because most of us numskulls don't remember that 1/2 "power" is the same as a square root. But it is. This function

```
=SQRT(number)
```

gives you the same answer as this function:

```
=POWER(number,1/2)
```

The cube root then? It's the 1/3 power. So to get the cube root of a number you use this function:

```
=POWER(number,1/3)
```

And I can only pray that you never really have to use such a function in real life.

I'm Trying to Use SQRT but Keep Getting #NUM! Errors. Why?

Excel is unable to calculate the square root of a negative number. This opens up a wormhole in mathematics having to deal with imaginary numbers, flagged by the constant *i*. Excel doesn't really give a damn about *i*, so the solution is instead to filter out the possibilities of calculating the square root of a negative number.

To eliminate the possibilities of a negative number inside the SQRT function, you need to use the ABS function. ABS returns the "absolute value" of a number, or the value of any number minus the minus sign. So ABS(–15) is 15. And ABS(4) is 4. Here's how you would put such a thing to work:

1. Type the following values into cells J1 through J4:

   16 -4 10 -25

2. Into cell K1 type =SQRT(J1).
3. Fill-copy down from cell K1 through cell K4, and you'll see something similar to Figure 13.3. Obviously something in the universe is out of whack.

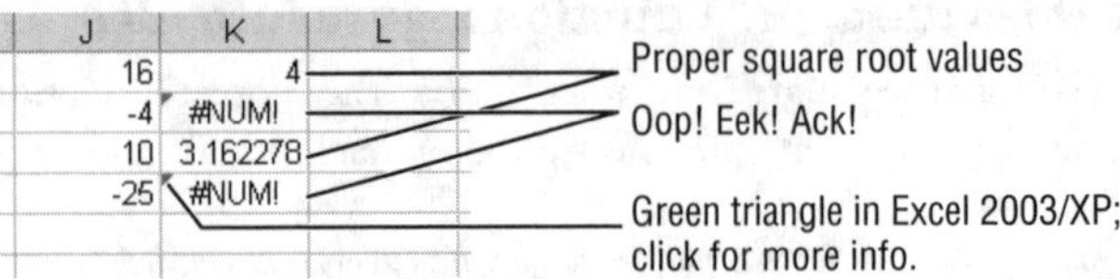

FIGURE 13.3 The dreadful result of finding the square root of negative numbers

NOTE *Don't fret over the negative numbers. They happen. The solution is merely to make them non-negative and try again.*

4. Edit the formula in cell K1 to read =SQRT(ABS(J1)).

NOTE *Remember the F2 key to edit!*

Formulas read from the inside out. So first you're converting the value of cell J1 into an absolute value—whacking off the negative part, if it exists. Then, with that guaranteed-to-be-positive number in there, you can safely and sanely calculate the square root, no errors possible.

5. Fill-copy down through cell K4, and the values should happily be calculated, negative numbers be damned.

I've done woodworking and shop work enough to know that I do occasionally end up trying to calculate the square root of a negative number. It typically happens because I measure a distance in a manner that yields a negative number. By recalculating the distance, it's possible to come up with a positive number that doesn't cause the SQRT function to vomit all over the place, but, generally speaking, the ABS function ends up giving you a proper result despite the original negative numbers.

How Can I Get My Answer to Display to Two Decimal Places?

The number of decimal places displayed is controlled by the cell's number format: Select the cell(s) and press Ctrl+1; then click the Number tab. The Number, Currency, and Accounting formats all have a setting for the number of decimal places to appear in the cell.

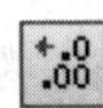

The decimal places can also be quickly set by using the Increase Decimal and Decrease Decimal buttons on the Formatting toolbar. Note that as the number of decimal places is changed, values are rounded up or down accordingly.

What's the Difference between Rounding and Truncating a Number?

The rounding functions take a number and bump it up or down to the next decimal place depending on which function you choose. Some functions round up, some round down, and some round depending on the number's value (like they taught in school).

Truncating functions are the executioner's axe: They just lop off part of a number, like WHACK! Leaving you with whatever is left over, again depending on the function.

There are various rounding and whacking functions available to you in Excel. Choose the proper one depending on how you want that value manipulated.

CEILING

Ceiling is a rounding-up function that lets you specify what to round the value up to. The format is

```
=CEILING(value,significance)
```

So if you want to round the value in cell A1 up to the nearest 10th spot, you would use

```
=CEILING(A1,0.1)
```

Or suppose they do away with the penny and everything has to be rounded up to the nearest nickel; then here is that function:

```
=CEILING(A1,0.05)
```

Or, worse, suppose they do away with the penny, nickel, and dime and you have to round everything up to the nearest quarter:

```
=CEILING(A1,0.25)
```

The companion function for CEILING is FLOOR.

NOTE *The advantage to using CEILING is that it rounds up to a given digit or interval. The disadvantage is the function's spelling: I before E except after C.*

EVEN

The EVEN function always rounds any value up to the next even integer (number without a decimal part). So

```
=EVEN(0.98)
```

produces the value 2, the next even number up from the value .98.

The companion function for EVEN is (logically) ODD.

FLOOR

The FLOOR function is the rounding-down version of the CEILING function. So when that day comes that they do away with the penny, pray that they use the FLOOR function to round *down* to the nearest nickel, not up. This would be that function:

```
=FLOOR(A1,0.05)
```

The above function takes the value in cell A1 and rounds it down to the nearest 0.05 value.

NOTE *Both the CEILING and FLOOR functions can round negative numbers, but both values in the function must be negative or you get a #NUM! error. For example, if A1 is negative, then =FLOOR(A1,-0.05) must be used; both values must be negative.*

INT

The INT function converts numbers of any type into integers. An integer is any number without a decimal or fractional part, including negative numbers.

For positive numbers, INT lops off any decimal part.

For negative numbers, INT lops off the decimal part and rounds *down.*

For example:

```
=INT(4.25)
```

The cell with the above formula displays the value 4—no fraction or decimal.

```
=INT(-11.01)
```

The cell above displays the value –12.

The most common reason I use the INT function is for generating a random number. The random number function, RAND, produces values in the range 0 to 1. So to get a value higher, you must not only multiply the RAND function's result but also lop off the fractional part. INT is handy for this.

My generic random number formula is

```
=INT(RAND()*value)+1
```

This formula produces a random number between 1 and *value.* So if you're trying to calculate rolls of the dice for some sort of Excel craps game, you would use this formula:

```
=INT(RAND()*6)+1
```

ODD

The ODD function is the companion of the EVEN function. It's job is to round any number up to the next whole odd number.

```
=ODD(0.98)
```

The cell with the function listed above displays the value 1.

ROUND

The ROUND function does the same rounding as they tried to teach you in school: It rounds up or down depending on whether the number ends in a 5 or not. Also, with this function, you can set which place before or after the decimal place to round. Here is the format:

```
=ROUND(value,precision)
```

The *value* is a cell or specific value. The *precision* is a positive or negative number that tells ROUND the number of digits to round to. Positive precision values round to the right of the decimal place; negative values round to the left.

The ROUND function is so much fun that I've devised a mini-worksheet for you to play with it, as shown in Figure 13.4.

FIGURE 13.4
Toying with the ROUND function

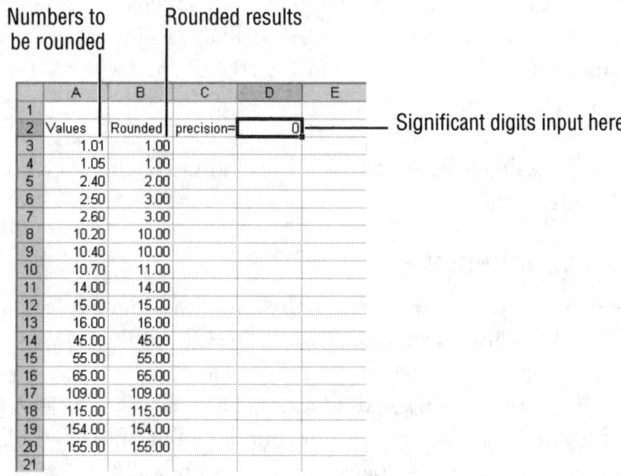

	A	B	C	D	E
1					
2	Values	Rounded	precision=	0	
3	1.01	1.00			
4	1.05	1.00			
5	2.40	2.00			
6	2.50	3.00			
7	2.60	3.00			
8	10.20	10.00			
9	10.40	10.00			
10	10.70	11.00			
11	14.00	14.00			
12	15.00	15.00			
13	16.00	16.00			
14	45.00	45.00			
15	55.00	55.00			
16	65.00	65.00			
17	109.00	109.00			
18	115.00	115.00			
19	154.00	154.00			
20	155.00	155.00			
21					

Follow these steps to create the worksheet and experiment with the ROUND function:

1. Into cell A2 type **Values.**
2. Into cell B2 type **Rounded.**
3. Into cell C3 type **precision=**.
4. Into cell D3 type **0**.
5. Name cell D3 **precision.**
6. Type these values in cells A3 through A20, as shown in Figure 13.4:

1.01 1.05 2.4 2.5 2.6 10.2 10.4 10.7 14 15 16 45 55 65 109 115 154 155

7. Format the cells in A3 through B20 to display two digits.
8. In cell B3 type **=ROUND(A3,precision)**.
9. Drag to fill the formula in cell B3 down through cell B20. Now your screen should look similar to Figure 13.4. Right away you can see how the numbers in column A are rounded up or down in column B; most notable are 1.05, 2.4, 2.5, and 2.6.
10. Type **1** into cell D2. Now the values in column B are rounded to the first digit after the decimal. This affects only the first two values, 1.01 and 1.05, which are rounded down and up, accordingly.
11. Type **2** into cell D2. Nothing changes. Rounding to the second digit after the decimal doesn't affect any of the numbers in the table. That's because none of the numbers hold any digits that far out on the right.

12. Type **-1** into cell D2. Now the rounding happens on the left of the decimal. Note how the first five values in column B are now zero? They're all rounded down. Other values in column A are rounded up or down to the nearest 10, which is where –1 sets things.

13. Type **-2** into cell D2.

Now the rounding happens to the nearest hundreds digit. To go any higher you'd need to restack column A with larger numbers.

ROUNDDOWN, ROUNDUP

These are two companion functions to the ROUND function, and they behave as their names imply: ROUNDDOWN always rounds down and ROUNDUP always rounds up. (The ROUND function rounds up or down depending on the value.)

Like ROUND, each of these functions has a precision value, which tells you which digit to the left or right of the decimal place is used for rounding. But unlike ROUND, the direction of rounding is set by the function, not the value of the digit rounded off.

TRUNC

The final rounding function isn't rounding at all; it's *truncating*, or lopping off, any given portion of a number. In its simplest format, TRUNC merely lops off the decimal part of any value:

```
=TRUNC(2.3)
```

The above function displays the value 2 in the cell. Whack! Off goes the .3.

TRUNC can also sport an optional precision value, which works like the precision value in the ROUND function:

```
=TRUNC(3.141,2)
```

This function displays 3.14 in the cell; the digits after the second decimal place are lopped off. Likewise:

```
=TRUNC(12345,-2)
```

This function displays 12300 in the cell; the two digits to the left of the decimal place are lopped off.

I don't use TRUNC myself. Then again, I drive a pickup truck and it doesn't have a TRUNC.

How Can I Assure That the Result of This Operation Will Always Be Positive?

This is the ABS function, which was discussed earlier in this chapter on how to deal with the square root of negative numbers ("I'm Trying to Use SQRT but Keep Getting #NUM! Errors. Why?").

What's the Word I'm Looking for That Means the Remainder of One Value Divided by Another?

The "leftover" value when dividing one number into another is known as the *remainder*. To determine what the remainder is you use the *modulus* function, named after evil Dr. Modulus who developed it.

As anyone who's ever struggled through division knows, not every number cleanly divides into any other number. Typically there is something left over. For example:

```
=22/7
```

The result displayed in the cell is 3.142857. So you could say that 7 goes into 22 three times "plus change." But back in math class, you most likely wrote, "7 goes into 22 3 times with 1 remainder." Alas, .142857 doesn't look anything like "1 remainder." So that's where the modulus or MOD function comes into play. Write this into a cell:

```
=MOD(22,7)
```

This reads, "What is the remainder of 22 divided by 7?" Press Enter and you'll see the value 1 displayed in the cell. Or try this:

```
=MOD(24,5)
```

Before pressing the Enter key can you guess what the remainder of 24 divided by 5 could be? Yup, it's 4.

When the MOD function returns 0, it means the number divides in cleanly:

```
=MOD(52,13)
```

The above function returns 0 because 13 gazinta 52 four times.

NOTE *Use the MOD function in conjunction with dividing a value that cannot return a fractional number.*

Why not write one of those old chestnut math problems to demonstrate how MOD works? Assume that there are three of you: yourself, Smelly Kelly, and Dirty Berty. You would like to split up the apples you stole from Mr. Magillicutty's tree evenly between you all. Any apples left over you're going to toss back at Mr. Magillicutty's kitchen window. Create a table that shows numbers of apples from 3 on up to 30 and how many apples for each value you would have left to throw back at the kitchen window.

Don't spaz! I've done this for you, as shown in Figure 13.5.

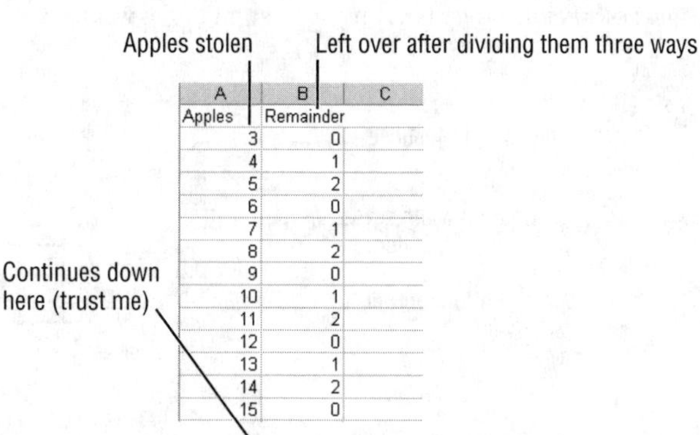

Apples	Remainder
3	0
4	1
5	2
6	0
7	1
8	2
9	0
10	1
11	2
12	0
13	1
14	2
15	0

FIGURE 13.5 The dreaded solution to the math word puzzle

It's really easy, thanks to the MOD function:

1. Into cell A1 type **Apples.**
2. Into cell B1 type **Remainder**. These are the apples you get to toss at the kitchen window (which is closed, so the intent here is to break the glass—but it's only a story so don't get all moral and ethical on me).
3. Into cell A2 type **3**, and then drag-fill with the right mouse button down to cell A29; select "Fill Series" from the pop-up menu when it appears.
4. Into cell B2 type **=MOD(A2,3)**. This reads, "the remainder of dividing the value in cell A2 (the number of apples) by the 3 of you."
5. Copy-fill down from cell B2 through cell B29.

And there you have it: Depending on the number of apples you stole, you will have a 2/3 chance that you'll get to throw one or two of them at the window.

The SUM of All Things

The handiest function of them all is the SUM function. It's one of the original functions from the very first spreadsheet, VisiCalc. And evidence of its importance is seen right there on the Standard toolbar; it's the only function that sports its own button. Golly! I suppose that merits the glut of interesting sections that follow.

Why Bother with the SUM Function When I Just Love Typing + Signs Over and Over Again?

The reason the SUM function exists is to handle the extremely common task of totaling a column of values, such as shown in Figure 13.6: Select the bottom cell, click the AutoSum button on the Standard toolbar, and achieve the total. Instant sum! Very smart.

NOTE *The name of the function is SUM, which includes a range of cells that are totaled and displayed. The symbol for the AutoSum toolbar button is the Greek character* sigma [Σ], *which could be the Greek word for SUM but probably isn't.*

FIGURE 13.6
Instant sum

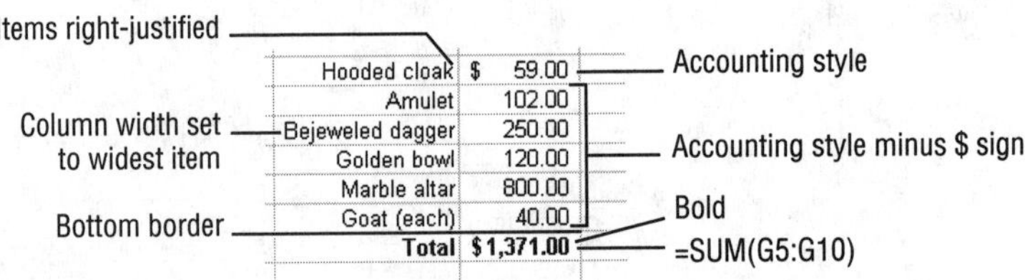

You Say the AutoSum Button Is Very Smart, but Sometimes It Can Be Very Stupid

Actually, the AutoSum button knows only as much as it assumes. Sometimes you need to give it a little help.

Suppose you have a worksheet similar to the one shown in Figure 13.7. Go ahead and type it in, if you dare; that's the first part.

The second part is detailed below. This covers how you finish off the report by using the SUM function sometimes and not other times:

1. Click to select cell C6.
2. Click the AutoSum button on the toolbar. The SUM function is inserted and smartly selects the four cells above, C2 through C5. Smart. Smart. Smart.
3. Press the Enter key to lock in the formula.
4. Format cell C6 bold.
5. Click to select cell C11.
6. This time manually type =SUM(. Type only the first part of the function.
7. Now select cells C8 through C10 with the mouse, and they're plugged into the function.

NOTE *You can actually click and select individual cells or values for the SUM function; it doesn't always have to be a slew of cells.*

FIGURE 13.7
Yet another sample worksheet

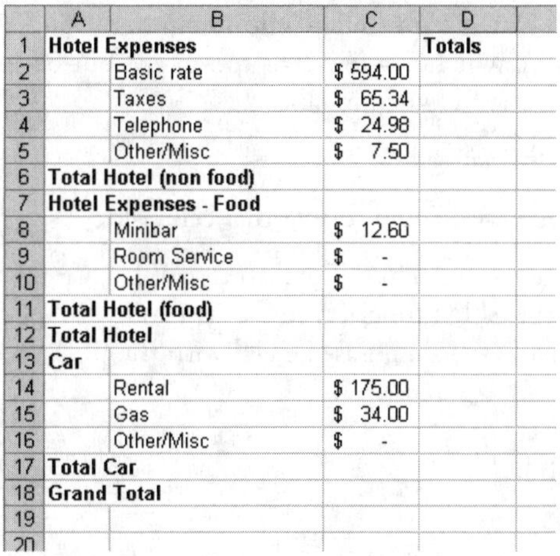

	A	B	C	D
1	**Hotel Expenses**			**Totals**
2		Basic rate	$ 594.00	
3		Taxes	$ 65.34	
4		Telephone	$ 24.98	
5		Other/Misc	$ 7.50	
6	**Total Hotel (non food)**			
7	**Hotel Expenses - Food**			
8		Minibar	$ 12.60	
9		Room Service	$ -	
10		Other/Misc	$ -	
11	**Total Hotel (food)**			
12	**Total Hotel**			
13	**Car**			
14		Rental	$ 175.00	
15		Gas	$ 34.00	
16		Other/Misc	$ -	
17	**Total Car**			
18	**Grand Total**			
19				
20				

8. Type the closing) and press Enter.
9. Make cell C11 bold as well.
10. Click to select cell C17.
11. Click the AutoSum button on the toolbar again, and the values are smartly selected. (Yes, spaces interfere with the cells the SUM command automatically selects. More on that in a second.)
12. Press the Enter key.
13. Make cell C17 bold.
14. Now to do the Totals column: In cell D6, type **=C6**. This copies the nonfood Hotel subtotal over into the Totals column; no need to reuse the SUM function in D6 because it's already used in C6.
15. Format cell D6 bold.
16. Into cell D11, type =.
17. Click cell C11 with the mouse and press Enter.
18. Make cell D11 bold.
19. Click to select cell D12.
20. Time to calculate the Hotel subtotal: Click the AutoSum button on the toolbar. Oops! It selects only cell D12.
21. Use the mouse to drag from cell D6 down through cell D11. Now the formula reads =SUM(D6:D11), which is a few cells too many, but occasionally such lassoing of cells is necessary with the SUM command.
22. Press Enter and format cell C12 bold.
23. Into cell D17 type **=C17** and format that cell bold.
24. Finally you come to the Grand Total: Into cell D18 type **=SUM(D12,D17)**. Again, remember that the SUM function can accept individual cells. And they need not even be in the same row or column as the cell with the SUM function.
25. Press Enter.
26. Format cell D18 bold.

I Want the Sum off to the Left

The best way to sum a row of cells instead of a column is to select a cell to the right of the row of cells and then click the AutoSum button on the toolbar.

Excel looks up, and then it looks to the left to see if there are any numbers needing to be totaled. Otherwise, you have to manually select the cells using the mouse, as shown in Figure 13.8.

FIGURE 13.8
Pulling a sum from the left

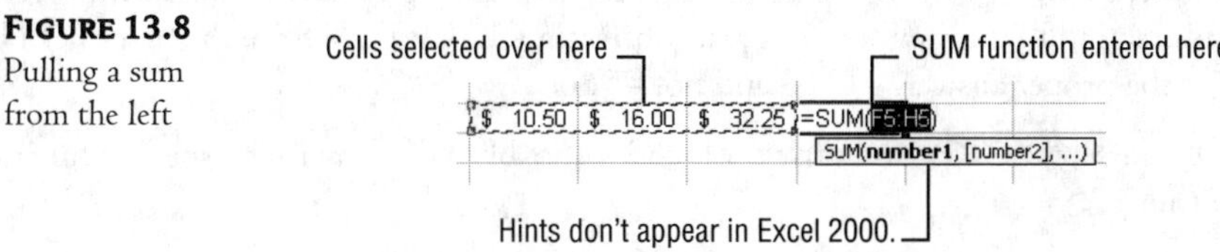

Can I Use the SUM Function on More Than a Row or Column?

Sure: The SUM function can total up a whole block of numbers, as shown in Figure 13.9. It can even total up multiple blocks of functions, as shown in Figure 13.10.

FIGURE 13.9
Totaling a block of values

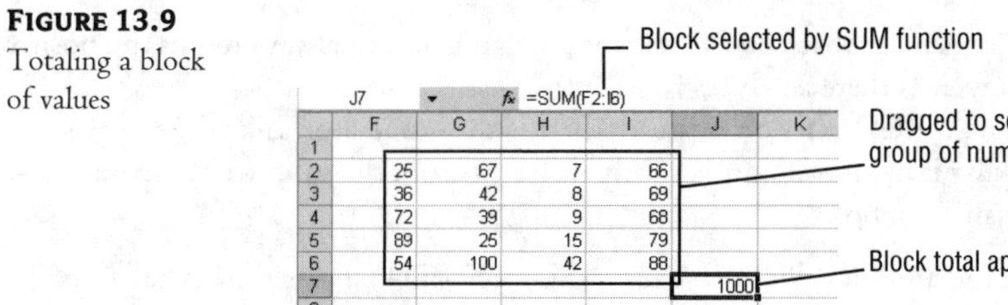

FIGURE 13.10
The Sum of three different blocks of values

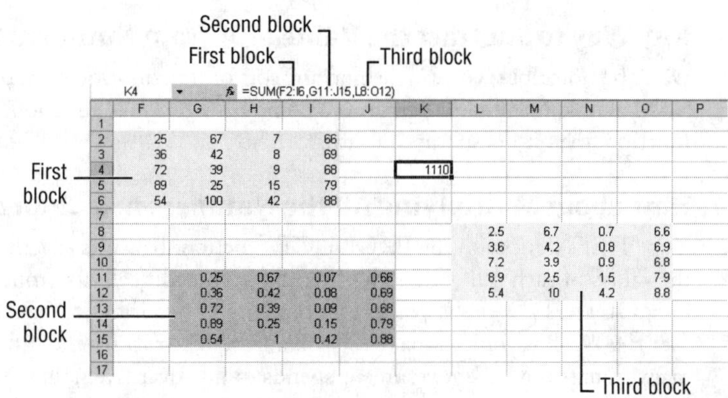

Any Way to Subtract a Large Swath of Numbers?

Not with a function. The only way to subtract a column of numbers is to create a formula where you subtract the value of each cell from each cell, which you can do in the following steps:

1. Type the values **125**, **99**, **801**, and **191** into cells D1 through D4.
2. Into cell D5, type the formula: **=0-D1-D2-D3-D4**. You have to start with 0 because you're subtracting all the numbers, not just subtracting the last three from the first one. That way you get the proper answer, –1216 and not –966.

   Of course, there's an easier trick, which is probably why there isn't a specific function for such a thing:

3. Click to select cell D5.
4. Click the AutoSum button on the toolbar, and SUM naturally selects the four numbers above.
5. Press the Enter key.

Did you notice anything about the result? Yes, it's 1216, which is the positive value of the result you got in step 2. Thus looms the question: How do you turn a positive value into a negative one in Excel?

You should remember that you can use the ABS function to always return the positive value of a function or number. Is there a NEGS function?

No, there is no NEGS function. Instead, there is the – operator. Like the % operator, it affects a number by making it negative. This is subtly different from the subtraction operator, –, though it's essentially the same symbol.

6. Edit the function in cell D5 to read **=-SUM(D1:D4)**. Press the F2 key to edit the cell and simply insert a minus sign before the SUM function. This negates the result and gives you the subtracted total of the column—or the end result you originally requested.

Keep the values in cells D1 through D4 for the next section's example.

Any Way to Subtract the Value of π from Numbers Using the SUM Function?

Don't be ridiculous; you can fashion any sort of function you want by mixing and matching formulas. SUM is unique in that it performs a common worksheet function. If it's not a common worksheet function, then it doesn't need to exist, right?

How about Multiplying All the Numbers in a Chunk?

Yup: That's done with the PRODUCT function. It works exactly like SUM, but it multiplies all the values of each cell with each other. So if you edit cell D5 from the previous set of steps to read =PRODUCT(D1:D4), you get a number so huge it has to be displayed in scientific notation: 1.89E+09. (But you can make the cell a little wider to see the value 1,893,263,625, which is how many dollars the U.S. government spends in just over five hours.

What's the Point of Using the AutoSum Button on the Toolbar Like a Menu?

If the AutoSum button is the king of functions, then it must have a royal court. In Excel 2003/XP (but not in Excel 2000) the AutoSum button has a drop-down menu, as shown in Figure 13.11. This menu lists four other functions similar to SUM and almost as popular. You can instantly insert these functions by choosing them from the menu. (Excel 2000 users can still manually type in each function.)

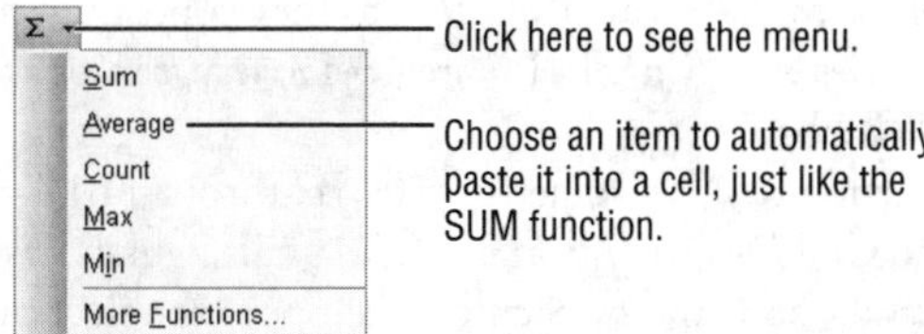

FIGURE 13.11
The royal cousins to the SUM function on its toolbar menu

Is AVERAGE Just an Average Function or Does It Really Calculate the Average?

You remember hating averages from school, right? The idea was to total up a bunch of numbers and then divide that result by the number of numbers. So:

```
125 + 99 + 801 + 191 = 1216
```

You know this from earlier in this chapter. Now to get the average you have to divide 1216 by 4 (the number of numbers). But screw that! Instead, and using the same values in cells D1 through D4 as shown earlier, complete these steps:

1. Click to select cell D5.
2. In Excel 2003/XP, choose AVERAGE from the AutoSum button's menu; in Excel 2000, type =AVERAGE(D1:D4).
3. Press Enter. It's 304!

Now teachers can really figure out the class average, baseball nuts can do batting averages, and all of us below- or above-normal people can simply sit back and appreciate the AVERAGE function.

NOTE *Though I'm not getting into them here, Excel has a surplus of statistical functions, logically kept in the Statistical category of the Insert Function dialog box. So if you need to cast a standard-deviation spell on a group of numbers, you'd use the STDEV function, similar to the way AVERAGE is cast above.*

Why Would I Ever Use the COUNT Function?

You gotta figure: How does the AVERAGE function know how many numbers it's reading in? Obviously, somewhere in Excel's bowels must be a function that counts the number of numbers. That function is, logically, the COUNT function.

The COUNT function merely returns how many cells contain values. So if you select a swath of cells—say some huge block—COUNT tells you how many of those cells have values in them. It does not count any cells with text, nor does it count blank cells.

I can imagine a situation where there is some sort of tally being kept in a worksheet. For example, in Figure 13.12 results are posted for an election as they come in. A popular statistic on election night is the number of counties reporting. In Figure 13.12, that can be calculated in cell D2 by using the function =COUNT(B2:B17).

The COUNT function reads the range of cells, B2 through B17, and counts how many have values.

A variation on the COUNT function is COUNTIF, which bases its results on the number of items in a group matching something specific. So suppose the election is over, and Figure 13.13 shows the winning results by each county according to political party.

FIGURE 13.12
An example of using the COUNT function

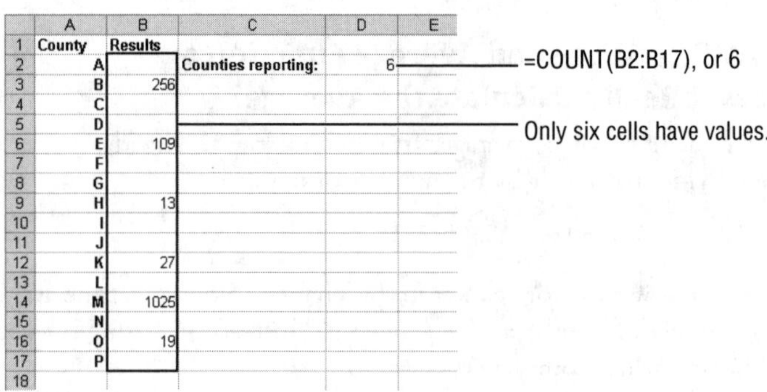

FIGURE 13.13
Election results by party

	A	B	C	D	E
1	County	Results			
2	A	Rep	Counties reporting:	ALL	
3	B	Dem	Republican:		
4	C	Dem	Democratic:		
5	D	Rep			
6	E	Rep			
7	F	Rep			
8	G	Dem			
9	H	Rep			
10	I	Dem			
11	J	Dem			
12	K	Dem			
13	L	Rep			
14	M	Rep			
15	N	Dem			
16	O	Dem			
17	P	Dem			
18					

Totals go here.

Either "Dem" or "Rep" text

Don't Forget These Common Comparison Things!

Here are some more symbols you learned and have since forgotten since high school. These are comparison operators, primarily used in the various IF formulas:

= Is equal to; is TRUE if the values are equal.

> Is greater than; is TRUE if the value on the left is more than the value on the right.

>= Is greater than or equal to; is TRUE if the value on the left is equal to or more than the value on the right.

< Is less than; is TRUE if the value on the left is smaller than the value on the right.

<= Is less than or equal to; is TRUE if the value on the left is equal to or smaller than the value on the right.

<> Not equal to; is TRUE if the values are not equal

To total them up without using your fingers, into cell D3 you would type this formula:

```
=COUNTIF(B2:B17,"Rep")
```

This reads, "Count the number of cells between B2 and B17 that match 'Rep.'" Or, actually, the "IF" implies to count the cells if they are equal to or match a logical expression that could be included in the function. More on that in a sec.

Into cell D4 enter the following formula:

```
=COUNTIF(B2:B17,"Dem")
```

And that displays the total number of counties that are represented by Democrats.

Mathematically, suppose you had a series of test results in cells D4 through D44 and you wanted to determine how many were above 60. If so, then you could use COUNTIF to determine that value:

```
=COUNTIF(D4:D44,">60")
```

Above, COUNTIF examines cells D4 through D44. If any are "greater than 60," they are counted and the total number is displayed in the cell.

What Are the Advantages to MIN and MAX?

The MIN and MAX functions are used to find the lowest and highest values in a swath of selected cells, like this:

1. In cells F3 through F8, type the following values:

   325 456 197 224 380 210

2. Select all the cells, F3 through F8, and name them **scores**.

3. Into cell G3, type the formula **=IF(F3=MAX(scores),"Winner!","")**. So if the cell on the left (F3) is equal to the highest value in the list of scores, the cell displays the text "Winner!" Otherwise, nothing "" is displayed.

4. Drag-fill to copy the formula down from cell G3 through cell G8.

And we have a winna, as shown in Figure 13.14.

To determine the lowest score, MIN would be used: Simply edit the formula in cell G3 to read

```
=IF(F3=MIN(scores),"Loser!","")
```

Then drag-fill down to copy the formula into the rest of the cells.

And now the thought puzzle: How can you get both "Winner!" and "Loser!" to display, as shown in Figure 13.15?

No, the answer isn't to use a logical function, such as OR.

The answer is not to use two IF statements in the same cell.

The answer is to hide your work elsewhere and use text concatenation to create the illusion of too much work in one cell. Figure 13.16 explains it all.

First, the same "Winner!" formula is used in cells G15 down through G20:

```
=IF(F3=MAX(scores),"Winner!","")
```

This produces the same results, with the winner being displayed well below the original set of scores.

Second, the same "Loser!" formula is put into cells H15 through H20:

```
=IF(F3=MIN(scores),"Loser!","")
```

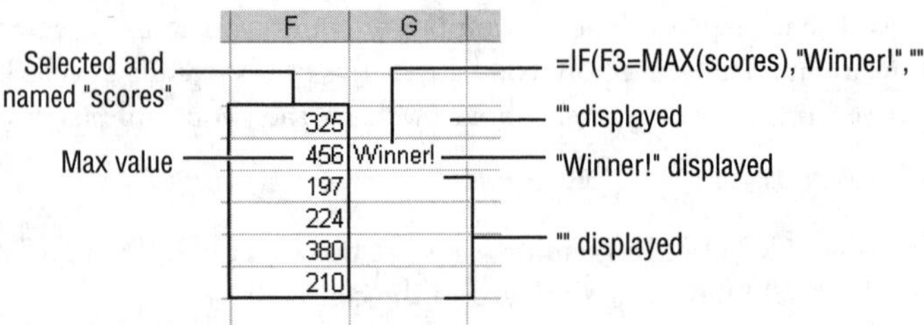

FIGURE 13.14
Determining who is the winner by using the MAX function

FIGURE 13.15
The MIN and MAX values are highlighted.

F	G
325	
456	Winner!
197	Loser!
224	
380	
210	

FIGURE 13.16
Hiding your work

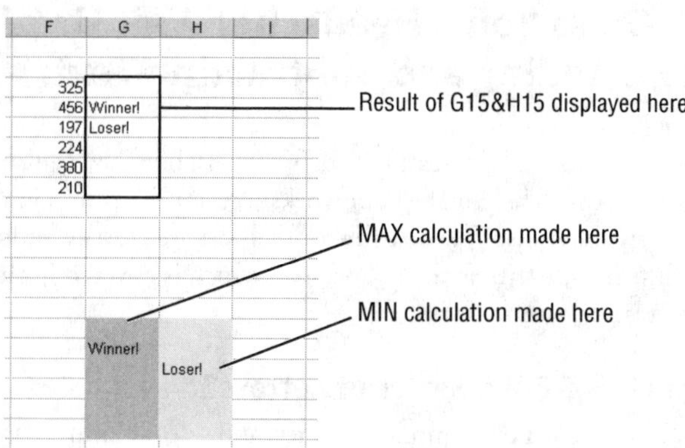

Again you get the same results, just away from the action.

At this point you have both the "Winner!" text and "Loser!" text displayed in the cells. Because they should never be the same cell (that would mean everyone tied), you can use the & operator to add the text from one cell to the text from another cell. So:

Third, the formula =G15&H15 is placed into cell G3. This tells Excel to display the text from cell G15 plus the text from cell H15 into cell G3. Because G15 and H15 are blank, nothing is displayed.

When the formula is copied down, however, the cells containing text are duplicated. So the result of cell G16 "Winner!" & H16 "" is "Winner!" And that is displayed in cell G4.

The result of cell G17 "" & H17 "Loser!" is stuck together and placed into cell G5. And so on.

That's one way you can get the MIN *and* MAX values to display in one column.

NOTE *Yes, it's cheating. But it's a great way to lead into the next subject: text functions.*

ANOTHER WAY TO GET "WINNER!" OR "LOSER!" TO DISPLAY

Yet another way to get either "Winner!" or "Loser!" to display is by "nesting" IF statements.

In a programming language there would be a companion ELSE statement for an IF. So you could say "IF this item is the maximum value, do this, ELSE (or otherwise) do that." The equivalent of this in Excel is the following:

```
=IF(F3=MAX(scores),"Winner!",IF(F3=MIN(scores),"Loser!",""))
```

What's being done above is that the "Value_if_false" part of the IF function is being replaced by yet another IF function—perfectly legal. That way a second comparison can be done in the same cell. The results come out the same as the example in the main part of the text.

There is no real limit on how many IF commands you can nest inside of each other, though I suppose after a certain number the logic would be hard to follow and tough to test.

If Math Gives You a Headache, Wait Until You Start Adding and Subtracting Text

I'm kidding! Relax.

Excel has a number of interesting text functions, but they can't really do much unless you add in the power of macros to help make your worksheet hop, skip, and jump. Alas, this book does not cover macros, so there are only a few text functions I feel are worthy enough to take up your time with. In fact, one of the most useful is the & operator, which is covered in the previous section and also helps solve an interesting puzzle there.

How Can I Drag-Fill a Series of Letters?

You can have a series of days, months, values, and so on. But if you want to fill column A with letters A through Z you must use a text function to make that happen. Here's how:

1. Click to select cell A1.
2. Type in the formula =CHAR(ROW()+64).
3. Press Enter.
4. Reselect cell A1.
5. Drag the cell down to fill and copy it, down to cell A19 or so. As you drag, you copy the formula into each subsequent cell, which creates a range of letters, A through as low as you want to go.

The CHAR function is used to display a character in a cell—any character. You can enter values from 1 through 255, though only a few of those numbers display recognizable characters; most of the characters are "blank" or display foreign language letters or symbols.

NOTE *The values used by the CHAR function are ASCII codes. ASCII is a common scheme for assigning letters, numbers, and other symbols to code values. It's used by almost all computers worldwide.*

You don't need to know all the codes to use CHAR; only a handful are worthy of attention:

- Characters 65 through 90 display the uppercase letters A through Z.
- Characters 97 through 122 display the lowercase letters a through z.

Pretty much everything else is some symbol or dingbat that you'd probably never want in a cell by itself. (And if you do, I'm certain that you're clever enough to figure out how to make a table in Excel to display all 255 variations of the CHAR function.)

In this function, =CHAR(ROW()+64)), I'm using the value returned by the ROW() function to help calculate the letter displayed in a cell. ROW() returns the current row number, or 1 for cell A1. That calculates out to =CHAR(65), which displays the letter A.

Alas, you cannot drag-fill with the CHAR function. Remember that CHAR displays text, not a value, so there is really nothing to fill (just as you cannot drag-fill text).

So if you want to display letters A through J in cells C8 through C18, you could do this:

1. Click cell C8.
2. Enter the formula =CHAR(65).
3. Click cell C9 and enter the formula =CHAR(66).
4. Repeat this for each cell down to C18, incrementing the value in the CHAR function by one each time.

BORING!

Or you could do this:

1. Click cell C8.
2. Enter the formula =CHAR(ROW(A1)+64). Rather than have the ROW() function return the current row—which means you'd have to do math in your head (65-current_row)—you can simply have Excel calculate the row number for cell A1, which is always 1. Add 64 and you get an A.
3. Drag cell C8 down through cell C18 to copy and fill. As you drag, the relative reference A1 changes to the next row, which increases for each cell down and gives you the next letter in the alphabet.

How Can I Use CONCATENATE to Make My Worksheet More Polite?

Concatenation is the art of sticking two or more pieces of text together. It's a fancy term for what's basically "word glue." You already saw an example with the & operator earlier in this chapter. Basically & just takes text from one cell and combines it with text in another cell to create a longer, combined piece of text.

As an example, consider Figure 13.17. All the lines of text say basically the same thing, "Pay up or die!" The difference is in the formatting. In both cases, the second line of text looks better than the first. That's because the second line uses concatenation to build the line of text as opposed to stuffing the text and values into separate cells (which is how the first line does things).

FIGURE 13.17
Using CONCATENATE to clean up some text

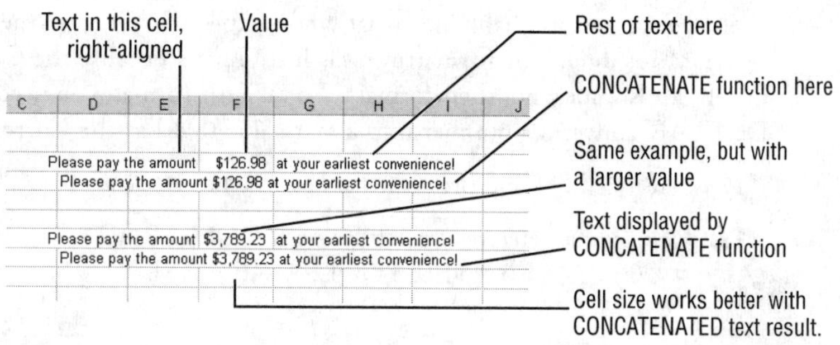

The following steps show you how to use concatenation by building the example in Figure 13.17:

1. Into cell E3, type **Please pay the amount.**
2. Right-justify cell E3.
3. Type **126.98** into cell E4.
4. Format cell E4 with the Currency format. Do not click the Currency button to do this; remember that the Currency button on the toolbar uses the Accounting format. You want the dollar sign close to the number to make it look good.
5. Into cell E5 type **at your earliest convenience!**

This is the way most folks would format a calculated dollar amount into a worksheet, such as an invoice or purchase order. But the cell containing the value still isn't wide enough to make the sentence appear continuous. Instead, it looks like one of those "You have won!" junk mails where your name has obviously been added after the fact.

Now you could adjust the cell's width for column F. But look at the second example in Figure 13.17. It still doesn't look as good as it could—not when compared to the two "perfect" sentences below the examples.

The way to clean up the situation is to concatenate everything so that one string of text is displayed, not two pieces of text and a value. That's done with the CONCATENATE function, as follows:

6. Into cell D4, type **=CONCATENATE(**.
7. Click cell E3. That's the first bit of text.
8. Type a comma.
9. Click cell E4 and type a comma.
10. Click cell E5 and type a closing parenthesis. The function should now read = CONCATENATE(E3,F3,G3).
11. Press Enter.

The results are probably not what you're expecting. Though the value did survive into the final sentence, it's ugly. The formatting was lost. That's because the CONCATENATE function merely reads values, not their formats. To fake the format, you need to use the DOLLAR function. DOLLAR converts a number into a text value that has the Currency format. Keep working:

12. Select cell D4 and press the F2 key to edit.
13. Replace the reference to cell F3 with **DOLLAR(F3)**. The function should now read = CONCATENATE(E3,DOLLAR(F3),G3).

14. Press Enter. Alas, still not there. You need to add some spaces around the number. Spaces are merely text, and the CONCATENATE function accepts text in a cell or text you can type in directly. So:

15. Select cell D4 and press the F2 key to edit.

16. Insert blank spaces—" "—before and after the DOLLAR function as follows:

```
= CONCATENATE(E3," ",DOLLAR(F3)," ",G3)
```

17. Press Enter, and finally the text looks good.

The moral of the story is that CONCATENATE, aside from being a booger to type, accepts text from a cell, values from a cell, or even text you directly type in, such as the spaces in this section's example. In fact, you could concoct a function like this:

```
= CONCATENATE("Please pay the amount ",DOLLAR(F3), " at your earliest
convenience!")
```

This includes the text directly (plus the blank spaces), which may save you from crowding up your worksheet too much.

Chapter 14

Fun with Charts and Graphs

Charts are fun.

OH, NO: I MEAN, charts are *hard work*. Toil! Dread! Endless effort! Some charts take *weeks* to create and tune. And the results are worth it: High and lofty, frequently overpaid individuals can look at a chart and rub their dour chins in deep contemplation. These individuals appreciate the frankness and honesty of an XY plot or pie graph over the pages of numbers—the "real work." That's because the aristocratic brain just isn't attuned to seeing the trees. No, they want the forest—preferably a *National Geographic*–type photograph of one.

Aw, what the heck: I just can't help myself. Charts are fun! Even when the data they illustrate is as dismal as Minnesota in February, there is just this certain joy that comes when playing with charts. This is going to be a fun chapter—probably a review for most because nothing induces the joy of play like charts in Excel.

- Cooking up a chart in Excel (review)
- Using the Chart Wizard and Chart toolbar
- Repairing a chart after it's made
- Adjusting chart fonts and colors
- Adding and removing chart chunks
- Changing the way the chart appears

Basic Chart Tricks

Charts are rather easy to "get" in Excel. There are only a few basic things to remember, so if this is your first exposure—or even your first in-depth exposure—read over the next several sections to get up to speed. The next major part in this chapter, "Redoing the Chart," is where most of the common chart puzzles are solved and questions are answered.

What's the World's Second-Fastest Way to Create a Chart?

Aside from theft, the fastest way to create a chart is to lasso a group of numbers in a worksheet and click the Chart Wizard button on the Standard toolbar. When the wizard appears, click the Finish button. Voila: instant chart.

Okay, it's instant *ugly* chart, but it's a chart or "graph" of the numbers you lassoed. Now some answers to your deepest questions:

Q: Can you lasso only one number and make a chart?

A: Yes, but this produces a useless chart. Charts are designed for overview and comparison—the"Big Picture" thing. Charting only one value is hardly useful.

Q: What if I lasso a table of numbers?

A: Then you get a multidimensional chart.

Q: The chart looks ugly.

A: That's because you didn't work all the way through the wizard, so as a punishment Excel coughs up its ugliest chart.

Q: How can I fix things?

A: Keep reading.

How Can I Force the Chart onto a New Sheet?

To create a chart on a new sheet in Excel, you must use the first-fastest way of creating a new chart. Simply lasso the numbers you want represented on the chart, then press the F11 key.

Instantly a new sheet—a Chart sheet—is created in the workbook, as shown in Figure 14.1. It contains a graph of the numbers you selected. And, yes, it is a dumb graph, just as if you had used the second-fastest chart-creating method described in the previous section.

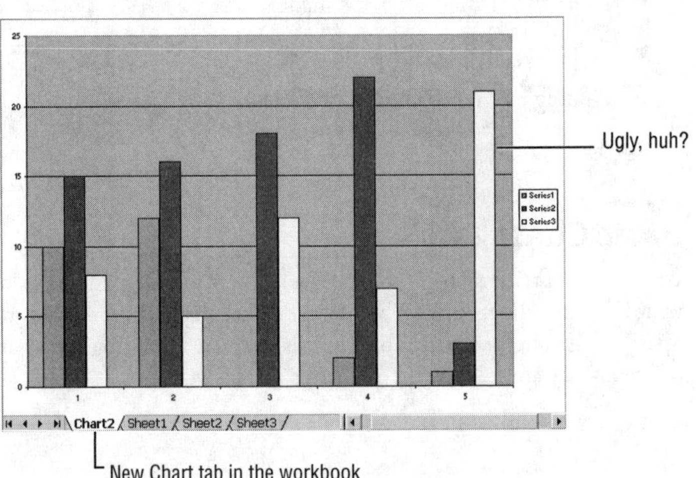

FIGURE 14.1
The new chart is instantly created when you press the F11 key.

Creating a New Chart

Here are the fastest and next-fastest ways to create a chart in Excel:

F11 Create new Chart sheet in the workbook based on selected cells.

Alt+F1 Same as F11 though not as easy to remember.

Alt+I, H, Alt+F Using the wizard, places a chart in the current worksheet.

Can I Copy a Chart from a Chart Sheet Back into a Workbook?

Yes, but the results are ugly. It's much better just to create the chart in the workbook by using the wizard as opposed to copying the chart from the Chart sheet.

NOTE *If you work the entire wizard through, then the final option lets you decide whether to put the chart into the current worksheet or create a new Chart sheet for it.*

If You Use the Wizard Properly, Then You Won't Have to Redo the Chart

Most of the advice in the next part of this book covers undoing things that could have been done right, had you paid full attention to the wizard. The problem is that the wizard has so many steps, seemingly disorganized, that it's tough to tell where the bodies are buried. Therefore, the next few pages outline the wizard process, telling you what's where and what you might be missing. This should save you time when you next need to create a chart.

1. Create a nifty little table in your document. To best test the various chart types, I created the table shown in Figure 14.2—just a simple silly thing. Note that it is labeled. The Chart Wizard will pick up the labels, as Excel's List commands did.

NOTE *If you want labels on the chart, then first put them on your data in the worksheet.*

2. Select the table. You can select the whole table, labels and all, or just click one cell in the table 'cause Excel is smart and knows where the table is.
3. Choose Insert ➤ Chart. This is just another way to click the Wizard button. (I'm required by the *Computer Book Author's Handbook* to show all the variations.)

The wizard begins.

FIGURE 14.2
A silly table I whipped up

	Jordan	Simon	Jonah	Jeremiah
Breakfast	0%	100%	50%	100%
Lunch	75%	100%	25%	25%
Dinner	100%	100%	75%	100%

Percentages of meals consumed

THREE-DIMENSIONAL CHARTS IN A TWO-DIMENSIONAL WORLD

Excel charts fall into two categories: two-dimensional and three-dimensional. This has nothing to do with the graphics that appear on the chart. You can have a two-dimensional graph using three-dimensional objects, such as cones or cylinders. No, it refers to the dimensions of the graph itself.

A two-dimensional graph has an x-axis and a y-axis. The x-axis goes left and right. The y-axis goes up and down. This is just as you would expect from your nightmarish experiences in high school geometry class.

- The x-axis is the *Category* axis, and it goes left and right.
- The y-axis is the *Value* axis, and it goes up and down.

A three-dimensional graph has x-, y-, and z-axes. Here things get screwy:

- The x-axis is the *Category* axis, and it goes in and out—the third dimension. (This would have been the z-axis in geometry glass.)
- The y-axis is the *Series* axis, and it goes left and right. (It would have been the x-axis in geometry class.)
- The z-axis is the *Value* axis, and it goes up and down. (The y-axis in geometry class.)

Don't punish yourself trying to memorize this. If it's something you refer to often, then just dog-ear this page. (I've never bothered memorizing it.)

STEP 1: CHOOSE THE TYPE OF CHART

The first choice you must make in the wizard is the overall look of the chart. There are chart types and subtypes, as shown in Figure 14.3.

Which type is proper? It depends on your data, but also your audience. The cool thing is the handy Press and Hold to View Sample button, which I recommend you use liberally before clicking the Next button.

FIGURE 14.3
Selecting a chart type

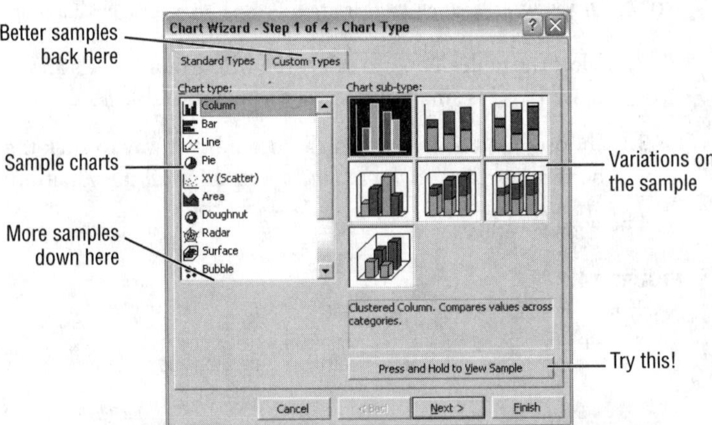

Another buried treasure in this step is the Custom Types tab. It contains even more variations, though it lacks the Press and Hold to View Sample button as well as the subtypes.

4. Select a chart type. Do not worry if the chart is labeled or positioned properly at this point. You're just picking out a general type. The labels and axes can be fixed later in the wizard. For my sample, I've chosen the "Area Blocks Chart" type from the Custom Types tab. I don't know why. I may change my mind later.
5. Click the Next button.

STEP 2: CHECK YOUR DATA

I suppose Step 2 is really required only if you didn't first select any data from your worksheet. But more importantly, it's also where you can change the way the data in the table runs in the chart, from XY to YX (so to speak), as shown in Figure 14.4.

6. Click to select Columns or Rows, whichever isn't selected now. Observe how this changes the perspective on your table.

NOTE *The row values from the table are the key to the chart. They're the values that can be manipulated more than the column values. If the table wasn't set up properly, then you can swap the rows/columns as shown in Step 6.*

7. Click the Series tab. This part of the dialog box lets you add or remove rows from the chart. Remember: If you'd rather manipulate the columns, then return to the Data Range tab and swap the rows/column again.

   Normally you wouldn't mess with this stuff. In fact, instead of manipulating the table here, do it in the worksheet instead. For example, if you notice that one row tends to block another (such as Simon blocking Jordan in Figure 14.5), then click Cancel to quit the wizard, and rearrange the rows in your table before re-creating the chart.
8. Click the Next button.

FIGURE 14.4
Putting the table into the chart

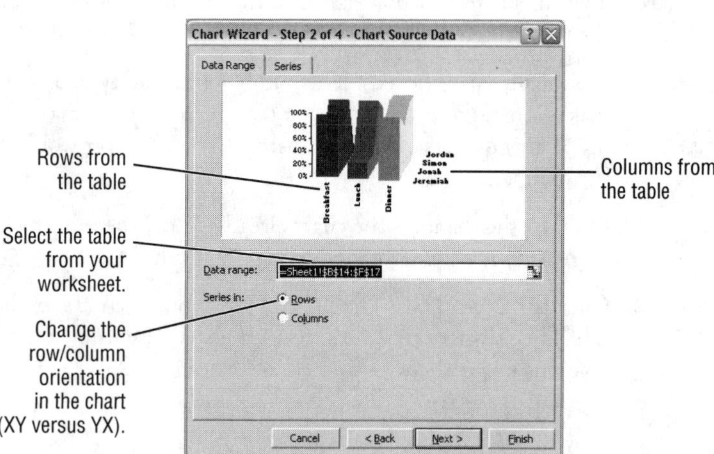

FIGURE 14.5
Messing with the rows in the chart

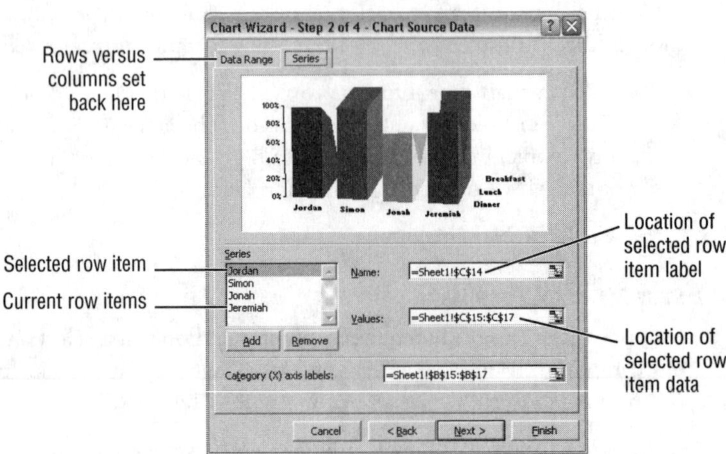

STEP 3: ADJUST THE CHART'S APPEARANCE AND VISIBLE OPTIONS

Step 3 my butt! There are six tabs in this dialog box! Six different things to do. It's Steps 3 through 8 if you ask my opinion. Add another two steps for the other tabs in the other dialog box boxes and, dang it, I'm starting a letter-writing campaign!

9. Click the Titles tab (if you need to). Here you can optionally add a title to the chart plus labels for each of the axes. (Three-dimensional charts have a z-axis; other charts just have x- and y-axes.)

NOTE *If you want to give your chart a title and some labels, then this is the place to do it. It's much more difficult to do this after the chart has been created.*

10. Type in a name for the chart into the "Chart Title" box. The title appears over the chart, on the top, centered.

11. Optionally label the axis. The number and variety depend on the chart type. Sometimes this makes sense. For example, if you have merely numbers on an axis, you can clarify them by saying "Part numbers" or "Sales districts" or whatever would help you make more sense out of the numbers.

    On the other hand, if the chart already shows the months January through December, then there is no need to add a redundant "Months" label.

12. Click the Legend tab. The Legend tab should be next, as shown in Figure 14.6, not the Axes tab. This is where you can save a little space by using a legend instead of labeling individual columns or pie slices.

FIGURE 14.6
Adding a legend

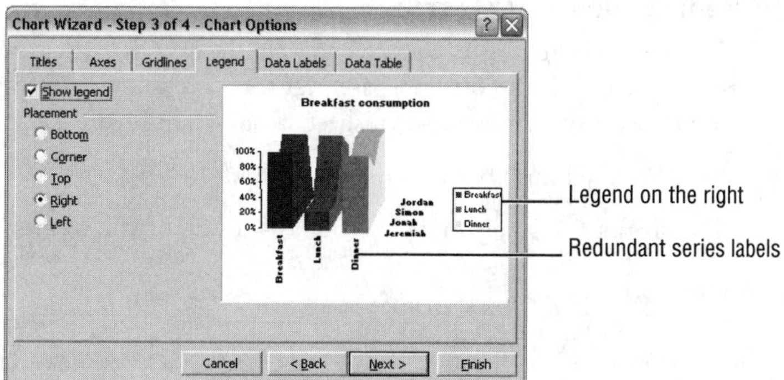

13. Click the Show Legend button.

14. Optionally click the Placement buttons to put the legend where you want it in the chart.

In Figure 14.6, I've put the legend off to the right. But notice how the legend repeats the labels on the Series (bottom) axis? Even the colors in the legend match the block graphs in the chart. So the labels on the Series axis are now no longer needed.

15. Click the Axes tab.

16. Click to remove the labels on the bottom axis. For 2-D charts that's the Category (x) axis; for the 3-D charts it's the Series (y) axis. But don't bother memorizing that: Just click the various check boxes until the bottom labels are removed.

17. Click the Gridlines tab. Another place to play: Click to check and uncheck the various gridline options. I find the value gridlines come in handy.

18. Click the Data Labels tab. This tab lets you put information right on the graph part of the chart, labeling individual bars or pieces of the chart. I think it looks too crowded with that information showing.

NOTE *If it's too crowded now, don't fuss: You can always space the bars farther apart, which is covered in the section "How Can I Space the Bars Farther Apart?" later in this chapter.*

19. Click the Data Table tab. Only one job to tackle here: whether you want the original table from the worksheet to be included with the chart or not. Clicking the "Show Data Table" item gives you a preview of how junky it looks. It looks less junky if you create the chart in its own sheet in the workbook. And you can always add the data table later.

20. Click the Next button.

STEP 4: ALL-DONE SILLY LAST STEP

It all comes down to this: Where do you want the new chart? As a new sheet or as an object in a worksheet? If you're printing off transparencies for a slideshow or incorporating the chart into another Office application, choose its own sheet, as shown in Figure 14.7.

21. Click the Finish button, and you're done.

The chart sits lovingly in its new home—ready for you to mess with it further.

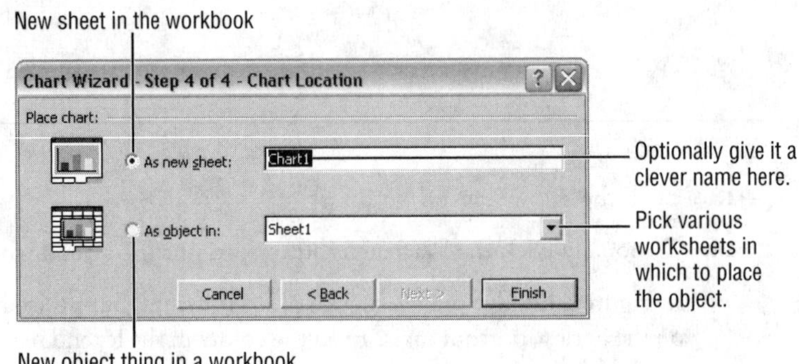

FIGURE 14.7
Picking a place for the new chart

Yes, Indeed, I'm Grossly Unhappy and Must Redo the Chart

Who is ever happy with their charts? And consider this: Modifying (or "playing") with a chart most definitely does fall under the category of "working." So if you have a slow afternoon, you can spend gobs of time honing and perfecting an Excel chart.

The best part of messing with a chart is that Microsoft understands the need. Therefore there are many, many tools available for hammering out new charty things. The following sections describe them all.

NOTE *Throughout the chapter, remember: a chart updates if you change the values in the worksheet.*

The Handy Chart Redoing Helper: the Chart Toolbar

If you're lucky, then the Chart toolbar pops up after you slap down a chart into a worksheet. Hands down, the Chart toolbar is the best way to mess with a chart. Forget pocking and right-clicking with the mouse. If that's ever frustrated you, then the Chart toolbar is the answer you've been seeking.

To summon the Chart toolbar, choose View ➤ Toolbars ➤ Chart. Figure 14.8 tells you what's what on the toolbar. Between that and a few of the tricks in the next several sections, you can fix your chart in no time.

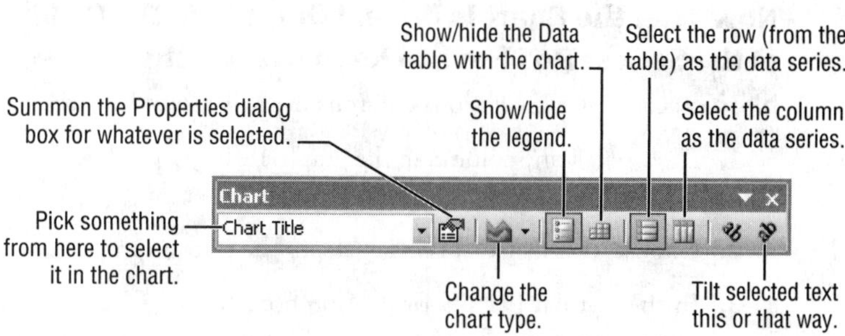

Show/hide the Data table with the chart.
Select the row (from the table) as the data series.
Summon the Properties dialog box for whatever is selected.
Show/hide the legend.
Select the column as the data series.
Chart
Pick something from here to select it in the chart.
Chart Title
Change the chart type.
Tilt selected text this or that way.

FIGURE 14.8
The Chart toolbar, your friend and pal

NOTE *The following sections assume that the Chart toolbar is floating near your chart.*

How Can I Quickly Convert the Chart into a Chart of Another Type?

Use the Chart toolbar's Chart Type button to quickly change the chart type. When you click this button (on the Chart toolbar), a drop-down palette of options appears, as shown in Figure 14.9. Just click one of the options to see your chart reformed. Sadly, the options aren't as vast as in the Chart Wizard.

NOTE *If you really want to mess around, note that the drop-down palette can be "torn off" the Chart toolbar and dragged away to create the Chart Type toolbar. Point and drag the mouse as indicated in Figure 14.9.*

Do I Have to Redo the Whole Wizard if I Don't Find a Chart Type I Like on the Wee Li'l Palette?

No. If you want the vast options from the Chart Wizard, then just right-click anywhere on your chart. Choose "Chart Type" from the pop-up menu, and you'll once again see the Chart Type dialog box, similar to the Chart Wizard's first step (Figure 14.3). That way, you can reset your chart to any of the examples Excel offers.

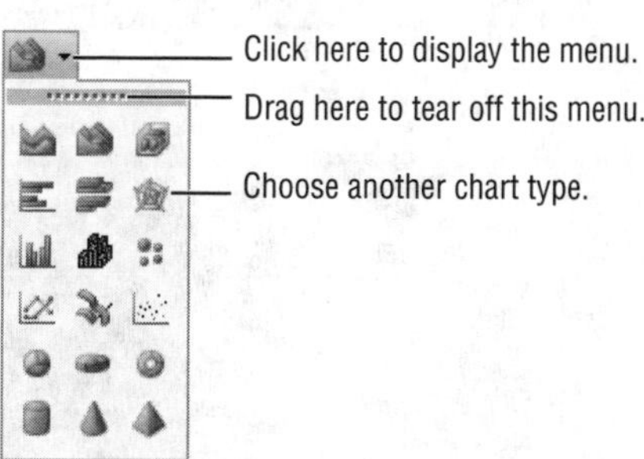

Click here to display the menu.
Drag here to tear off this menu.
Choose another chart type.

FIGURE 14.9
Choose another chart from this list.

Now That the Chart Is Done, I Don't Like the Order of the Series. Do I Have to Redo Everything?

No. You can move the various columns or rows around whichever way you like. Follow these steps:

1. Right-click any column in the graph. If the graph doesn't have columns, click an element that represents the data, such as a dot in a scatter graph.
2. Choose "Format Data Series" from the pop-up menu.
3. In the Format Data Series dialog box, click the Series Order tab. Now you can rearrange the columns by selecting one and clicking the Move Up or Move Down button, as shown in Figure 14.10.
4. Click OK when you're done moving.

What if I Want to Get Rid of a Column?

Cheating, huh? Seriously, it's easy to get rid of a column or any chunk of data in a chart. Use Figure 14.11 as an example.

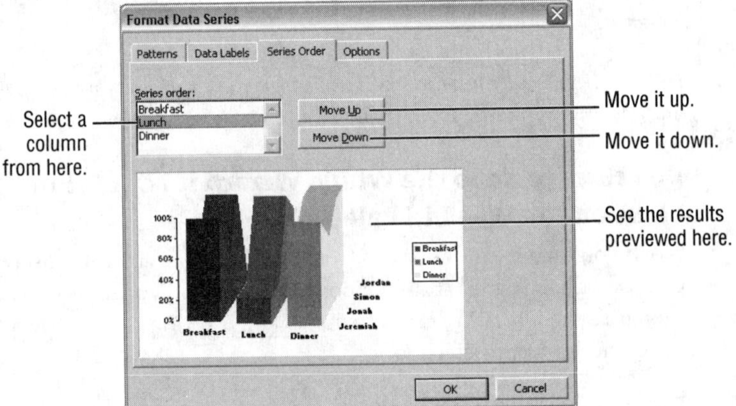

FIGURE 14.10
Rearranging the columns in a graph

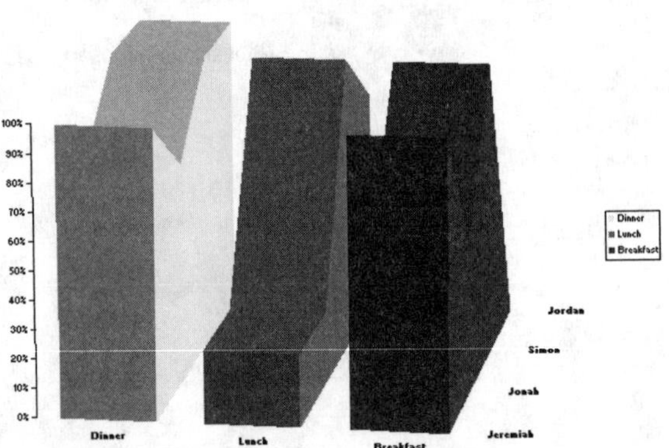

FIGURE 14.11
An example

Say you wanted to get rid of the Breakfast column in Figure 14.11. From the Chart toolbar, select Series "Breakfast" from the drop-down list; then press the Delete key on the keyboard. It's gone.

You could also just right-click the thing and choose Clear from the pop-up menu, but with some charts removing a column or row can be tricky.

Now I Want My Column Back!

If you're too slow with the Undo command, then you have to manually re-add your row by telling the chart, once again, where to find its data. You'll need two buttons for this process, which I call the "Go-Get-Her" button and the "Return Gizmo" button. Heed these carefully worded steps:

1. Right-click the chart.
2. Choose "Source Data" from the pop-up menu. If you don't see that menu item, then try clicking again, this time on a column or other important bit in the chart.
3. Click the Series tab in the Source Data dialog box. You'll see something similar to Figure 14.12, where you can re-add any column you deleted from a chart.

NOTE *You can also add new columns simply by selecting that information from any worksheet. This is a way to modify any chart you've already created.*

4. Click the Add button.

5. Click the Go-Get-Her button on the right end of the Name box.
6. Click the tab of the sheet that has the chart's original table. You may think Excel is broken here; it's not. The dialog box is hidden, and you're looking at the chart underneath. You need to click a worksheet tab to return to the worksheet from whence the chart got its data.
7. Click the cell that contains the name of the column you zapped. In Figure 14.11 it was Breakfast, which happens to be in Sheet1, cell B15 on my screen.

FIGURE 14.12
Adding a column back into a chart

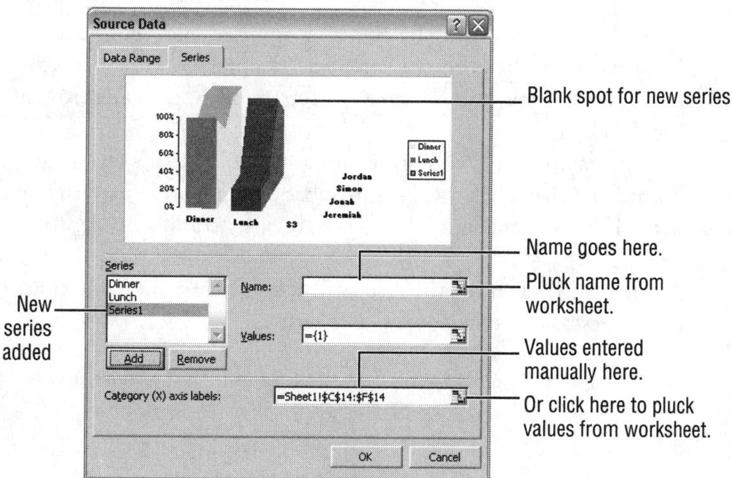

8. Click the Return Gizmo button, and you're back in the dialog box.
9. Click the Go-Get-Her button on the right end of the Values box.
10. Click the tab of the worksheet that contains the values you're looking for.
11. Select the cells containing the data for the new column.
12. Click the Return Gizmo button, and that should be it.
13. Click OK; the chart is restored.

What About Deleting a Row of Data?

The data that series charts prefer to work with is the bottom, left-to-right values. If you want to work with values on other scales, you'll have to rotate the chart so that those values are in front.

For example, in Figure 14.11 the names are on the right side, not the bottom. To fix this, click the By Column button on the Chart toolbar. Then you can remove the item as outlined in the section, "What if I Want to Get Rid of a Column?" covered earlier in this chapter.

NOTE *The By Row and By Column buttons will not work if you've messed with the chart too much. Especially, moving or removing data series will render the buttons useless.*

Any Way to Change the Colors Used by the Chart?

If you don't like the color of a line or grapfollow these steps to fix it:

1. Right-click the offending line. Blue! How dare they. Especially this late in the spring!
2. Choose "Format Data Series" from the pop-up menu.
3. Click the Patterns tab in the Format Data Series dialog box.
4. Choose a new color from the Area area, as shown in Figure 14.13.
5. Click OK.

Rather than be boring by choosing another color, consider clicking the Fill Effects button in the Patterns tab of the Format Data Series dialog box. When you do, you'll find a great dialog box that lets you select gradients, textures, patterns, and even images from graphics files elsewhere on your disk for the chart.

For example, say you want your bar to look like it's faced with marble. If so, click the Fill Effects button and then click the Texture tab. Select a marble pattern from the list, and then click OK. Back in the Format Data Series dialog box, be sure to add a border to the artwork so that it can more easily be seen.

Figure 14.14 shows the results of reformatting the same chart from Figure 14.11, but using various types of fill styles for the data series.

NOTE *The availability of patterns, textures, gradients, and pictures depends on the type of chart selected.*

FIGURE 14.13
Changing the color of a bar in a chart

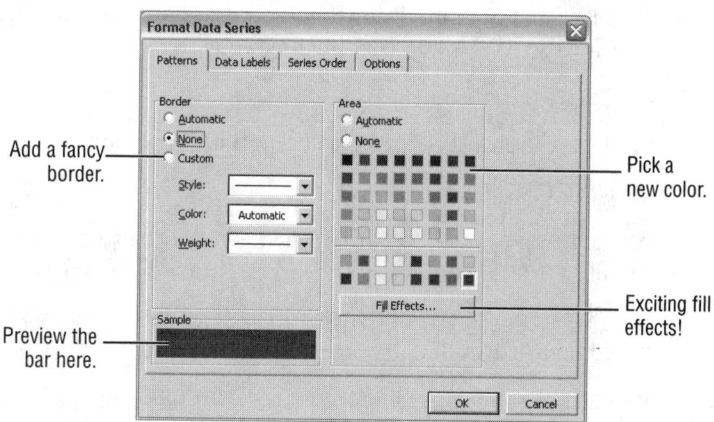

FIGURE 14.14
Way different colors for the chart

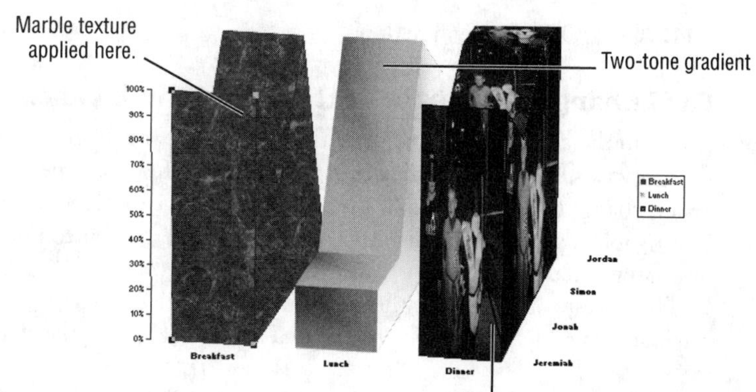

Now I Want a Title! And a Legend!

Adding a legend is cinchy, thanks to the Chart toolbar: Just click the Legend button on the toolbar. Ta-da! It alternately adds or removes the legend from your chart.

A missing title is easy to fix:

1. Right-click anywhere on the chart.
2. Choose "Chart Options" from the pop-up menu. If you don't see this command, then you clicked in the wrong place! In this case, unlike the previous sections, do not click on the chart's data.

3. The Chart Options dialog box appears. It looks similar to the dialog box you see in Step 3 of the Chart Wizard. In fact, anything you forgot to do back there can be redone or undone here.
4. Click the Titles tab.
5. Type the chart title into the "Chart Title" text box.
6. Click OK.

A problem now, and even back when you ran the Chart Wizard (if you did), is that you're given only a title and not really a chance to format it. If you want to format it, then continue with these steps:

7. Choose "Chart Title" from the drop-down list on the Chart toolbar.
8. Click the Properties button on the Chart toolbar.
9. In the Format Chart Title dialog box, click the Font tab.
10. Work the gizmos in the Font tab to select the title formatting you want.
11. Click OK when you're done.

Can I Change the Font or Text for the Chart's Labels?

Labels in the chart are referred to in the Chart toolbar's drop-down list as "Axis." These are the Category axis, Series axis, Value axis, and more (or fewer), depending on the type of chart.

To change the font, color, or other properties of these labels, choose the one you want from the Chart toolbar's drop-down list; then click the Properties button on the toolbar. Click the Font tab in whatever dialog box appears, and you're on your way.

The easiest way to change the label names themselves is to return to the worksheet containing the original data table. Change the labels used on the table, and the chart will be updated instantly.

The Value Axis Is Displeasing Me to No End. Where Can I Modify It?

"Value axis" is the name given to the part of the chart that tells you what the bars represent, as shown in Figure 14.15. Here's how you mess with that part of the chart:

1. Choose "Value Axis" from the drop-down list on the Chart toolbar.
2. Click the Properties button. The Format Axis dialog box is displayed.
3. Click the Scale tab. This is where you can mess with the axis, as shown in Figure 14.16.

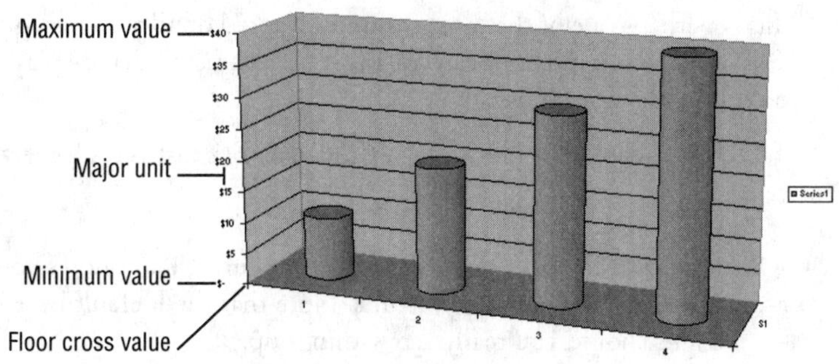

FIGURE 14.15
Things to play with on the Value axis

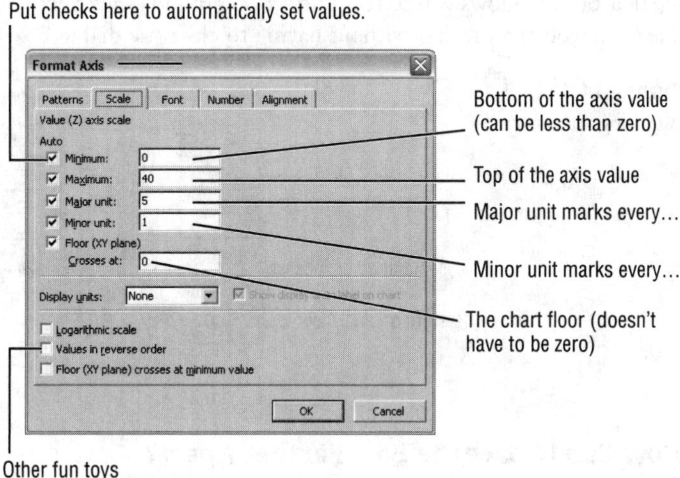

FIGURE 14.16
Various things to play with in the Scale tab of the Format Axis dialog box

4. Set the various options in the dialog box as please you. For example, if you want the Value axis to be shorter, uncheck the Minimum value and input something new. Or if you want it taller, put in a higher value. Leaving the check mark lets Excel decide where to put things.
5. Click the Patterns tab. Note the two areas for setting the Major and Minor tick marks. Normally the Minor tick marks aren't shown, so None is selected. But you can see them if you specify an option other than None.
6. Click OK, and hopefully the Value axis is formatted in a manner that does not tweak you.

Can I Redo the Angle of This 3-D Chart?

This is perhaps one of the most commonly asked of all the chart questions. That is, after you create a 3-D view on a graph, how can you move the "camera" that displays the graph? It's simple, providing you follow these secretive steps:

1. Right-click the chart. Not on any data, but just on the chart's background.
2. Choose "3-D View" from the pop-up menu.
3. Play with the 3-D View dialog box. Figure 14.17 shows you the gizmos, though this dialog box more than invites playtime. Note that the Default button is used to recover the original angle, should you really screw things up.
4. Click OK when you're done.

Note that the 3-D View dialog box is one of the rare ones in Office with an Apply button. Clicking that button allows you to see (in the background) the effect your adjustments have on the chart. That way you can preview without having to close the dialog box.

FIGURE 14.17
Adjusting your view

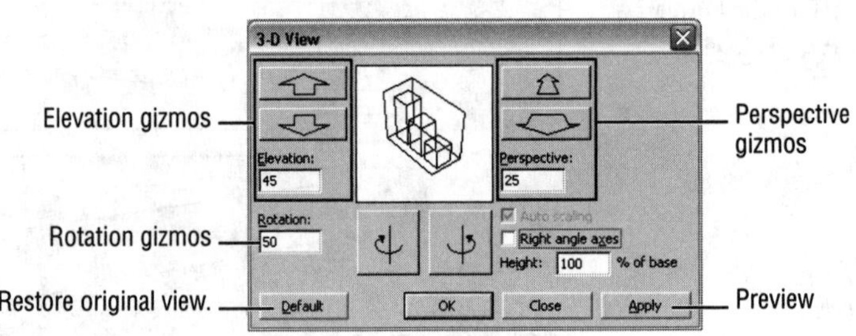

How Can I Space the Bars Farther Apart?

Some of those charts do get crowded. It really depends not only on how much data you're putting into the chart but also on the chart type. Some charts show a mess of data better than others; you just have to preview things to see which looks best.

There are some after-creation adjustments you can make to a chart to space out the bars. Compare Figures 14.18 and 14.19.

Here are the steps taken to make those bars appear farther apart:

1. Right-click the mouse on any bar.
2. Choose "Format Data Series" from the pop-up menu. The Format Data Series dialog box appears.

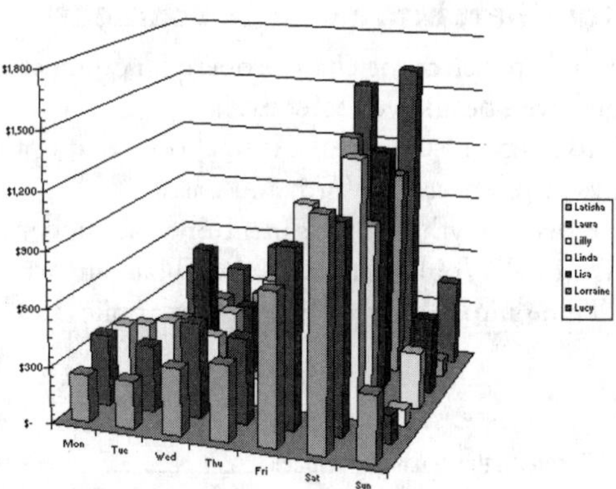

FIGURE 14.18
Bars too close together

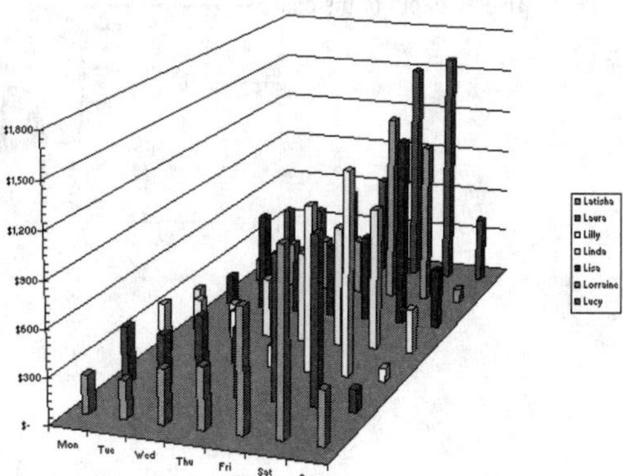

FIGURE 14.19
Bars just right

3. Click the Options tab. If there is no Options tab, then you have a chart type that cannot be adjusted in this manner. Figure 14.20 shows the dialog box and its pertinent parts.
4. Adjust the depths and widths. Refer to Figure 14.20 for how this works, though you can have fun just playing on your own.
5. Click OK when you're done.

Also consider combining the adjustments made here with the 3-D View adjustments described in the previous section to truly customize how your chart is presented.

I Need to Paste the Chart into a Word Document!

The key here is to be able to select the chart properly. You must select the whole thing, the Chart Area. If not, you won't even be allowed to copy.

The quickest way to select the Chart Area is to choose that option from the Chart toolbar's drop-down list. Then copy, switch over to Word, and paste.

Beyond that basic move, everything that is mentioned about copying a worksheet into Word (from Chapter 10, "Why the Hell Would Anyone Other Than an Accountant Use Excel?" the section "Plopping an Excel Thing into a Word Thing") also applies to charts.

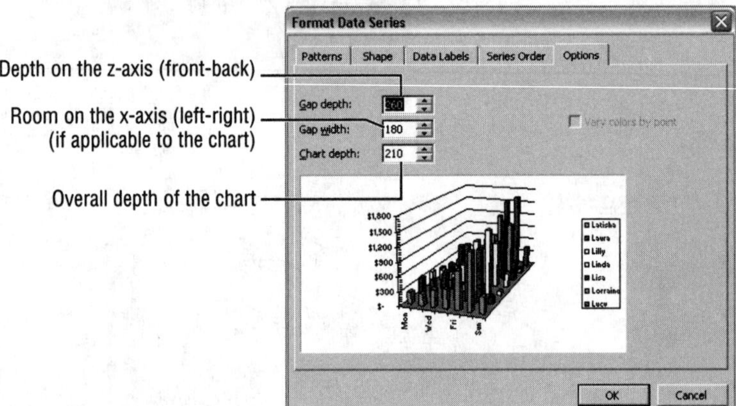

FIGURE 14.20
Adjusting the room between bars

Chapter 15

Excel Templates, Samples, and Web Mischief

THIS CHAPTER IS THE "show me a picture" chapter. Sometimes it's just easier to point at the picture and say, "This is what I want!" So what I've done is concocted a few worksheet examples. Some of them illustrate concepts I haven't yet presented—things that I'd like to show you but that didn't fit into the other chapters. The rest of the examples are of some common worksheets. They're enough to build upon or at least inspire you to create bigger, better, and bolder worksheets in the future.

- Creating, using, and changing workbook templates
- Designing the special BOOK and SHEET templates
- Using the handy Split and Freeze commands
- Formatting rows and columns to create a calendar
- Importing data from the Web into a worksheet

The Document You Use Over and Over: The Template

The examples that dot the rest of this chapter may eventually form the basis for some common worksheets—stuff you use over and over. In Microsoft Office parlance, the stuff you use over and over is potential template material. After all, why keep rebuilding the same worksheet over and over when you can start with a basic template and get most of the job done ahead of time?

Saving a Template: Duh

You've built the basics. Formatted. Created styles even. Everything about the workbook is set for reuse. The only things you haven't entered are the things that change in specific cells: information that will be input later, such as dates, values, text, other numbers, and la-di-da. It's Miller Time! But before you walk into the sunset with your pals in a beer commercial, you need to save the workbook to disk as a template. Here's how your fumbling fingers would do that:

1. Choose File ➤ Save As.
2. From the "Save As Type" drop-down list, choose "Template (*.xlt)." When you do this, note that the folder changes. Excel saves the template in your own personal Templates folder. Its location varies depending on your version of Windows. See the sidebar, "Where the Templates Lurk on the Hard Drive" for the boring details.
3. Give the template a memorable filename.
4. Click the Save button.
5. Close the file. I recommend this step to cease any further modification of the template at this time. If you want to use the template, then it's best to start up a new document and do it that way.

A template can come from any source. You can build one off a workbook you've already created or you can make one from scratch. My advice is to create a workbook first, then customize it over time, and finally save it to disk as a template.

NOTE *Saving a template focuses Excel's attention on the Templates folder. To return to the My Documents folder when you go to open another workbook, click the My Documents button on the left end of the Open dialog box.*

And to Use the Template?

Templates ain't no good unless you can use them over and over. To create a new workbook based on a template, obey these steps:

1. Choose File ➤ New.
   - In Excel 2003/XP this action displays the New Workbook task pane. You're not done yet. However, if you do see the template you want to use displayed near the bottom of the task pane, you can click it now and get on with things. But that's not the point of these steps.
   - In Excel 2000, you'll see the New dialog box, similar to the Templates dialog box shown in Figure 15.1.
2. In Excel 2003, click the "On My Computer" link in the task pane; in Excel XP, click the "General Templates" link in the task pane. Now you see what your Excel 2000 brothers saw already (the price of upgrading), which is the Templates dialog box, shown in Figure 15.1.
3. Select a template to use and click the OK button, and you're using that template.

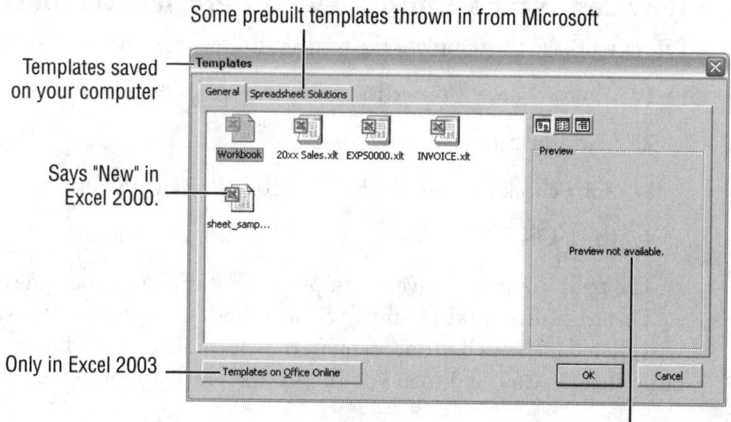

FIGURE 15.1
Pluck a template from this place.

Everything from the template is imported into your current workbook. With all that work done, you just need to fill in the missing parts. But do not forget to save! Give the file a new, proper name, and then save it in a logical location when you're done. Or, better still, do that first so you don't have to be reminded of it later.

What's the Best Way to Change a Template?

Rather than search all over the hard drive for a template you want to fix, just start up a new document using that template. Fix stuff. Then save the document back to disk as a template again, which is covered earlier in this chapter.

NOTE *Rename the file back to the original template name! The file will probably have a "1" in it. Delete that 1, and then you'll have the original template name.*

Be sure to answer "Yes" when you're asked if you want to replace the original.

WHERE THE TEMPLATES LURK ON THE HARD DRIVE

Excel tends to save its template files in the most random of locations. It would take me a few paragraphs to describe these locations for each version of Windows. Instead of wasting your time reading that, here's a big tip:

Create a folder specifically for your Excel templates. For example, create a folder in the My Documents folder and call it `Excel Templates`. Then store all your Excel templates there, instead of the place Excel uses—which, as I've said before, isn't easy to get to and varies depending on which version of Windows you're using (and whether you've upgraded Office or installed it new).

How Can I Save a Template with a Preview Window?

Before you save the template file to disk, follow these steps:

1. Choose File ➤ Properties.
2. Click the Summary tab.
3. Put a check mark in the box by "Save Preview Picture."
4. Click OK.

The template is now saved with preview information you can see when selecting the template.

This trick also works for any Excel workbooks. For example, to see the preview in the Open dialog box, click the Views button/menu in the Open dialog box (Figure 15.2). Choose Preview from the menu that appears, and then you can see the preview (for regular documents that have them).

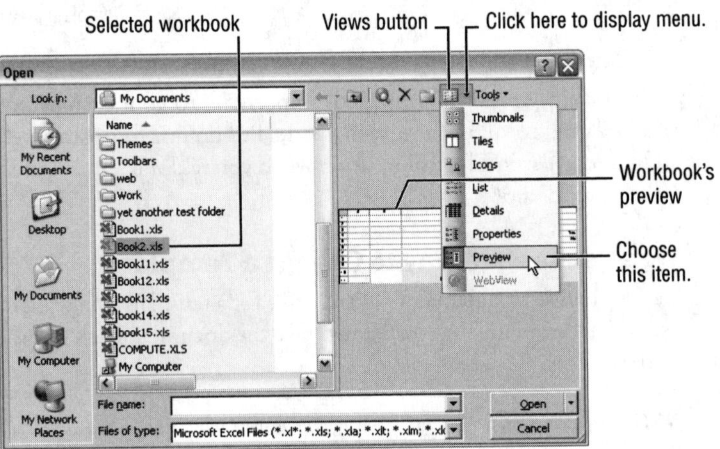

FIGURE 15.2 Preview documents in the Open dialog box.

Other Users on My Windows XP Computer Cannot Find the Template!

No, they can't! That's because each user on a Windows XP computer has their own account area, separate from other users and typically password-protected as well.

The least awkward solution is to copy the template files you want to share into the Shared Documents folder. Then have the other users copy them from the Shared Documents folder into their own folders.

Or if you want to be magnanimous, simply direct everyone on the computer to save their Excel templates directly into the Shared Documents folder (or a subfolder of Shared Documents).

What's the Equivalent in Excel to the NORMAL.DOT Template in Word?

Excel has two equivalents to `NORMAL.DOT`, which is the main document template in Word. One is called `BOOK.XLS`, and the other is called `SHEET.XLS`.

As an example, suppose that every sheet you add to your workbook must be the same. Say they are invoices or yearly financial summaries—whatever—the bottom line is that whenever you add a new worksheet, you'd like it to be preset with certain things. If so, then what you need is a SHEET template. Here's how to make one:

1. Start a new, blank workbook.
2. Delete Sheets 2 and 3, so that you have only one sheet remaining. This is very important. If you don't delete the extra sheets, then this technique doesn't work.
3. Gussy up the one sheet as your single-sheet template. For example, you can set various styles, name ranges of cells, or preformat dates and times. Do whatever it is you want to appear in every new sheet you add to a worksheet. An example is shown in Figure 15.3.

NOTE *Obviously if you prefer not to have preformatted sheets but blank sheets, you do not need to create a SHEET template.*

4. When you're ready, choose File ➤ Save As.
5. Choose "Template (*.xlt)" from the "Save As Type" drop-down list. You are saving a template to disk.
6. Name the document **SHEET**. So the full name would be `SHEET.XLT`, for an Excel template.

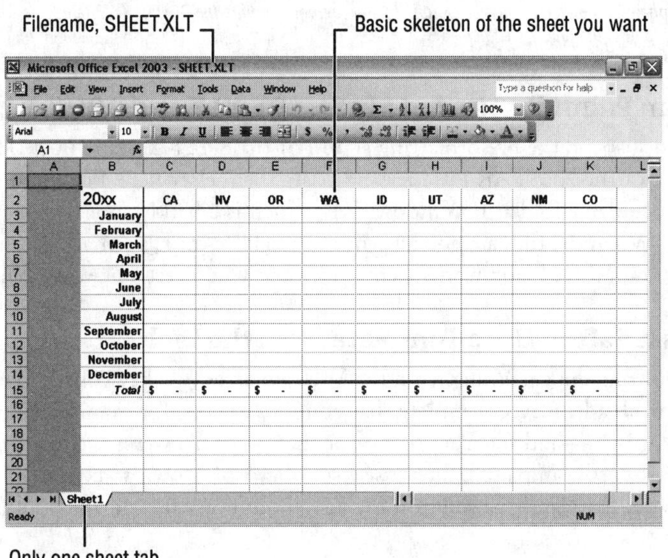

FIGURE 15.3
A sample sheet template

7. Choose the folder `C:\Program Files\Microsoft Office\Office\XLSTART` from the "Save In" drop-down list. If you've upgraded Microsoft Office, then there will be several subfolders named Office inside the Microsoft Office folder. Choose the one with the highest number. Or perhaps the only folder there may have a number at the end of its name, such as Office10.
8. Click the Save button to save.

NOTE *This resets Excel's working folder to the XLSTART folder. The next time you use the Save As or Open dialog box, click the My Documents folder button (on the left side of the dialog box) to return to your computer's main My Documents folder.*

To test how this works, simply add a new sheet to any workbook; choose Insert ➤ Worksheet from the menu or press Shift+F11. All new sheets added to the workbook look like the `SHEET.XLT` file you saved in the XLSTART folder.

What's the Purpose of the BOOK.XLT Template?

The `BOOK.XLT` template provides a template for all new workbooks you create in Excel. It works like the `SHEET.XLT` template, though `BOOK.XLT` can contain multiple sheets formatted how you like them—or it may only need to contain some styles you enjoy using.

Like `SHEET.XLT`, the `BOOK.XLT` template must be saved in the XLSTART folder; refer to the previous section for details.

After `BOOK.XLT` is saved, all new workbooks you create will carry whatever features are found in the `BOOK.XLT` template—unless you use another template to create a workbook.

NOTE *Remember that a* `BOOK.XLT` *template need not contain any preformatted cells at all. Perhaps it just needs to contain some styles you like to use. However you format the* `BOOK.XLT` *template, that's how all your new workbooks will appear and work in Excel.*

I'm Painfully Tired of My SHEET.XLT and BOOK.XLT Templates

To suspend the preformatting action of the `SHEET.XLT` and `BOOK.XLT` templates, merely move them out of the XLSTART folder and paste them elsewhere. For example, I moved them to the Shared Documents folder in Windows XP, which is a handy spot for anyone to get at them.

When the files are gone, then Excel behaves as it normally does: New workbooks are blank and contain three blank worksheets, and when you insert a new worksheet, it comes up blank as well.

Is It Safe to Use a Template from the Web?

Downloading anything from the Web involves two keywords, "reliable source." It's possible to download an Excel template that contains a virus, for example. So when you go web browsing for templates—and there are many out there—find a web page that you feel is trustworthy. If you're trustworthy-impaired, then just visit Microsoft's own web page, which has literally thousands of useful templates—a solution for just about every puzzle you could imagine.

To visit the Web for templates in Excel 2003, click the "Templates Home Page" link in the New Workbook task pane.

In Excel XP, click the link that says "Templates on Microsoft.com," also in the task pane.

For Excel 2000, visit the following page on the Internet:

`http://officeupdate.microsoft.com/TemplateGallery/`

From what I can gather, each version of Office appears to have its own home plate on the Microsoft web page. Yet I don't see anything that says specifically that templates from one version of Excel will not work on another.

What's the Need for the Save Workspace Command?

The File ➤ Save Workspace command can be very handy for the busy Excel user. What it does is save the size and position of all your open Excel workbooks, charts, and what-have-you. That way, if you're a stickler for positioning your stuff "just so" on the screen, you can get that position back by saving the workspace.

To reload the workspace, simply choose the saved workspace file when you start Excel. Because of that, obviously, it helps to save your workspace using a memorable filename.

For example, Stella works at a major television production studio (not Fox) and every day she's e-mailed the overnight ratings. She likes to open up that window on the left and then enter data for her shows into a worksheet on the right edge of the screen. Rather than spend four or five minutes positioning each worksheet's window just so (and because her boss is too cheap to buy an 18-inch LCD display), she just uses the Save Workspace command. To start her day, she opens the workspace and the worksheets are already positioned, opened, and ready for her to report the "overnights."

Some Simple Sample Documents

The following sections show how to set up and use some sample documents. These could be future templates, or they could be handy examples of new things you didn't know about, or they may just show you a few tricks you haven't yet thought of.

The Big Worksheet with the Seemingly Stable Headings

Not every worksheet is going to fit neatly on the screen. Consider at the minimum that a worksheet with the months January through December requires 12 columns. That may barely fit on your screen. The problem isn't seeing them all at once; Excel scrolls over to display any part of a large worksheet. The problem comes when you use column or row headings. They disappear as you scroll into the meat of a worksheet.

Consider Figure 15.4. August through December are off to the left—just a scrollbar away—but when you scroll over that far, the row headings in column A disappear! Note that I've color-coded the major headings, so that's one helpful clue. But otherwise, there will be a lot of left-right scrolling going on as you fill in the months August through December.

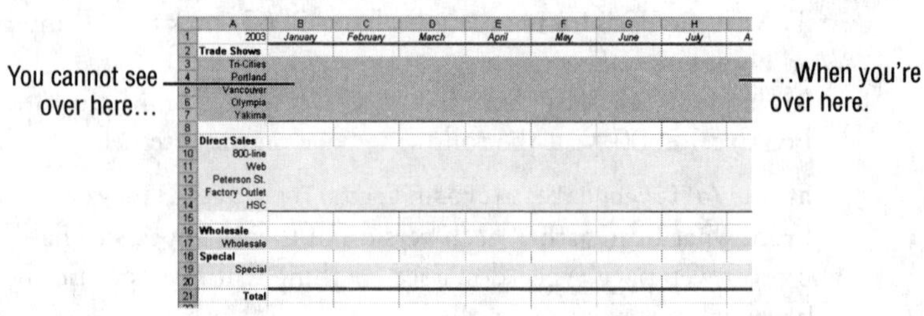

You cannot see over here…
…When you're over here.

FIGURE 15.4
The wide problem

And that's just not my idea of a computer trying to save you time!

Fortunately there is a handy solution, which I call split and freeze. First the split:

Excel lets you split a single worksheet into two or four panes. Each pane scrolls independently of each other pane, which is the key to seeing a larger piece of a worksheet without losing sight of another piece. Follow these peaceful steps:

1. Click a cell somewhere in the middle of your screen. Say, cell E12, which looks middlish on the screen.
2. Choose Window ➤ Split. Holy smokes! A cross is nailed to your worksheet, but what you actually see are split-pane bars that allow you to scroll each of the four areas individually. Figure 15.5 shows what's up.

   Each pane shows you a different part of the worksheet. They're all scrollably independent. Or they can all show you the same view:
3. Scroll each pane so that cell A1 is visible in each.
4. Click to select cell A1.
5. Type **echo** into cell A1. And what you see should look like Figure 15.6. Scary that you can click one pane and see three echoes.

   Scary. Downright frightening.

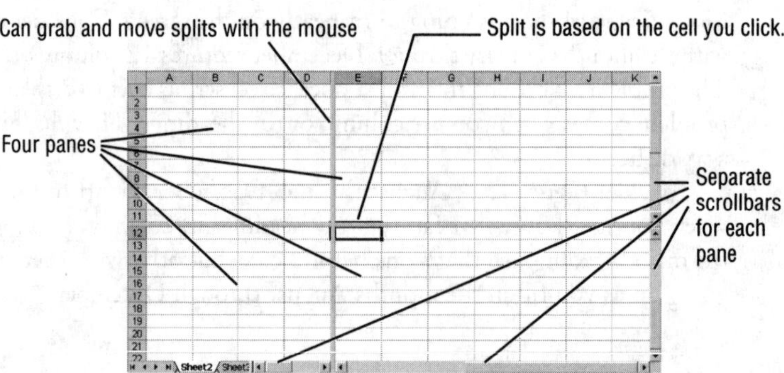

FIGURE 15.5
Not a banana split, but a worksheet split

FIGURE 15.6
Four views of the same set of cells

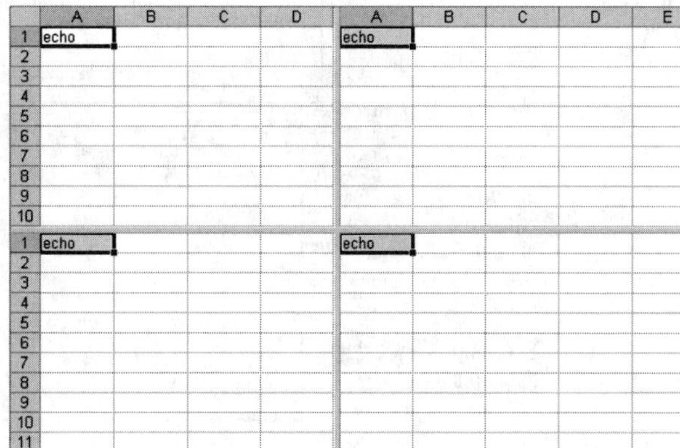

You can also arrange to have the worksheet split manually.

6. Choose Window ➤ Remove Split. And the three bogus panes are gone.
7. Grab the horizontal split gizmo with the mouse and drag down. Use Figure 15.7 as your guide. When you're done moving the split bar, you'll have two views on the worksheet.
8. To split vertically in a manual manner, use the vertical split gizmo: Grab the vertical split gizmo and drag to the left. Refer to Figure 15.8 for information on how this one works.

FIGURE 15.7
The horizontal split, manual style

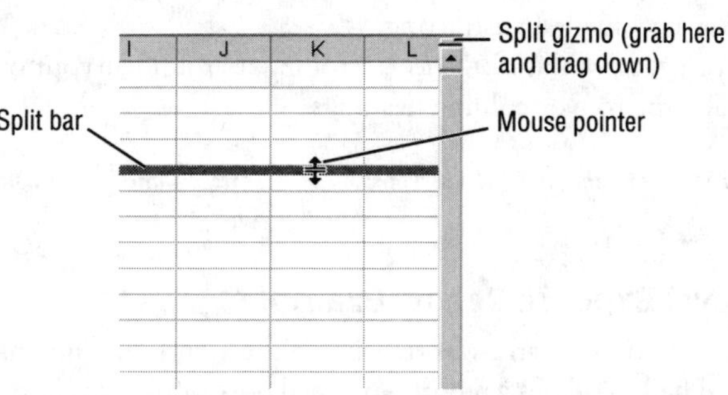

FIGURE 15.8
The vertical split, manual style

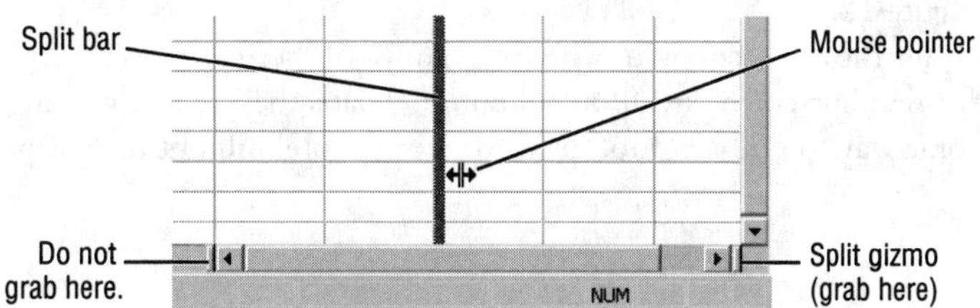

FIGURE 15.9
The split-screen solution to the large worksheet

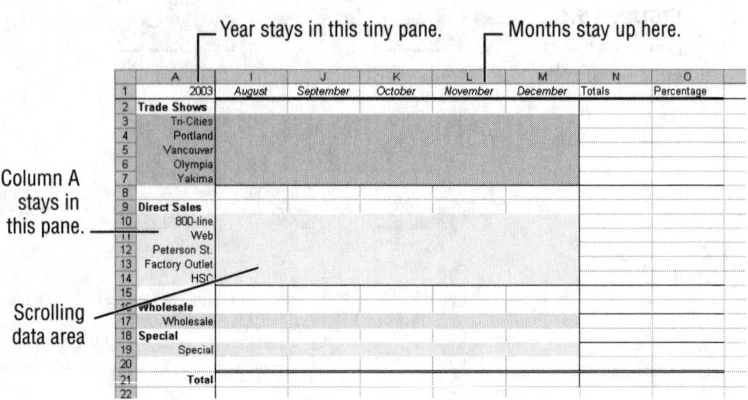

Returning to the example in Figure 15.4, what's needed are split bars just below row 1 and to the left of column A. This solution is shown in Figure 15.9.

See how part of the sheet can scroll over to display August through December? The rows and columns on the worksheet are still visible. But there's one more trick:

9. Choose Window ➢ Freeze Panes.

This command does two things. First it locks the split bars in place, which essentially freezes the top, top-right, and bottom-left panes. Those panes cannot be scrolled. Second, the split bars narrow so that they become less distracting.

Now you can use the worksheet, scrolling it around at your own whim, and not have to worry about losing the row or column headings.

NOTE *To unfreeze the panes, choose Window ➢ Unfreeze Panes. Then optionally choose Window ➢ Remove Split to get rid of the split bars.*

The Travel Expense Report Example

There was one time when I was traveling quite a bit in my line of work, at least twice a month. For every trip, I had to fill out a report or my evil boss wouldn't reimburse me. That taught me a lot about worksheets, because my original quick-and-dirty expense report eventually grew to include all kinds of categories for things I could be reimbursed for. The final evolution of that worksheet is shown in Figure 15.10.

It's the evil accountant who forced most of the "logic" in this travel expense report. The categories for reimbursement are all in column F. That's the key to the thing. Because of that, I had to devise some way to pull any food paid for on the hotel bill out of that part of the bill and onto a separate food bill. (Some companies make you do the same thing with the phone bill charges.) Here's how I did that:

1. The total hotel bill is input on line 11. There are four columns for inputting the expenses, depending on how the expense was paid: corporate American Express card, personal MasterCard, check, or cash. The source didn't matter to the company, but it did to me for when I filled out my expenses at home on the computer.
2. The total for all the phone calls is put into line 13.
3. The total for any miscellaneous charges is put into line 14.
4. Line 15 shows any food purchases made at the hotel. This included hotel restaurants, room service, the minibar, and those overpriced soda machines in the ice room.
5. The nonfood, nonphone, nonmisc part of the hotel bill is then calculated in line 12. The formula is =B11-SUM(B13:B15), which is copied into columns C, D, and E as well. That's how the lodging portion of the bill is separated from the phone, food, and whatever.
6. The totals in column F are simply the sums of the four cells to the left.
7. Cell F18 equals the sums of the block of cells B15 through E17.
8. The totals on row 26 are for each column. This determines which account gets reimbursed what amount.
9. And the final total cell, F26, contains the entire cost of the trip.

Note that there are spaces at the top of the worksheet to type in the name of the event, the cities visited, departure and return times, and attendees. For multiple cities, however, it's best to do one sheet per stay.

Now the only question that remains will be, "Is liquor considered 'food'?"

NOTE *When it comes to naming my expense reports, I use the start date of the trip. So a trip on February 9 would be EXPS0209. A trip on June 17 would be EXPS0617. This naming scheme allows the files to be sorted in chronological order when the folder is sorted alphabetically.*

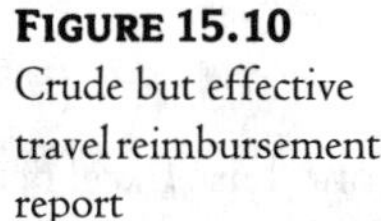

FIGURE 15.10
Crude but effective travel reimbursement report

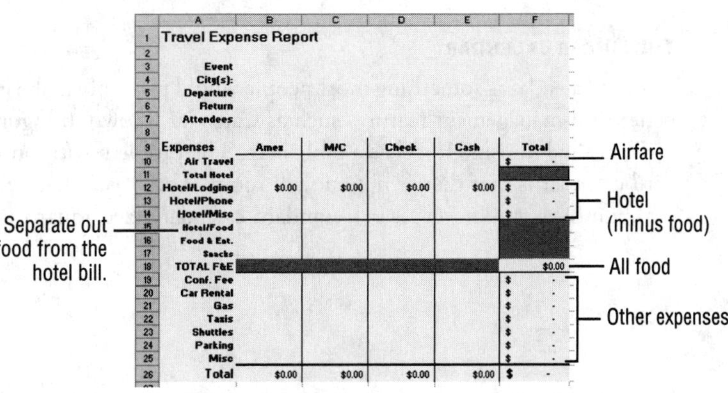

Basic Tricks for Getting More Information on the Screen

You may not be stuck with a tiny aperture through which you must view Excel's worksheet. There are many tricks for getting more information on the screen, all of which are basic computer tricks but which are also easy to forget. Here's my short list:

- Use the Zoom tool. Choose View ➤ Zoom or use the Zoom drop-down list on the Standard toolbar to "zoom out" and show more information in Excel's window. The drawback here is that when you zoom back too far, the screen becomes impossible to read.
- Change monitor resolution. The higher the resolution, the more junk you can see on the screen. I have a large monitor with a resolution of 1600 × 1200 pixels. A new worksheet in Excel shows columns A through W and rows 1 through 63—wonderful, if your monitor can support it. The drawback? Stuff gets tiny and harder to read.
- Adjust all the column widths so that no column is wider than it needs to be. Remember: Double-click the line between one column and the next to make the first column as wide as necessary.
- Choose a smaller font.
- Remove toolbars. You can also switch the Windows taskbar to Auto-hide, which can be a frustrating option, but it does give you at least two more rows on the screen. (Refer to your favorite Windows book for information on auto-hiding the taskbar.)
- Use the View ➤ Full Screen command to do away with all of Excel's gizmos. Refer to Chapter 9, "Customizing Word," for information on how this works with Word; the command is similar for Excel.

Making a Calendar

Excel can make beautiful calendars, and I'm not going to waste any of your time here giving the step-by-steps when so many prebuilt templates exist. So if you want to use Excel to print out a pretty calendar (and even add pictures of the kids), visit the Web and browse through the many calendar templates available.

In my own experience, I'm stubborn and so I make my own calendars, but usually not the wall-hanging kind (which I can still pick up free at various car part stores around town—and some credit unions still hand them out). What I need calendars for is *scheduling*. I've used both linear and two-dimensional calendars for this purpose.

The Linear Calendar

A linear calendar is something most people would probably make in Word. I use Excel because it has better grid-management features such as Calendar, shown in Figure 15.11.

Basically I'm using Excel as a table here. The problem with putting such information into a standard calendar is that there's not enough room. The "cast" that needs to be present in Figure 15.11 (column D) would never fit in a standard calendar-sized square.

FIGURE 15.11
A linear calendar done in Excel

Date	Time	Subject	Who needs to be at the Theater!
Tue, March 23	7:00 PM	*Work Act 3*	Lys, Dem, Hermia, Helena, Quince, Snug, Bottom, Flute, Snout, Starveling, Oberon, Titania, Puck, Peaseblossom, Cobweb, Moth, Mustardseed
Thu, March 25	7:00 PM	*Work Act 4*	Theseus, Hyppolyta, Egeus, Athenians, Lys, Dem, Hermia, Helena, Quince, Snug, Bottom, Flute, Snout, Starveling, Oberon, Titania, Puck, Peaseblossom, Cobweb, Moth, Mustardseed
Sat, March 27	10:00 AM	*Set building!*	Entire cast!
	1:00 PM	Pizza Party!	
	4:00 PM	*Work Act 5*	Entire cast!
Wed, March 31	7:00 PM	*Work Acts 1 and 2*	Entire cast (all Fairies, Athenians, Indian Boy too!)
Fri, April 2	7:00 PM	*Work Act 3*	Lys, Dem, Hermia, Helena, Quince, Snug, Bottom, Flute, Snout, Starveling, Oberon, Titania, Puck, Peaseblossom, Cobweb, Moth, Mustardseed
Sat, April 3	10:00 AM	Painting	All Cast

THE MORE TRADITIONAL CALENDAR

I typically use this linear calendar when I direct large-cast shows at my community theater. For smaller-cast shows, people are more familiar with—and actually use—the traditional calendar make-up, as shown in Figure 15.12. It's actually not that difficult to create, once you know a few shortcuts.

The key I've found when creating a traditional calendar is to allocate four cells for each date, as illustrated in Figure 15.13. That way you can stick a variety of information into a "date" by cheating. And it also helps to know how to squeeze text into cells using text wrapping and alignment tricks.

1. Start a new worksheet in Excel.
2. First you format the columns: Click the A heading to select all of column A.

FIGURE 15.12
A more traditional calendar done in Excel

April 2003

Sunday	*Monday*	*Tuesday*	*Wednesday*	*Thursday*	*Friday*	*Saturday*
		1	2	3	4	5
6	7	8	9	10	11	12
13	14	15	16	17	18	19
20	21	22	23	24	25	26
27	28	29	30			

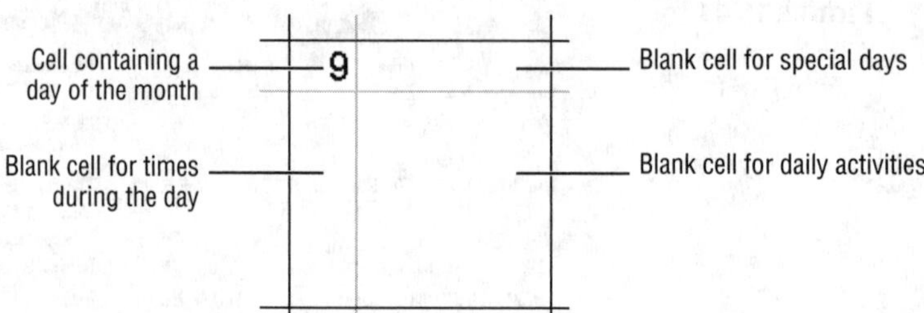

FIGURE 15.13
Detail of a day in the life of the traditional Excel calendar

3. Ctrl-click to select columns C, E, G, I, K, and M. These are the cells that will hold the days of the month.
4. Choose Format ➤ Column ➤ Width.
5. Set the width to **2.6** and click OK. This works as long as you're using standard Arial 10 pt as your calendar's font. If you're not, it's easy to fix later by reselecting the columns and making the width wider.
6. Select columns B, D, F, H, J, L, and N. Use the Ctrl key to click and select the multiple columns.
7. Format their column width to **9**.

That takes care of seven days a week. The next step is to format the rows for the dates. Most months can fit into a 7 by 5 grid, though occasionally there are months requiring a sixth row. The following steps do a five-week grid:

8. Click to select rows 4, 6, 8, 10, and 12. Use the Ctrl key to select multiple rows at once.
9. Choose Format ➤ Row ➤ Height.
10. Set the row height to **56**.
11. Now you enter the text for the calendar: Type the month and year into cell F1.

NOTE *To ensure that Excel accepts exactly what you type, prefix the month by a single tick (') or apostrophe. That prevents Excel from formatting the month and year as a time value.*

12. Into cell A2 type **Sunday**.
13. Into cell C2 type **Monday**.
14. Into cells E2, G2, I2, K2, and M2 type the rest of the days of the week. Nope, you cannot drag-fill here because you're skipping every other cell.

15. Format the days of the week and the month and year as you see fit. I used *italics*. You can play around, but do be careful: The day text is supposed to hang over into the next cell. That may look wrong now, but it looks proper when printed.
16. Next, the calendar dates: Type **1** for the first day of the month in the proper column in row 3.
17. Continue to fill in the rest of the days of the month.

NOTE *If you need an extra row for the last week of the month, select row 14 and set its row height to 56.*

Finally, format the lines. There are numerous ways to do this, but you've got to be careful because you're surrounding four cells with a single border. Here's a quick way I did it, though this is by no means the only way:

18. Select the cells for one day of the month. For example, E3, E4, F3, and F4.
19. Press Ctrl+1 to bring up the Format Cell dialog box.
20. Click the Border tab.
21. Choose the thin line style.
22. Click the Outline preset button.
23. Click OK.

Now to repeat this:

24. Select the next four cells that make up a date on the calendar.
25. Press the F4 key. This reapplies the border command to those four cells.
26. Repeat steps 24 and 25 for the rest of the days of the month. If you screw up, you'll have to return to the Format Cell dialog box and do steps 20 through 23 again. But you won't screw up, will you?

This by no means completes the calendar. There are still lots of fun things you can do with color, borders, text formatting, and even inserting pictures. But do keep in mind that Excel does have a nice selection of predesigned calendar templates on the Web, should you want to save some time.

NOTE *If you're trying to create a personal calendar with due dates and appointments,* stop! *Microsoft Outlook has this ability built in, plus the ability to print its calendars in a manner much quicker than those 26 steps listed in this section.*

The Worksheet That Shows You How to Cheat on Your Taxes

You wish.

Can I Grab Data from the Web and Use It in a Worksheet?

Oh, absolutely. This all depends on the web page, however. Some web pages don't cough up Excel-friendly information. Some do. In any event, once you find the information, provided that it's held in a table on the web page (which most information is), you can easily import that table's information into your worksheet.

NOTE *You cannot grab information from all web pages. Some web pages have only text or perhaps display their information in a format Excel cannot read. If that's the case, then try to find another web page that offers similar information. Or just give up.*

Before starting out, you need to know that most, if not all, of the material you find on the Web is copyrighted. This means it cannot be taken and used for profit or distributed without permission. Even so, there is something called "fair use," which says that you can use information personally, but you cannot profit from it.

For example, if you want to make your own Larry King shrine on your hard drive, that's fine. But if you want to mass-produce Larry King memorabilia, you need his (or his owner's) permissions. Keep that in mind, and also understand that's why the following sections have fictitious websites as their examples.

Outright Web Theft with Excel 2003/XP

Be thankful you upgraded; the web connection in your version of Excel is dead sexy. It makes stealing, er, borrowing stuff from the Web as easy as cheating on your taxes. (Sadly, that section had to be cut from the chapter.)

Here you go:

1. Choose Data ➤ Get External Data ➤ New Web Query. A very sweet dialog box opens displaying a mini web browser. Very cool, so I'm showing it to you in Figure 15.14. Just be amazed at its wonder.

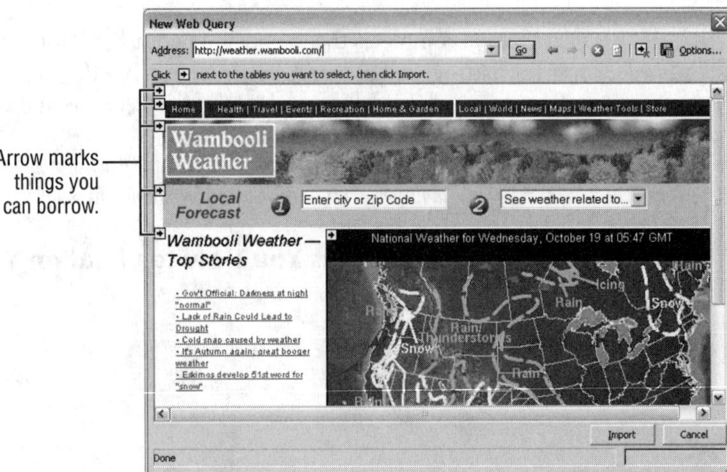

FIGURE 15.14
Web theft begins here.

2. Type in the address of the web page you want to thieve from and click the Go button. For this example, visit any of the several online weather forecasting websites. (These are great examples of websites that have regularly changing information).

3. Once you're at the website, enter your ZIP code or take whatever steps are necessary to summon your local weather page. When you see the local weather page, locate the local forecast. Or if you're borrowing from any web page, ensure that you're on the page you need to borrow from before continuing with the next step.

4. Click the arrow next to the item you want to stick into your worksheet; the arrow changes to a check mark. You can select more than one item, though if you're doing this for the first time, pick only one to download, such as the current temperature on your local weather page.

   If the arrows are having trouble showing up, click the Show/Hide Icons button on the toolbar in the New Web Query dialog box.

5. Click the Import button. An Import Data dialog box appears, letting you choose between sticking the data in an existing worksheet or creating a new worksheet for it. For now:

6. Click to select a new worksheet, and then click OK.

And the information appears in a collection of cells in your worksheet. Actually it's a "table" because the table format was originally used on the web page. Also, no pictures or images are transferred, merely the pertinent text data—which may include hyperlinks. Figure 15.15 shows what the new imported worksheet looks like on my computer.

Don't fuss over the format just yet. Skip ahead to the section, "Fixing That Ugly Web Data."

FIGURE 15.15
The final result for a typical April day where I live

	A	B	C
1		37°F	
2	Partly Cloudy	Feels Like	
3		31°F	
4			

Stealing from the Web in Excel 2000

Alas! Excel 2000 and the Internet just aren't that well married to make this task as seamless as it is in the more recent versions of Excel. But who's complaining? Just follow these steps:

1. Choose Data ➤ Get External Data ➤ New Web Query. This opens the dreadfully dull New Web Query dialog box. Ignore it.

2. Click the Browse Web button. Your web browser starts up all bright and gay. Your job is to browse to a web page that contains data you want to steal. How about the weather?

3. Visit a weather forecasting web page.

4. Enter your ZIP code to look up your local weather. Hopefully, without too many pop-ups or annoying ads or surveys to fill out, you will eventually arrive at a page that displays the weather for your locale. I'll assume that you can get there on your own. When you're at that page, continue:
5. Switch back to Excel. Press Alt+Tab to do this, or just click the Excel button on the taskbar. You'll be amazed to find that web page address listed in the New Web Query dialog box.

The next steps are harder here because you're operating blindly:

6. Select only the tables from step 2 in the dialog box.
7. Click the OK button.
8. Choose "New Worksheet" from the new dialog box that appears.
9. Click OK.

Excel attempts to load the pertinent information from the web page and place it into your worksheet. The problem here is that everything from that page will be loaded—not just the weather info you need but advertisements and other information as well.

As an example, the weather page for my home downloaded into a chunk of cells and some very wide columns. It took me a while to find the pertinent information, which ended up in cells B17 through C19. That's fine! It's the best Excel 2000 can do, but you can do better on your own, as covered in the next section.

Fixing That Ugly Web Data

Remember earlier on how I explained that not all the raw data in a worksheet needs to be seen? Some stuff you can put way off the normal viewing area and just pull in the SUM totals or other important information. That same philosophy must go with web information as well.

From Figure 15.15, the current temperature is stored in cell B1. (Excel 2000 put it in cell C17.) That's fine because that cell can be referenced by another cell in another worksheet, something formatted more to your liking: Simply copy and paste special the cell; paste it as a link, as shown in Figure 15.16. Then format it all nice and pretty.

NOTE *In Excel 2000, you must choose Edit ➤ Paste Special from the menu to paste in the cell's value as a link; choose Paste Link from the Paste Special dialog box, and then click OK.*

A better need for this type of reformatting would be if you're pulling in financial or stock data from some website. The stock data may appear in a vast table with other information, but you may just want the up-to-the-minute price quote. If so, you just select the proper cell in the imported data worksheet, and copy–paste special that cell's data into your main financial wizard worksheet—one you most likely have set up to better monitor such things.

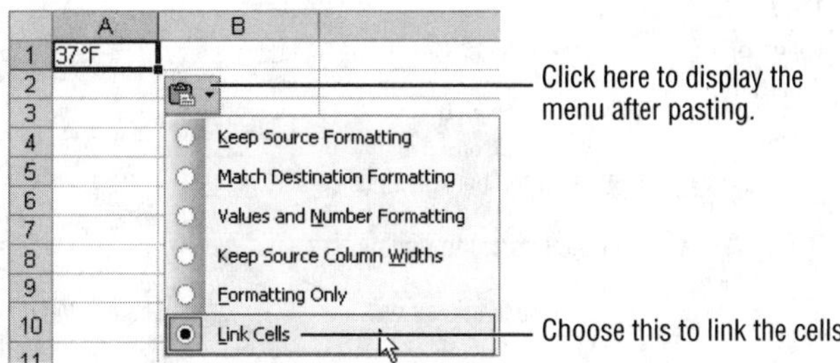

FIGURE 15.16
Pasting the temperature in a special way

It's Getting Hotter Out but the Temperature in My Worksheet Hasn't Changed

While you can paste-link items from one worksheet to another on your own computer, hot-linking to the Web just isn't done yet. So instead you must manually set refresh times for your web data. If you don't, then the information is updated only when you open the worksheet after saving it to disk. And you can also force an update if you like. This applies not only to the weather example here, but also to stock quotes, news items, or whatever else you've imported that needs updating.

The secret here is the External Data toolbar, shown in Figure 15.17. To summon this toolbar, choose View ➤ Toolbars ➤ External Data.

To set a refresh schedule, first click to select a cell in the table imported from the web page. Then click the Data Range Properties button. This displays the nifty dialog box shown in Figure 15.18, where you can tell Excel how often to venture out to the Web. Refer to Figure 15.18 for what to set and what to ignore.

If you'd rather just quickly update, click the Refresh button. That way if the stock market is churning your soul with angst, you can view those near-real-time quotes in your worksheet as they're really happening. Boy, will that make the hairdos on CNBC seethe with jealousy!

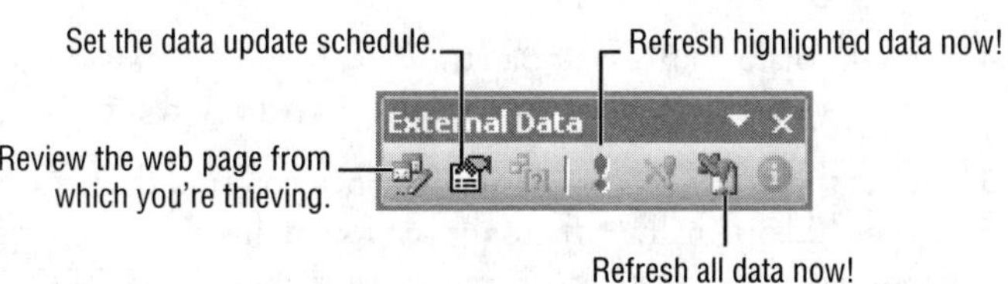

Set the data update schedule.
Refresh highlighted data now!
External Data
Review the web page from which you're thieving.
Refresh all data now!

FIGURE 15.17
The handy External Data toolbar palette thing

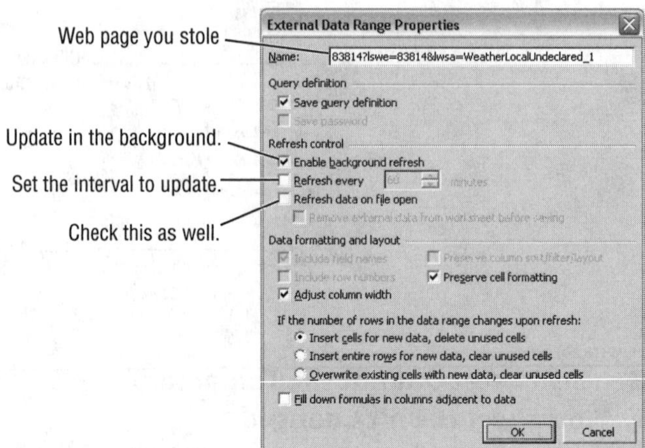

FIGURE 15.18
Set a web page update schedule here.

The Web Page Has Changed or Something, and I'm Not Pulling in the Data I Once Did

Web pages do change. This is a constant truth of the Web. Because of this, linking to a web page means that one day you may open your favorite external data worksheet and discover something unknown or silly in place of the weather, the latest headline, stock news, or computer tip. When that happens, follow these steps:

1. Return to the worksheet that contains the imported information from the web page. Note that it's *imported* information now and no longer stolen.
2. Display the External Data toolbar.
3. Click the Edit Query button. This redisplays the original Web Query dialog box (Figure 15.14), showing the web page you're stealing from. (Now it's theft again.)
4. Use the dialog box to relocate the data. If you're lucky, the data may have just changed location on the same page. Otherwise, you may have to start browsing all over again to find the new data.
5. Select the data when you locate it. Once you find the data, continue to select it for importing as you did originally; refer to the section in this chapter specific for your version of Excel. Then continue with the steps for importing there.

Again this points out the advantage of keeping the web data on one sheet in the workbook and copying the valuable stuff to another sheet. Even if the web page changes, all you need to do is relocate the data on the new worksheet and then copy–paste special–link it to the "real" worksheet you use for examining the data.

Index

Note to the Reader: Throughout this index **boldfaced** page numbers indicate primary discussions of a topic. *Italicized* page numbers indicate illustrations.

E

G

H

I

J

K

L

M

S

U

V

W

X

Y

Z